Quantitative Modelling
in Marketing and Management

Edited by

Luiz Moutinho
University of Glasgow, UK

Kun-Huang Huarng
Feng Chia University, Taiwan (ROC)

 **World Scientific**

NEW JERSEY · LONDON · SINGAPORE · BEIJING · SHANGHAI · HONG KONG · TAIPEI · CHENNAI

Published by

World Scientific Publishing Co. Pte. Ltd.

5 Toh Tuck Link, Singapore 596224

USA office: 27 Warren Street, Suite 401-402, Hackensack, NJ 07601

UK office: 57 Shelton Street, Covent Garden, London WC2H 9HE

Library of Congress Cataloging-in-Publication Data
Moutinho, Luiz.
    Quantitative modelling in marketing and management / by Luiz Moutinho
(University of Glasgow, UK) and Kun-Huang Huarng (Feng Chia University,
Taiwan (ROC)).
        p. cm.
    ISBN 978-9814407717 (alk. paper)
    1. Management--Mathematical models. 2. Marketing--Mathematical models.
    I. Huarng, Kun-Huang. II. Title.
    HD30.25.M68 2012
    658.80072'7--dc23

                                                    2012031583

British Library Cataloguing-in-Publication Data
A catalogue record for this book is available from the British Library.

In-house Editor: Dipasri Sardar

Typeset by Stallion Press
Email: enquiries@stallionpress.com

Printed in Singapore.

Quantitative Modelling
in Marketing and Management

CONTENTS

v

PREFACE

After having been involved for a number of years in quantitative modelling, both editors felt that there was a need to have a comprehensive research text aimed at advanced researchers in marketing and management that would encapsulate a myriad of techniques and applications. We have also felt that to structure the content of the book into statistical (more commonly known), computer, mathematical, and other modelling approaches, would provide a framework to analyse the issues, tools and examples associated with each technique. The rationale for this book is to demonstrate the applicability of the methods, describe its key features and highlight the potential utilisation of each methodology. The overarching concept underlying this research book lies in one common denominator — the use of a research (quantitative) modelling approach. A number of relevant considerations about modelling itself are contained in the final chapter. We would like to thank all the excellent contributors for their superb chapters, as well as Sandlyon, our editor, other previous editors at World Scientific for their understanding and patience with regard to the completion of this book.

We sincerely hope that you will find its content useful and relevant for academic research in the marketing and management fields!

Best wishes
Luiz Moutinho
Kun-Huang Huarng
January 2012

INTRODUCTION

After having been involved for a number of years in quantitative modelling, both editors felt that there was a need to publish a comprehensive research text aimed at advanced researchers in marketing and management that would encapsulate a myriad of techniques and applications. We also felt that by structuring the content of the book into statistical (more commonly known), computer, mathematical, and other modelling approaches, it would provide a framework to analyse the issues, tools and examples associated with each technique. Accordingly, this book is composed of three parts, each with several related articles.

Part 1. Statistical Modelling

The coverage of statistical modelling includes multidimensional scaling (MDS) models, structural equation modelling, partial least squares path models, and data envelopment analysis.

The MDS comprises a family of various geometric models representing the structure in data and the corresponding set of methods for fitting such spatial models. Major applications of MDS in marketing include positioning, market segmentation, new product design, consumer preference analysis, etc. DeSarbo and Kim present several popular MDS models for the analysis of consumer preference or dominance data. First, vector or scalar products model represents brands by points and consumers by vectors in a T dimensional derived joint space. They describe both individual and segment level vector MDS models. Second, multidimensional simple unfolding or ideal point model represents both brands and consumers jointly by points in a T dimensional derived joint space. Next, they discuss two more complex variants of multidimensional unfolding called the weighted unfolding model and the general unfolding model. A real application of consideration to buy large sport utility vehicles is provided and the empirical results from each type of models at the individual level are discussed.

Structural equation modelling (SEM) is a popular statistical technique for testing and estimating causal relations using a combination of statistical data and qualitative causal assumptions, which are typically based on a theory. This technique is widely used by social scientists for theory testing and development. SEM is a combination of factor analysis and multiple-regression and includes path analysis and confirmatory factor analysis. SEM helps researchers to generate and test hypotheses about relationships among theoretical constructs. The tight specification model in SEM makes it a uniquely powerful statistical tool. SEM can help a researcher answer substantive questions and validate measurements. Manhas, Manrai, Manrai, and Ramjit intend to provide an overview and some insights to how SEM works and what its benefits are to a social scientist. They discuss automated manhole opening system (AMOS) procedure and several aspects of SEM including model identification, specification, estimation, modification and issues of sample size and interpretation and communication of results. They illustrate many of the key ideas and concepts pertaining to SEM by providing an example.

Since Jöreskog (1967) provided an operative algorithm for maximum likelihood (ML) estimation of latent variable models, covariance-based procedures are tautologically synonymous of SEM techniques (Chin, 1998). However, Herman Wold questioned the applicability of covariance structure models estimation *via* ML (Fornell and Cha, 1994) because it requires heavy distribution assumptions and high sample sizes. Tenenhaus *et al.* (2005) propose a new 'soft modelling' alternative (here, few distribution assumptions and few cases suffice), later named partial least squares path modelling (PLSPM). PLSPM was scarcely used in management and marketing research until 10 years ago. Aldás-Manzano intends to illustrate and provide guidelines regarding the use of PLSPM as a

SEM tool and to reveal its strengths and weaknesses based on a practical example.

Data envelopment analysis (DEA) is getting more popular in evaluating performance among candidates. On the basis of the underlying relationship between inputs and outputs, the mathematical measurement of performance can be expressed as an efficiency computation, often described as productivity. Total factor productivity presents a ratio which allows an investigation of multitude combinations of these factors. There are strengths and weaknesses in the mathematical models, such as DEA. Hence, it is necessary to pay attention to these weaknesses to evaluate DEA's suitability for solving particular problems. Manzoni and Islam present an in-depth introduction to DEA and show that DEA is a powerful non-parametric tool for analysing efficiencies of decision making units in the same cohort.

Statistical models are commonly used to provide evidence of relationships and processes that are important in the population. Interpreting these models is never straightforward as estimates for the model parameters and significance levels are dependent upon the methods used to build them, the so-called 'variable selection problem'. Hutcheson investigates how parameter estimates and significance values may be related to the methods used for their construction. He uses simulated and real-world data to demonstrate that models may not always provide valid indications of 'actual' relationships and processes in the population. The validity of conclusions drawn from the research may be affected by the use of single-model selection, which forces analysts to report just one instance of what might be a multi-model solution. It states that many published reports and papers interpret statistical models that are invalid because little or no consideration is taken as to how they were constructed or whether single-solution reporting is appropriate. Hutcheson demonstrates these problems and proposes a solution in the form of a modelling procedure that uses a restricted-set of variables and a reporting method which enables multiple-models to be described.

Part 2. Computer Modelling

Computer modelling covers topics ranging from neural networks, logical discriminant models (LDM), meta-heuristic methods, fuzzy correlation, fuzzy index, fuzzy Delphi, and fuzzy composite score.

Artificial neural networks (ANNs) are able to discover complex non-linear relationships in data (Donaldson and Kamstra, 1996; Indro *et al.*, 1999). The SEM can be used to measure the reliability and validity of the observed variables and latent variables. It can estimate the overall structural model to examine the fitness between the overall model and the observed data as well as the causal relationship among the latent variables. Coelho, Moutinho, and Silva intend to compare the usefulness and the potential contributions of ANNs in the marketing field and compare the traditional modelling based on SEM. It uses ANN modelling and SEM to evaluate loyalty in the bank industry in Brazil. ANNs highlight the role of the relationship quality on customer loyalty while SEM confirms six of the seven hypotheses of the proposed model. The findings highlighted the point that micro-, small-, and medium-sized companies' loyalty to their main bank is strongly influenced by affective commitment. Some similarities can be found by comparing the results achieved from both methodologies. This result suggests that, for this marketing problem, ANNs and SEM seem to be complementary to each other.

ANNs have been applied to various problem domains, including credit ratings (Kumar and Bhattacharya, 2006), Dow Jones forecasting (Kanas, 2001), customer satisfaction analysis (Gronholdt and Martensen, 2005), stock ranking (Refenes *et al.*, 1993), stock index forecasting (Huarng and Yu, 2006; Yu and Huarng, 2010; Yu *et al.*, 2009) and tourism demand (Law, 2000; Law and Au, 1999; Martin and Witt, 1989; Palmer *et al.*, 2006), etc. However, there is a need for an increased awareness in other areas of marketing and management to complement the limited work undertaken in retailing and direct marketing. Indeed, Hruschka (1991) and Krycha and Wagner (1999), drew attention to the scarcity of articles applying ANN techniques to marketing and management issues. Coelho, Moutinho, and Silva intend to show different fields where ANNs can successfully be used and how they can help researchers to better capture and understand management problems, as well as to provide different linkages between variables. Some examples are: New ICT adoption, loyalty in the banking industry, entrepreneurial orientation and small firm performance, the influence of external market orientation, entrepreneurial orientation, innovation and resources on export performance, and the determinants of the involvement of university researchers in spin-off creation, etc.

Discriminant or classification analysis is a supervised learning that formulates the association between a set of entities' attributes (predictors) and a categorical target attribute imposing classes to those entities. Discriminant analysis can be viewed as a data analysis task that may be accomplished by statistical, data mining, or statistical learning techniques. Cardoso analyses different models of discriminant analyses. In linear discriminant analysis, the discriminant scores are a weighted sum of predictors and the derivation of classification rules requires Gaussian data and a common predictor covariance matrix. Logistic regression models the log-odds or logit transformations of classes probabilities as linear combinations of predictors and it makes less assumptions regarding data when compared to linear discriminant analysis (Hair *et al.*, 2005). Some alternative discriminant functional approaches are built using data mining techniques (Hastie *et al.*, 2001). As opposed to statistical approaches, these methods do not generally require distributional assumptions on the data to infer the models to the population, thereby establishing a degree of uncertainty. However, they generally have to rely on large datasets that can provide a holdout set (data not used for model estimation) in order to obtain alternative estimates of models' uncertainty. The logical discriminant models (LDM) emerge in the context of discriminant techniques, within the data mining framework, as providing results that are very easy to interpret — trees and rules — making them very appealing, namely in management decision support. The LDM (also referred as symbolic learning systems), have some additional advantages when compared to other techniques, namely the capacity to deal with explanatory variables of different measurement levels (quantitative and qualitative), good handling of missing data and robustness. For demonstration, Cardoso also uses LDM to classify the data of 440 customers of a wholesale distributor.

During the 1980s, general interest in the so-called meta-heuristic methods dramatically increased. This was due to their apparent widespread success in solving a variety of difficult problems in a wide range of disciplines. Hurley and Moutinho describe three such meta-heuristics: evolutionary algorithms (EA), simulated annealing (SA) and tabu search (TS). Their development for discrete optimisation problems that arise in marketing will be discussed. Meta-heuristics are a class of approximate methods that are designed to solve difficult combinatorial optimisation problems. They provide general frameworks that allow for the creation of new hybrids by combining different concepts derived from classical heuristics, artificial intelligence, statistical mechanics, biological systems, evolution and genetics. In particular, meta-heuristics use one or more of these concepts to drive some subordinate heuristic, such as local neighbourhood search. Whereas specialised heuristics or optimisation procedures can usually only be applied to a narrow band of problems, meta-heuristics can be applied to a wide variety of problems. However, this robustness comes at the sacrifice of domain specificity. Meta-heuristics would generally have a much more satisfactory performance on such problems.

How to evaluate correlation with fuzzy data properly is always interesting. Traditionally, Pearson's Correlation Coefficient is used to measure the correlation between data with real value. However, when the data are composed of fuzzy numbers, Pearson's Correlation Coefficient may not be applicable. Yang, Cheng, Wu, and Sriboonchitta define the fuzzy correlation and propose a method to calculate fuzzy correlation with fuzzy data, and interval, triangular and trapezoidal data. Empirical analysis is used to illustrate the application of the proposed method for evaluating the fuzzy correlations. Furthermore, the related practical phenomena can be explained by the appropriate definition of fuzzy correlation.

Contemporary community colleges have drawn wide attention on their performance management when they face dramatic challenges worldwide. Lee, Wu, and Su aim to measure the performance from customer capital and propose solutions that can effectively improve the performance measurement methods for community colleges. They utilise a soft computing method to design the performance evaluation model. By fuzzy statistical methods, they retrieve the community college management features and build up the performance indicators, such as enrolment, satisfaction, and attendance for customer capital. Empirical results show that community colleges can perform effective decision making on performance evaluation by adapting the analysis of customer capital.

In the globalised era with dramatic challenges, schools leaders have been facing more stress from their jobs. Wu and Liu intend to analyse and evaluate job stress factors of school leaders. They present the assessment program by using the Fuzzy Delphi method and fuzzy questionnaire sampling survey. They propose the index of job stress of school leaders by using fuzzy evaluation methods as well as soft computations. The empirical analysis shows that the three dimensions with eight indicators can explain the state of job pressure of school leaders. This analysis implies that the proposed index of job stress for school leaders could be an efficient index in the job stress research.

Chiou and Ou propose a mechanism based on fuzzy composite score (FCS) to integrate multiple scoring methods for situational judgement test (SJT). In addition to dealing with various scale types, the proposed operating mechanism can provide fuzzy space for linguistic judgment so as to compare the difference of SJT score under different degrees of linguistic vagueness. Based on the current SJT scoring method, Chiou and Ou simulate sample responses for four types of different scales to explain the FCS operation. The comparison between five different degrees of vagueness is also conducted in this fuzzy frame. Empirical analysis shows that (1) the proposed FCS operation can integrate multiple scoring methods, and provide advanced adjustment of linguistic vagueness to more closely match authentic cognition; (2) as the degree of linguistic vagueness increases, the diversity in FCS between high score and low score samples is reduced, but moderated by different SJT scoring methods. To conclude, practical and academic points of view about FCS of SJT are discussed for future study.

Part 3. Mathematical and Other Models

Mathematical and other models cover cluster analysis, fuzzy questionnaire, qualitative comparative analysis, data warehouse solutions, growth models, preference ranking organisation method for enrichment evaluations (PROMETHEE), clique communities, and k-clique.

Cluster analysis provides insights into data, such that objects in an identified cluster are more similar to each other than to objects in other clusters (Duda *et al.*, 2001). The term cluster analysis does not identify a particular statistical method or model, quite unlike the discriminant analysis, factor analysis, and regression. The role of a clustering technique, in order to perform cluster analysis, is to facilitate the partitioning of the data into such clusters, based on specified cluster characteristics. Beynon and Daunt offer a background to the general approach termed cluster analysis, including an illustrative cluster analysis of a real world problem. At the technical level, one dominant issue when considering cluster analysis is the wide range of clustering techniques available to be employed. Two of the most commonly applied clustering techniques are employed (Mingoti and Lima, 2006), such as the hierarchical Ward's method (WM) (Ward, 1963; Janssens *et al.*, 2003) and the non-hierarchical k-means (KM) (MacQueen, 1967; Kanungo *et al.*, 2002). The hierarchical and non-hierarchical nature of these two techniques is one example of the variability prevalent in different clustering techniques available to undertake cluster analysis. A further example of their variability is in their effectiveness when outliers are present in the investigated data, with the hierarchical techniques affected by their inclusion, while the non-hierarchical techniques are considered to be more robust (Mingoti and Lima, 2006). In addition to technique issues, the 'clustering' attained is also interpreted and validated, to ensure that it is theoretically and practically meaningful (Frayley and Raftery, 1998). Validation refers to procedures that evaluate the results of cluster analysis in a quantitative and objective fashion (Jain and Dubes, 1988). Beynon and Daunt demonstrate the issue of cluster analysis through the analysis of a pertinent marketing problem, namely the investigation of the relationship between personality and dysfunctional customer behavior.

Numerous studies have indicated that the use of membership functions and fuzzy interval data are more realistic and suitable for social science research. Chang and Jiang design a fuzzy questionnaire to calculate how much Chinese consumers care about the superstitious number 'four'. The fuzzy questionnaire is used to estimate Chinese consumers' purchasing intentions and the price reduction that would induce them to purchase items featuring the number four. The empirical results from using fuzzy statistics and soft computing accurately reflect the intentions of these consumers. Their study finds that the respondents care about phone numbers containing the number four and fourth floors equally. Additionally, groups categorised according to age, ethnicity, religion, and education differed significantly in their perception of the superstitious number four.

Beynon and McDermott offer a description of qualitative comparative analysis (QCA). Introduced by Ragin (1987), QCA is an analytical tool grounded in set theory that allows analysts to make causal claims about the structure of relationships between variables, attributes and outcomes (Rizova, 2011), in ways that account for multiple conjunctural causation. Although the name of the technique suggests an emphasis on the derivation of findings from qualitative data, the underlying mechanics of QCA are wholly quantitative. As a result, it is considered an innovative technique for case-oriented research, that aims to *bridge the gap* between qualitative (case study oriented) and quantitative (variable oriented) approaches to social scientific research (Grofman and Schneider, 2009). The underlying objective of QCA is to compare similar cases (as similar as possible) (Maggetti, 2009) that differ only in the causal conditions (independent variables), which should explain the variation in an outcome (dependent variable). The intention is to identify the necessary and sufficient causes leading to that outcome (*ibid*). The key difference between QCA and traditional case-oriented methods is that QCA facilitates the extension of analysis beyond a small number of cases (Ragin and Rihoux, 2004). The purpose of this chapter is to give an overview of the theoretical and practical fundamentals of QCA. As a result, it combines theoretical discussion with worked examples. The first hypothetical example clearly illustrates the technical rudiments of QCA. A second real-world example from healthcare management is then utilised to fully demonstrate the potential application of QCA. The problem considers whether the use of a clinical directorate management structure in hospitals is associated with the involvement of clinical staff in hospital decision making.

Extracting knowledge from data is the major objective of any data analysis process, including the ones developed in several sciences as statistics and quantitative methods, database/data warehouse and data mining. The data mining is the most ambitious because it intends to analyse and extract knowledge from massive and often badly structured data with many specific objectives. It is also used for relational database data, network data, text data, log file data, and data in many other forms. Hence, there is no surprise that a myriad of applications and methodologies have been and are being developed and applied for data analysis functions; cross industry standard process for data mining (CRISP-DM) and sample, explore, modify, model, assessment (SEMMA) are two such examples. The need for a roadmap is, therefore, critical. The entire knowledge discovery process includes many phases. Mendes, Cavique, and Santos walk through each phase, outlining typical tasks and methods involved and present cases of application. They present the CRISP-DM process model with the CRISP-DM methodology, and by working upon the successful results of those earlier experiences, developed a very well specified process model.

Mendes, Cavique, and Santos report two projects for supporting decisions of the Company of Electricity in Azores Islands, Electricidade dos Açores. There were several decisions to support, such as whether communications between islands should be moved from the present telephone lines to VoIP, and if better models to support forecast power consumption should be adopted. The solution established integrating OLAP cubes in a data mining project, based on CRISP-DM process model. The objective was to secure accurate data, build a data warehouse and to use appropriate tools to analyse them in order to properly inform the decision makers, both for strategic and more operational decisions. These decision support system (DSS) translates big comma-separated values (CSV) flat files or acquire data in real time from operational databases to update a data warehouse, including importing, evaluating data quality and populating relational tables. Multidimensional data cubes with numerous dimensions and measures were used for operational decisions and as exploration tools in the strategic ones. Data mining models for forecasting, clustering, decision trees and association rules identified several inefficient procedures including fraud situations. It was, therefore, possible to support necessary decisions, but several other models were also displayed so that control decision makers and strategists could support new problems.

Growth models represent similarities between growth in nature and growth in economy. They are widely used in quantitative research for time series data analysis and enable better understanding of forces that influence growth in a sense of its dynamics, market capacities as well as forecasting of a future growth. The growth models can be unbounded or bounded assuming that limit or saturation level of growth exists as the time increases. The diffusion of innovation and new technology, market adoption of consumer durables, products/services that do not include repeat sales, subscription services (e.g., telecommunications services) and allocations of restricted resources are examples of the S-shaped bounded growth. Sokele focuses on the models that describe such bounded growth and cumulative volume (sales) of market adopted products/services (or similar). In general, during its life cycle, after the design phase, every product/service passes through the following phases: introduction, growth, maturity and decline, resembling the profile of the technology life cycle and its associated market-growth profile. The understanding of each segment of the product/service life cycle (P/SLC) for business planning purposes is especially important in highly competitive market environment and for products/services resulting from emerging technologies. The growth model in a form of differential equation is created as the result of analysis and understanding of growth for the specific product/service.

The PROMETHEE method was introduced in Brans (1982) and further developed in Vincke and Brans (1985) and Brans *et al.* (1984, 1986). It is used as a multi-criteria decision aid to rank a finite set of decision alternatives, based on evidence from a selection of criteria. The ranking achieved by PROMETHEE produces a series of final 'net' values which are used to rank alternatives, found from the aggregation of constituent 'criterion' values, which express the levels of preference of the alternatives over the different criteria. Beynon and Barton introduce the original PROMETHEE analysis and illustrate its technical progression. They offer an understanding of the application of PROMETHEE within a pertinent management problem, namely performance management. A specific example problem is the relative performance ranking of individual police forces, in the East England region in the UK. The performance in this case is measured by each police force's levels of sanction detections (percentage levels of clear-up rates).

After Berners-Lee (2006) communication on the three ages of the Web in the *International World Wide Web Conference WWW2006*, there has been an explosion of interest in the social networks associated with Web 2.0 in an attempt to improve socialising. A new model for knowledge management has been proposed — social network analysis is a very relevant technique that has emerged in modern sociology which studies the interaction between individuals and organisations (Scott and Carrington, 2011; Wasserman and Faust, 1995). The social network analysts need to survey each person about their friends, ask for their approval to publish the data and keep a track of that population for years. Also, the applications, implemented on internet, that use the concept of establishing links between friends and friends of friends, like Facebook © or LinkedIn (LinkedIn Corporation ©), provide the required data. According to Linton Freeman's comprehensive Development of Social Network Analysis, the key factors defining the modern field of social network analysis are: The insight that the structure of networks affects the outcome of aggregate actions, and the methodological approach that uses systematic empirical data; graphic representation; and, mathematical and computational models to analyse networks. These attributes of social network analysis were established through the work of scientists from the fields of psychology, anthropology, and mathematics over the last decades (Freeman, 2004). The visualisation of a small number of vertices can be completely mapped. However, when the number of vertices and edges increases, the visualisation becomes incomprehensible. Graph mining can be defined as the science and the art of extracting useful knowledge, like patterns and outliers provided, respectively, by repeated and sporadic data, from large graphs or complex networks (Faloutsos *et al.*, 1999; Cook and Holder, 2007). As these authors put it, there are many differences between graphs; however, some patterns show up regularly, the main ones appearing include small worlds, degree distribution and community mining. In this chapter, Cavique, Mendes, and Santos introduce the clique communities using the graph partition approach, based on the k-clique structure. A k-clique is a relaxed clique. A k-clique in a graph is a sub-graph where the distance between any two vertices is no greater than k. It is a relevant structure to consider when analysing large graphs like the ones arising in social network analysis.

In social network analysis, a k-clique is a relaxed clique. A k-clique in a graph is a sub-graph where the distance between any two vertices is no greater than k. The visualisation of a small number of vertices can be easily performed in a graph. However, when the number of vertices and edges increases, the visualisation becomes incomprehensible. Cavique, Mendes, and Santos propose a new graph mining approach based on k-cliques. The concept of a relaxed clique is extended to the whole graph, to achieve a general view, by covering the network with k-cliques. The sequence of k-clique covers is presented, combining small world concepts with community structure components. Computational results and examples are also presented.

The objective of quantitative research is to develop and employ mathematical models, theories and/or hypotheses pertaining to phenomena. In the social sciences, **quantitative research** refers to the systematic empirical investigation of social phenomena via statistical, mathematical or computational techniques. Quantitative research is used widely in social sciences such as in marketing and management. In the social sciences, the 'quantitative' term relates to empirical methods, originating in both philosophical positivism and the history of statistics. Quantitative methods can be used to verify which research hypotheses are true. In the last chapter, both editors list a number of relevant considerations about modelling itself. The evaluation of quality calls for an examination for four key stages is also illustrated.

References

Berners-Lee, T (2006). The next wave of the web plenary panel. *15th International World Wide Web Conference*, WWW2006, Edinburgh, Scotland.

Brans, JP (1982). Lingenierie de la decision. Elaboration dinstruments daide a la decision. Methode PROMETHEE. In *Laide a la Decision: Nature, Instrument set Perspectives Davenir*, R Nadeau and M Landry (eds.), pp. 183–214. Qu ebec, Canada: Presses de Universite Laval.

Brans, JP, B Mareschal and PH Vincke (1984). PROMETHEE: A new family of outranking methods in MCDM. *International Federation of Operational Research Studies (IFORS 84)*, North Holland, pp. 470–490.

Brans, JP, PH Vincke and B Mareschal (1986). How to select and how to rank projects: The PROMETHEE method. *European Journal of Operational Research*, 24, 228–238.

Chin, WW (1998). The partial least squares approach to structural equation modelling. In *Modern Methods for Business Research*, GA Marcoulides (ed.), pp. 295–336. Mahwah, NJ: Lawrence Erlbaum Associates.

Cook, DJ and LB Holder (eds.) (2007). *Mining Graph Data*. New York: John Wiley & Sons.

Donaldson, RG and M Kamstra (1996). Forecast combining with neural networks. *Journal of Forecasting*, 15(1), 49–61.

Duda, R, P Hart and D Stork (2001). *Pattern Classification*. New York: Wiley.

Faloutsos, M, P Faloutsos and C Faloutsos (1999). On power-law relationships of the Internet topology. In *Proceedings of SIGCOMM*, pp. 251–262. New York: ACM.

Fornell, C and J Cha (1994). Partial least squares. In *Advanced Methods of Marketing Research*, RP Bagozzi (ed.), pp. 52–78. Cambridge, MA: Blackwell Publishers.

Frayley, C and E Raftery (1998). How many clusters? Which clustering method? Answers via model-based cluster analysis. *The Computer Journal*, 41(8), 578–588.

Freeman, LC (2004). *The Development of Social Network Analysis: A Study in the Sociology of Science*. Vancouver: Empirical Press.

Grofman, B and CQ Schneider (2009). An introduction to crisp set QCA, with a comparison to binary logistic regression. *Political Research Quarterly*, 62, 662–672.

Gronholdt, L and A Martensen (2005). Analysing customer satisfaction data: A comparison of regression and artificial neural networks. *International Journal of Market Research*, 47(2), 121–130.

Hair, JF, W Black, BJ Babin and RE Anderson (2005). *Multivariate Data Analysis — A Global Perspective*, 6th edn. New Jersey: Prentice Hall.

Hastie, T, R Tibshirani and JH Friedman (2001). *The Elements of Statistical Learning — Data Mining, Inference and Prediction*. New York: Springer-Verlag.

Hruschka, H (1991). Einsatz Kunstlicher Neuronaler Netzwerke zur Datenanalyse. *Marketing ZFP*, 37(4), 217–225.

Huarng, K and H-K Yu (2006). The application of neural networks to forecast fuzzy time series. *Physica A*, 363(2), 481–491.

Indro, DC, CX Jiang, BE Patuwo and GP Zhang (1999). Predicting mutual fund performance using artificial neural networks. *Omega*, 27, 373–380.

Jain, A and R Dubes (1988). *Algorithms for Clustering Data*. Englewood Cliffs, NJ: Prentice Hall.

Janssens, M, L Sels and I Van Den Brande (2003). Multiple types of psychological contracts: A six-cluster solution. *Human Relations*, 56, 1349–1378.

Jöreskog, KG (1967). Some contributions to maximum likelihood factor analysis. *Pshychometrika*, 32, 443–482.

Kanas, A (2001). Neural network linear forecasts for stock returns. *International Journal of Finance and Economics*, 6(3), 245–254.

Kanungo, T, DM Mount, NS Netanyahu, CD Piatko, R Silverman and AY Wu (2002). An efficient k-Means clustering algorithm: Analysis and implementation. *IEEE Transactions on Pattern Analysis and Machine Intelligence*, 24(7), 881–892.

Krycha, KA and U Wagner (1999). Applications of artificial neural networks in management science: A survey. *Journal of Retailing and Consumer Services*, 6 (September), 185–203.

Kumar, K and S Bhattacharya (2006). Artificial neural network vs. linear discriminant analysis in credit ratings forecast: A comparative study of prediction performances. *Review of Accounting & Finance*, 5(3), 216–227.

Law, R (2000). Back-propagation learning in improving the accuracy of neural network-based tourism demand forecasting. *Tourism Management*, 21, 331–340.

Law, R and N Au (1999). A neural network model to forecast Japanese demand for travel to Hong Kong. *Tourism Management*, 20, 89–97.

MacQueen, JB (1967). Some methods for classification and analysis of multivariate observations. In *Proc 5th Berkeley Symposium on Mathematical Statistics and Probability*, pp. 281–297. Berkeley: University of California Press.

Maggetti, M (2009). The role of independent regulatory agencies in policy-making a comparative analysis. *Journal of European Public Policy*, 16(3), 450–470.

Martin, CA and SF Witt (1989). Accuracy of econometric forecasts of tourism. *Annals of Tourism Research*, 16, 407–428.

Mingoti, SA and JO Lima (2006). Comparing SOM neural network with fuzzy c-means, K-means and traditional hierarchical clustering algorithms. *European Journal of Operational Research*, 174, 1742–1759.

Palmer, A, JJ Montaño and A Sesé (2006). Designing an artificial neural network for forecasting tourism time series. *Tourism Management*, 27, 781–790.

Ragin, CC (1987). *The Comparative Method: Moving Beyond Qualitative and Quantitative Strategies*. Berkeley: University of California.

Ragin, CC and B Rihoux (2004). Qualitative comparative analysis (QCA): State of the art and prospects. *Newsletter of the American Political Science Association Organized Section on Qualitative Methods*, 2(2), 3–13.

Refenes, AN, M Azema-Barac and AD Zapranis (1993). Stock ranking: Neural networks vs. multiple linear regression. *IEEE Int Conf on Neural Networks*, 3, 1419–1426.

Rizova, PS (2011). Finding testable causal mechanisms to address critical public management issues. *Journal of Comparative Policy Analysis: Research and Practice*, 13(1), 105–114.

Scott, JP and P Carrington (eds.) (2011). *The SAGE Handbook of Social Network Analysis*. UK: Sage Publications.

Tenenhaus, M, VE Vinzi, YM Chatelin and C Lauro (2005). PLS path modeling. *Computational Statistics & Data Analysis*, 48, 159–205.

Yu, TH-K and K-H Huarng (2010). A neural network-based fuzzy time series model to improve forecasting. *Expert Systems with Applications*, 37(4), 3366–3372.

Yu, TH-K, K-H Huarng and R Rianto (2009). Neural network-based fuzzy autoregressive models of different orders to forecast Taiwan stock index. *International Journal of Economics and Business Research*, 1(3), 347–358.

Vincke, JP and P Brans (1985). A preference ranking organization method. The PROMETHEE method for MCDM. *Management Science*, 31, 641–656.

Ward, JH (1963). Hierarchical grouping to optimize an objective function. *Journal of the American Statistical Association*, 58(301), 236–244.

Wasserman, S and K Faust (1995). *Social Network Analysis: Methods and Applications*. Cambridge: Cambridge University Press.

PART 1

STATISTICAL MODELLING

Chapter 1

A REVIEW OF THE MAJOR MULTIDIMENSIONAL SCALING MODELS FOR THE ANALYSIS OF PREFERENCE/DOMINANCE DATA IN MARKETING

Wayne S. DeSarbo*
Smeal College of Business
Pennsylvania State University
University Park, PA.
wsd6@psu.edu

Sunghoon Kim
Smeal College of Business
Pennsylvania State University
University Park, PA.
suk220@psu.edu

Multidimensional scaling (MDS) represents a family of various spatial geometric models for the multidimensional representation of the structure in data as well as the corresponding set of methods for fitting such spatial models. Its major uses in Marketing include positioning, market segmentation, new product design, consumer preference analysis, etc. We present several popular MDS models for the analysis of consumer preference or dominance data. The first spatial model presented is called the vector or scalar products model which represents brands by points and consumers by vectors in a T dimensional derived joint space. We describe both individual and segment level vector MDS models. The second spatial model is called the multidimensional simple unfolding or ideal point model where both brands and consumers are jointly represented by

*Communicating author.

points in a T dimensional derived joint space. We briefly discuss two more complex variants of multidimensional unfolding called the weighted unfolding model and the general unfolding model. Here too, we describe both individual and segment level unfolding MDS models. We contrast the underlying utility assumptions implied by each of these models with illustrative figures of typical joint spaces derived from each approach. An actual commercial application of consideration to buy large Sports Utility Vehicle (SUV) vehicles is provided with the empirical results from each major type of model at the individual level is discussed.

Keywords: Multidimensional scaling; vector model; unfolding model; positioning analysis; market segmentation; clusterwise models.

1. Introduction

Using the Carroll and Arabie (1980) broad conceptualisation, we define multidimensional scaling (MDS) as a family of various geometric models for the multidimensional representation of the structure in data as well as the corresponding set of methods for fitting such spatial models. Carroll and Arabie (1980) present a taxonomy of the area of MDS based on the properties of the input measurement data (e.g., number of modes, number of ways, power of the mode, scale type, conditionality, completeness of the data, replications, etc.) and properties of the underlying multidimensional measurement model (e.g., type of geometric model, number of sets of points in the derived space, number of derived spaces, degree of constraints on model parameters, etc.). Thus, their definition extends classical MDS which typically deals only with spatial models for proximity data (e.g., similarities/dissimilarities) to various other forms of continuous and discrete representations, as well as to other data types. Our focus will be upon the two major types of models utilised for the analysis of dominance (i.e., preference, consideration to buy, choice, etc.) data as is typically collected in Marketing Research: The vector MDS model and the unfolding MDS model (Scott and DeSarbo, 2011). Readers interested in a more comprehensive discussion of this broad area of MDS are encouraged to consult the excellent book on MDS by Borg and Groenen (2005) for an in-depth treatment of these and other types of MDS approaches for the analysis of such data (e.g., correspondence analysis). For expositional purposes, we will assume that the data to be analysed is a two-way dataset of metric brand preferences where the rows of this data matrix ($\underline{P}$) reflect a sample of consumers and the columns of the matrix represent brands in a designated product/service class. The general entry in this data matrix (P_{ij}) is the metric preference rating given for brand j by consumer i. The objective of the MDS models to be described is to estimate a spatial configuration (a joint space) of both row (consumers or derived market segments) and column (brands) objects such that their particular geometric interrelationships most parsimoniously recovers the input preference data $\underline{P}$. We will describe both traditional individual level MDS models and more recent segment level or clusterwise MDS models for the analysis of such preference or dominance data.

2.   The Vector MDS Model

2.1.   *The individual level vector MDS model*

Tucker (1960) and Slater (1960) were the first to independently formulate this scalar products based model for geometrically displaying the structure in such two-way data (Carroll, 1972, 1980). Related to factor analysis, the underlying model can be mathematically represented as:

$$P_{ij} = \sum_{t=1}^{T} a_{it}b_{jt} + e_{ij}, \tag{1}$$

where:

$i = 1,\ldots,I$ consumers;
$j = 1,\ldots,J$ brands;
$t = 1,\ldots,T$ dimensions;
$a_{it} =$ the tth coordinate of the terminus of the preference vector for consumer i in the derived space;
$b_{jt} =$ the tth coordinate of the location of brand j in the derived space;
$e_{ij} =$ error.

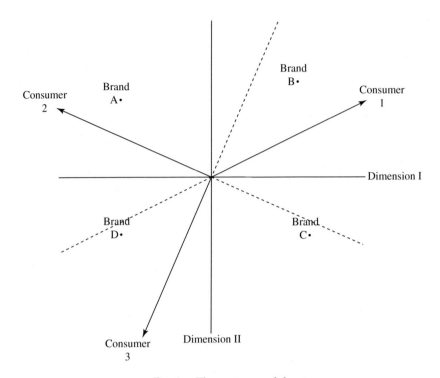

Fig. 1.   The vector model.

We describe this particular geometric representation *via* Fig. 1 which illustrates the workings of the vector MDS model in Eq. (1) for the simple case of two dimensions, four brands, and three consumers. The two dimensions are labelled in the figure and represent typical scatter plot axes. The brand coordinates (b_{jt}) are plotted here for each of the four brands (A, B, C, and D) and represent the positions of the brands in this derived space. Note, the consumer locations (a_{it}) are represented in this model (labelled Consumers 1, 2, and 3) as vectors emanating thru the origin whose orientations point in the direction of increasing preference or utility for each consumer. Each of the three consumers' vectors point in different directions reflecting heterogeneity (i.e., individual differences) in their respective tastes and preferences. (Note that we draw the tails of the vectors here as dashed lines reflecting the areas of the space that are dispreferred for each consumer). The predicted cardinal preference values are given by the orthogonal projection of each of the brands onto each consumer's preference vector. Thus, Consumer 1 has the following order of predicted preference: B, C, A, D; Consumer 2: A, D, B, C; and, Consumer 3: D, C, A, B. Note, the consumer vectors are typically normalised to equal length in such joint space representations although, under certain data pre-processing conditions, the raw lengths of such vectors can be shown to be proportional to how well each consumer's preferences are recovered by the vector representation. The goal of such an analysis is to simultaneously estimate the vectors and brand coordinates in a given dimensionality that most parsimoniously captures/recovers the empirical preference data. The analysis is typically repeated for $t = 1, 2, 3, \ldots, T$ dimensions and the dimensionality is selected by inspection of a scree plot of the number of estimated dimensions *versus* a goodness of fit statistic (e.g., variance accounted-for) that measures how well the model predictions in Eq. (1) match the input preference data given the number of model parameters being estimated. Note, the cosines of the angles each consumer vector forms with the coordinate axes render information relating to the importance of these derived dimensions to that consumer. The iso-preference contours for this vector MDS model in two dimensions for a particular consumer vector (i.e., locations of equal preference) are perpendicular lines to a consumer vector at any point on that vector since brands located on such lines would project at the same point of predicted preference onto the vector. Thus, it is important to note that this vector model is not a distance based spatial model. Also, one can freely rotate the joint space of vectors and brand points and not change the model predictions (the orthogonal projections of the brand points onto the consumer vectors) or goodness-of-fit results. As noted by Carroll (1980), one of the unattractive features of this vector model is that it assumes that preference changes mono-tonically with respect to all dimensions. That is, since a consumer's vector points in the direction of increasing preference or utility, the more of the dimensions in that direction implies greater preference; i.e., *the more the better*. In marketing, this can create conceptual problems depending upon the nature of the underlying dimensions.

This assumption may not be realistic for many latent attributes or dimensions underlying brands in a product/service class. For example, it is not clear that consumers prefer infinite amounts of size and sportiness (assuming those were the two underlying dimensions driving their vehicle preferences) in their family Sports Utility Vehicle (SUV). In addition, it would imply that the optimal positioning of new brands would be located towards infinity in the direction of these consumer vectors which is most often not realistic. However, the vector MDS model has been shown to be very robust and estimation procedures such as MDPREF (Carroll, 1972, 1980) based on singular value decomposition principles provide globally optimum results while being able to estimate all orthogonal dimensions in one pass of the analysis.

Recently, Scott and DeSarbo (2011) have extended this individual level deterministic vector MDS model to a parametric estimation framework and have provided four variants of the individual level vector MDS model involving reparameterisation options of the consumer and/or brand coordinates. There are occasions or application where the derived dimensional coordinates regarding $\underline{A} = ((a_{it}))$ and/or $\underline{B} = ((b_{jt}))$ in Eq. (1) are either difficult to interpret or need to be related to external information (e.g., brand attributes/features, subject demographics, etc.). One can always employ property fitting methods (Borg and Groenen, 2005) where methods such as correlation or multiple regression can be employed to relate $\underline{A}$ and/or $\underline{B}$ to such external information. Unfortunately, given the rotational indeterminacy inherent in the vector model, such methods can mask tacit relationships between these estimated dimensions and such external information. As such, the model defined in (1) can be generalised to incorporate additional data in the form of individual and/or brand background variables. The coordinates for individuals (vector termini) and/or brands, as the case might be, can be reparameterised as linear functions of background variables (see Bentler and Weeks, 1978; Bloxom, 1978; de Leeuw and Heiser, 1980; and Noma and Johnson, 1977, for constraining MDS spaces). If stimulus attribute data is available, then b_{jt} can be reparameterised as:

$$b_{jt} = \sum_{k=1}^{K} x_{jt}\gamma_{kt}, \qquad (2)$$

where x_{jk} is the value of feature k $(k=1,\ldots,K)$ for brand j and γ_{kt} is the impact of feature k on dimension t. As in CANDELINC (Carroll et al., 1979), Three-Way Multivariate Conjoint Analysis (DeSarbo et al., 1982), GENFOLD2 (DeSarbo and Rao, 1984, 1986), Restricted Components Analysis (Takane et al., 1995), and various clusterwise or latent class MDS approaches (DeSarbo et al., 2008), one can model the location of stimuli to be a direct function of their respective features. Thus, the x_{jk} are quantified features which are related to brand attributes (Lancaster, 1966, 1979). Similarly, when individual respondent background data is available, a_{it} can be reparameterised as:

$$a_{it} = \sum_{r=1}^{R} z_{ir}\alpha_{rt}, \qquad (3)$$

where z_{ir} is the value of characteristic r $(r = 1,\ldots,R)$ for individual i and α_{rt} is the impact of the rth individual characteristic on dimension t. When both stimuli and individual background data are available, both sets of coordinates can be so reparameterised. (Note that one always has the option of performing general property fitting analyses in the non-parameterised model with $\underline{A}$ or $\underline{B}$ if, for example, one did not have the full set of background variables to describe $\underline{A}$ or $\underline{B}$ completely). An option in the Scott and DeSarbo (2011) methodology also exists to estimate a stretching/shrinking parameter when a_{it} is so reparameterised to avoid potential problems with placing constraints on individual vectors as discussed in Carroll et al. (1979) and DeSarbo et al. (1982). This parameter would appear as a consumer specific multiplicative term on the right-hand side of Eq. (3). Maximum likelihood involving non-linear optimisation methods is utilised in estimating the desired set of model parameters.

2.2.   *The segment level or clusterwise vector MDS model*

Recently, DeSarbo *et al.* (2008) have developed a clusterwise bilinear vector MDS model which enables one to *simultaneously* perform market segmentation and positioning analyses. This model is mathematically represented as:

$$P_{ij} = \sum_{s=1}^{S} \theta_{is} \sum_{t=1}^{T} a_{st} b_{jt} + c_i + e_{ij}, \qquad (4)$$

where:

$s = 1, \ldots, S$ market segments (unknown);

$a_{st} = $ the tth coordinate of the terminus of the preference vector for segment is in the derived space;

$\theta_{is} = 0$, if ith consumer is not classified in segment s, 1, otherwise;

$\theta_{is} \in \{0, 1\}$;

$c_i = $ an additive constant.

This clusterwise bilinear MDS model is designed to *simultaneously* derive a single joint space where the derived segments (not individual consumers) are represented by vectors (a_{st}) and brands by coordinate points (b_{jt}), and their interrelationship in the space denotes aspects of the underlying data structure. Thus, it estimates the brand coordinates, market segment composition, and the segment vectors all at the same time. In essence, the geometry of the clusterwise vector MDS model is nearly identical to that described in Fig. 1 with the exception that individual consumer vectors are replaced by segment level vectors. Here too, the orientations of the estimated segment vectors give the direction of highest utility for each segments, and a brand has higher preference the further out in the direction of the vector (i.e., the larger the orthogonal projection of the brand onto the segment's preference vector). A major benefit of the DeSarbo *et al.* (2008) model is that it does not require distributional assumptions unlike latent class MDS models (see DeSarbo *et al.*, 1991), and provide a concise spatial representation for the analysis of preference/dominance data. Here too, an option to reparameterise brand locations as a linear function of attributes via Expression (2) is available. The alternating least-squares and combinatorial optimisation estimation procedures are fast and efficient, and can accommodate large datasets. In addition, within a complete cycle of iterations, it estimates conditional globally optimum values of the parameters via analytic closed form expressions. Within each major iteration, the procedure performs four cycled steps to estimate the parameters b_{jt}, a_{st}, θ_{is}, and c_i. It monitors convergence by calculating an overall VAF (variance accounted for — akin to R^2) statistic after each cycle. Model selection (i.e., selecting R and S) is determined on the basis of scree plots of VAF versus sequential values of R and S. In addition, as with all MDS procedures, model selection is also guided by interpretation of the results and parsimony. Lastly, this model accommodates both overlapping segmentation structures as well as hard partitions.

3.   The Unfolding MDS Model

3.1.   *The individual level simple unfolding model*

Coombs (1950) (unidimensional unfolding) and Bennett and Hayes (1960) (multidimensional unfolding) introduced a different type of geometric MDS model for the analysis of such metric preference/dominance data called the simple unfolding model. Mathematically, the model can be represented as:

$$F(P_{ij})^{-1} = \sqrt{\sum_{t=1}^{T} (a_{it} - b_{jt})^2 + e_{ij}}, \qquad (5)$$

where we use the same notation as used in the vector model in Eq. (1) with some striking differences relating to the nature of how consumers' preferences are represented in this approach. In particular, in the simple unfolding model, both brands and consumers are represented as coordinate points in the derived T dimensional joint space. Here, the closer in distance between a consumer and a particular brand, the higher the predicted preference is for that particular brand. Thus, distance is *inversely* related to preference

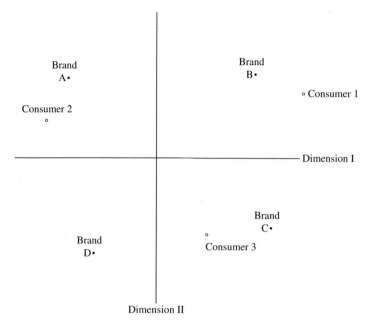

Fig. 2.   The simple unfolding model.

and that is why one sees an inverse function for preference on the left hand side of Eq. (5) above. Figure 2 illustrates this model in two dimensions with three consumers and four brands. Consumer 1's order of predicted preference would be B, C, A, D; Consumer 2: A, D, B, C; and, Consumer 3: C, D, B, A. This geometric model is Euclidean distance based, and the consumer locations are often called *ideal points* as they reflect the optimal combination of the dimensions for that consumer. Thus, unlike the vector model where higher preference tends off to infinity in the direction of the estimated consumer vector, the simple unfolding model posits highest utility at the ideal point, and preference trails off uniformly in any direction from that ideal point. The farther a brand is from a consumer ideal point, the less preferred that brand is. Here, the iso-preference contours in two dimensions are concentric circles around an ideal point since all brand points of fixed radius around the particular brand point would reflect equal preference by this model. Both the brand locations and consumer ideal points are estimated to best recover the empirical preference data. As in the vector model, the analysis is conducted in $t = 1, 2, 3, \ldots, T$ dimensions, and the dimensionality is selected in terms of contrasting goodness-of-fit versus the number of dimensions estimated. Like the vector model, one can rotate the joint space configurations and not affect distances. The simple unfolding model also is indeterminate with respect to the origin of the derived joint space. Nonetheless, the simple unfolding model is more appealing to marketers given its finite preference utility assumptions and intuitive underlying Euclidean distance model. Ideal points often represent targets for marketers who try to attempt to position their brands near target segment ideal points (DeSarbo and Rao, 1986). DeSarbo and Rao (1984,1986) have implemented the linear reparameterisations of brand and/or ideal points as written in Eqs. (2) and (3) to allow for policy simulations and optimal positioning strategies. Carroll (1980) also introduced the weighted and general unfolding models which provide for additional forms of individual differences in a multidimensional unfolding context, but these more complex models involve the estimation of many additional parameters, and successful applications of these highly parameterised unfolding models in the marketing literature are lacking (we describe each in more detail below).

As first noted by Carroll (1980), while the vector and ideal point model appear to be quite different geometric representations, one can easily show that the vector model is a special case of the simple ideal point model. If one were to move an ideal point for any individual consumer further and further out along a fixed line from the origin while holding the brand locations fixed, one ends up with a vector utility model for that consumer in the limit where the ideal point tails off to infinity. The family of concentric circles surrounding that ideal point begins to flatten out and resemble the iso-preference lines of the vector model. Thus, there is additional flexibility involved in the simple unfolding model which can accommodate the vector model as a special case. However, despite its greater flexibility and intuitive appeal, the simple unfolding model suffers from frequent degenerate, uninformative solutions where the brand points and consumer ideal points are estimated to be excessively separated from each other (see Borg and Groenen (2005) for more elaborate definitions and a discussion of attempts to resolve this difficulty).

As mentioned earlier, Carroll (1980) also introduced two more general forms of multidimensional unfolding called the *weighted* and *general unfolding* MDS models. The weighted unfolding model allows each individual to have the differently weighted dimensions in addition to different ideal points. Mathematically, the weighted unfolding model can be represented as:

$$F(P_{ij})^{-1} = \sqrt{\sum_{t=1}^{T} w_{it}(a_{it} - b_{jt})^2 + e_{ij}}, \qquad (6)$$

where w_{it} is an estimated weighting factor which represents the importance of the tth dimension for the ith consumer. Assuming $w_{it} > 0$, this parameter allows for a stretching or shrinking of a particular dimension that is individual specific. Figure 3 illustrates the weighted unfolding model in two dimensions with three consumers and four brands. Different from the simple unfolding model, this model has ellipse shaped iso-preference contours (instead of concentric circles in the simple unfolding model) in two dimensions where the larger the weight for a particular dimension, the smaller the corresponding axis of the iso-preference ellipse. In Fig. 3, Consumer 1 equally weights the two dimensions and orders brands A, B, C, D regarding his predicted preference; Consumer 2 weights Dimension I more than Dimension II with the preference order of C, D, A, B; and Consumer 3 weights Dimension II more than Dimension I with the preference order of B, D, A, C. This geometric model is constructed on the basis of the weighted Euclidean distance defined in Eq. (6). Problems arise when the estimated w_{it} are negative with respect to respective interpretation. If for a specific consumer in two dimensions both weights are negative, then the location of that individual's ideal point becomes an *anti-ideal point* and refers to the point in the joint space of *least* preference. There, preference increases as one travels *further away* from the anti-ideal point in either direction. When the weights are mixed (i.e., in two dimensions, one

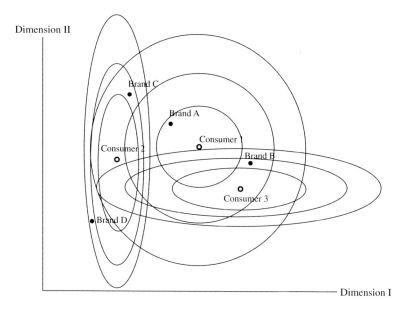

Fig. 3.   The weighted unfolding model.

is positive and the other is negative), the location of the ideal point is a *saddle point* where preference increases on one direction as you go further away from the ideal point, while preference increases with the other dimension as you get closer to the ideal point. Given the dramatic increase in the number of estimated parameters and the associated difficulties involved with the interpretation of negative weights, it is no wonder why there have not been many published applications involving this particular model.

Another more complex generalisation of the simple and weighted unfolding models is the general unfolding model that can be characterised by individual specific differential rotations as well as differential weightings. The differential rotations can be conducted by allowing linear transformation on matrices $\underline{A} = ((a_{it}))$ and $\underline{B} = ((b_{it}))$. Mathematically, this general unfolding model can be represented as:

$$F(P_{ij})^{-1} = \sqrt{\sum_{t=1}^{T} w_{it}(a_{it}^* - b_{jt}^*)^2 + e_{ij}}, \qquad (7)$$

where $((a_{it}^*)) = \underline{A}^*$ and $\underline{A}_i^* = \underline{A}_i T_i (\underline{A}_i$ is the ith row of the matrix $\underline{A}$ and $\underline{T}_i$ is an orthogonal transformation matrix for the ith consumer). Here, $((b_{jt}^*)) = \underline{B}^*$ and $\underline{B}_j^* = \underline{B}_j T_i (\underline{B}_j$ is j-th row of the matrix $\underline{B}$). While the weighted unfolding model allows distinct individuals to differently weight dimensions, the general unfolding model *additionally* modifies the assumption that all individuals utilise the same set of dimensions. Here, the general unfolding model allows each individual to choose idiosyncratic sets of reference dimensions in the joint space. That is, each individual is allowed to rotate the reference frame of perceptual space and then to differentially weight these dimensions. Figure 4 illustrates (for one hypothetical consumer) that the general unfolding model also has iso-preference ellipse contours for different $\underline{T}_i$, but the ellipses need not be parallel to the dimension axes depending on $\underline{T}_i$. Because rotation alone does not make the model different from the simple unfolding model, it is the combination of differential rotations and differential weighting of dimensions that makes this a more general unfolding model.

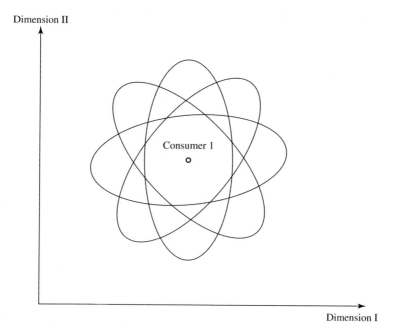

Fig. 4.   Illustration of general unfolding model.

Like weighted unfolding models, there is a dramatic increase in the number of parameters involved with such a model compared to the simple unfolding model, and a paucity of any known published marketing applications exists.

3.2. *The segment level or clusterwise multidimensional unfolding model*

DeSarbo *et al.* (2008) more recently developed a two- and three-way clusterwise unfolding MDS model which simultaneously estimates a joint space of stimuli and (multiple) ideal points by derived segment, as well as the segments themselves. This model is mathematically represented as:

$$F(P_{ijr})^{-1} = \sum_{s=1}^{S} \theta_{is} \sum_{t=1}^{T} w_{rt}(a_{srt} - b_{jt})^2 + c_r + e_{ijr}, \tag{8}$$

where:

$r = 1, \dots, R$ consumptive situations (e.g., time, usage occasion, goal, etc.);

$P_{ijr} =$ the preference for brand j given by consumer i in situation r;

$a_{srt} =$ the tth coordinate of the ideal point for market segment s in situation r;

$w_{rt} =$ weighting parameters for dimension t in situation r;

$c_r =$ an additive constant for situation r;

$e_{ijr} =$ error (deterministic).

This clusterwise unfolding MDS model can be used for the analysis of any type of two- or three-way metric preference/dominance data. In case of three-way data, the model shows how multiple ideal points can represent preference changes over situations, and it provides a concise spatial representation for the analysis of contextual/situational preferences. As an illustration, Fig. 5 presents a hypothetical solution for $S = 3$ segments, $J = 10$ brands, and $R = 3$ consumptive situations. The figure illustrates the spatial solution provided by this three-way clusterwise unfolding MDS model where a_{sr} labels the associated ideal point set of coordinates for the sth

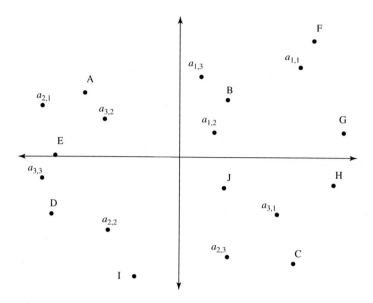

Fig. 5.   Clusterwise unfolding joint space.

segment in the r-th situation, and the letters A–J label the brands. As shown in the figure, Segment 1 has three ideal points which fall into the first quadrant and the ideal points seem not to be much affected by situational factors. In contrast, Segment 2 and Segment 3 have their ideal points located in quadrants 2, 3 and 4, and the points show large ideal point movements associated with these situational factors.

This three-way clusterwise unfolding MDS model allows for a number of diverse options. First, either two-way or three-way data are accommodated by this model. Second, one can choose either stationary ideal points a_{st} or situation/context dependent ideal points a_{srt}. Third, one can estimate either non-overlapping or overlapping segments. Fourth, one can impose constraints on w_{rt} (weighting parameter) including positivity constraints or equality constraints $w_{rt} = w_r$ for all t (the equality constraint allows for a simple clusterwise unfolding model). Fifth, one can perform either internal or external analyses regarding the brand coordinates b_{jt}. Last, users can select from a variety of starting options such as given starting values, random starting values or rational starting values.

With regard to estimation procedure, the three-way clusterwise unfolding MDS model utilises an alternating least-squares iterative estimation procedure. Within each iteration, w_{rt}, c_r, a_{srt}, θ_{is} and b_{jt} are estimated by minimising the error sums of squares:

$$\sum_{i=1}^{N}\sum_{j=1}^{J}\sum_{r=1}^{R} q_{ijr}[F(P_{ijr})^{-1} - F(\hat{P}_{ijr})^{-1}]^2, \qquad (9)$$

where q_{ijr} is a user specified weighting function that is adapted to prevent degenerate solutions as introduced by DeSarbo and Rao (1984) and DeSarbo and Carroll (1985). The dimensionality and number of segments are determined based on scree plots of VAF versus T and S, interpretation of the derived solutions, parsimony, etc.

4. A Marketing Application

In this section, we present a detailed Marketing application of the two individual level MDS joint space models (the vector and simple unfolding models) using customer consideration-to-buy data from a tracking study conducted in 2002 by a large U.S. automotive consumer research supplier. This particular application is modified from DeSarbo and Scott (2011). The study has been conducted semi-annually in June and December for over 20 years across several different vehicle segments. It is used to gauge automotive marketing awareness and shopping behavior among vehicle intenders. An "intender" is defined as a prospective buyer that will be "in market" or has plans to purchase a new vehicle within the next 6–12 months. The surveys used in these tracking studies were conducted among new vehicle intenders and were collected from an automotive consumer panel of more than 600,000 nationally represented households (see DeSarbo *et al.* (2008) for additional details). Using a 4-point preference response scale (4 – "Definitely Would Consider", 3 – "Probably Would Consider", 2 – "Probably Would Not Consider", and 1 – "Definitely Would Not Consider"), the respondents rated each brand in terms of their consideration-to-buy (preference) corresponding to the product segment in which he or she intends to purchase.

For this illustration, we used the large sport utility vehicle segment which included the following 16 brands: Chevy Suburban, Chevy Tahoe, Cadillac Escalade ESV, Cadillac Escalade EXT, Ford Expedition, Ford Excursion, GMC Yukon, GMC Yukon Denali, H1 Hummer, H2 Hummer, Lexus LX470, Lincoln Navigator, Mercedes G-Class, Range Rover, Toyota Land Cruiser, and Toyota Sequoia. Using this product class, we estimate both the vector model and the ideal-point (unfolding) model. The data matrix for both models consists of the same individual stated consideration-to-buy from 278 respondents on the set of 16 large SUV vehicles listed above. Thus, the input data is a two-way dataset of metric brand considerations/preferences where the rows of this data matrix are the 278 consumers and the columns represent the 16 brands.

4.1. *The vector model results*

We first consider the results of the Scott and DeSarbo (2011) stochastic vector model where the goal is to simultaneously estimate the consumer vectors and brand coordinates in a given dimensionality while best recovering the empirical consideration data. Figure 6 shows the resulting configuration in two dimensions with brand locations represented as diamond shaped points and the consumers as vectors emanating from the origin (we normalise the vectors to equal length for convenience and drop the tails of the vectors in an attempt to reduce the clutter in the figure). With respect to Dimension I (horizontal axis), we see that the GM vehicles are separated from the non-GM vehicles. We thus label this dimension as GM versus non-GM. Dimension II (vertical) represents price with the least expensive vehicles at the top of the axis and increasing in price as you travel down the vertical axis. For instance, the majority of vehicles below the horizontal axis listed for more than $60,000, whereas the Expedition or Yukon listed in the mid $30K range at this time. The figure also reveals that brands sharing the same manufacturer are located close together. This means that consumers give these particular brands similar consideration in their purchase plans. Note that four of the GM vehicles are closely located in the first quadrant. Similarly, the two Cadillac Escalades (also GM vehicles) are grouped

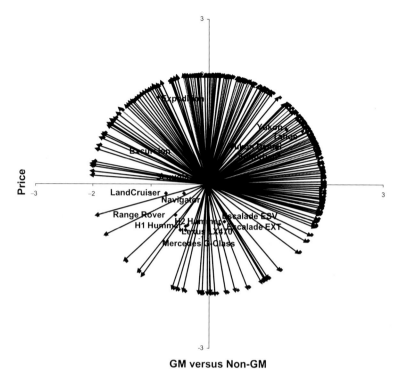

GM versus Non-GM

Fig. 6.   Vector model — SUV application.

together, but given their premium pricing they are located with the higher priced vehicles. Other manufacturer groupings include the Ford Expedition and Ford Excursion, Toyota Land Cruiser and Toyota Sequoia, as well as the H1 and H2 Hummers. This particular joint space positioning map is problematic for this set of manufacturers in failing to make their own subset of brands sufficiently distinctive from each other and appealing to different sets of consumers in this particular product segment.

From Fig. 6, we also note a heavier concentration of vectors in the top half of the graph near the Chevy and GMC products. We may conclude that for this vehicle product segment, consideration-to-buy is greatest for the Chevy/GMC brands, followed by the Ford Expedition where we find the next largest concentration of consumer vectors. In this figure, note that a number of consumer vectors are superimposed on one another. This merely represents consumers with very similar consideration-to-buy ratings on all 16 brands. The lower part of Fig. 6 shows much less segment consideration for the large luxury sport utility vehicles like the unique Range Rover and H1 Hummer.

4.2. *The simple unfolding model results*

For the simple unfolding model representation, we first reverse scaled the same input data $(5 - P_{ij})$ given Eq. (5). Figure 7 displays the derived two-dimensional joint space spatial map for the simple unfolding or *ideal point* model obtained from the DeSarbo and Rao (1986) GENFOLD2 model. Recall that both brands and consumers are represented as points in this two-dimensional space. Here, brands are labelled and represented as diamonds for ease of identification and the 278 consumer are represented by points. The closer a consumer ideal point is to a brand, the higher the

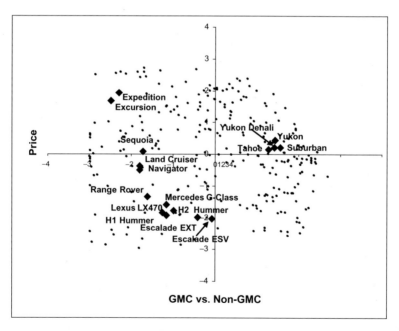

Fig. 7.   Simple unfolding model — SUV application.

consideration-to-buy for that particular brand. Figure 7 shows a similar configuration of brand locations to Fig. 6 (derived from the vector model), and we label these two dimensions accordingly with Dimension I representing a GM versus non-GM factor, and Dimension II as price. Like Fig. 6, the more expensive vehicles are located lower on the vertical axis while the GM vehicles are separated from the non-GM vehicles along the horizontal axis. As indicated above, brands sharing the same manufacturer are located near one another suggesting similar consideration-to-buy and similar positioning difficulties. The ideal-point model shows a clustering of consumer points near the GM vehicles (Yukon, Yukon-Denali, Tahoe, and Suburban). There are also a good number of points in the fourth quadrant, the area between the Suburban and Tahoe and the premium priced vehicles. Because of the Euclidean distance present in the interpretation of the unfolding model, we might interpret this as potential consumer demand for different varieties of large GM SUV's given the underlying dimensions which define the space.

5. Discussion

Both Fig. 6 (vector model) and Fig. 7 (unfolding model) depict a two-dimensional joint space with 16 brands and 278 consumers. We find that the two figures are quite similar with respect to their respective brand configurations and interpretation of the underlying dimensions. Since MDS seeks to reveal the underlying structure in data, this result is not surprising given we use the same data matrix to estimate both models. Both representations reveal potential Marketing positioning problems where each manufacturer's own brands appear to compete more against their own brands than against those brands of other manufacturers.

References

Bennett, JF and WL Hays (1960). Multidimensional unfolding: Determining the dimensionality of ranked preference data. *Psychometrika*, 25, 27–43.

Bentler, PM and DG Weeks (1978). Restricted multidimensional scaling models. *Journal of Mathematical Psychology*, 17(2), 138–151.

Bloxom, B (1978). Constrained multidimensional scaling in n spaces. *Psychometrika*, 43(3), 397–408.

Borg, I and PJF Groenen (2005). *Multidimensional Scaling*, 2nd edn. Mannheim, Germany: Springer.

Carroll, JD (1972). Individual differences and multidimensional scaling. In *Multidimensional Scaling: Theory and Applications in the Social Sciences*, RN Shepard, AK Romney and S Nerlove (eds.), Volume I: Theory, pp. 105–155. New York: Seminar Press, Inc.

Carroll, JD (1980). Models and methods for multidimensional analysis of preferential choice (or other dominance) data. In *Similarity and Choice*, ED Lantermann and H Feger (eds.), pp. 234–289. Bern Stuttgart, Vienna: Hans Huber Publishers.

Carroll, JD and P Arabie (1980). Multidimensional scaling. *Annual Review of Psychology*, 31, 607–649.

Carroll, JD, S Pruzansky and JB Kruskal (1979). CANDELINC: A general approach to multidimensional analysis of many-way arrays with linear constraints on parameters. *Psychometrika*, 45 (March), 3–24.

Coombs, CH (1950). Psychological scaling without a unit of measurement. *Psychological Review*, 57, 148–158.

de Leeuw, J and W Heiser (1980). Multidimensional scaling with restrictions on the configuration. In *Multivariate Analysis*, PR Krishnaiah (ed.), Vol. 5, pp. 501–522. New York: North Holland.

DeSarbo, WS, AS Atalay and SJ Blanchard (2009). A three-way clusterwise multidimensional unfolding procedure for the spatial representation of context dependent preferences. *Computational Statistics and Data Analysis*, 53, 3217–3230.

DeSarbo, WS, JD Carroll, DR Lehmann and J O'Shaughnessy (1982). Three-way multivariate conjoint analysis. *Marketing Science*, 1(4), 323–350.

DeSarbo, WS, DJ Howard and K Jedidi (1991). MULTICLUS: A new method for simultaneously performing multidimensional scaling and cluster analysis. *Psychometrika*, 56(1), 121–36.

DeSarbo, WS and VR Rao (1984). A set of models and algorithms for the general unfolding analysis of preference/dominance data. *Journal of Classification*, 1, 147–186.

DeSarbo, WS and VR Rao (1986). A constrained unfolding methodology for product positioning. *Marketing Science*, 5, 1–19.

DeSarbo, WS, R Grewal and CJ Scott (2008). A clusterwise bilinear multidimensional scaling methodology for simultaneous segmentation and positioning analyses. *Journal of Marketing Research*, 45, 280–292.

DeSarbo, WS and CJ Scott (2011). A review of multidimensional scaling joint space models for the analysis of preference data. In *Wiley International Encyclopedia of Marketing*, J Sheth and N Malhotra (eds.), Marketing Research, Vol. 2, pp. 198–205. West Sussex: John Wiley & Sons.

Lancaster, K (1966). A new approach to consumer theory. *Journal of Political Economy*, 74(2), 132–157.

Lancaster, K (1979). *Variety, Equity, and Efficiency*. New York, NY: Columbia University Press.

Noma, E and J Johnson (1977). Constraining nonmetric multidimensional scaling configurations. Technical Report No. 60, The University of Michigan, Human Performance Center, Ann Arbor, MI.

Takane, Y, HAL Kiers and J de Leeuw (1995). Component analysis with different sets of constraints on different dimensions. *Psychometrika*, 60(2), 259–280.

Tucker, LR (1960). Intra-individual and inter-individual multidimensionality. In *Psychological Scaling: Theory and Applications*, H Gullikson and S Messick (eds.). New York, NY: Holt, Rinehart, & Winston.

Scott, CJ and WS DeSarbo (2011). A new constrained stochastic multidimensional scaling vector model: An application to the perceived importance of leadership attributes. *Journal of Modelling in Management*, 6(1), 7–32.

Slater, P (1960). The analysis of personal preferences. *The British Journal of Statistical Psychology*, 13(2), 119–135.

Chapter 2

ROLE OF STRUCTURAL EQUATION MODELLING IN THEORY TESTING AND DEVELOPMENT

Parikshat S. Manhas
University of Jammu, Jammu, India

Ajay K. Manrai
University of Delaware, Newark, Delaware, USA

Lalita A. Manrai
University of Delaware, Newark, Delaware, USA
manraia@udel.edu

Ramjit
University of Jammu, Jammu, India

Structural equation modelling (SEM) is a popular statistical technique for testing and estimating causal relations using a combination of statistical data and qualitative causal assumptions, which are typically based on a theory. This technique is widely used by social scientists for theory testing and development. SEM is a combination of factor analysis and multiple-regression and it includes path analysis and confirmatory factor analysis. SEM helps researchers to generate and test hypotheses about relationships among theoretical constructs. The tight specification model in SEM makes it a uniquely powerful statistical tool. SEM can help a researcher answer substantive questions and validate measurements. This chapter is intended to provide an overview and some insights to readers as to how SEM works and what are its benefits to a social scientist. We discuss AMOS procedure and several aspects of SEM including model identification, specification, estimation, and modification as well as issues of sample size and interpretation and communication of results. We illustrate many of the key ideas and concepts pertaining to SEM by providing an example.

Keywords: Structural equation modelling (SEM); analysis of moment structures (AMOS); general linear model (GLM); statistical techniques; theory testing; theory development.

1. Introduction

Structural equation Modelling (SEM) can trace its history back more than 100 years. At the beginning of the 20th century Spearman (1904) laid the foundation for factor analysis and the theory for measurement model in SEM (Spearman, 1904). Spearman tried to map different dimensions of intelligence back to a general intelligence factor. Thurston (1947) invented multifactor analysis and factor rotation (more or less in opposition to spearman) and thereby founded the modern factor analysis.

About 20 years after Spearman, Wright started the development of the so-called path analysis (Wright, 1918, 1921). A young geneticist published the first application of path analysis, which modelled the bone size of rabbits. Wright (1921, 1934) presented the method of path analysis for estimating causal relations among variables based on the correlation matrix of observed variables, emphasising path coefficients (standardised regression coefficients) but also using 'path regressions' (unstandardised coefficients). He invented a graphical method of presenting causal relations using path diagrams, consisting of variable labels connected by arrows for direct effects, double headed arrows for unanalysed correlations, and the estimated path coefficients listed over single headed arrows. From path diagrams, Wright could read off total, direct, and indirect effects, and quickly decompose correlations into various causal sources, such as direct effects, indirect effects, common causes, and the like. Among the models Wright estimation by path analysis was what later became known as the MIMIC model.

In the early seventies path analysis and factor analysis were identified and combined to form the General Structural Equation Model. Foremost in its development was Joreskog, who created the well-known linear structural relations (LISREL) program for analysing such models (Joreskog, 1973).

However, LISREL is not alone on the scene. Other similar computer programs are Equations (EQS) (Bentler, 1985) and reticular action model ('RAM') (McArdle and McDonald, 1984), which is included in the ('SYSTAT') software programs under the name Reticular action model or near approximation ('RAMONA') by Arbuckle (1989).

1.1. *Structural equation modelling*

SEM has considerably advanced particularly in the social sciences. The direction of advances has varied by the substantive problems faced by individual disciplines. For example, path analysis developed to model inheritance in population genetics, and later to model status attainment in sociology. A review of the literature in the field of psychology suggests that the factor analysis was developed to understand the structure of intelligence, and simultaneous equation models were developed in economics to examine supply and demand. The discipline-specific advances in SEM came about in the early 1970s to create a multidisciplinary approach to SEM. Later, during the 1980s, responding to criticisms of SEM for failing to meet assumptions implied by maximum likelihood estimation and testing, SEM proponents responded with estimators for data that departed from multivariate normality, and for modelling categorical, ordinal, and limited dependent variables. More recently, advances in SEM have incorporated additional statistical models (growth models, latent class growth models, generalized linear models, and multi-level models), drawn upon artificial intelligence research to attempt to 'discover' causal structures, and finally, return to the question of causality with formal methods for determining causality with non-experimental data.

SEM techniques such as LISREL and partial least squares (PLS) are second generation data analysis techniques (Bagozzi and Fornell, 1982) that can be used to test the extent to which research meets recognised standards for high quality statistical analysis. That is to say, they test for statistical conclusion validity in the tradition of

Cook and Campbell (1979). In contrast to first generation statistical tools such as regression, SEM enables researchers to answer a set of interrelated research questions in a single, systematic, and comprehensive analysis.

SEM refers to such assorted techniques as path analysis, confirmatory factor analysis (CFA), causal modelling with latent variables, and even analysis of variance and multiple linear regressions. SEM permits complicated variable relationships to be expressed through hierarchical or non-hierarchical, recursive or non-recursive structural equations, to present a more complete picture of the entire model (Bullock *et al.*, 1994, Hanushek and Jackson, 1977). SEM is an extension of the general linear model (GLM) that enables a researcher to test a set of regression equations simultaneously. SEM software can test relationship models, but it also allows you to examine more complex relationships and models, such as CFA and time series analyses. SEM is an extension of the GLM that enables a researcher to test a set of regression equations simultaneously that you cannot do by applying the simple regression. It also implements percentile intervals and bias-corrected percentile intervals (Stine, 1989), as well as Bollen and Stine's (1992) bootstrap approach to model testing. A structural equation model thus consists of two components, the 'measurement model', in which latent variables are proposed and tested through CFA, and the 'Structural Model', in which the latent variables are linked together in a relational way. Structural Equation model is a comprehensive statistical approach to testing hypotheses about relations between observed and latent variables and is sometimes called covariance structure analysis, causal modelling, LISREL and many other things. The consensus these days is to call it — SEM. It combines features of factor analysis and multiple regressions for studying both the measurement and the structural properties of theoretical models. It allows the estimation of causal relationships among 'latent' (unobserved) variables as well as between 'measured' (observed) variables. Unlike older procedures it also allows for measurement error and correlated residuals. Path analysis is a form of structural equation model in which 'causal' relationships are hypothesised between observed variables only and the concept of latent variables is ignored. Structural equation model is also involved in testing the 'causal' links between variables. Because of the historical, logical and philosophical issues that forever remain unresolved, the notion of statistically being able to establish a 'causal' model has been largely replaced by the term 'structural' model. This implies adscription of more or less permanent or fixed relationships between various inter connected social conditions or social facts that can be uncovered and tested by statistical techniques. Thus, SEM tests the theoretical relationships between certain hypothesised structural conditions.

In order to apply the SEM technique, the researcher first specifies a model on the basis of literature and theory, and then conducts the fitness test of data for the specified model. The input to the analysis is usually a covariance matrix of measured variables such as survey item scores, and one could use matrices of correlations. In practice, the data analyst usually supplies SEM programs with raw data, and the programs convert these data into co-variances and means for its own use. The model consists of a set of relationships among the measured variables and these relationships are then expressed as restrictions on the total set of possible relationships. We have organised the remainder of the chapter in three sections. Next, we discuss the common terminology as well as some rules and conventions in SEM applications including issues related to sample size. After that we have introduced a SEM example to motivate and illustrate the ideas of model identification and model specification. In the context of the example, we also discuss several criteria for the goodness-of-fit of a SEM model. Finally, we provide a discussion on Model estimation, model modification as well as interpretation of results.

1.2. *Terminology, rules, and conventions*

SEM is a flexible and powerful extension of the GLM and there is a certain terminology that is prevalent in its use. We are giving some of the commonly used terms as the same will be helpful and in particular to a new user. For example, 'Exogenous variables' — variables used as predictors that are not predicted by other variables;

'Endogenous variables' — variables that are predicted by other variables; 'Mediating variables' — endogenous variables in the middle of a causal chain 'Observed/manifest variables' — variables that are directly measured; 'Unobserved/latent variables' — variables that are not directly measured but constructed based on relationships among other observed variables; 'Recursive models' — in these models causality goes in one direction only and error terms are uncorrelated. 'Non-recursive models' — models, which include bi-directional causal relationships (two or more variables that influence each other) and/or correlations between two or more error terms; 'Model parameter' — a coefficient (mean/ variance/ covariance/ regression coefficient) of a structural equation model; 'Path diagram' — a structural equations model represented according to the graphical conventions listed below; 'Free parameters' — unknown coefficients estimated by the model; 'Fixed parameters' — coefficients set equal to a particular value by the researcher prior to model estimation and 'Constrained parameters' — coefficients set equal to one another by the researcher prior to model estimation.

As mentioned previously, AMOS is a popular software to conduct SEM. In AMOS for the default estimation procedure, all endogenous variables ought to be interval or ratio scale. SEM produces diagrams with the variables arranged from left to right in temporal/causal order (causes before effects). Observed variables are always represented by rectangles and unobserved variables are represented by ellipses in SEM diagrams. There is a clear distinction between associations and causal relationships (both in theoretical terms and in terms of graphical representation of a structural equations model). Non-causal (association) relationships are represented by curved double-headed arrows. Causal relationships are represented by straight single-headed arrows (with the arrow pointing towards the effect).

Associations (non-causal relationships) can only be modelled among exogenous variables. Associations between two endogenous variables or between an endogenous variable and an exogenous variable are not possible in the SEM framework. The model should include all possible influences on the endogenous variable(s).

The influences that cannot be accounted for by the predictors included in the model are included in the error term. The error term also includes measurement error in the endogenous variable. In short, this means that each endogenous variable in the model must have an associated 'Error' term. Exogenous variables are assumed to be measured without error. In other words, exogenous variables do not have an associated error term. Error terms are considered to be unobserved variables and as such are represented by ellipses. All the variable in the model (including latent variables) must have unique variable names. Observed variables' names are their names in the dataset. For the latent variables one can choose any name, provided these names are different from the names of observed variables in the active dataset. All latent variables in the model must have a scale. This is accomplished by imposing some constraints either on the variance of the latent variable (not recommended in multi-group analyses), or on a regression coefficient associated with the latent variable (the default option in AMOS). For a latent variable with multiple indicators, by default one of the loadings is set to one. This makes the latent variable 'borrow' the scale of the indicator for which the loading has been set to one. For latent variables representing error terms, by default the associated error path is set to one. AMOS is a WYSIWYG (What You See is What You Get) program: The covariance between two exogenous variables is assumed to be zero if the diagram does not include a curved double-headed arrow between these two variables. The effect of a variable on another variable is zero if the diagram does not include a straight single-headed arrow between these two variables. A model will not output results if it has negative degrees of freedom (DF < 0). DF > 0 is a necessary but not sufficient condition for the model to be identified and estimated.

After reviewing the literature, the investigator should plan on collecting at least 100 cases, with 200 being better if possible (Tanaka, 1987). Consequences of using smaller samples include more convergence failures improper solutions (including negative error variance estimates for measured variables), and lowered accuracy of parameter estimates and, in particular, standard errors. When data are not normally distributed or are otherwise flawed in some way (almost always the case), larger samples are required.

2.   Structural Equation Modeling — Example

2.1.   *Model identification*

SEM requires each equation to be properly identified. Models in which there is only one possible solution for each parameter estimate are said to be just-identified. Models for which there are an infinite number of possible parameter estimate values are referred as under identified. Finally, models that have more than one possible solution (but one best or optimal solution) for each parameter estimate are considered over-identified. For a better understanding of the SEM process it is important to identify the different types of causal relationships that may make two variables co-vary. In essence, four different types can be described:

1. Direct causal relationships, where one variable directly causes an effect on the other (Fig. la). Direct relationships can also be reciprocal as shown in Fig. 1b.
2. Indirect causal relationships, where one variable causes an effect on another through a Third variable (Fig. 1c).
3. Spurious relationships, where the two variables of reference have a common variable that causes effects on both of them (Fig. 1d).
4. Association without causation (i.e., correlation). The two variables of reference have a common variable, but it is not possible to determine if the common variable contributes to co-variation between the two former variables through indirect or spurious relationship (Fig. 1e).

The model shown in Fig. 2 is exactly as it would look if the paragraph interface were used for programming. The two headed arrows indicate possible collinearity among the independent variables.

Model specification

'Model specification' refers to formally stating a model by doing translation of theory into mathematical equations. The path diagram

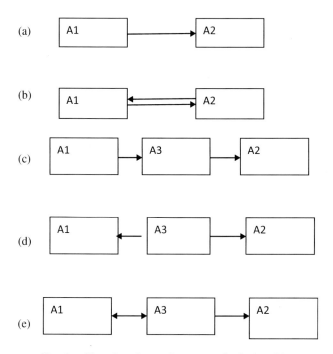

Fig. 1.   Showing the various causal relationship.

shows the causal relationships among all variables in the system. It should be based upon *a priori* knowledge of such relationships which are ultimately related to previous experience or theoretical basis (Coenders *et al.*, 2003). Thus, the path diagram represents the working hypothesis about the causal relationships among variables. Relationships between variables are uni-directionally causal (indicated by a straight, single-headed arrow on path diagrams), correlations (indicated by a double-headed arrow on path diagrams) or residual unexplained variances (arrows not originating in a variable).

It usually helps to draw a path diagram, showing the independent and dependent variables. The independent variables are often referred to as 'exogenous' variables meaning their causes are determined outside the model. The dependent variables are often referred to as 'endogenous' variables because their causes are presumed to be determined from within the model. One must

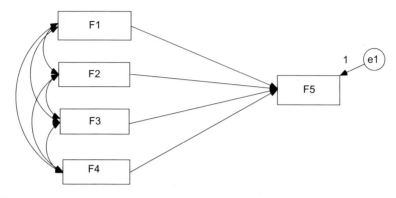

Where

F1—'Satisfaction with hotel staff and employees' (four items summated scale)

F2—'Quality services provided by the hotel' (four items summated scale)

F3—'Restaurants and cafes in the hotel' (four summated scale)

F4—'Price / value of the money provided by the hotel' (four summated scale)

F5—'Overall guest satisfaction with the hotel' (three summated scale)

Fig. 2.   Dimensions of guest satisfaction.

specify the relevant constructs, both latent and observed and specify the relationships between the constructs. The problems may arise pertaining to the identification but can usually be handled. One reason for under identification is the use of very few indicators for a latent variable, i.e., (one or two only). Two indicators will produce under identification; three will produce just identification; and four will produce over identification. Thus, one should try to have three or more indictor variables. After identification and specification of model the model is estimated.

2.2.   *Goodness-of-fit*

A non-significant chi-square indicates that the parameters that were estimated for the model fit the data. In order to check the model has a good fit or not one would need to examine the values of different indices, such as listed in Table 1.

LISREL (Joreskorg, 1973) includes four indices, namely, root mean square residual (RMR), goodness-of-fit Index (GFI), adjusted goodness of fit index (AGFI), and CMIN. Bentler (1985) in EQS

Table 1.   Fit indices and summary of default model.

Tests	Criteria	Model fit summary (current example)
χ^2 test		
χ^2	$P > 0.05$	0
$\chi^2/\text{d.f}$	< 5	0.00 (Just identified)
Fit Of Indices		
GFI	> 0.90	0.91
AGFI	> 0.90	0.94
RFI	> 0.90	0.92
NFI	> 0.90	0.96
MNFI	> 0.90	0.94
Alternative Indices		
CFI	> 0.95	0.97
RMSEA	< 0.08	0.04
RMR	< 0.05	0.03

includes those as well as his own the comparative fit index (CFI), normed fit index (NFI), and non-normed fit index (NNFI). The CFI is generally regarded as the best, but there are disagreements. It is wise to report them all. The CFI tests the improvement of fit between a so-called independence model, where there is no relationships between variables, and the proposed model. The Fit indices are generally set to range from 0–1. The fit indices are considered acceptable if the numerical value is above 0.90, although this, like the $p = 0.05$ level, is arbitrary and depends on the researcher preference. Another popular measure is the root mean square error of approximation (RMSEA). This measure is reported in decimal. RMSEA value below 0.05 is considered acceptable.

Other than above-mentioned fit indices those are mentioned in Amos output Table 2 are CMIN is one of absolute fit measure, it gives the idea about the minimum discrepancy levels of the models. RMR usually based on correlation less than 0.05 is taken as a sign of good fit. NCP and FMIN are measures based on the population discrepancy, Use \ ncplo and \ ncphi to display the lower and upper limits of the 90% confidence interval.

Based on their experience with RMSEA, Browne and Cudeck (1993) suggest that a RMSEA of 0.05 or less indicates a 'close fit'.

Table 2.　Model estimation for example regression weights: default model.

			Estimate	S.E.	C.R.	P	Label
F5	←	F3	0.819	0.544	15.056	***	par_1
F5	←	F2	0.839	0.030	28.369	***	par_2
F5	←	F1	0.905	0.122	7.449	***	par_3
F5	←	F4	0.619	0.070	8.870	***	par_8

Employing this definition of 'close fit', PCLOSE gives a test of close fit while P gives a test of exact fit. AIC the Akaike Bayesian information criterion and (ECVI) Expect for constant scale factor compares the ML estimation of goodness-of-fit Indices (dimensionality and parsimony) of each model (Alkaike, 1974). These criteria can be used not only to compare two alternative models of similar dimensionality, but how the models compare to the 'independence model' at one extreme and the 'saturated model' at the other. The model that yields smallest value of each criterion is considered best. *Hoelter* measure falls in a class of its own and it pinpoints the connection between sample size and significance of chi-square.

2.3.　*Model fit summary for the current example*

Based on the fit indices reported in Table 1, the model in our current example is identified and meets with the fit criteria like CMIN, GFI, AGFI, RFI, RMSEA, RMR etc.

3.　Model Estimation, Modification and Interpretation

Model estimation refers to testing the model and for that one should have enough number of cases/data that was previously discussed in sample size in this chapter. One needs to make sure that one should not get more value of kurtosis and skewness and also take care of missing values.

As shown in Table 2, all the regression coefficients (or weights) are statistically significant. Thus, all the factors F1, F2, F3, F4, are considered meaningful in predicting the guest satisfaction (F5). The reader may note that the C.R. values are greater than two for each of the predictor variables and the corresponding *p*-values are in the acceptable range indicating statistical significant. Furthermore, one could test several hypotheses in this context, such as,

Hypothesis-1: Satisfaction with hotel staff and employees (Fl) does not determine overall guest satisfaction (F5),

Hypothesis-2: 'Quality Services provided by the hotel' (F2) do not determine overall guest satisfaction (F5),

Hypothesis-3: 'Restaurant and Cafes in the hotel' (F3) do not determine overall guest satisfaction (F5),

Hypothesis-4: 'Price/value for money provided by the hotel' (F4) does not determine overall guest satisfaction (F5).

The regression coefficient for Fl is 0.905 and the C.R. value is 7.44. We, therefore, reject Hypothesis-1 that is 'Satisfaction with hotel staff and employees' (Fl) does not influence overall guest satisfaction (F5). The regression coefficient of F2 is 0.839 and C.R. value is 28.369. Thus, we reject Hypothesis-2, that is 'Quality Services provided by the hotel' (F2) do not effect overall guest satisfaction (F5). F3 has a regression coefficient of 0.819 and C.R. value of 15.056. Thus, we reject Hypothesis-3, that is 'Restaurant and cafes in the hotel' do not effect overall guest satisfaction (F5). Likewise we reject Hypothesis-4, that is 'price/value for money provided by the hotel' (F4) does not effect overall guest satisfaction (F5) in view of the regression coefficient for F4 being 0.619 and C.R. value of 8.870. Thus, all four predictor variables (Fl through F4) are significant in predicting overall guest satisfaction (F5) in this example.

SEM programs also provide two sets of information that allow you to improve your model. In AMOS and LISREL they are called modification indices (MI). In EQS they are called the Lagrange Multiplier (LM) test and the Wald test. The Mis suggests paths to add to your model to improve its fit. If you have any missing data AMOS will not report MIs and you must modify your model without this aid. This is controversial because mindless use of the tests allows capitalisation on chance. The issue is not so much using the tests but the basis for using the test. Just going in and adding paths without concern for the underlying theory is a questionable research practice. However, if there are sound theoretical reasons for adding or dropping paths then it would be appropriate to do so. After making theory based modifications suggested by the SEM procedure, the model estimation is repeated until one achieves a satisfactory solution or desired goodness-of-fit for the model.

The model is then interpreted along the lines discussed above. One can then make claims about the relationship among theoretical constructs, based on the best fitting model. Caution should always be taken when making claims of causality even when experimentation or time-ordered studies have been done. The term *causal model* must be understood to mean: 'a model that conveys causal assumptions', not necessarily a model that produces validated causal conclusions. Collecting data at multiple time points and using an experimental or quasi-experimental design can help rule out certain rival hypotheses but even a randomised experiment cannot rule out all such threats to causal inference. Good fit by a model consistent with one causal hypothesis invariably entails equally good fit by another model consistent with an opposing causal hypothesis. No research design, no matter how clever, can help distinguish such rival hypotheses, save for interventional experiments. As in any science, subsequent replication and perhaps modification will proceed from the initial findings.

References

Alkaike, H (1974). A new look at the statistical identification model. *IEEE Transaction on Automatic Control*, 19, 716–723.

Arbuckle, JL (1989). AMOS: Analysis of movement structures. *The American Statisticians*, 43, 66–77.

Bagozzi, RP and C Fornell (1982). Theoretical concepts, measurements, and meaning. In *A Second Generation of Multivariate Analysis*, C Fornell (ed.), Vol. 1, pp. 24–38. New York, NY: Praeger.

Bentler, PM (1985). *Theory and Implementation of EQS, A Structural Equation Program*. Los Angeles: BMDP statistical software.

Browne, MW and R Cudeck (1993). Alternative ways of assessing models fit. In *Testing Structural Equation Models*, KA Bollen and JS Lon (eds.), pp. 136–162. New bring Park, CA: Sage.

Bollen, KA and RA Stine (1993). Bootstrapping goodness-of-fit measures in structural equation models. In *Testing Structural Equation Models*, A Bollen and JS Long, pp. 111–135. K. Newberry Park: Sage Publications.

Bollen, KA and RA Stine (1992). Bootstrapping goodness-of-fit measures in structural equation models. *Sociological Methods and Research*, 21, 205–229.

Bullock, HE, LL Harlow and SA Mulaik (1994). Causation issues in structural equation modeling research. *Structured Equation Modeling*, 3(1), 253–267.

Coenders, G, J Bisbe, WE Saris and JM Batista-Foguet (2003). Moderating effects of management control systems and innovation on performance. Simple methods for correcting the effects of measurement error for interaction effects in small sample. *Working Paper*, Department of Economics, University of Girona, Spain (June, 1–21).

Cook, T and DT Campbell (1979). *Quasi-Experimentation: Design and Analysis Issues for Field Settings*, pp. 20, 31, 39–47. Boston: Houghton-Mifflin Co.

Hanushek, EA and JE Jackson (1977). *Statistical Methods for Social Scientists*. Orlando, FL USA: Academic Press.

Joreskog, KG (1973). A general method for estimating a linear structural equation system. In *Structural Equation Models in The Social Science*, AS Goldberger and OD Duncan (eds.). N.Y: Seminar press.

McArdle, JJ and RP McDonald (1984). Some algebraic properties of the reticular action model for moment structures. *British Journal of Mathematical and Statistical Psychology*, 37(2), 234–251.

Spearman, C (1904). General intelligence,objectivity determined and measured. *America Journal of Psychology*, 15, 201–293.

Stine, RA (1989). An introduction to bootstrap methods: Examples and ideas. *Sociological Methods and Research*, 18, 243–291.

Tanaka, JS (1987). How big is big enough? Sample size and goodness of fit indices in structural equation models with latent variables. *Child Development*, 58, 134–146.

Thurston, LL (1947). *Multiple Factor Analysis*. Chicago, IL: University of Chicago Press.

Wright, S (1918). On the nature of size factors. *Genetics*, 3, 367–374.

Wright, S (1921). Correlation and causation. *Journal of Agricultural Research*, 20, 557–585.

Wright, S (1934). The method of path coefficients. *The Annals of Mathematical Statistics*, 5(3), 161–215.

APPENDIX

Steps To Launch Amos Graphics

One can launch Amos Graphics in any of the following ways:

- *Click Start on the Windows task bar, and choose Programs → Amos 16 → AmosGraphics.*
- *Double-click any path diagram (*.amw).*

- *Drag a path diagram (*.amw) file from Windows Explorer to the Amos Graphics Window.*
- *Click Start on the Windows task bar, and choose Programs → Amos 16 → View Path*
- *Diagrams. Then double-click a path diagram in the View Path Diagrams window.*
- *From within SPSS, choose Analyze.*

Chapter 3

PARTIAL LEAST SQUARES PATH MODELLING IN MARKETING AND MANAGEMENT RESEARCH: AN ANNOTATED APPLICATION

Joaquín Aldás-Manzano*

Universitat de València. Facultat d'Economia. Avda. de los Naranjos s/n.
46022-Valencia (Spain)
joaquin.aldas@uv.es

Since Jöreskog (1967) provided an algorithm for maximum likelihood estimation of latent variables structural models, covariance-based approaches (CBSEM) are tautologically synonymous of structural equation modelling. However, when Diamantopoulos and Winklhofer (2001) alerted that formative configuration should be considered as a reasonable alternative to model certain constructs, academic realised that CBSEM had many limitations to deal with this kind of constructs. Partial least squares path modelling (PLSPM) has recently arises as an alternative to CBSEM as its algorithm easily manages formative constructs. Proposed as a soft modelling alternative to CBSEM by Jöreskog's thesis advisor Herman Wold, PLSPM has addtional properties that explained its growing use in marketing and management research: Few distribution assumptions and can be estimated with small sample sizes. The objective of this chapter is, on the basis of a practical example, to illustrate and provide guidelines regarding the use of PLSPM as a structural equation modelling tool, revealing its strengths and weaknesses, in order to allow researchers to decide on the adequacy of this approach for their particular investigation.

Keywords: Partial least sqaures path modelling (PLSPM); structural equations models; formative constructs, second order constructs.

---

*Corresponding author.

1. Introduction

Since Jöreskog (1967) provided an operative algorithm for maximum likelihood estimation (ML) of latent variable (LV) models and mainly, after he included it in LISREL, a commercial software (Jöreskog, 1970), covariance-based procedures are tautologically synonymous of structural equation modelling (SEM) techniques (Chin, 1998).

However, Herman Wold (Jöreskog's doctoral adviser) questioned the applicability of covariance structure models estimation *via* ML (Fornell and Cha, 1994) because of its heavy distribution assumptions and high sample sizes needed. In fact, according to Tenenhaus *et al.* (2005) he opposed this 'hard modelling' to a new 'soft modelling' alternative (few distribution assumptions, few cases can suffice) he called partial least squares (PLS). The first general PLS algorithm Wold (1973) offered was called nonlinear iterative pArtial least squares (NIPALS) and a final presentation of the PLS approach to path modelling with LVs is present in Wold's (1982) paper.

As Tenenhaus *et al.* (2005) point out, some terminological confusion has arisen due to the common use of PLS regression in the chemometrics. So, following these authors recommendation to distinguish these two related but different tools we will refer here, in advance, to the use of the PLS approach for SEM as partial least squares path modelling (PLSPM).

PLSPM has been scarcely used in management and marketing research until 10 years ago. The main reason may rely in the absence of a friendly software to deal with the estimations, as LVPLS 1.8 (Löhmoller, 1987, last version) has been the only software available for years. However, the efforts of Chin (2000) with PLS-Graph (beta), Ringle *et al.* (2005) with SmartPLS (beta), Fu with VisualPLS, ScriptWarp Inc, with WarpPLS (commercial) o Tenenhaus, Vinzi, Chatelin y Lauro con XLSTAT-PLSPM (commercial), allow researchers now to easily implement their PLSPM estimations. This fact has provoked an increasing numbers of papers to be published using this methodology. Good recent reviews of this increasing popularity can be found in Henseler *et al.* (2009) or Reinartz *et al.* (2009).

In our opinion, another factor that has contributed to the increasing interest in PLSPM is related to the academia concerning the adequate LVs configuration as either reflective or formative. Since Diamantopoulos and Winklhofer (2001) alerted that formative configuration should be considered as a reasonable alternative to model certain constructs, and Jarvis *et al.* (2003) warned that mis-specification was a common practice in marketing and management journals, alternatives were considered to deal with the difficulties of CBSEM to estimate formative constructs. In a review of papers that address formative measurement, Diamantopoulos *et al.* (2008) show that nearly half of them used PLSPM to model this type of constructs, showing that the easy way in which PLSPM algorithm integrates formative constructs, is enabling PLSPM to be considered as an alternative by researchers.

The objective of this chapter is, on the basis of a practical example, to illustrate and provide guidelines regarding the use of PLSPM as a SEM tool, and revealing its strengths and weaknesses, to allow researchers to decide on the adequacy of this approach in their particular investigation. The rest of the chapter is structured as follows: First, the PLSPM algorithm will be presented with detail, as the main weaknesses and strengths of the techniques arise directly from it. Second, the advantages and disadvantages of PLSPM to estimate structural equation models are presented, and orientation regarding when to choose it in place of CBSEM are provided. Third, a real research structural model is presented and estimated with PLSPM in a step-by-step process: second order factors consideration, validation of the measurement model, assessment of the structural model and hypotheses testing. A conclusion section closes the chapter.

2. The PLSPM Algorithm

Figure 1 illustrates the terminology that will be followed to describe the PLSPM algorithm. The classical structural equation model terms of measurement model and structural model are renamed in PLSPM algorithm to outer model (measurement) and inner model (structural). Outer model can be either reflective (if the indicators are

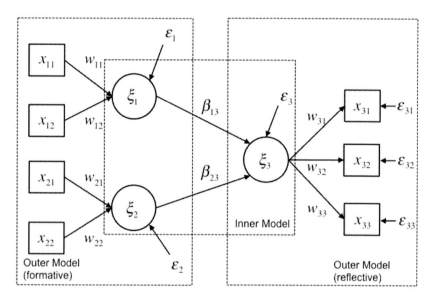

Fig. 1.   An example of PLSPM model.

caused by the LV) or formative if the LV is caused by its indicators. Figure 1 is just an example, no restrictions apply regarding the formative or reflective nature of the LVs: A model can be formed only by formative or by reflective LV and dependent and independent LV can be both formative or reflective. The decision regarding the formative or reflective nature of LV is strictly conceptual. Good guidelines to decide are provided by Diamantopoulos and Winklhofer (2001), Jarvis *et al.* (2003), or Diamantopoulos *et al.* (2008).

In the covariance-based approach of SEM (CBSEM), the difference between the sample covariance's and the covariance's implied by the theoretical model are minimised. That is, the model solution are those parameters which minimise the differences between both matrices (Chin and Newsted, 1999), unless covariance-based SEM, PLSPM focuses on maximising the variance of the dependent variables explained by the independent ones instead of reproducing the empirical covariance matrix (Hacnlein and Kaplan, 2004). While CBSEM first estimates model parameters and then case values (if requested), PLSPM starts calculating case values of LVs as linear combinations of their empirical indicators (Fornell and Bookstein,

1982). The weights used to determine these case values are estimated so that the resulting case scores capture most of the variance of the independent variables that is useful for predicting the dependent one (Haenlein and Kaplan, 2004). Finally, these case values are used in a set of regressions to determine the parameters for structural relations.

Let us try to describe this process in a more formal way. To make it readable, it will be illustrated by applying the algorithm to the example model of Fig. 1. The PLSPM algorithm description is based on Henseler *et al.* (2009) and can be structured in seven stages. More detailed statistical descriptions (and variations) of this algorithm can be found in Tenenhaus *et al.* (2005) and Fornell and Cha (1994).

Stage 1. Initialisation. The LV scores (LV values for each case) are calculated as linear combinations of their indicators. In the first iteration, they are calculated as the mean of the indicators (that is, weights are assumed to be 'one' in this first iteration, although other arbitrary combination of weights can be provided depending on the software). The 'outer' subscript of the LV proxies ($\hat{\xi}^{outer}$) refers to the fact that it is calculated using the outer part of the model as described in Fig. 1 that is, the indicators of the LV. The LV proxies are standardised (mean of 'zero' and standard deviation of 'one').

$$\hat{\xi}_1^{outer} = x_{11} + x_{12}$$

$$\hat{\xi}_2^{outer} = x_{21} + x_{22}$$

$$\hat{\xi}_3^{outer} = x_{31} + x_{32} + +x_{33}$$

$$w_{11} = w_{12} = w_{21} = w_{31} = w_{32} = w_{33} = 1.$$

Step 2. Inner weights estimation. Inner weights are calculated for each LV. There are different schemes for that. The centroid scheme (Wold, 1982) that uses the sign of the correlation between the LV proxies, the factor weighting scheme (Löhmoller, 1989) that uses the correlation, and the path weighting scheme takes into account the direction of the paths. We will illustrate this step using the factor weighting scheme. If two LVs are adjacent (linked by a path), the weight is calculated as the correlation between the LV scores. If they are not adjacent, this weight is set to zero. In Fig. 1 this weights (e_{13}, e_{23}) would be the weight estimation for the paths β_{13}, β_{23}.

$$
e_{jh} = \begin{cases} \text{cov}(\hat{\xi}_j^{outer}, \hat{\xi}_h^{outer}) & \xi_j, \xi_h \text{ adjacent} \\ 0 & \text{rest of cases} \end{cases} \tag{1}
$$

Step 3. Inner approximation of the LV. Inner proxies of the LV are calculated. As we have an outer proxy for each LV, the structural part of the model can be used now to calculate a proxy of the LV. The term inner refers to the fact that the structural part of the model is used. The weights used in these linear combinations are the inner weights of Step 2, that is:

$$
\hat{\xi}_h^{inner} = \sum_j e_{ij} \hat{\xi}_{jh}^{outer} \tag{2}
$$

When applied to our example, we get:

$$
\begin{cases} \hat{\xi}_1^{inner} = e_{13} \hat{\xi}_3^{outer} \\ \hat{\xi}_2^{inner} = e_{23} \hat{\xi}_3^{outer} \\ \hat{\xi}_3^{inner} = e_{13} \hat{\xi}_1^{outer} + e_{23} \hat{\xi}_2^{outer}. \end{cases}
$$

Step 4. Outer weights estimation. It is now time to improve the initial outer estimation of the weights (we arbitrarily fixed them to 'one' in Step 1). The outer weights are calculated by regressing (ordinary least squares) each indicator on the inner estimation of the LV it is connected (reflective LV) or by regressing each LV on its indicators (formative LV). In the case of reflective LV, as they are standardised the estimation is reduced to the covariance. In its general form:

$$
x_{ij} = c_{ij} + w_{ij} \hat{\xi}_j^{inner} + \varepsilon_{ij} \quad \text{(reflective LV)},
$$

$$
\hat{\xi}_h^{inner} = c_j + \sum_i w_{ij} x_{ij} + \varepsilon_j \quad \text{(formative LV)}. \tag{3}
$$

That applied to the example of Fig. 1 makes:

$$\begin{cases} x_{13} = c_{13} + w_{13}\hat{\xi}_3^{inner} + \varepsilon_{13} \\ x_{23} = c_{23} + w_{23}\hat{\xi}_3^{inner} + \varepsilon_{23} \\ x_{33} = c_{33} + w_{33}\hat{\xi}_3^{inner} + \varepsilon_{33} \end{cases}$$

$$\rightarrow \hat{w}_{13}, \hat{w}_{23}, \hat{w}_{33} \qquad (4)$$

$$\begin{cases} \hat{\xi}_1^{inner} = c_1 + w_{11}x_{11} + w_{21}x_{21} + \varepsilon_1 \\ \hat{\xi}_2^{inner} = c_2 + w_{21}x_{21} + w_{22}x_{22} + \varepsilon_2 \end{cases}$$

$$\rightarrow \hat{w}_{11}, \hat{w}_{12}, \hat{w}_{21}, \hat{w}_{22}$$

Step 5. Outer approximation of the LV scores. We reproduce now Step 1 but with this new set of weights estimators ($\hat{w}_{ij}$) instead of the arbitrarily set to 'one' initial weights:

$$\hat{\xi}_j^{outer} = \sum_i \hat{w}_{ij}x_{ij}. \qquad (5)$$

In our example, we get:

$$\begin{cases} \hat{\xi}_1^{outer} = \hat{w}_{11}x_{11} + \hat{w}_{12}x_{12} \\ \hat{\xi}_2^{outer} = \hat{w}_{12}x_{12} + \hat{w}_{22}x_{22} \\ \hat{\xi}_3^{outer} = \hat{w}_{13}x_{13} + \hat{w}_{23}x_{23} + \hat{w}_{33}x_{33}. \end{cases} \qquad (6)$$

Step 6. Stop criterion. Now these five steps should be repeated until no significant change can be observed in the weight estimation. Different stop criteria can be selected. Smartpls (Ringle *et al.*, 2005) stops when the difference between two consecutive estimations of the weights is lower than 10^{-5} (this parameter can be modified in the options menu). Formally:

$$\sum_{i,j} \left| w_{ij}^{(k)} - w_{ij}^{(k-1)} \right| < 10^{-5}. \qquad (7)$$

Step 7. Final solution. After the last iteration, loadings and inner regression coefficients are calculated as follows. The LV scores are the last outer estimation of them.

$$\hat{\xi}_j = \hat{\xi}_j^{outer}.$$

The loadings estimation of formative (π) and reflective (λ) LV are calculated with the formula in Step 4, but using the final estimation of the LV scores:

$$x_{ij} = c_{ij} + \lambda_{ij}\hat{\xi}_j + \varepsilon_{ij} \quad \text{reflective} \tag{8}$$

$$\hat{\xi}_j = c_j + \sum_i \pi_{ij}x_{ij} + \varepsilon_j \quad \text{formative.}$$

The path coefficients are determined conducting a multiple linear regression for each endogenous LV:

$$\hat{\xi}_h = \sum_j \beta_{jh}\hat{\xi}_j + \zeta_j. \tag{9}$$

3. PLSPM Properties: Strengths and Weaknesses

The algorithm described above in the previous section provokes PLSPM to have certain statistical and operational characteristics that configure the main advantages and disadvantages of this technique for researchers. They could be summarised as follows:

1. As no sample covariance matrix is compared to the covariance matrix implied by the model, no global fit indices can be calculated.
2. Each LV should be connected to at least another LV by a path. This implies that confirmatory factor analysis (CFA) is not an option to validate the measurement (outer) model, following the classical two-step approach proposed by Anderson and Gerbing (1988), as covariances and not structural paths link the LV. Alternatives will be provided in brief.
3. Each LV should be associated at least to one indicator. This means that second order constructs cannot be easily used in PLSPM models. The example that will illustrate this chapter provides alternatives to deal with this kind of models.

4. Non-recursive models (A causes B and B causes A) are not estimable. The same happens with logical loops between LVs (A causes B; B causes C; C causes A).
5. Formative LVs are very easily treated by the algorithm. In fact, a formative construct is just a multiple regression with as many regressors as indicators in the construct (see Step 4 of the algorithm). In CBSEM, these types of constructs are much more difficultly incorporated (see Jarvis *et al.* (2003) or Diamantopoulos and Winklhofer (2001) for a good explanation of how formative constructs can be incorporated in a CBSEM using MIMIC models, loading on two reflective constructs or combinations of both).
6. PLSPM requires relatively small sample sizes. If attention is paid to model represented in Fig. 1, it can be seen that the most complex computational step in the algorithm is a multiple linear regression with two independent variables. Classical rules of thumb recommend 15–20 cases for each independent variable (Hair *et al.*, 1998), so the model in the example could be estimated with as few as 40 cases. This statement will be qualified afterwards, as statistical power considerations should apply. Rules of thumb for this model to be estimated through CBSEM indicate that it would require 200 cases or more (Boomsma and Hoogland, 2001).
7. Being a limited information approach, PLSPM has the advantage that it involves no assumptions about the population or scale of measurement (Fornell and Bookstein, 1982). Looking at the algorithm, we realise that multiple OLS regressions are developed, so, how can we say no assumptions about the data distributions are assumed? We know OLS regression requires, for instance, multivariate normality. PLSPM uses OLS regression to get an estimation of the parameters, but it does not use the OLS *t*-values to evaluate their significance. OLS assumptions are necessary to assure that the *t*-statistic will follow a known distribution but not to estimate the parameters. We will need an alternative procedure to estimate parameters significance, and it will be based on resampling as we will illustrate in the example that will follow.

8. The LV estimations are inconsistent. As Chin (1998) or Haenlein and Kaplan (2004) point out, the LV scores in PLSPM are aggregates of manifest variables that involve measurement error, and they will converge on the parameters of the true LV scores only when both the sample size and the number of indicators become infinite (McDonald, 1996). This bias tends to provoke higher estimates of the loadings (measurement-outer model) and lower estimates of the path coefficients (structural-inner model). This problem is known as 'consistency at large'. It not only affects the sample size, but also the number of indicators per LV. To get unbiased estimations, the number of indicators per LV should be high, which makes PLSPM attractive when CBSEM reach their limit: When the number of indicators per LV becomes excessively large (Haenlein and Kaplan, 2004).

The immediate question is: When should a researcher use PLSPM instead of CBSEM to estimate a path model? We review the more frequent advices in the literature and we will finally provide our own opinion. A good reading for this topic is Reinartz *et al.* (2009) as they review more than 30 papers on marketing and management research, indicating the argument the authors used to select PLSPM instead of CBSEM as analytical tool. PLSPM should be the choice if:

1. The phenomenon in question is relatively new or changing and the theoretical model or measures are not well formed (Chin, 1998: 333).
2. The model is relatively complex with large numbers of indicators and/or LVs (Chin, 1998: 333; Chin and Newsted, 1999: 314).
3. There is an epistemic need to model the relationship between LV and indicators in different models (i.e., formative and reflective measures) (Chin, 1998: 333; Fornell and Cha, 1994: 73; Chin and Newsted, 1999: 314).
4. The data conditions relating to normal distribution, independence, or sample size are not met (Chin, 1998: 333; Chin and Newsted, 1999: 314).
5. There is a need for more flexibility in modelling beyond those afforded by first-generation techniques (Chin, 1998: 333).

6. The main objective of the researcher is prediction, not parameter estimation (Fornell and Cha, 1994: 73; Chin and Newsted, 1999: 314).

In our opinion, some of these arguments, being true, do not usually apply to typical marketing or management research problems and others are being questioned by recent research. Our experience demonstrates that PLSPM in marketing and management research is nearly always used in a confirmatory approach. That would make situations 1, 5 and 6 very rare in our knowledge area.

A recent research by Reinartz *et al.* (2009) conducted a large-scale Monte-Carlo simulation comparing the performance of PLSPM and CBSEM with a variety of sample sizes, number of indicators, and indicator distribution.

Focusing on distributional assumptions (argument #4), their results show that when assumptions regarding indicator distributions are not met, ML based CBSEM behaves very robustly even in cases of extreme kurtosis and skewness. The distribution of the indicators neither impacts the amount of improper solutions nor parameter accuracy in a substantial manner. They conclude that justifying the choice of one approach over the other in the basis of this factor alone is not sufficient.

With regards to sample size (argument #4), their results confirm the recommendation. Average relative error in parameters' estimation depends much less on sample size within PLS than it docs within ML-based CBSEM. They conclude that PLSPM should be the method of choice for in situations where the number of observations is lower than 250.

In relation to argument #6, their results demonstrate that the statistical power of PLSPM is always larger than or equal of ML-based CBSEM and, in many cases, PLS requires only half as much information as ML-based CBSEM. PLS can achieve a statistical power of 0.80 for medium population effect sizes, with a sample size as small as 100.

According to these results and to the more common objectives of research in marketing and management, our opinion is that PLSPM is a good option both when the researchers are dealing with small but representative samples and when their model includes formative constructs that cannot be identified defining a MIMIC model or loading on a couple of reflective constructs. Obviously, although not usual in our opinion, if the focus of the research is prediction or theory development, PLSPM should be the option.

4. Applied Example: The Role of Trust on Consumers Adoption of Online Banking

The present example is based on previous research of the authors (Bigné *et al.*, 2008; Ruiz *et al.*, 2009; Aldás *et al.*, 2009a; Aldás *et al.*, 2009b; Aldás *et al.*, 2009). Although a literature review is developed and theoretical basis is provided to formulate the different hypotheses, the objective of this section is basically to illustrate the way PLSPM should be applied. Consequently, readers should refer to the above-mentioned papers for a more detailed presentation of the theoretical relationships and a more in-depth discussion and implications of the results. Smartpls (Ringle *et al.*, 2005) will be used to estimate the model.

4.1. *The model*

As Sarel and Marmorstein (2003) point out, despite heavy investment by banks in developing online capabilities, many online consumers are inactive or use online banking sporadically, focusing mainly on verification tasks and avoiding more complex transactions. As moving consumers to the online channel has a clear cost savings goal, succeeding in this objective becomes very important for banks, as meaningful savings are only possible with a significant migration of consumers to online banking. Understanding the key drivers of users attitude to the service, become a relevant topic for the banking sector.

Much of the research (Eriksson *et al.*, 2005; Pikkarainen *et al.*, 2004; Wang *et al.*, 2003) into user acceptance of E-banking services has used an extended Davis' (1989) Technology Acceptance Model (TAM) to predict user acceptance of technology as a valid conceptual framework. The TAM posits that perceived usefulness and perceived ease of use are two key determinants of technology acceptance. Attending Davis *et al.* (1989), the perceived ease of use was defined as the degree to which a person believes that using a particular system would be free of effort. Perceived usefulness was described as the degree to which a person believes that using a particular system would enhance his or her job performance. According to the TAM, both perceived usefulness and perceived ease of use influence the attitude of individuals towards the use of a particular technology. Perceived usefulness is also influenced by perceived ease of use.

Previous research focused on distance banking adoption reported evidence of the significant influence of perceived ease of use on actual usage (Eriksson *et al.*, 2005; Pikkarainen *et al.*, 2004) or Internet and Mobile banking services usage intention (Luarn and Lin, 2005; Wang *et al.*, 2003), either directly or indirectly through its impact on perceived usefulness. Internet banking websites need to be both easy to learn and easy to use, because when an application is perceived to be easier to use than another, it is more likely to be accepted by users.

The following hypotheses summarise the core TAM proposals:

H1: *Perceived ease of use of online banking services has a positive influence on the perceived usefulness of online banking services.*

H2: *Perceived ease of use of online banking services has a positive influence on attitude to online banking.*

H3: *Perceived usefulness of online banking services has a positive influence on attitude to online banking services.*

Previous research has found trust to be a crucial driver of Internet banking adoption (Bradley and Stewart, 2002; Mukherjee and Nath, 2003; Wang *et al.*, 2003). Thus, in virtual environments, it is fundamental to increase consumer trust, as the risk associated to possible losses from the online banking transaction is greater than in traditional environments.

Trust occurs when one party has confidence in an exchange partner's reliability and integrity (Morgan and Hunt, 1994). Previous studies consider confidence to be a multidimensional construct with three different dimensions: Honesty, benevolence, and competence

(Donney and Canon, 1997; Ganesan, 1994; Sirdeshmukh *et al.*, 2002). Honesty indicates consumer certainty over the company's sincerity and determination to keep promises. Benevolence concerns the consumer's belief that the company is interested in his welfare, has no intention of behaving opportunistically and it is motivated by the quest for mutual benefit. Competence refers to the perception of the other party's skill and ability. Nowadays, many companies largely base trust on the competences their customers perceive, especially in high perceived risk environments like Internet.

Studies focused on online banking (Kassim and Abdulla, 2006; Kim and Prabhakar, 2000; Mukherjee and Nath, 2003) point that trust is a critical factor in stimulating online banking operations. The uncertainty which an individual often assumes makes trust a necessary component (Gerrard and Cunningham, 2003; Pikkarainen *et al.*, 2004). Otherwise, the consumer is reluctant to use online banking services (Kassim and Abdulla, 2006; Mukherjee and Nath, 2003).

Hence the following research hypothesis:

H4: *Consumer trust in online banking has a positive influence on attitude to online banking use.*

Research by Wu and Chen (2005) posits that perceived ease of use is an antecedent of trust. Perceived ease of use has a positive influence on trust as it promotes a favourable impression towards the online seller in the initial adoption of the service. Research by Koufaris and Hampton-Sousa (2002) also evidences the role of trust as a consequence of perceived ease of use.

Gefen *et al.* (2003) has demonstrated that perceived ease of use increases trust, because it increases the perception that e-vendors are investing in their relationship with customers. Ease of searching, transaction interaction, broken links and navigation have all been associated with changes in online trust (Igbaria *et al.*, 1997; Nielsen *et al.*, 2000).

Accordingly,

H5: *Perceived ease of use has a positive influence on consumer trust in online banking.*

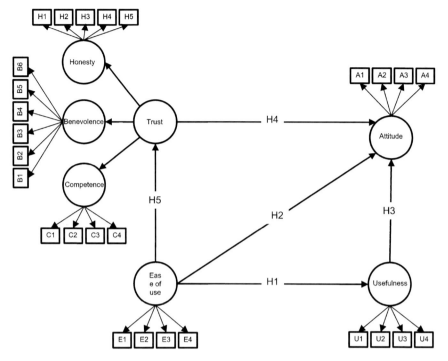

Fig. 2.   Theoretical model proposed.

Figure 2 summarises the proposed model.

4.2. *Method*

A field survey of Internet banking users was employed to empirically test the research model proposed earlier. Data for this study was collected *via* an online survey of 511 Internet banking adopters. Pre-test questionnaires were administered to 20 Internet banking services users and 20 experts in financial services with experience as purchasers of online banking services during the past year. As a result of the pre-tests, some redundant questions were eliminated and some of the scales were adapted in order to facilitate understanding and to avoid erroneous interpretations.

Respondents are Internet users of 16 years of age or older, who had used Internet banking services in the previous year. Intervie- wees answered a survey through a web page that was designed

Table 1.   Sample demographics.

Characteristics	Column percentage ($N = 511$)
Gender	
Male	61.6
Female	38.4
Education	
Primary	4.9
Secondary	32.7
University	62.4
Age	
16–24	9.5
25–34	35.0
35–44	30.9
45–54	16.5
55–64	6.5
65+	1.6

specifically for this research study. A total of 2,025 Spanish Internet banking users were contacted during the online survey; 759 agreed to participate. A final sample of 511 (67.3%) valid questionnaires has been analysed.

Profile of respondents is shown in Table 1. The total sample is composed of 61.6% men and 38.4% women. A large percentage of the sample belongs to the age segment between 25 and 34 (35.0%) and 35–44 (30.9%). In terms of educational level, university educated individuals predominate (62.42%).

Gender and age quotas based on Internet user characteristics examined by the Instituto Nacional de Estadística [Spanish National Statistics Office] study on Internet banking (INE, 2007).

The constructs used in our study were adapted from previous studies and measured by multiple items seven-point Likert-type scales as can be examined in more detail in Table 2.

4.3.   *Estimating a PLSPM. Step 1. Dealing with second order factors*

As indicated, after the algorithm was presented, one of the limitations the algorithm provokedwas that all the LVs should have at least one indicator. If we pay attention to Fig. 2, it should be noticed

Table 2.   Measurement scales.

Construct	Construct dimensions	Item coding	Item descriptions	Source
Trust	Honesty	H1	I think that this banking web site usually fulfils the commitments it assumes	Adapted from Donney and Canon (1997), Kumar et al. (1995), Roy et al. (2001), and Siguaw et al. (1998)
		H2	I think that the information offered by this banking site is sincere and honest	
		H3	I think I can have confidence in the promises that this banking web site makes	
		H4	This banking web site does not make false statements	
		H5	This web site is characterised by the frankness and clarity of the services that it offers to the consumer	
	Benevolence	B1	I think that the advice and recommendations given on this web site are made in search of mutual benefit	
		BE	I think that this banking web site is concerned with the present and future interests of its users	
		B3	I think that this banking web site takes into account the repercussions that their actions could have on the consumer	
		B4	I think that this banking web site would not do anything intentional that would prejudice the user	
		B5	I think that the design and commercial offer of this banking web site take into account the desires and needs of its users	
		B6	I think that this banking web site is receptive to the needs of its users	

(Continued)

Table 2.   (*Continued*)

Construct	Construct dimensions	Item coding	Item descriptions	Source
Competence		C1	I think that this banking web site has the necessary abilities to carry out its work	Adapted from Davis (1989) and Suh and Han (2002)
		C2	I think that this banking web site has sufficient experience in the marketing of the products and services that it offers	
		C3	I think that this banking web site has the necessary resources to successfully carry out its activities	
		C4	I think that this banking web site knows its users well enough to offer them products and services adapted to their needs	
Usefulness		U1	Using online banking services makes it easier to do my banking activities	Adapted from Davis (1989) and Suh and Han (2002)
		U2	Using online banking services enables me to accomplish banking activities more quickly	
		U3	I find using online banking websites useful for my banking activities.	
		U4	Using online banking sites enhances the productivity of my banking activities	
Ease of use		E1	It is easy for me to learn how to utilise Internet banking sites	Adapted from Davis (1989) and Suh and Han (2002)
		E2	I find Internet banking sites easy to use	
		E3	Using online banking services do not requires a lot of mental effort	
		E4	I find it easy to get Internet banking sites to do what I want to do following the instructions available on these websites.	
Attitude		A1	Using online banking is a good idea	Adapted from Suh and Han (2002)
		A2	Using online banking is a wise idea	
		A3	Using online banking is a positive idea	
		A4	Using online banking is an appealing idea	

that trust has been defined as a second order construct of its three first order dimensions: Benevolence, honesty and competence, not having indicators itself, and making the model not estimable.

Different procedures have been proposed to treat second order constructs. We will follow Wilson and Henseler (2007) to present the two more common approaches: The hierarchical components approach and the two-step approach.

The hierarchical components approach (also known as the repeated indicators approach, was initially proposed by Wold (1982) and it solves the problem by using all the indicators of the first order dimensions as indicators of the second order construct, as illustrated for our example in Fig. 3. Some of the limitations of this approach arise when the number of indicators of each first order factor is very different, making the second order factor more related to one dimension than to other. In the same sense, when the epistemic relationship between the second order dimension and the first order one is formative, the second order construct is perfectly explained

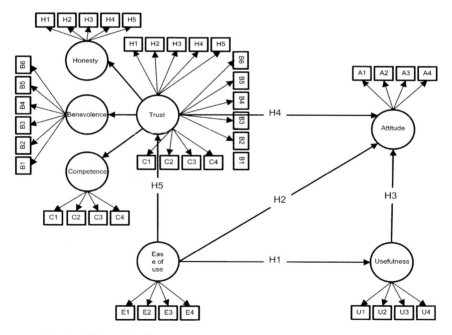

Fig. 3.   Hierarchical components approach to second order constructs.

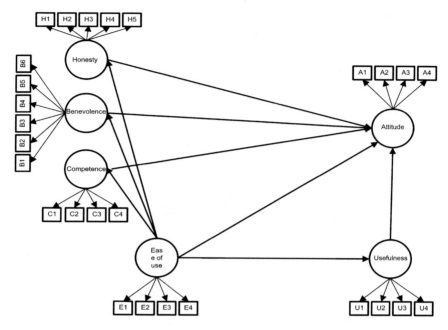

Fig. 4.   Two-step approach to second order constructs. Step 1.

by the first order dimensions (they share indicators). This provokes that any other LV can influence significantly the second order LV as there is no residual variance to be explained.

In the two-step approach (Agarwal and Karahanna, 2000; Henseler *et al.*, 2007), the first step starts by deleting the second order construct and relating the first order ones to those LVs of which the second order one was dependent or caused (Fig. 4). Then the LV scores of the first order factors are estimated. In the second step, the first order factors are no more LV, as the LV scores are used as indicators of the second order construct (Fig. 5). This model is now an estimable model. We will follow this approach in our example.

4.4.   *Estimating a PLSPM. Step 2. Validating the measurement (outer) model*

We already indicated when the algorithm was presented that the classical two-step approach proposed by Anderson and Gerbing (1988) to estimate a CBSEM was not applicable to PLSPM. The reason

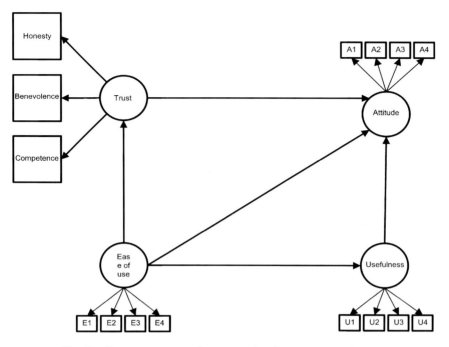

Fig. 5. Two-step approach to second order constructs. Step 2.

is that in the first step, a CFA must be applied to get the necessary information to evaluate the reliability, convergent and discriminant validity of the measurement model. A CFA cannot be applied in PLSPM as the algorithm needs one LV to be connected by structural paths to at least another LV.

The solution to this question is simple: The PLSPM will be estimated including its structural (inner) part, but no attention will be paid to the estimation of the regression coefficients. Only the weights and loadings of the outer model will be considered and classical reliability and validity criteria will be applied. After excluding those indicators that provoke LV not to fit the standard criteria, that is, after having got a reliable and valid measurement model, the PLSPM will be re-estimated and attention will be focused then on the inner model.

Let us refresh our memory on the reliability and validity criteria the measurement model should accomplish with our example model. We will focus on reflective constructs as these criteria are not applicable to formative constructs.

4.4.1. Reliability

Reliability is tested by checking that, for each LV:

- Cronbach's (1951) α is higher than the recommended value of 0.70 (Churchill, 1979). Being:

$$\alpha = \frac{k\rho}{1 + (k-1)\rho},$$

where k is the number of indicators of the LV and ρ the average correlation among those indicators.
- Composite reliability (Werts *et al.*, 1974) should also be higher than 0.70 (Fornell and Larcker, 1981).

$$CR_i = \frac{\left(\sum_j \lambda_{ij}\right)^2}{\left(\sum_j \lambda_{ij}\right)^2 + \sum_j Var(\varepsilon_{ij})},$$

being λ_{ij} the loading estimation of the j indicator of the i-th LV. $Var(\varepsilon_{ij})$ is related to the loadings as follows:

$$Var(\varepsilon_{ij}) = 1 - \lambda_{ij}^2.$$

4.4.2. Convergent validity

- The variance that a LV explains of its indicators should be higher than the variance due to the measurement error. An average variance extracted index (AVE) higher than 0.50 assures this requirement (Fornell and Larcker, 1981).

$$AVE_i = \frac{\sum_j \lambda_{ij}^2}{\sum_j \lambda_{ij}^2 + \sum_j Var(\varepsilon_{ij})},$$

being all the notation equivalent to the composite reliability formula.

AVE is an average index for the set of indicators of each LV. It makes sense to demand that each indicator individually should also be reasonably explained by its LV. The usual criterion is that each indicator's loading should be significantly different from zero and at least as high as 0.70 which indicates that half of that indicator variance is explained by its LV (as $0.70 \approx 0.50$).

4.4.3. *Discriminant validity*

Briefly said, one LV should share more variance with its indicators than with another LV. Fornell and Larcker (1981) operationalised this criterion by checking that the squared correlation between two LVs (the variance that one explains of the other) is always lower than the corresponding AVE of both LVs (the variance shares with their indicators).

Tables 3 and 4 summarise the application of the above-mentioned criteria to our example model. It can be seen that, according to them,

Table 3.   Validation of the measurement model. Reliability and convergent validity.

Variable	Indicator	Factor loading	*t*-value (bootstrapping)	CA	CR	AVE
Usefulness	U1	0.93**	84.67	0.94	0.96	0.84
	U2	0.93**	90.03			
	U3	0.94**	103.13			
	U4	0.87**	55.33			
Ease of use	E1	0.89**	69.47	0.93	0.95	0.82
	E2	0.94**	78.83			
	E3	0.89**	54.36			
	E4	0.90**	61.73			
Attitude	A1	0.92**	85.91	0.93	0.95	0.84
	A2	0.93**	78.89			
	A3	0.93**	82.28			
	A4	0.88**	54.91			
Trust	Honesty	0.94**	169.70	0.93	0.94	0.85
	Benevolence	0.91**	94.12			
	Competence	0.92**	94.89			

Note: CA = Cronbach's alpha; CR = Composite reliability; AVE = Average Variance Extracted **$p < 0.01$; *$p < 0.05$.

Table 4.   Validation of the measurement model.
Discriminant validity.

	1	2	3	4
1. Usefulness	**0.84**			
2. Ease of use	0.64	**0.82**		
3. Attitude	0.67	0.55	**0.84**	
4. Trust	0.34	0.34	0.40	**0.85**

Note: Diagonal represents the average variance extracted; while below the diagonal the shared variance (squared correlations) are represented.

the measurement model exhibits adequate levels of reliability, convergent and discriminant validity. That helps us avoid unnecessary deletion of the indicators and allows us to proceed to the next stage: Assessing the structural model.

A very important question should be addressed here. The reader will notice that a column with *t*-values has been provided in Table 3 to evaluate the significance of each indicator (as they not only need to be higher than 0.70, but also significant). However, we indicated at the beginning of this chapter that PLSPM does not assume any distributional assumption regarding the indicators. How can we calculate a *t*-value then? The answer will be developed later, but these *t*-values are obtained by a re-sampling procedure: Bootstrapping. As these *t*-values are necessary to evaluate not only the significance of the loadings and weights, but also the significance of the structural coefficients, we will present this point after assessing the structural model.

A final point before focusing in the inner model is related to LV with formative indicators. Although formative measures are not the focus of this chapter, and some readings have been recommended to get introduced to them (Diamantopoulos and Winklhofer, 2001; Diamantopoulos *et al.*, 2008), some rationale should be provided regarding why the previous criteria do not apply to formative measures. In a reflective measure, all the indicators share a common cause, the LV, which makes it necessary for all the indicators to behave similarly (thereby, should be correlated). Most of the indices we have provided are just a measure of the degree of that correlation (very clearly in the case of Cronbach's α).

But when the indicators cause the LV these high correlations among the indicators cannot be expected, as they are not sharing any common cause. The criteria to evaluate a formative construct are strictly conceptual (Henseler *et al.*, 2009 and Jarvis *et al.* (2003) provide a good guidance). The only statistical caution a researcher should have is related with the degree of correlation among the indicators. We can see a formative construct as a regression: A set of independent variables (indicators) that are influencing a dependent one (the LV) where multicollinearity is also a problem in PLSPM as it is in regression. The researcher should calculate the variance inflation factor (VIF) in order to detect this problem (higher than 10 is a critical degree but levels higher than five should also alert of a careful reading of the results).

4.5.   *Estimating a PLSPM. Step 3. Assessing the structural (inner) model*

In CBSEM this step is fairly easy.[1] Several goodness-of-fit indices are calculated (GFI, AGFI, TLI, RMSEA, etc.) with well-known acceptable values. We even have a statistical test based on the χ^2 that allow us to accept or reject the null hypothesis of perfect fit (sample matrix equals model matrix). But as derives from the study of the PLSPM algorithm, there is no matrix fit in it and thus, no similar statistic can be calculated. We can only get one R^2 for each dependent LV of our model.

So, before interpreting the model results in terms of acceptance or rejection of our model hypotheses that we transformed into paths in the inner model, we need some guidance on the 'quality' of the estimations it provides. Two criteria are commonly used.

---

[1]Of course this statement is a conscious simplification of reality, as the debates on the adequacy of goodness-of-fit indices or the recommendation of trusting only on the χ^2 test is an open debate in the academy. See Barret (2007) for a good presentation of the topic.

4.5.1. R^2 *of dependent LV*

A common criterion is providing a minimum level for the R^2 of each LV. Chin (1998: 323) talks of a 'substantial' R^2 of 0.67, a 'moderate' level of 0.33 and a 'weak' level of 0.19 for different dependent LV of his model. In our opinion, this arbitrary (although probably reasonable standards) should be revised under the light of the statistical power of the test that the R^2 is significantly different from zero. We think that what is really relevant is being quite sure (Cohen's (1988) criterion of 80% can be a good baseline) that we are going to reject the null hypothesis that R^2 deviates significantly from zero when his hypothesis is false. Taking that into account, and considering our example, the more complex regression the algorithm performs is that of attitude regressed on the other three LVs. Figure 6 provides the power analysis developed with G*Power 3 (Faul *et al.*, 2007) for a regression with three independent variables for different sample sizes. It can be seen that for that regression, sample sizes higher than 75 can provide enough evidence that the R^2 we get is significantly different from zero (our sample size is 511).

Table 5 provides the R^2 of our model that could be considered as substantial or moderate according to Chin (1998) criterion but, apart from that, we are reasonably sure we are explaining a significant part of those LV variances, according to the power analysis.

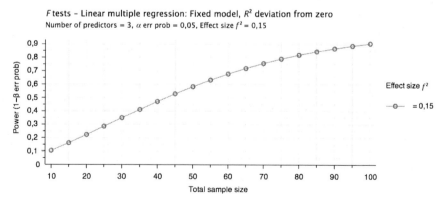

Fig. 6.   Power analysis.

Table 5.   Inner model assessment indicators.

Factor	R^2	Q^2
Attitude	0.72	0.58
Trust	0.34	0.28
Ease of use	0.64	0.52
Usefulness	—	—

4.5.2.   *Predictive relevance*

As the R^2 criterion may look someway arbitrary, a second test is commonly proposed. Its rationale is very straightforward. Let us delete a part of our database (that is, we create artificial missing values of our manifest variables). If we use the inner model to predict some data (the indicators missing data we have created), our prediction should improve a *naïve* estimation of those data (e.g., the mean of the non-missing values of those indicators). If the estimation that uses the model added value (the structural relationships) is not improving the estimation based on means, our model will not enjoy of predictive relevance.

The process is called *blindfolding*, and these are the steps that follows (a very good description can also be found in Tenenhaus *et al.* (2005)):

1. The data matrix is divided in G groups (G is usually set to five or seven, but the only requirement is that this value, called omission distance, should not be a perfect divisor of the sample size). Wold (1982) recommends values between five and ten.
2. The first group is removed from the database (if $G = 7$, one of each seven data are deleted).
3. A PLSPM is estimated on the database without those data. Weights that we described in the algorithm are obtained and also the LV scores.
4. With those weights and the LV scores, we can get a prediction of each indicator just by using the formulas described in the step 4 of the algorithm. For instance for a reflective LV:

$$x_{ij} = c_{ij} + w_{ij}\xi_h^{\text{inner}} + \varepsilon_{ij}. \tag{10}$$

5. But we can also get a prediction of that indicator, without using the PLSPM model information (without weights nor LV scores), by calculating the average of that indicator for the non-missing cases.

6. The process will be repeated for the next 1/7 group of cases until all the database has been out of the model in a certain step.

If we call x_{kn} to the case n of the indicator k that has been deleted, and $\hat{x}_{kn}$ to the estimation of that case by using the information from the PLSPM (weights and LV scores) and $\bar{x}_{kn}$ to the estimation of the case without using that information (the mean of the rest of the non-missing cases), we can obtain the average error we have got in both estimations (E_k using PLSPM information and O_k without using it) as follows:

$$E_k = \sum_{n=1}^{N} (x_{kn} - \hat{x}_{kn})^2,$$

$$O_k = \sum_{n=1}^{N} (x_{kn} - \bar{x}_{kn})^2.$$

If $E_k < O_k$, our model will have predictive relevance. Another way of putting it is by writing Stone–Geisser Q^2 statistic (Stone, 1974; Geisser, 1975) as follows:

$$Q_k^2 = 1 - \frac{E_k}{O_k}.$$

Our model will have predictive relevance if $Q^2 > 0$ (equivalent to $E_k < O_k$). Table 5 shows no problem with this criterion as all the statistics are positive.

4.6. *Estimating a PLSPM. Step 4. Hypotheses testing*

Once the inner model shows adequate level of predictive relevance, as indicated by the R^2 of the dependent LV and Stone–Geisser's Q^2, the last step is analysing the significance of the estimation of the inner model paths what will lead to the acceptance or rejection of the model hypotheses.

As we stated in a previous step, PLSPM does not make any distributional assumption regarding the indicators. Consequently, when the algorithm performs the OLS estimation of the path coefficients (also the loadings and weights), *t*-values from OLS estimation cannot be used, as that would force to assume, among others, the multivariate normal distribution of the data.

Bootstrapping is the alternative PLSPM used to compute the significance of both, the regression coefficients of the inner model and the significance of the weights or loadings of the outer model. N random subsamples are extracted from the original data. The size of any of these subsamples must be the same that the original data sample size, what forces a sampling with replacement procedure. N usually ranges from 300–500 subsamples. The PLSPM model is estimated for each of those N subsamples, providing us N estimations of each parameter (path coefficients, loading and weights). Accordingly, the mean of the estimations of each parameter can be computed as well as their standard errors. The bootstrapped *t*-statistic used to test the null hypothesis that the parameter (β, λ, or w) equals 'zero', can be now computed as (Chin, 1998):

$$t - statistic = \frac{\beta}{se(\beta)}$$

where *t*-statistic follows a Student's *t*-distribution with $N - 1$ degrees of freedom, β is the original estimation of the path coefficient (loading or weight) and se(β) is the bootstrapping standard error of that parameter estimation.

Henseler *et al.* (2009) make an important consideration regarding the bootstrapping procedure. Depending on the initialisation procedure of the outer weights, the sign of the LV estimation can change (although being the same in absolute value). As the bootstrapping procedure implies many estimations of the same model, the LV sign indeterminacy affects the bootstrap path model estimations, by approaching the mean estimation to zero, biasing the bootstrap standard error upward and diminishing accordingly the null hypothesis rejection probability. These authors recommend using the individual sign change option that merely reverses the sign

Table 6. Hypotheses testing.

Hypothesis	Path	Standardised path coefficients	t-value (bootstrap)
H1	Ease of use → Perceived usefulness	0.802**	34.56
H2	Ease of use → Internet banking attitude	0.158**	3.14
H3	Perceived usefulness → Internet banking attitude	0.567**	10.64
H4	Trust → Internet banking attitude	0.214**	5.58
H5	Ease of use → Trust	0.585**	16.07

R^2 (Attitude) = 0.72; R^2 (Trust) = 0.34; R^2 (Ease of use) = 0.64;
Q^2 (Attitude) = 0.58; Q^2 (Trust) = 0.28; Q^2 (Ease of use) = 0.52;

**$p < 0.01$; *$p < 0.05$.

of the bootstrap estimation for each parameter if this sign is different to the one of the original estimation.

In our example, Table 3 offered the bootstrapped t-values for the outer model, showing that all the loadings are significant which reinforces our conclusion of measurement model reliability and convergent validity. Table 6 offers the structural (inner) model estimation with the corresponding bootstrapped t-values.

Results show that the favourable attitude to the use of online banking has a rational basis, as its main antecedent is the perceived usefulness of the service ($H3$: $\beta = 0.567$; $p < 0.01$), as it makes easier and quicker banking activities, increasing perceived productivity. However, the role of the 'ease of use' is also very relevant. Results show that it becomes difficult to perceive a technology as useful which is not easy to use, as easiness is usefulness's main antecedent ($H1$: $\beta = 0.802$; $p < 0.01$). The effect of the perceived ease of use of internet banking on the attitude to this technology is not only mediated by perceived usefulness but the direct influence is also positive and significant ($H2$: $\beta = 0.158$; $p < 0.01$). These results confirm, once more, the applicability of TAM to explain a wide variety of technology adoption processes, including online banking.

But, when focusing on the role that trust, an external variable to TAM, plays on the attitude to online banking, the results show that this effect is positive and significant ($H4$: $\beta = 0.214$; $p < 0.01$). Accordingly, developers should notice that, although important, it is not only necessary to focus on usability when designing a web site for performing financial operations online. As Suh and Han (2002) point out, external signs that allow users to trust on the web become necessary: Privacy protocols or trust seals should explicitly be present on the web sites.

Finally, it should be taken into account that unusable web designs are also a thread to trusting an online banking site ($H5$: $\beta = 0.585$; $p < 0.01$). If a customer finds difficult to perform any operation, a psychological risk of lack of control on the process would arise. Even if honesty and benevolence are not questioned by this feeling, at least the perception of competence of the bank can suffer consequences.

5. Conclusion

The recent attention paid in marketing and management literature to the formative configuration of many latent constructs, altogether with the usual difficulties of researchers to work with big sample sizes, explains the growing number of papers that make use of PLSPM to estimate their structural equation models.

The description of the algorithm provided in this chapter, shows that including formative constructs in the model docs not represent a technical problem for PLSPM, as these constructs just generate a multiple OLS regression with as many independent variables as indicators of the formative construct. The more complex effort PLSPM performs is a multiple OLS regression with as many independent variables as indicators are present in the more complex formative constructs or as the higher number of paths a dependent LV receives. This fact makes the sample requirements to be significantly lower that classical CBSEM.

The PLSPM makes no distributional assumptions regarding the manifest variables, where ease in dealing with real world data where normality is not the rule. However, we have provided evidence of recent research that demonstrates that ML estimation CBSEM can perform as well, if not better, than PLSPM when normality assumptions are violated. The absence of distributional assumptions makes PLSPM to calculate the significance of the weights, loadings and paths *via* re-sampling procedures, like bootstrapping.

This chapter has shown that one of the main limitations of PLSPM when it is used as a substitute of CBSEM, that is, for confirmatory purposes, arises from the fact that no global fit indices can be provided, as the estimation is done by sequential OLS regressions and not by fitting a sample covariance matrix to a covariance matrix implied by the model. The PLSPM, as indicated in the chapter, bases the predictive relevance of the inner (structural) model in the size of the R^2 of the dependent LV and in Stone–Geisser Q^2 obtained again by a re-sampling procedure: blind folding.

As PLSPM algorithm requires all the LVs to be connected by a structural path, CFA is not an option to validate the outer (measurement), as proposed by Anderson and Gerbing (1988). This chapter has shown that PLSPM estimates the model first, ignoring the inner part and focusing in the outer part, applying the classical criteria of reliability, convergent and discriminant validity. After eliminating poor indicators, the model is re-estimated to evaluate the inner part to contrast hypotheses.

All these characteristics of PLSPM have been illustrated with an annotated real research example that has analysed the role of trust on the attitude of consumers to online banking.

References

Aldás, J, C Lassala, C Ruiz and S Sanz (2009a). The role of consumer innovativeness and perceived risk in online banking usage. *International Journal of Bank Marketing*, 27(1), 53–75.

Aldás, J, C Lassala, C Ruiz and S Sanz (2009b). Key drivers of internet banking services use. *Online Information Review*, 33(4), 672–695.

Aldás, J, C Ruiz and S Sanz (2009). Exploring individual personality factors as drivers of M-shopping acceptance. *Industrial Management & Data Systems*, 109(6), 739–757.

Anderson, JC and DW Gerbing (1988). Structural equation modeling in practice: A review and recommended two-step approach. *Psychological Bulletin*, 103(3), 411–423.

Agarwal, R and E Karahanna (2000). Time flies when you're having fun: Cognitive absorption and beliefs about information technology usage. *MIS Quarterly*, 24(4), 665–694.

Bigné, E, C Ruiz, J Aldás and S Sanz (2008). Influence of online shopping information dependency and innovativeness on internet shopping adoption. *Online Information Review*, 32(5), 648–667.

Boomsma, A and JJ Hoogland (2001). The robustness of LISREL modeling revisited. In *Structural Equation Modeling: Present and Future*, R Cudeck, S Du Toit and D Sörbom (eds.), pp. 139–168. Chicago, IL: Scientific Software International.

Bradley, L and K Stewart (2002). A Delphi study on the drivers and inhibitors of internet banking. *International Journal of Bank Marketing*, 20(6), 250–260.

Chin, WW (1998). The Partial Least Squares approach to structural equation modeling. In *Modern Methods for Business Research*, GA Marcoulides (ed.), pp. 295–336. Mahwah, NJ: Lawrence Erlbaum Associates.

Chin, WW and PR Newsted (1999). Structural equation modeling analysis with small samples using partial least squares. In *Statistical Strategies for Small Sample Research*, RH Hoyle (ed.), pp. 307–341. Thousand Oaks, CA: Sage Publications.

Chin, WW (2000). Frequently asked questions — partial least squares and PLS-Graph homepage. Available at http://disc-nt.cba.uh.edu/chin/plsfag.htm.

Churchill, GA (1979). A paradigm for developing better measures of marketing constructs. *Journal of Marketing Research*, 16(1), 64–73.

Cohen, J (1988). *Statistical Power Analysis for the Behavioral Sciences*, 2nd edn. Hillsdale, NJ: Lawrence Erlbaum Associates.

Cronbach, LJ (1951). Coefficient alpha and the internal structure of tests. *Psychometrika*, 16(3), 297–334.

Davis, FD (1989). Perceived usefulness, perceived ease of use, and user acceptance of information technology. *MIS Quarterly*, 13(3), 319–340.

Davis, FD, RP Bagozzi and PR Warshaw (1989). User acceptance of computer technology: A comparison of two theoretical models. *Management Science*, 35(8), 982–1002.

Diamantopoulos, A and H Winklhofer (2001). Index construction with formative measurement models: Interpretation and modeling implications. *Journal of Marketing Research*, 38(2), 269–277.

Diamantopoulos, A, P Riefler and KP Roth (2008). Advancing formative measurement. *Journal of Business Research*, 61, 1203–1218.

Donney, PM and JP Cannon (1997). An examination of the nature of trust in buyer-seller relationships. *Journal of Marketing*, 61(2), 35–51.

Eriksson, K, K Kerem and D Nilsson (2005). Consumer acceptance of internet banking in Estonia. *International Journal of Bank Marketing*, 23(2), 200–216.

Faul, F, E Erdfelder, A-G Lang and A Buchner (2007). G*Power 3: A flexible statistical power analysis program for the social, behavioral, and biomedical sciences. *Behavior Research Methods*, 39, 175–191.

Fornell, C and F Bookstein (1982). Two structural equation models: LISREL and PLS applied to consumer exit-voice theory. *Journal of Marketing Research*, 19, 440–452.

Fornell, C and J Cha (1994). Partial Least Squares. In *Advanced Methods of Marketing Research*, RP Bagozzi (ed.), pp. 52–78. Cambridge, MA: Blackwell Publishers.

Fornell, C and DF Larcker (1981). Structural equation models with unobservable variables and measurement error: Algebra and statistics. *Journal of Marketing Research*, 18(3), 328–388.

Ganesan, S (1994). Determinants of long-term orientation in buyer-seller relationships. *Journal of Marketing*, 58, 1–19.

Gerrard, P and JB Cunningham (2003). The diffusion of internet banking among Singapore consumers. *International Journal of Bank Marketing*, 21(1), 16–28.

Gefen, D, E Karahanna and DW Straub (2003). Trust and TAM in online shopping: An integrated model. *MIS Quarterly*, 27(1), 51–90.

Geisser, S (1975). A predictive approach to the random effect model. *Biometrika*, 61(1), 101–107.

Haenlein, M and AM Kaplan (2004). A beguinner's guide to Partial Least Squares analysis. *Understanding Statistics*, 3(4), 283–297.

Henseler, J, CM Ringle and RR Sinkovics (2009). The use of Partial Least Squares path modeling in international marketing. *Advances in International Marketing*, 20, 277–319.

Henseler, J, B Wilson, O Götz and C Hautvast (2007). Investigating the moderating role of fit on sports sponsoring and brand equity: A structural model. *International Journal of Sports Marketing and Sponsorship*, 8(4), 321–329.

Igbaria, M, N Zinatelli, P Cragg and ALM Cavaye (1997). Personal computing acceptance factors in small firms: A structural equation model. *MIS Quarterly*, 21(3), 279–305.

INE (Spanish National Statistics Offixe) (2007). Encuesta sobre equipamiento y uso de tecnologías de la información y comunicación en los hogares. Primer semestre 2007. Available at www.ine.es/inebase/cgi [accessed on 12 July 2007].

Jarvis, CB, SB MacKenzie and PM Podsakoff (2003). A critical review of construct indicators and measurement model misspecification in marketing and consumer research. *Journal of Consumer Research*, 30(2), 199–218.

Jöreskog, KG (1967). Some contributions to maximum likelihood factor analysis. *Pshychometrika*, 32, 443–482.

Jöreskog, KG (1970). A general method for analysis of covariance structures. *Biometrika*, 57, 239–251.

Kassim, N and A Abdulla (2006). The influence of attraction on internet banking: An extension to the trust-relationship commitment model. *International Journal of Bank Marketing*, 24(6), 424–442.

Kim, K and B Prabhakar (2000). Initial trust, perceived risk, and the adoption of internet banking. In *Proc. 21st Int. Conf. Information Systems*, WJ Orlikowski, P Weill, S Ang and HC Kromar (eds.), pp. 537–543. Brisbane: Association for Information Systems.

Koufaris, M and W Hampton-Sousa (2002). Customer trust online: Examining the role of the experience with the web site. *CIS Working Papers Series*. Available at http://cisnet. baruch.cuny.edu/papers/cis200205.htm [accessed on 23 February 2007].

Kumar, N, L Scheer and J Steenkamp (1995). The effects of supplier fairness on vulnerable resellers. *Journal of Marketing Research*, 32(1), 42–53.

Löhmoller, JB (1987). *LVPLS Program Manual, Version* 1.8. Zentralarchiv für Empirische Sozialforschung. Köln: Universität Zu Köln.

Löhmoller, JB (1989). *Latent Variable Path Modeling with Partial Least Squares.* Heidelberg: Physica.

Luarn, P and HH Lin (2005). Toward and understanding of the behavioural intention to use mobile banking. *Computers in Human Behaviour*, 21(6), 873–891.

McDonald, RP (1996). Path analysis with composite variables. *Multivariate Behavioral Research*, 31(2), 239–270.

Morgan, R and S Hunt (1994). The commitment trust theory of relationship marketing. *Journal of Marketing*, 58(July), 20–38.

Mukherjee, A and P Nath (2003). A model of trust in online relationship banking. *International Journal of Bank Marketing*, 21(1), 5–15.

Nielsen, J, R Molich, C Snyder and S Farrell (2000). *E-commerce User Experience: Trust*. Nielsen NormanGroup, Freemont, CA. Available at www.nngroup.com/ reports/ecommerce/ [accessed on 4 January 2008].

Pikkarainen, T, K Pikkarainen, H Karjaluoto and S Pahnila (2004). Consumer acceptance of online banking: An extension of the technology acceptance model. *Internet Research*, 14(3), 224–235.

Reinartz, W, M Haenlein and J Henseler (2009). An empirical comparison of the efficacy of covariance-based and variance-based SEM. *International Journal of Research in Marketing*, 26, 332–344.

Ringle, CM, S Wende and A Will (2005). *SmartPLS 2.0 (beta)*. Hamburg, Germany: University of Hamburg.

Roy, M, O Dewit and B Aubert (2001). The impact of interface usability on trust in web retailers. *Internet Research*, 11(5), 388–398.

Ruiz, C, S Sanz and J Aldás (2009). Drivers and barriers to online airline ticket purchasing. *Journal of Air Transport Management*, 15, 294–298.

Sarel, D and H Marmorstein (2003). Marketing online banking services: The voice of the customer. *Journal of Financial Services Marketing*, 8(2), 106–118.

Siguaw, J, P Simpson and T Baker (1998). Effects of supplier market orientation on distributor market orientation and the channel relationship: The distributor perspective. *Journal of Marketing*, 62, 99–111.

Sirdeshmukh, D, J Singh and B Sabol (2002). Consumer trust, value and loyalty in relational exchanges. *Journal of Marketing*, 66, 15–37.

Stone, M (1974). Cross-validatory choice and assessment of statistical predictions. *Journal of the Royal Statistical Society*, 36, 111–147.

Suh, B and I Han (2002). Effect of trust on customer acceptance of internet banking. *Electronic Commerce Research and Applications*, 1(3/4), 247–263.

Tenenhaus, M, VE Vinzi, YM Chatelin and C Lauro (2005). PLS path modeling. *Computational Statistics & Data Analysis*, 48, 159–205.

Wang, YS, YM Wang, HH Lin and T Tang (2003). Determinants of user acceptance of internet banking: An empirical study. *International Journal of Service Industry Management*, 14(5), 501–159.

Werts, CE, RL Linn and KG Jöreskog (1974). Intraclass reliability estimates: Testing structural assumptions. *Educational and Psychological Measurement*, 34(1), 25–33.

Wilson, B and J Henseler (2007). Modeling reflective higher-order constructs using three approaches with PLS path modeling: A Monte Carlo comparison. In *Proc. ANZMAC 2007 Conf.*, M Thyne, KR Deans and J Gnoth (eds.), pp. 791–800. New Zealand: Australian and New Zealand Marketing Academy.

Wold, H (1973). Non-linear iterative partial least squares (NIPALS) modelling. Some currents developments. In *Multivariate Analysis*, PR Krishnaiah (ed.), Vol. III, pp. 383–407. New York: Academic Press.

Wold, H (1982). Soft modeling: The basic design and some extensions. In *Systems Under Indirect Observation*, part 2, KG Jöreskog and H Wold (eds.), pp. 1–54. Amsterdam: North Holland.

Wu, IL and JL Chen (2005). An extension of trust and TAM model with TPB in the initial adoption of on-line tax: An empirical study. *International Journal of Human-Computer Studies*, 62(6), 784–808.

Chapter 4

DEA — DATA ENVELOPMENT ANALYSIS: MODELS, METHODS AND APPLICATIONS

Dr. Alex Manzoni
CSES/Victoria Graduate School of Business
Victoria University
300 Flinders St
MELBOURNE VIC 3000
Australia
alex.manzoni@bigpond.com

Professor Sardar M.N. Islam
Centre for Strategic Economic Studies
Victoria University
300 Flinders St
MELBOURNE VIC 3000
Australia
Sardar.Islam@vu.edu.au

Data employment analysis is a non-parametric optimisation technique for the assessment of productivity when expressed as an input–output ratio. Decision making units (DMU) are established as discrete units of observation located on or near the piecewise frontier. Each DMU is measured as virtual input–virtual output calculation of efficiency. The study needs many DMUs so that the model can discriminate between them and assign the best rating of 100%. This is the benchmark against which all the others are ranked. Variations to the model are possible. These include constant increasing and decreasing returns to scale. There are a number of strenghts to this model with the absence of the need for an absolute efficiency as the theoretical maximum to compare against. It has been widely applied and can be partnered with other quantitative techniques.

Keywords: Data envelopment analysis; efficency; productivity.

1. Introduction

The mathematical measurement of performance expressed as an efficiency computation based on the underlying relationship between inputs and outputs, often described as productivity, is increasingly computed by the application of data envelopment analysis (DEA). Its early-day origins came from the necessity to develop a measurement tool for application in not-for-profit driven organisations which have less tangible business outcomes.

Total factor productivity, which considers all inputs and outputs, presents a ratio which allows an investigation of multitude combinations of these factors, as viewed from the vantages of often bounded external constraints, with the objective of entity optimisation. There are a number of strengths in mathematically-based models such as DEA, but also some weaknesses, which need to be addressed to evaluate DEA's suitability for solving particular problems. The first DEA model that successfully optimised each individual observation (Decision Making Unit), with the objective of calculating a discrete piecewise frontier was proposed by Charnes *et al.* (1978) and was based on the work of Farrell (1957). They designed a model, known as the Charnes, Cooper and Rhodes (CCR) Model, 'that generalised the single-output/input ratio measure of efficiency for a single DMU in terms of a fractional linear-programming formulation transforming the multiple output/input characterisation of each DMU to that of a single *virtual* output and virtual input' (Charnes *et al.*, 1994: 6).

2. Basic DEA Model

In a DEA model, the efficiency of an arbitrary unit i is defined as:

$$Efficiency\ of\ unit\ i = \frac{\sum_{j=1}^{n_O} O_{ij}\, w_j}{\sum_{j=1}^{n_I} I_{ij}\, v_j}, \tag{1}$$

$$Where: Efficiency\ of\ unit\ i = \frac{Weighted\ sum\ of\ unit\ i's\ outputs}{Weighted\ sum\ of\ unit\ i's\ inputs}.$$

Here, O_{ij} represents the value of unit i on output j;
   I_{ij} represents the value of unit i on input j;
   w_j is the nonnegative weight assigned to output j;
   v_j is the nonnegative weight assigned to input j;
   n_I is the number of input variables; and
   n_O is the number of output variables.

A linear programming solution is iterated for each DMU in the sample, under a set of pre-defined constraints. One of these is the value of the weighting factors. In arriving at the solution, no unit is allowed to select weights that would cause that unit to obtain efficiency greater than 100%. Thus, the weighted sum of the units' outputs must be less than or equal to the weighted sum of the units' inputs.

$$\sum_{j=1}^{n_O} O_{kj}w_j \leq \sum_{j=1}^{n_I} I_{kj}v_j \quad \text{for} \quad k = 1 \text{ to } n \text{ units.} \tag{2}$$

Also, to prevent unbounded solutions we need the sum of the weighted inputs for each unit to equal one.

$$\sum_{j=1}^{n_I} I_{ij}v_j = 1. \tag{3}$$

Note: Since DEA also assumes that for input variables 'less is better' and for output variables 'more is better' the variables chosen should conform to this logic.[1]

A linear programming problem is solved for each DMU in the sample given a set of constraints. In arriving at the solution, the unit under investigation cannot select weights that will cause any unit to obtain efficiency greater than 100%. Thus the weighted sum of the units' outputs must be less than or equal to the weighted sum of the units' inputs.

$$\sum_{j=1}^{n_O} O_{kj}w_j \leq \sum_{j=1}^{n_I} I_{kj}v_j \quad \text{for} \quad k = 1 \text{ to } n \text{ units.}$$

---

[1]This has been addressed in the most recent models so that 'more is worse' can be an output factor. For example, pollution generated in a production process fits this reality.

Also, to prevent unbounded solutions we need the sum of the weighted inputs for each unit to equal one.

$$\sum_{j=1}^{n_I} I_{ij} v_j = 1.$$

Suppose there are n DMUs and for each there are $j = 1, \ldots n$ inputs and outputs, where the input data for DMU_j, $(x_{1j}, x_{2j}, \ldots x_{mj})$, are represented by the $\mathbf{X}$ $(m \times n)$ matrix and the output data, $(y_{1j}, y_{2j}, \ldots y_{sj})$, are represented by the $\mathbf{Y}$ $(s \times n)$ matrix as follows:

$$\mathbf{X} = \begin{pmatrix} x_{11} & x_{12} & \cdots & x_{1n} \\ x_{21} & x_{22} & \cdots & x_{2n} \\ \vdots & \vdots & \cdots & \vdots \\ x_{m1} & x_{m2} & \cdots & x_{mn} \end{pmatrix},$$

$$\mathbf{Y} = \begin{pmatrix} y_{11} & y_{12} & \cdots & y_{1n} \\ y_{21} & y_{22} & \cdots & y_{2n} \\ \vdots & \vdots & \cdots & \vdots \\ y_{s1} & y_{s2} & \cdots & y_{sn} \end{pmatrix}.$$

The efficiency of each DMU is measured as the 'virtual output' divided by the 'virtual input' once, so there needs to be n optimisations for whole DMU set. The following fractional programming problem is solved to obtain the output and input 'weights' which maximises the DMU ratio.

$$(F.P_0) \max \theta = \frac{u_1 y_{1o} + u_2 y_{2o} + \cdots + u_s y_{so}}{u_1 x_{1o} + u_2 x_{2o} + \cdots + u_m x_{mo}},$$

$$\text{subject to } \frac{u_1 y_{1j} + u_2 y_{2j} + \cdots + u_s y_{sj}}{u_1 x_{1j} + u_2 x_{2j} + \cdots + u_m x_{mj}} \leq 1 \ (j = 1, \ldots, n),$$

$$v_1, v_2, \ldots, v_m \geq 0,$$

$$u_1, u_2, \ldots, u_s \geq 0.$$

The above fractional program (FP_o) can now be replaced by a linear program (LP_o) as follows:

$(L.P_0)$ max $\theta = \mu_1 y_{1o} + \cdots + \mu_s y_{so}$.

Subject to $v_1 x_{1o} + \cdots + v_m x_{mo} = 1$,

$\mu_1 y_{1j} + \cdots + \mu_s y_{sj} \leq v_1 x_{1j} + \cdots + v_m x_{mj}$ $(j = 1, \ldots, n)$,

$v_1, v_2, \ldots, v_m \geq 0$,

$\mu_1, \mu_2, \ldots, \mu_s \geq 0$.

The arbitrary unit (DMU) for which the efficiency is calculated is typically any productive entity that is chosen by the researcher, contingent on the aspects of output and input factors of interest. The broadness of definability of DMU allows researchers to investigate efficiency relationships beyond traditional views, an important feature noticeable in later and more recent research.

Needless to say, there are a number (usually many) of DMUs in the study cohort as it is implicit in the DEA technique that these are assessed and ranked relative to one another. The DMUs can number as few as 15 or 20 and as many as 10,000 (Beasley, 1990) but the quantity is important because of its impact on the model's ability to discriminate between DMUs. There are some heuristics that suggest the optimum quantities of DMUs (sample size), input and output factors; the sample size should be greater than the sum of inputs times outputs, the sample size should also be equal or greater than three times the sum of inputs and outputs, and finally, the one third rule states that the sample size is acceptable if the number of fully efficient DMUs is no greater than one-third of the total number of DMUs in the sample (Cooper *et al.*, 2006; Avkiran, 2006; Ramanathan, 2003).

Each DMU is characterised by output and input factors which are of differing importance to the best operational efficiency of the unit, but DEA automatically assigns weights to each factor to optimise the overall efficiency of the unit (in the CCR model). This automatic assignment however, can be overridden by the researcher (Golany and Roll, 1989).

One important reason for doing a DEA study is to find inefficient DMUs so that they can be projected onto the *efficient frontier*. Fully efficient DMUs lie on this *frontier* so all others are inefficient. The amount by which these are inefficient is their distance from the frontier. To reach the frontier, movement must be origin-seeking i.e., input focused, or origin-leaving i.e., output focused and both distances can be computed. If a DMU is closer to the origin and needs to travel outwards to achieve efficiency, it is seeking to better use existing resources. More output can be achieved from the same inputs so that this *technical efficiency* is a score of under-achievement. For example, a technical efficiency of 80% suggests that 20% more output is possible from the existing inputs.

When the output quantities are acceptable and need to be maintained, the inefficiency displayed by a DMU is the achievement of this output at a cost of inputs higher than efficient DMUs. Allocative (price) efficiency, therefore, shows how much reduction in inputs is necessary for the DMU to become fully efficient. For example, an allocative efficiency of 70% suggests that inputs can be reduced by 30% for the DMU to achieve full efficiency compared to other DMUs. This 'price efficiency' usually shows how the DMU falls short of achieving efficiency due to a failure to make input substitutions or reallocations, in other words, to find better priced equivalent alternatives. The third efficiency is the overall efficiency when both technical and allocative efficiencies are considered.

3.   Slack and Returns to Scale

Those DMUs that are efficient allow us to empirically estimate the efficiency frontier and to approximate it piecewise linearly and by definition these DMUs are 100% efficient and conversely those not on this frontier are inefficient. *Slack* is the amount of inefficiency exhibited by these non-efficient DMUs and may be a consequence of poor performance of inputs, outputs or both therefore, we have *input slack*, and alternatively *output slack*.

The *returns to scale* (RTS) concept represents the relationship between inputs and outputs when one or other is changed. It primarily refers to increasing or decreasing efficiencies based on size of change, and in economics this is called 'elasticity'. The possibilities for efficiency are:

- A change in input or output results in a directly proportional change in the other, called *Constant RTS*.
- An increase in inputs may result in an increase in outputs in greater proportion than the input increase, called an *Increasing RTS*.
- A proportional increase in inputs leading to a proportionally lesser increase in output, known as *Decreasing RTS*.

The RTS properties that an organisation possesses may reflect the nature of the industry, the size of the company, its mode of operation, and a variety of other reasons which constrain efficiency-seeking strategies. The CRS assumption for example, is only appropriate when firms are operating at optimal scale with no imperfect competition, no constraints on supplies, labour of finance etc.

4. Assumptions, Strengths and Limitations

The unique feature of DEA is that it has a reported usefulness in cases where other tools have failed because of the complexity and often unknown nature of the relationship between multiple input and output variables. In fact this robustness is demonstrated in the ability of DEA to use data of imperfect knowledge to the extent that such data may be expressed in ordinal relations such as 'more than' or less than for some DMUs and more conventional tangible data for others. The levels of measurement, i.e., nominal, ordinal interval, and ratio for DMUs may differ but the ability to include them in the dataset ensures that the efficiency calculation for each DMU occurs with the contributions of all factors weighted according to their individual influence.

The fundamental assumption underlying DEA is that as an 'extreme point' method if one DMU is capable of achieving 100% efficiency through the correct ratio of output and input factors optimally weighted, then other inefficient DMUs should be capable of doing the same if they operate efficiently. Implicit in this assumption is that the inputs and outputs are homogeneous when in fact there may be differing amounts of heterogeneity in not only the factors of the DMUs but within the DMUs themselves. Other considerations that warrant attention when applying DEA include:

- The exclusion or poor selection of input and output data, by design or omission, may produce a bias in the results.
- Measurement error in the data can produce biased results.
- Extraneous environmental (e.g., regulatory or physical) factors may impact on operational performances of different DMUs.
- Efficiencies of DMUs are cohort dependent and could be quite different if the wider population were included.
- The DEA computation does not necessarily account for operational decisions regarding management's risk aversion or longitudinal optimisation strategies.

Charnes *et al.* (1994: 8) provide 12 strengths of DEA:

(1) The focus is on individual DMUs in contrast to population averages.
(2) Each DMU has a single aggregate measure for the utilisation of input factors (independent variables) to produce desired outputs (dependent variables).
(3) DEA can simultaneously utilise multiple outputs and multiple inputs with each being stated in different units of measurement.
(4) Adjustments can be made for extraneous variables.
(5) Categorical (dummy) variables can be included.
(6) Computations are value-free and do not require specification or knowledge of *a priori* weights of prices for the inputs or outputs.
(7) There is no restriction on the functional form of the production relationship.
(8) DEA can accommodate judgment when desired.
(9) DEA can produce specific estimates for desired changes in inputs and/or outputs for projecting DMUs below the efficient frontier onto the efficient frontier.
(10) Results are Pareto optimal.

(11) Focus on revealed best-practice frontiers rather than on central-tendency properties of frontiers.

(12) Satisfy strict equity criteria in the relative evaluation of each DMU.

The non-parametric nature of DEA means it does not allow the application of inferential statistics and traditional mechanisms such as hypothesis testing, etc. As an extreme point technique it can be significantly influenced by outliers and is susceptible to the 'noise' (even symmetrical noise with zero mean) such as measurement error. DEA is good at estimating relative efficiencies but poor at absolute values. It converges slowly to 'absolute efficiency' not allowing a comparison to the 'theoretical maximum' and DEA requires that each DMU has a separate linear programming formulation, thus resulting in many LP iterations. For large problems with many DMUs this can be computationally intensive and demanding, and sometimes beyond the capabilities of some programs when traditional mathematics is applied. Another concern is the lack of definitive operational parameters, such as the maximum and minimum numbers of DMUs, inputs and outputs.

5. Applications, Examples and Computation Programs

The body of knowledge surrounding DEA and its applications is growing steadily and becoming diverse. It is not expected that all issues will be explained here but some additional commentary may give a perspective on DEA's applicability. The earlier models were implicit in the notion that more outputs and less inputs were positive achievements, and consequently were designed around this axiom with no provision for alternatives. In recent times, however, the focus on operational efficiencies has broadened to include their impact beyond the organisation. For example, increased productive output may be seen positively by stockholders, economists, government and company staff, yet be frowned upon by the community. Increased output may mean increased waste, pollution or environmental damage at the perceived affordability of a decrease in the purchase cost per unit. Traditional DEA models could not accommodate such negative outputs but contemporary models can include such factors. There are many examples of its success in traditional applications such as, in education, health care, police forces, transport, housing and public sector utilities but a forthcoming book by the authors highlights significant contemporary developments in the application of DEA to corporate governance, organisation behaviour and supply chain management. For example, the corporate social responsibility (CSR) of a large national (Australian) bank, publicly acknowledged for its corporate citizenship by winning a number of 'gold star' awards for CSR, was measured using DEA. The algorithm identified which business units were the most efficient users of the cultural input variables; stakeholder engagement, ethical business behaviour, social accountability, value attuned communication and dialogue in achieving the best corporate social responsiveness (output). This was done without resorting to grass-roots operations research, and while DEA is bedded in the mathematics of linear programming, this example illustrates how the advent of powerful spreadsheet programming and DEA-specific proprietary software has increased its appeal and application. Because of its new utility, an in-depth knowledge of operations research is no longer required to understand or use DEA.

6. Conclusion

DEA is a powerful non-parametric tool for analysing efficiencies of DMUs in the same cohort by allowing direct peer, and peer to grouped-peers comparisons on the basis of a multitude of input and output factors through a now diverse range of models, and with various application software.

An *a priori* knowledge or assignment of weights is not necessary (although sometimes preferable) for the model as results are still legitimate, albeit arguably conservative, and there is no need to make assumptions about the functional form of inputs or outputs as the relational analysis of results provides different perspectives of efficiency, thus revealing opportunities for improvement.

A key feature of DEA is its wide appeal and application resulting from its utility in ease of use and the number of variations to the basic model which is available. It can also be successfully partnered with other quantitative techniques.

Acknowledgement

This article is adopted from Manzoni, A. and Islam, S.M.N. (2009) *Performance Measurement in Corporate Governance: DEA Modelling and Implications for Organisational Behaviour and Supply Chain Management*. Heidelberg: Springer Science and Business Medi. The authors thank Springer for kindly giving the permission for publishing this chapter.

References

Avkiran, NK (2006). *Productivity Analysis in the Service Sector with DEA*, 3rd edn. Qld: Avkiran.

Beasley, JE (1990). Comparing university departments. *Omega*, 18(2), 171–183.

Charnes, A, WW Cooper and EL Rhodes (1978). Measuring the efficiency of decision making units. *European Journal of Operational Research*, 2(6), 429–444.

Charnes, A, WW Cooper, AL Lewin and LM Seiford (1994). *DEA: Theory, Methodology, and Application*. Boston: Kluwer Academic Publishers.

Cooper, WW, LM Seiford and K Tone (2006). *Introduction to DEA and its Uses with DEA-Solver Software and References*. New York: Springer.

Farrell, MJ (1957). The measurement of productive efficiency. *Journal of the Royal Statistical Society*, 120(3), 253–290.

Golany, B and Y Roll (1989). An application procedure for DEA. *Omega*, 17(3), 237–250.

Manzoni, A and SMN Islam (2009). *Performance Measurement in Corporate Governance: DEA Modelling and Implications for Organisational Behaviour and Supply Chain Management*. Heidelberg: Springer.

Ramanathan, R (2003). *An Introduction to DEA: A Tool for Performance Measurement*. New Delhi: Sage Publications.

Chapter 5

STATISTICAL MODEL SELECTION

Graeme D Hutcheson
Manchester University

Statistical models are basic features of quantitative analysis and are commonly reported in academic articles and books to provide evidence of relationships and processes that are of importance in the population. Interpreting these models is, however, rarely straight forward as estimates for the model parameters and significance levels are dependent upon the methods used to build them, the so-called 'variable selection problem'. This chapter investigates how parameter estimates and significance values may be related to the methods used for their construction and uses simulated and real-world data to demonstrate that models may not always provide valid indications of 'actual' relationships and processes in the population. In particular, the use of subset-selection methods may enable variables that are not important in the population to enter into models simply due to chance. In addition to this, the validity of conclusions drawn from the research may be affected by the use of single-model selection, which forces analysts to report just one instance of what might be a multi-model solution. It is proposed that many published reports and papers (including undergraduate and postgraduate projects) interpret statistical models that are invalid as little or no consideration is taken as to how they were constructed or whether single-solution reporting is appropriate. This chapter aims to demonstrate these problems and proposes a solution in the form of a modelling procedure that uses a restricted-set of variables and a reporting method which enables multiple-models to be described.

Keywords: Variable selection; stepcoise selection; model-fit criteria; multi-model presentation.

1. Introduction

A popular research 'strategy' is to collect a lot of data (usually from a questionnaire or survey) about a certain research area, use a statistical technique to identify those variables that are 'significant' and then attempt to interpret these results in relation to the population. This type of research is very common, particularly for those projects that are essentially exploratory in nature and involve the analysis of many variables. The goal of such research is often to identify the 'important' variables and only include these in a single parsimonious model. Although the selection of variables to include in a model is a major part of the analysis process, the procedures used are rarely discussed in detail and are sometimes omitted from written reports entirely. This is problematic as the variable selection procedure is intimately linked to how the parameter estimates and significance levels that are reported relate to the actual relationships and processes that may be present in the population. This ultimately affects the validity of the conclusions drawn from the research.

2. Some Example Analyses

It is useful at this point to describe a couple of example analyses that provide a fairly typical illustration of those presented in the literature and the type of analyses commonly used in undergraduate and postgraduate research projects. Although these examples are based on 'exploratory' analyses where the object was to identify a small subset of important variables from a much larger set of data, the issues discussed here is applicable to any analysis where a subset of variables is selected for inclusion in a model.

2.1. *Tourism in Portugal*

Over 8,500 visitors to Portuguese airports were helped to complete a questionnaire containing over 100 questions in order to investigate their behaviour, profile and preferences for travel. A multinomial logit procedure was used to select a final parsimonious model from a range of explanatory variables to predict the travellers' destination. The analysis of deviance statistics for this model are shown in Table 1

Table 1. An analysis of deviance table for a multinomial logit model of the destination of travellers at Portuguese airports.

	Deviance (LR Chisq)	df	p-value
Coefficients			
TourType	370.7	48	$< 2.7e{-}09$
Country	168.2	36	$< 2.2e{-}06$
Age	30.1	6	0.00061
Gender	15.4	6	0.02360
Earnings	25.1	6	0.00012

(see Hutcheson and Moutinho (2008) for a detailed explanation of the use of analysis of deviance tables with logit models).

2.2. *Union membership*

Data taken from the current population survey (see Berndt, 1991) was used to model the probability of someone being a member of a Union (see Hutcheson and Moutinho (2008, chapter 3) for a detailed discussion of these data). Information was collected on a large number of variables from 534 individuals and a binary logit model used to determine those that were significant. These were then represented in a final parsimonious model of Union membership. Tables 2a and 2b show the deviance statistics and the individual regression parameters for this model.[1]

Typical (albeit naïve) interpretations of these models tend to interpret the importance of the variables on the basis of the p-values (either estimated from the deviance measure or the z-statistic) and describe the effect these have on the response using the parameter estimates. For example, from Table 1 we are led to conclude that the type of tourism (TourType; golf, beach, cultural, etc.) is by far the most 'important' variable out of those which were considered

---

[1] Although the p-values shown in Tables 2a and 2b are slightly different (see 'gender', for example), they are derived from the same data. Table 2a shows estimates of significance based on a measure of deviance ($-2LL$) whilst Table 2b shows significance based on the large-sample approximation to the z-statistic.

Table 2a.   An analysis of deviance table for a binary logit model of union membership.

	Deviance (LR Chisq)	df	p-value
Coefficients			
Wage	11.788	1	0.0006
Age	8.301	1	0.0040
Gender	4.708	1	0.0300
Occupation	36.521	5	7.47e−07

Table 2b.   A binary logit model of union membership. The letter T. denotes a treatment contrast where the indicated category is compared to a reference category. The letter S. denotes a sum contrast where the indicated category is compared to the average of all categories (see Hutcheson (2011) for a discussion of contrast coding in regression models).

	Estimate	Standard error	z-statistic	p-value
Coefficients				
	−4.475	0.566	−7.904	2.7e−15
Wage	0.088	0.025	3.477	0.001
Age	0.030	0.01	2.886	0.004
Gender[T.male]	0.614	0.287	2.142	0.032
Occupation				
[S.clerical]	0.095	0.394	0.241	0.810
[S.management]	−1.370	0.570	−2.402	0.016
[S.other]	1.174	0.282	4.163	3.1e−05
[S.professional]	0.615	0.305	2.015	0.044
[S.sales]	−1.588	0.870	−1.825	0.068

for travellers selecting a destination (it accounts for a reduction in deviance of 370.7 and is highly significant), followed by the nationality of the traveller (Country), age, earnings and gender. Similarly, we may conclude from Table 2a that union membership is most significantly related to the type of occupation, followed by wage, age and gender. In addition to this, conclusions are often drawn about the direction and size of the relationship through interpreting the parameter estimates. For example, the statistics in Table 2b (after taking into account the fact that the estimates are provided in log-odds) suggest that those employees in professional occupations are more highly unionised than those in sales or management and males are more likely to be members of a union than females.

The models above appear to *make sense* and include variables that can be 'sensibly interpreted' in relation to the population. For example, the type of holiday the respondent is having is likely to have a highly significant effect on the destination, and this is what the model suggests. The model also suggests that gender is related to destination (albeit, less significantly than the type of holiday), a result that can be 'explained' in terms of gender preference (males and females 'obviously' have different holiday preferences). Similarly, union membership is significantly related to occupation, a result that is not surprising as some occupations are likely to be more unionised than others. This model also suggests that gender is related to union membership (albeit, less significantly than occupation), a result that can be 'explained' in terms of a gender preference.

Although these conclusions may be rather simplistic, they are indicative of the type that are commonly drawn from statistical models. Indeed, conclusions are often based solely on such statistical output (this is inevitable as this output is often the only information presented in a research paper) and are interpreted as being directly illustrative of processes in the population. However, just because the models appear to 'make sense', it does not mean that the conclusions are valid. Having carefully selected which variables are to be 'measured' and considered for inclusion in the model, it is, in all probability, easy to interpret a whole range of different results and 'sensibly' apply them to the population. For example, models which show that females have a significantly greater probability of joining a union also 'make sense' and can be interpreted in relation to gender preferences operating in the population. Similarly, a finding that the probability of union membership decreases with age (as opposed to the increase of 0.03 in the logit score for each unit increase in age for the present model) would also 'make sense'. The exploratory nature of the research means that a wide range of models could be accepted and interpreted in relation to the population and published.

Although it is tempting to interpret the models above as being valid, there are some serious potential problems with doing so. At a very basic level, there are two main mistakes that can be made when selecting a model to represent a population. First, variables that are not really important may be included in the model (this is related to a Type I error) and, secondly, variables that are important may be left out (this is related to a Type II error). The use of the word 'important' here simply indicates a relationship that exists in the population rather than in a specific sample. The models in the examples shown above may well include variables that are not important for the population and may also omit other variables that are. These basic problems are described in detail below.

3. Problem 1: Including Non-Important Variables in the Model

An effective demonstration of how variables which are actually unrelated to a particular response in the population may end up being included in a model can be achieved using simulated data. The use of simulated data is effective for this purpose, as samples are drawn from 'known' populations, which enables the validity of the final models to be evaluated. For example, if two variables are sampled from two independent random populations, any significant relationship found between the variables in the samples would not provide a valid indicator of the actual relationship in the population.

3.1. *Simulating data*

We can obtain samples from known populations using a number of statistical and spreadsheet packages. For example, the R statistical package (see R Development Core Team, 2011) can easily generate samples from a number of different populations. A random sample of 25 cases from a normal distribution (with mean of 61 and standard deviation of 12) can be obtained using the rnorm() command.

```
rnorm(25, 61, 12)
```

which provides the following sample.[2]

```
34.40471 66.41870 53.32622 73.76648 85.04754 54.63265 87.45254 29.16693
48.61117 53.79831 65.71053 71.65768 53.09116 54.24071 60.12678 83.03730
58.66673 50.12326 55.24686 59.05064 61.37380 47.73879 55.70801 60.04294
74.17387
```

A different random sample of 25 cases from the same distribution can be obtained by simply re-running the command.

```
rnorm(25, 61, 12)
```

```
55.29956 50.38143 60.42785 55.30428 55.26533 52.54686 55.37105 77.86334
63.01067 60.12576 49.73424 81.28471 42.61243 65.18957 63.85451 56.27865
57.34389 54.58902 85.33915 51.28923 59.04998 61.84161 66.93960 61.45486
86.26911
```

These two samples are independent and are unlikely to be significantly correlated (for the data above, this is indeed the case, as the Pearson correlation coefficient is -0.09, $p = 0.67$). Categorical variables can be derived in a similar fashion. A random sample of 25 cases selected from two groups (one having the probability of 0.57) can be obtained using the rbinom() command in R.

```
rbinom(25, size=1, prob=0.57)
```

which provides the following sample.

```
1 1 0 0 1 1 0 1 0 1 1 1 1 0 0 0 1 0 0 1 1 0 0 0 0
```

A different random sample of 25 cases from the same distribution can be obtained by simply re-running the command.

```
rbinom(25, size=1, prob=0.57)
0 1 0 0 0 0 0 0 1 0 0 0 1 0 1 1 1 1 0 0 1 1 0 1
```

The 0 and 1 output can easily be relabelled (for example, male/female, yes/no, pass/fail, reply/no reply) and represented as categorical data.

Using these commands it is easy to obtain repeated samples from defined populations. It is easy to alter the sample size, mean, standard deviation, number and relative size of categories, and

---

[2]This is a random sample and changes each time the command is run. Running the rnorm(25, 61, 12) will not reproduce the sample shown here.

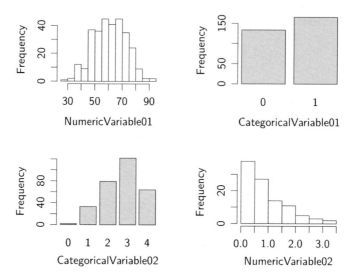

Fig. 1.   Graphs showing typical samples ($n = 300$) obtained from a number of random distributions. NumericVariable01 provides a sample from a normal distribution using the function `rnorm(300, 61, 12)`, NumericVariable02 provides a sample from a gamma distribution using the function `rgamma(100, shape=1, scale=1)`. CategoricalVariable01 and CategoricalVariable02 show 2 and 4 category variables derived using the functions `rbinom(300, size=1, prob=0.57)` and `rbinom(300, size=4, prob=0.67)`.

also obtain samples from other distributions (for example, the Weibull, Poisson, or Gumbel). Figure 1 shows the distributions of four independent random variables that have been selected using commands similar to those shown above.

3.2.   *Models derived from simulated data*

Using these simple commands, a number of datasets were constructed containing numeric variables that had a range of mean values and standard deviations, and categorical variables that had different numbers and sizes of categories. These datasets provided different samples of the population and were used to construct regression models of one of the simulated variables. A simple automated script selected a 'best model' for each dataset based on one of the many 'model-fit criteria' that can be used (e.g., AIC, BIC, Mallow's CP, Rsquare) using a stepwise automated variable selection technique that tested each variable sequentially for entry into the model (automated variable selection is very common and is provided by most statistical software; a detailed explanation of the procedure is provided by Fox and Weisburg, 2011).

The following models were derived from datasets composed of 27 simulated variables (i.e., 27 variables that were independently generated using commands similar to those described above). One variable was chosen as the response (this was a numeric variable and was given the label 'success') and the other 26 variables comprised the explanatories that were considered for entry into the model. The variable selection procedure used a backwards/forwards selection process based on the AIC criteria to select models. The four models shown in Table 3 are illustrative of the models obtained using this procedure. It is important to note that these models are not particularly 'unusual' with respect to the levels of significance or the number of variables retained. In order to make things easier for descriptive purposes, the simulated variables are given names such as Gender, Ethnicity, MathsScore, EnglishScore, Course, SES, FirstLanguage, etc.

We could continue to run models of the variable labelled 'success' and obtain many different final models containing different combinations of significant explanatory variables (i.e., those variables retained in the model on the basis of the AIC statistic). The important thing to note is that the significant associations found in these models do not tell us anything about the actual relationship between the variables in the population. For example, although 'Language' is highly significant in model 4, it would be wrong to conclude that 'Language' and 'success' are related **in the population**. These are just two random variables which showed an association *purely due to chance*. The variables included in the models shown in Table 3 are all randomly and independently generated — any statistically significant associations therefore apply to the sample, rather than the population.

The number of variables that are likely to enter into a model is directly related to the number of variables that are considered in the modelling process — the more variables that are tested for

Table 3. A selection of models that were derived from independently-sampled random variables. OLS regression was used to model a numeric variable using 26 explanatory variables. Models were derived using an automated backwards/forwards selection technique on the basis of AIC values.

	Sum Sq	Df	*F* value	Pr(>F)
Model 1				
MathScore3	2.436	1	2.4065	0.1219
EnglishScore1	2.023	1	1.9982	0.1586
SES1	6.370	3	2.0972	0.1007
Model 2				
MathScore1	4.905	1	5.6873	0.017729*
Pedagogy	7.160	1	8.3010	0.004257**
Disposition	2.823	1	3.2733	0.071448
SelfEfficacy	2.584	1	2.9963	0.084515
Ethnicity	8.491	4	2.4612	0.045512*
Model 3				
GeographyScore	4.458	1	4.4856	0.03501*
Model 4				
ScienceScore	3.450	1	3.5836	0.059337
BiologyScore	4.347	1	4.5153	0.034430*
SES1	14.993	3	5.1913	0.001654**
Language	16.197	1	16.8250	$5.316e-05$***

a relationship with the response variable, the higher the likelihood that some will be significant. In the models above, there were 26 explanatory variables, all of which were multiply tested (on their own and in combination with other explanatory variables) for an association with the response. Even when we just consider the main effects (i.e., no interaction or polynomial terms are considered for the models) the number of statistical tests applied is substantial. For 26 explanatory variables, a simple automated selection technique involves many hundreds of individual tests. If all potential models are considered (using an all-subsets selection procedure), the number of tests increases dramatically — 20 variables generate more than a million models and 30 variables more than a billion; see Burnham and Anderson (2002: 39). Given this number of tests, it is likely that some will show statistically significant associations purely due to chance. There is, therefore, considerable scope for including variables in the model that are not important. Although this has been highlighted in the literature and suggestions made about adjusting the α-levels, this issue has mostly been ignored by analysts:

> ... one might consider Bonferroni adjustments of the α-levels or
> *P*-values. However, if there were 1,000 models, then the α-level
> would be 0.00005, instead of the usual 0.05! Problems with data-
> dredging are often linked with the problems with hypothesis
> testing (Johnson, 1999; Anderson *et al.*, 2000). This approach is
> hardly satisfactory; thus analysts have ignored the issue and
> merely pretended that the data dredging is without peril and
> that the usual inferential methods somehow still apply.
>
> Burnham and Anderson (2002: 40).

Selecting variables from a large number of candidates in this way is commonly known as data-dredging, data-trawling, post-hoc data-analysis, data-snooping or data-mining, and is recognised as a poor practice that may lead to incorrect interpretations of effects when applied to the population. Such biases are clearly demonstrated in the models shown in Table 3. These models were derived using a stepwise procedure, which is a variable selection technique that tests a large number of models and has been strongly criticised:

> Stepwise variable selection has been a very popular technique
> for many years, but if this procedure had just been proposed as
> a statistical method, it would most likely be rejected because it
> violates every principle of statistical estimation and hypothesis
> testing.
>
> (Harrell, 2001: 56).

> *P*-values from subset selection software are totally without
> foundation, and large biases in regression coefficients are often
> caused by data-based model selection
>
> (Miller, 1990; quoted in Burnham and Anderson, 2002: 43).

Although the problems with stepwise selection are well-known, it is still commonly applied and remains a very popular technique for selecting a subset of variables. There are many warnings about the inherent dangers of subset selection (see, for example, Agresti, 2007; Burnham and Anderson, 2002; Harrell, 2001; Weisburg, 1985; Fox and Weisburg, 2011) and readers are encouraged to consult this literature for further information.

It is likely that the models presented in Tables 1 and 2 were carefully selected from a range of explanatory variables and many tests were conducted before the final selection was made (it is not possible to say how many variables were considered, as this information was not provided). The models of travel destination and union membership are, therefore, subject to the criticisms outlined above. The regression parameters and *p*-values reported for the models are suspect and any conclusions about relationships and processes in the population are, therefore, equally suspect.

Reported models are often the result of a protracted process of analysis, assessment, recoding and re-analysis that use multiple tests and inevitably 'trawls' the sample data for significant relationships. Without detailed knowledge of the actual modelling process used and the number of hypotheses tested, it is not possible to evaluate the validity of the models. Multiple testing is likely to be particularly problematic for information that has been measured a number of times. For example, indicators of socio-economic status may be represented using a number of variables including a child's access to free school meals, living in a low-participation neighbourhood (for University study), measures based on post-code (zip code), parental educational status, earnings, house ownership, etc. Assessing each of these variables individually will inevitably inflate the chances that a socio-economic status variable reaches significance in the model and eventually gets interpreted as a significant effect of socio-economic status in the population.[3]

4. Problem 2: Not Including Important Variables in the Model

In addition to including unimportant variables, it is also possible to exclude variables which are important and should have been

---

[3]Similar considerations can be applied to a number of factors that are typically measured using multiple variables (for example, work stress, happiness, attitudes, perceptions, etc.), although one may use factor analysis to alleviate some of these problems; see Moutinho and Hutcheson (2007) for an illustration of how multi-methods may be used in this context.

included in the model, thereby providing a misleading impression of relationships in the population. Leaving 'important' variables out is an issue in social research as we tend to rely on the identification of a single 'best model' to describe research findings. One of the major problems with selecting a single best-fitting model is that there are a number of different techniques that can be used to select it (forward selection, backward deletion, or a combination of these) utilising a number of different model-fit criteria (AIC, BIC, QAIC, FIC, Rsquare, Adjusted Rsquare, Mallow's CP, etc.). This often results in many 'best-fitting' models, containing different selections of variables, any of which may be chosen to represent the research findings. If you have enough time (and good enough software) you can probably find a model that you like (or at least, one that confirms your main hypothesis).

The selection process is further complicated if candidate explanatory variables are related to one another (multicollinearity), as regression parameters and significance estimates for individual variables can change drastically depending on which other explanatory variables are included in the model. When explanatory variables are related, the significance levels of individual parameters are affected, making it difficult to assess the 'true' relationship between the explanatory and response variables in the population. For example, the number of cigarettes smoked (the explanatory variable) may be a strong indicator of the health of an individual (the response variable). However, if information about the amount spent on smoking is also included in the model (as an additional explanatory variable), the significance of the relationship between the amount smoked and health will diminish as the amount smoked and amount spent on smoking are likely to be highly correlated. In this situation, it is likely that only one of the explanatory variables will be selected for the model. When explanatory variables are correlated, single-model selection becomes quite unstable with many models capable of being selected to represent the research findings and changes in variable selection resulting from relatively minor changes in the sample (for a detailed illustration of this, see Hutcheson and Sofroniou (1999: 78–82)). Correlated explanatory variables are very common in social science research and it is not unusual to see five or six separate indicators of what might be individual factors considered for entry into regression models (for example socio-economic status may be 'measured' using post-code, salary, educational level, being a recipient of free-school meals, type of school attended, etc; a single factor represented by many variables).

4.1. *Modelling fuel consumption*

The problem of selecting a single model to illustrate an analysis can be demonstrated using the Cars93 dataset[4] which contains variables that are highly inter-related (but not unusually so). A best-fitting model of the variable 'MPG.highway' derived using a stepwise procedure (in this case, a backward/forward selection using the bic criteria) selects the explanatory variables 'weight' and 'length':

$$\text{MPG.highway} = \alpha + \beta_1 \text{ Weight} + \beta_2 \text{ Length.}$$

Although this is the model that is best-fitting according to the procedure and criteria provided, no information is given about the other variables considered, or whether a slightly different sample may have resulted in the selection of other variables. Single model reporting ignores competing models and information about variables that have not been included in the models, but may still have influenced the selection.

In order to demonstrate that the single model above may not be providing a particularly clear picture of the analytical landscape, a regression procedure that presents multiple models was applied to the cars93 data. The 'regsubsets' function from the leaps package (Lumley, 2011)[5] was used to plot a graphic showing a number of the

---

[4]The Cars93 dataset contains information about 93 new cars including price, mpg (miles per gallon), engine size, body size, and indicators of features. The data and detailed information are available online at http://amstat.org/publications/jse/v1n1/datasets.lock.html. The Cars93 dataset is also part of the MASS library (Venables *et al.*, 2011) which is provided with the R statistical package (R Development Core Team, 2011).

best-fitting models of 'MPG.highway' (miles per gallon achieved on a highway) using 10 of the other variables in the dataset as potential explanatories.[6] A subset of these models is shown in Figs. 2a and 2b, which display the 10 best-fitting models for each number of model parameters using different selection criteria. Figure 2a shows the best-fitting models as determined by the bic criteria and Fig. 2b shows the best-fitting models as determined by the adjusted R-square statistic (adjR^2). Each entry on the graphs depicts a separate model with the number of explanatory variables indicated by the number. Better-fitting models have lower bic and higher adjR^2 scores. Each graphic shows 80 different models with their associated model-fit statistics indicated on the Y axis. Three models are identified on each graph for illustration purposes. For example, Fig. 2a shows that model 'MPG.highway $\sim$ RPM' has one explanatory variable and a bic score of -0.554 while the model 'MPG.highway $\sim$ Fuel.tank.capacity + Weight + Length' has three explanatory variables and a bic score of -95.618. The same models are shown in Fig. 2b along with their adjR^2 scores.

The important thing to note from the graphs in Fig. 2 is that a large number of models have similar fit statistics and the different criteria do not result in the same best-fitting model. Using the bic statistic, the best-fitting model contains the variables 'Length' and 'Weight' and has a bic score of -95.984, whereas using the adjR^2 statistic, the best-fitting model contains the variables 'EngineSize', 'Fuel.tank.capacity', 'Length', 'Rev.per.mile', 'Weight' and 'Width' and has an adjR^2 statistic of 0.7082. There are two different best-fitting models depending on the model-fit statistic chosen (the bic statistic tends to penalise larger models and this is obvious in Fig. 2a as the more parameters there are in a model, the higher the bic score tends

---

[5]This was implemented in R (R development core team, 2011) using the HH package (Heiberger, 2011a). An easy to use GUI of this package (RcmdrPlugin. HH, Heiberger, 2011b) is available as a plugin for the Rcmdr interface (Fox, 2005, 2011).
[6]The variables considered for entry into the models of MPG.highway were: Enginesize, Horsepower, Price, Rev.per.mile, Fuel.tank.capacity, Weight, Length, Width, Turn.circle, and RPM.

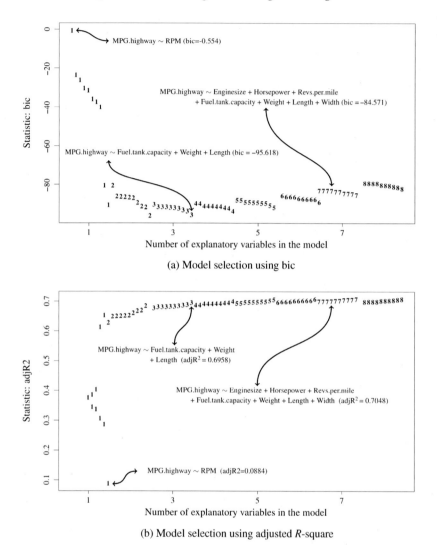

(a) Model selection using bic

(b) Model selection using adjusted R-square

Fig. 2.   An all-subsets regression output using bic and adjusted R-square model-fit criteria. Each model is designated by a single number (one to eight) that indicates the number of explanatory variables. The best-fitting models according to the bic statistic are those that are low on the graph. The best-fitting models according to the $\mathrm{adj}R^2$ statistic are those that are high on the graph. The x axis has been 'jittered' to help differentiate the models.[7]

[7]These graphics were obtained through using the HH Rcmdr Plugin (Heiberger, 2011b) and then edited using the tikzDevice package (Sharpsteen and Bracken, 2011; see also Tantau, 2010).

to be). Other model-fit criteria give other selections of variables. It is difficult to justify selecting one best-fitting model when there are so many with similar fit statistics to choose from.

Selecting a single best-fitting model from many potential candidates is a very common problem and is one that has been encountered by most researchers. This issue is often 'solved' by the analyst simply choosing to use one particular method and criteria to select a model and effectively ignore other models that may have been selected using another equally-valid procedure. Although a lot of effort may be spent in selecting the 'right' model, there is a question as to whether ANY single regression model can adequately describe the relationships in this set of data. Selecting one particular model will inevitably mean that some variables will not be considered and their possible contribution in the population not discussed; a particular problem if each variable considered for the model is of substantive interest (either to the researcher or to the reader). One possible solution to this problem is to present multiple models that provide a broad picture of the relationship between the variables of interest. Although information about competing models is valuable, it introduces considerable complexity to the analysis and may serve to obscure more than illuminate. This is demonstrated above as Fig. 2 may be useful for illustrating the number of competing models, but is unlikely to be of much use for illustrating individual models (there is only enough space on the graphic to provide details of a handful of individual models). Similarly, tables of model-fit statistics are complex and often prove difficult for readers to interpret. There are, however, some alternative graphics that can be used to effectively illustrate multiple models.

Figure 3 shows graphics from the leaps package (Lumley, 2011) that is available in R. The 'plot.regsubsets' command is used to plot a table showing which variables are in each model. The models are ordered by the specified model selection statistic (in this case, bic and adjR^2). These graphics can be simply drawn using the Rcmdr (R commander) graphical-user interface for R (Fox, 2005, 2011) and the Rcmdr plugin for the HH package (Heiberger, 2011b). Figure 3 shows models of 'MPG.highway' that can be constructed from the ten explanatory variables used in Fig. 2. The best four models are shown for models containing up to five parameters (for example, four for models with three explanatory variables and four for models with four explanatory variables). The variables that were considered for entry into the models are shown on the *x*-axis with each individual model shown as horizontal blocks on the graph. For example, the top line on the bic graph shows a model that includes the intercept and the variables 'weight' and 'length' and has a bic score of −96. The next best-fitting model includes the intercept and the variables 'Weight', 'Length' and 'Fuel.tank.capacity' and also shows a bic score of −96. The next best-fitting model repalces the variable 'Length' with 'Width' and shows a bic score of −94.

Figure 3 provides a detailed picture of the analysis that is much richer than any single model and allows individual variables to be assessed. For example, it is clear from Fig. 3a that when considering models with three explanatory variables (these are shown on the second and third lines down), either of the variables 'length' or 'width' may be used, as they both result in similarly fitting models. Similarly, when applying the adjR^2 criteria (Fig. 3b) the analyst could easily select a model that includes the variable 'Width', or one that includes the variable 'Engine.size' as both of these models also have similar fit statistics (these models are shown in the top two lines of the adjR^2 graphic). Selecting one model to represent the data inevitably leaves out a lot of information that may be of interest to readers of the research. The graphics are also interesting as they show which variables do not enter into any of the best-fitting models. For example, the variable 'Horsepower' is not included in any of the best-fitting models that are presented. If a single model is used to describe the research findings, it would be unclear whether 'Horsepower' might have been included in a model if the sample had been slightly different. Presenting the models using the graphics in Fig. 2, it is clear that 'Horsepower' is not part of any best-fitting model. This is important information, as showing that a variable does not enter into any of the best-fitting models provides more convincing evidence of its importance in the population than merely quoting a single model that does not include it.

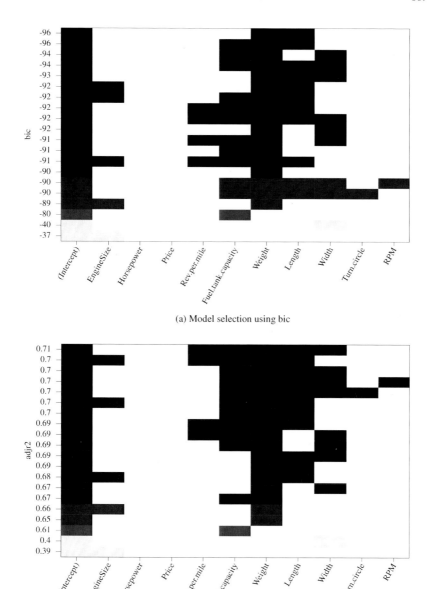

(a) Model selection using bic

(b) Model selection using adjR^2

Fig. 3. The best four models for each model size based on the bic criteria (3a) and adjR^2 (3b). Each horizontal line on the graph indicates an individual model. The models are ordered with the best-fitting depicted higher up.

One of the advantages of using a multi-model presentation such as that shown in Fig. 3, is that it provides a picture of the overall analytical landscape and allows patterns to be identified. For example, the models that were derived using the bic and adjR^2 criteria may look different, but they actually provide a consistent picture. Both techniques highlight the variables 'Weight', 'Length', 'Fuel.tank.capacity' and 'Width' as these commonly enter into the best-fitting models, and both techniques also show that the variables 'Horsepower', 'Price', 'Turn.circle' and 'RPM' commonly do not enter into the best-fitting models. Both techniques, therefore, provide a similar impression of the analysis, at least with respect to the selection of variables that seem to be important for predicting the response. This impression is also likely to be relatively 'robust' as changes in the sample or specific technique used to select the models is likely to only alter the position of the models in the hierarchy rather than changing the actual selection of variables. For example, if a larger sample resulted in the reversal of the top four models (i.e., the best-fitting model becomes the fourth best-fitting, the second became the third, etc.), the overall picture of the analysis would remain essentially unchanged. The absolute best-fitting model according to a specific criteria would have changed, but the analysis would still identify a similar selection of variables. In this way, the analyses gain a degree of robustness not possible with single model reporting. Identifying a set of best-fitting models also means that the analyst does not have to make what is often an arbitrary decision about which variables to include. All the variables that are of interest may be included to provide a picture of the analytical landscape, including those variables that do not, or only rarely, appear in the best-fitting models.

5. Conclusion

This chapter has demonstrated that the procedures used to derive models and the way in which they are presented are very important. In particular, selecting models from a large set of candidate variables is generally poor practice as it can greatly inflate the likelihood that variables enter into models due to chance factors rather than a reflection of their effect in the population. Also, the use of single-model reporting introduces a number of difficulties for analysts attempting to select a best-fitting model and for adequately describing the research findings.

As an illustration of these issues, it is likely that the analyses described at the start of this chapter (the models presented on tourist destination and union membership) may be misleading, or at least may provide a description of the analyses that is not optimal. The models were selected from many candidate variables and, as a result, it is likely that some variables have entered into the models more due to chance than due to a relationship in the population. In order to appropriately evaluate these models we need to know how many variables were considered and how many models were tested. It is also likely that there were a number of competing models that could have been selected had a slightly different sample or a different procedure or fit-statistic been used. The final model (the one presented in the research findings) may, therefore, represent only one out of many possible models. Whilst this may not be problematic for some research where the prediction of a particular response is of paramount importance, it is likely to be an important issue for research that aims to describe and explain complex inter-relationships between many variables.

These analyses could have been greatly improved through the use of the techniques outlined in this chapter. First, the careful selection of a small number of variables to consider for entry in the regression models will limit the damage caused by data-trawling. Variables to include in the models need to be carefully selected before any analysis is conducted as 'the best way to minimise model selection bias is to reduce the number of models fit to the data by thoughtful *a priori* model formulation' (Burnham and Anderson, 2002: 265). Results that have been obtained through data-trawling need to be identified and made clear in the analysis, or better still (at least according to Burnham and Anderson) 'should probably remain unpublished'. Second, the use of multiple model selection and presentation will help alleviate the problem of single model inference for what may be a multi-model solution.

> In many cases it is not reasonable to expect to be able to make inferences from a single (best) model; biology is not that simple; why should we hope for a simple inference from a single model?
>
> (Burnham and Anderson, 2002: 447).

The use of the kind of graphics illustrated in Fig. 3 allows multiple models to be presented and the analytical landscape mapped in a way that is simple for readers to digest. The use of these procedures and graphical tools will go some way to improving the quality of analyses conducted and reported in the social sciences. This position is made clear in the following quote from Burnham and Anderson (2002: 47).

> We cannot overstate the importance of the scientific issues, the careful formulation of multiple working hypotheses, and the building of a small set of models to clearly and uniquely represent these hypotheses.... We try to emphasise a more confirmatory endeavour in the applied sciences, rather than exploratory work that has become so common and has often led to so little.
>
> (Anderson *et al.*, 2000).

References

Agresti, A (2007). *An Introduction to Categorical Data Analysis*, 2nd edn. Hoboken, New Jersey: Wiley.

Anderson, DR, KP Burham and WL Thompson (2000). Null hypothesis testing: Problems, prevalence, and an alternative. *Journal of Wildlife Management*, 64, 912–923.

Berndt, ER (1991). *The Practice of Econometrics*. Boston: Addison-Wesley.

Box, GEP (1979). Robustness in the strategy of scientific model building. In *Robustness in Statistics*, RL Launer and GN Wilkinson (eds.). Chicago: Academic Press.

Burnham, KP and DR Anderson (2002). *Model Selection and Multimodel Inference: A Practical Information-theoretic Approach*, 2nd edn. New York: Springer.

Fox, J (2011). *R package 'Rcmdr' (version 1.7-3)*. A platform-independent basic-statistics GUI (graphical user interface) for R, based on the tcltk package. Available at http://cran.r-project.org/web/packages/Rcmdr.

Fox, J (2005). The R commander: A basic-statistics graphical user interface to R. *Journal of Statistical Software*, 14, 1–42.

Fox, J and S Weisburg (2011). *An R companion to Applied Regression*, 2nd edn. Thousand Oaks, California: Sage Publications.

Harrell, FE Jr. (2001). *Regression Modelling Strategies: With Applications to Linear Models, Logistic Regression, and Survival Analysis*. New York: Springer.

Heiberger, RM (2011a). *R package 'HH' (version 2.2-17)*. Support software for statistical analysis and data display by Heiberger and Holland, 2004. Available at http://cran.r-project.org/web/packages/HH.

Heiberger, RM (with support from Holland, B) (2011b). *R package 'RcmdrPlugin. HH' (version 1.1-29)*. Rcmdr support for the HH package. Available at http://cran.r-project.org/web/packages/RcmdrPlugin. HH.

Hutcheson, GD (2011). Categorical explanatory variables. *Journal of Modelling in Management*, 6(2), 225–236.

Hutcheson, GD and L Moutinho (2008). *Statistical Modeling for Management*. London: Sage Publications.

Hutcheson, GD and N Sofroniou (1999). *The Multivariate Social Scientist. Introductory Statistics using Generalized Linear Models*. London: Sage Publications.

Johnson, DH (1999). The insignificance of statistical significance testing. *Journal of Wildlife management*, 63, 763–772.

Lumley, T (2011). *R package 'leaps' (version 2.9)*. Regression subset selection. Available at http://cran.r-project.org/web/packages/leaps.

Miller, AJ (1990). *Subset Selection in Regression*. Boca Raton: Chapman and Hall.

Moutinho, L and GD Hutcheson (2007). Store choice and patronage: A predictive modelling approach. *International Journal of Business Innovation and Research*, 1(3), 233–252.

R Development Core Team (2011). *R: A Language and Environment for Statistical Computing*. R Foundation for Statistical Computing, Vienna, Austria. Available at http://www.R-project.org/.

Sharpsteen, C and C Bracken (2011). *R package 'tikzDevice' (version 0.6.2)*. A Device for R Graphics Output in PGF/TikZ Format. Available at http://cran.r-project.org/web/packages/tikzDevice.

Tantau, T (2010). *The TikZ and PGF Packages (version 2.10)*. Available at http://sourceforge.net/projects/pgf/.

Venables, WN, BD Ripley, K Hornik and A Gebhardt (2011). *R package 'MASS' (version 7.3-16)*. Functions and datasets to support Venables and Ripley, 'Modern Applied Statistics with S' (4th edn., 2002).

Weisburg, S (1985). *Applied Linear Regression*. 2nd edn. Hoboken, New Jersey: Wiley.

PART 2

COMPUTER MODELLING

Chapter 6

ARTIFICIAL NEURAL NETWORKS AND STRUCTURAL EQUATION MODELLING: AN EMPIRICAL COMPARISON TO EVALUATE BUSINESS CUSTOMER LOYALTY*

Arnaldo Coelho
Faculty of Economics, University of Coimbra
Av. Dias da Silva, 165, 3004–512, Coimbra, Portugal
acoelho@fe.uc.pt

Luiz Moutinho
Graeme D Hutcheson
Manchester University

Maria Manuela Santos Silva
Faculty of Economics, University of Coimbra
Av. Dias da Silva 165, 3004–5112 Coimbra, Portugal
nelinha@fe.uc.pt

This investigation aims to compare the usefulness and the potential contributions of Artificial Neural Networks (ANNs) in the marketing field, particularly, when compared to traditional modelling based on Structural Equations. It uses neural network modelling and structural equation modelling (SEM) to evaluate loyalty in the bank industry in Brazil. Based on a data collection of 229 bank customers (micro, small, and medium companies) from the Northeast of Brazil, the key objective of this study is to investigate the main drivers of customer loyalty in this industry. Neural networks highlight the role of the relationship quality on customer loyalty. The technique SEM confirmed six of the seven hypotheses of the proposed

---

*The Chapter 6 was done with the support of our doctoral research Sandra Maria Holanda.

model. The findings highlighted the point that micro, small, and medium companies' loyalty to their main bank is strongly influenced by affective commitment. Comparing the results achieved from both methodologies, some similarities can be found. Relationship quality is a second order construct that includes satisfaction and affective commitment as its key components, both of which are highlighted on the structural model. The strongest impact in this model is in the relation between satisfaction and affective commitment. This result suggests that, for this marketing problem, ANN and SEM seem to be complementary statistical tools, bringing complementary conclusions.

Keywords: Artificial neural networks; structural equation modelling; customer loyalty; services; SMEs; affective commitment.

1. Introduction

Relationship marketing assumes that retaining customer loyalty is much better than fighting for new customers (Berry, 2000), and its key objective is to identify and understand how antecedent variables influence customer loyalty (Hennig-Thurau *et al.*, 2002). Most of the literature in this field shows loyalty as an important relationship marketing outcome in services (Pritchard *et al.*, 1999; Johnson *et al.*, 2001; Mattila, 2001; Gastal, 2005).

In banking and financial services, the search for customer relationships is crucial, due to the great changes introduced in the last decades, within an increasingly competitive environment (Barnes, 1997). Competition in banking is growing and the financial business is being more and more fought between old and new operators in this industry. Banks have to deal with customer turnover, as well as with customers (both individuals and companies) who spread their banking activities across more than one bank (Adamson *et al.*, 2003; Guarita, 2005). Relationship marketing seems to be the main tool of the banks' differentiation strategy (Oliveira and Dutra, 2002), and loyalty seems to be essential for service business survival (Reichheld, 1994).

Not all a company's customers are searching for long-term relationships but all companies need to gather a set of loyal customers that can contribute to their business sustainability. Jones and Sasser (1995) suggest that customer loyalty is the best predictor of long-term financial performance. Thus, understanding how and why customers develop this sense of loyalty has become one of the crucial management issues of our day (Pritchard *et al.*, 1999).

Nonetheless, the antecedents of loyalty relationships are still not well-known, and a wide body of literature in this field still shows satisfaction as one of the best predictors of loyalty (Fornell, 1992; Ball *et al.*, 2004; Bick *et al.*, 2004). And whilst current discussion contends that satisfied customers are not necessarily loyal customers (Reichheld, 1994; Jones and Sasser, 1995), few can argue against the importance of customer satisfaction as one of the drivers of customer loyalty.

The search for the best predictors of customer loyalty in the bank industry, and specifically among micro, small, and medium companies in Brazil, is the main objective of this investigation. Using two different statistical tools, neural network modelling and structural equation modelling (SEM), the study takes relationship marketing and loyalty as a less structured problem and tries to find new links between marketing variables and loyalty. It does this by comparing the use of Artificial Neural Networks (ANNs) and SEM, particularly analysing the results, and the strengths and weaknesses of each.

2. Literature Review

2.1. *Loyalty*

Although satisfaction is a priority for all companies, customer loyalty is much more important and deserves special attention by companies' marketers and obviously by scholars (Phlesco and Baqer, 2008; Thuy and Hau, 2010). Loyalty seems to be a critical issue especially in the services sector, which in itself is a priority among researchers (Ostrom *et al.*, 2010).

Customer loyalty is a primary goal of relationship marketing and is sometimes even equated with the relationship marketing concept itself (Sheth, 1996). Most of the literature in this field seeks to define loyalty in terms of the process that makes customers loyal (Oliver, 1999) or, in a more operative approach, it tries to find metrics to measure loyalty (Dick and Basu, 1994; Prado and Santos, 2003).

The behavioural approach to loyalty, based on repeat buying, has been discussed since the 1970s, since researchers came to realise that repurchase is not enough evidence of brand loyalty (Newman and Werbel, 1973). Behavioural measures are based on a narrow perspective of loyalty, which ignores the dynamics of the underlying process (Day, 1969 in Bloemer *et al.*, 1999). Such measures are not capable of distinguishing between true loyalty and spurious loyalty (resulting from the lack of alternatives available for customers). Morgan and Hunt (1994) argue that in relational exchange, brand attitude becomes central to the repurchase decision.

Several researchers are now focusing on the importance of including both dimensions, behavioural and attitudinal, in any attempt to achieve a reliable measure for loyalty (Dick and Basu, 1994; Jones and Sasser, 1995; Prado and Santos, 2003; Ball *et al.*, 2004). And scholars continue to call for a more complete construal of customer loyalty and its determinants (Dick and Basu, 1994; Han *et al.*, 2008).

Nevertheless, there is a thin line between attitudinal and behavioural loyalty. They seem both to be closely interconnected: Repeated buying leads to the development of a positive emotion which motivates an emotional commitment towards being a part of the loyalty, and consequently, leads to a high level of connection and to the intention to continue buying (Oliver, 1999).

Oliver (1999) used the concept of latest loyalty, suggesting this to be based on a set of positive experiences (satisfactions) continuously lived by the customer. Although there are many antecedent factors influencing loyalty, the vast majority of the literature focuses on customer satisfaction (Fornell *et al.*, 1996), service quality (Aydin and Özer, 2005), trust and commitment (Morgan and Hunt, 1994). However, loyalty is a complex (Pritchard *et al.*, 1999) and emotional phenomenon (Mattila, 2001), and true loyalty cannot be found without emotions (Mattila, 2001; Shoemaker and Bowen, 2003). In the context of services, customers with a high level of affective commitment are more resistant to switching and are more likely to recommend the firm to others (Johnson *et al.*, 2001).

This particular investigation adopts the concept proposed by Oliver (1999) below:

[...] a deeply held commitment to rebuy or repatronise a preferred product-service consistently in the future, thereby causing
repetitive same-brand or same-brand — set purchasing, despite
situational influences or marketing efforts having the potential
to cause switching behaviour (Oliver, 1999: 34).

2.2. Loyalty determinants

Dick and Basu (1994: 99) developed a framework to understand
the antecedents of customer loyalty, defined as 'the strength of
the relationship between an individual's relative attitude and
repeat patronage'. Antecedents of relative attitude are classified
into three categories: Cognitive, affective, and conative. Cognitive
antecedents are associated with informational determinants, affective antecedents are related with feeling states involving the brand,
and conative are those concerned with behavioural dispositions
toward the brand.

Ball *et al.* (2004) divided the investigated antecedents of loyalty
by literature into four groups: Characteristics of the environment,
characteristics of the dyadic relationship, characteristics of the
consumer, and consumer perceptions of the firm. This last group
is considered to be most directly affected by the actions of the firm.

Han *et al.* (2008) categorise service loyalty determinants into
three models: quality, value, satisfaction (QVS), relationship-quality,
and relational-benefits. Each of these three approaches is considered
important to understand service loyalty. The most comprehensive
study of the QVS approach finds that satisfaction mediates the effects
of quality and value perceptions on loyalty (Cronin *et al.*, 2000).
Relationship-quality research focuses on trust and commitment
(Morgan and Hunt, 1994). Satisfaction has been added to its measures
to examine their combined impact on loyalty (Roberts *et al.*, 2003;
Francisco-Maffezzolli, 2007). Relational benefits models analyse the
benefits customers receive as a result of engaging in long-term relational exchanges with service providers and find that these benefits
are associated with customer loyalty (Hennig-Thurau *et al.*, 2002).

Nowadays, a wide range of constructs and dimensions are
being introduced and investigated as possible drivers of customer
behaviour. Previous investigations have identified, empirically, the

impacts on loyalty of relational closeness (Barnes, 1997), image (Nguyen and LeBlanc, 1998), monetary sacrifice (Johnson et al., 2001), perceived value (Cronin et al., 2000); emotions (Barnes, 1997), affective commitment (Johnson et al., 2001; Mattila, 2001); switching costs (Aydin and Özer, 2005), and dependence (Marques and Coelho, 2004).

Reichheld and Schefter (2000) show how loyalty drivers are changing and vary according to each situation, each context and each industry. Recent studies have demonstrated that loyalty in banking can be predicted by the quality of the relationship with the manager (Colgate and Danaher, 2000), and by availability of credit for businesses (Ibbotson and Moran, 2003). And emotions have been incorporated in contemporary conceptualisations of service loyalty (Barnes, 1997; Mattila, 2001; Jones et al., 2007). As noted by Barnes (1997: 774), '[a] relationship cannot be thought to exist without emotional content', and that includes commercial relationships. Hence, service encounters have the ability to produce positive and negative emotions, and as Sierra and McQuitty (2005) observed, if the strength of positive emotions toward a service provider increases, so too does service brand loyalty. Close relationships are characterised by positive affective ties (Berscheid et al., 1989). Relationship closeness will lead to repeat business and referrals. That said, it is also possible for customers to feel satisfied with a relationship without feeling that the relationship is particularly close (Barnes, 1997).

This suggests the need for much investigation in this field to improve the understanding of the nature and causes of the relationships between customers and suppliers. Especially, new metrics and new statistical tools should be found and used to find new links and provide a better appreciation of a problem that is far from being solved.

3. Research Method

The aim of the present study is to evaluate the antecedents of business clients' loyalty to their main provider of banking services. A convenience sample was used in the study, and the enterprises selected were contacted by interviewers and invited to participate. A total of

254 micro, small, and medium enterprises (SMEs) in the Northeast of Brazil were approached, and agreement was secured from 229 enterprises to participate in the study. The approach proved to be very successful, generating 229 completed (and usable) questionnaires, representing more than a 90% response rate. The survey on banking relationships was administered by personal interviews, previously scheduled, via questionnaire. The SME respondent was the highest individual responsible for the business's financial and banking decisions. As business customers may have accounts in more than one bank, the respondents were asked to indicate their main bank and answer the questions, based on the interactions with this bank.

All the constructs in the model were measured using a multiple-item scale that adopted a seven-point Likert-type response format, and all the metrics employed were developed based on the literature review related to the study. Specifically, the measures used were those developed by: Barnes (1997) — relationship closeness, positive and negative emotions; Bloemer and Odekerken-Schröder (2002) — image; Guarita (2005) — monetary and non-monetary credit sacrifice, perceived value; Colgate and Lang (2003) — relationship quality with the manager; Hennig-Thurau *et al.* (2002) — satisfaction; Ball *et al.* (2004) — trust; Prado and Santos (2003) — affective commitment and loyalty; Patterson and Smith (2001) — switching costs; Almeida *et al.* (2004) — dependence.

Due to the fact that 95% of the responding enterprises had either 1–19 or 20–99 employees, the findings of this study reflect the perspective of mainly the micro or small business segment of SMEs in the Northeast of Brazil. Returned questionnaires were analysed initially by using exploratory factor analysis and Chronbach's alpha. Thereafter, two statistical procedures, Neural Networks, and SEM were applied in order to model customer loyalty. These modelling approaches are presented and compared as are the results achieved.

3.1. *Artificial neural networks*

The Backpropagation (BP) algorithm was used to train a feedforward network in order to analyse the relationship between independent (loyalty) and dependent variables. Then structured equation modelling was used to test the proposed structural model with insights gained by the neural model, as suggested by the neural network.

The original inspiration for the ANNs approach comes from physiology and psychology, the aim being to work with a direct analogy of the human brain as a set of a large number of simple, highly-interconnected processing units, usually known as nodes or neurons operating in parallel. The basic element of a neural network, the neuron, executes two operations on the receiving values: It performs a weighted sum on the inputs received from the other nodes, and applies a function, f, called the activation function, to the resultant value of the previous function, generating a single scalar output that depends only on locally-available information stored internally or arriving via the weighted connections. This output is distributed to, and acts as an input to, other processing units. The simplest artificial neuron is the McCulloch-Pitts.

Different types of activation functions can be considered but the sigmoid function defined by:

$$f(x) = \frac{1}{1 + e^{-x}},$$

which is the activation function mainly used in the construction of a neural network.

Concerning the network topologies, we may identify three principal classes: Single-layer networks or single-layer Perceptrons, multi-layer networks or multi-layer Perceptrons (MLP), and recurrent networks. The single-layer Perceptron developed by Frank Rosenblatt (1958), suffers from some limitations referred to by Minsky and Papert (1969) in their book entitled 'Perceptrons'. To overcome such difficulties, one or more layers of neurons between the input and the output layers can be added. These internal layers designated as hidden layers are not directly observable from the inputs and outputs system. Each hidden neuron is linked to each input node and to each output neuron with the network computing values for each processing unit, as a weighted sum of the neurons in the preceding layer, in agreement with the connection weights. Neural networks with this architecture are usually designated by feedforward networks. By adding hidden layers, the network is enabled to extract high-order statistics because the network acquires a global perspective in spite of the extra set of links and the extra dimension of neural interactions. The incorporation of hidden layers within the neural network model provides more degrees of freedom and, therefore, offers substantially greater flexibility in building a complete model of human behaviour. Hornik *et al.* (1989) show that multi-layer networks using an arbitrary activation function are universal approximators. From a marketing viewpoint, a neural network with one hidden layer can also be of use in throwing light on latent or unobservable variables, for instance, underlying behaviours, traits or attitudes, which cannot be directly measured. Then, the hidden layer neurons can be labelled by reference to the weights of the connections from the input nodes which feed into them.

Another important characteristic in the construction of a neural network is its learning algorithm which is closely associated with neural architectures.

A vital feature of the network approach is that knowledge is acquired through a process of learning, and the inter-neuron connection strengths are used to store the knowledge. The learning is derived from examples presented to the network. These examples, known as training patterns, may consist of either inputs and desired outputs, or targets (supervised learning), or inputs only (unsupervised learning). It should be noted that neural networks do not require a knowledge base to be constructed, nor do they need an explicit inference procedure to be developed and subsequently encoded. Since, as we said, neural networks learn by examples, they have the potential for building computing systems that do not need to be programmed. Besides, their ability to represent both linear and non-linear relationships and to learn these interactions directly from examples, as well as their capacity for generalisation, and specifically the generation of reasonable outputs for inputs not founded in the course of the training, make it possible to reproduce complex systems whose behaviour rules are not known in detail or are difficult to analyse correctly. Indeed, the literature confirms that neural models outperform traditional statistical methods (Fadlalla and Lin, 2001;

Nguyen and Cripps, 2001; Wilson and Wragg, 2001; Audrain, 2002; Gronhold and Martensen, 2005).

For the perceptron model, the most common technique for supervised learning is an iterative procedure called the Delta rule whereby the weights for each connection are adjusted in proportion to the difference between the actual output layer values and the values predicted by the network, more concretely, in order to minimise an appropriate error quadratic function, usually the quadratic error function:

$$E^p = \frac{1}{2} \sum_{j=1}^{m} (d_j^p - y_j^p)^2,$$

where m is the number of outputs, and d_j^p and y_j^p are the desired and the correspondent output of the neuron j respectively, for pattern p.

As indicated earlier, adding hidden layers endows the network model with substantially increased representational power, but it also gives rise to computational problems: Obviously, it is impossible to compute prediction errors for hidden neurons, as they do not have observed values, and consequently this method cannot be applied. For feedforward networks, the BP algorithm which can be viewed as an extension of the Delta rule, is the most commonly employed procedure for the implementation of neural networks with supervised learning. The BP avoids that problem, by calculating imputed or implied values for the errors at each stage. This involves a *pro rata* division between hidden layer neurons of the observable errors calculated for the output layer. BP refers to this process of calculating errors by working backwards from the output neurons. It should be observed that the imputed errors are used to compute the adjustments to the weights at each stage in a way that will give the best improvement in the fit of the model. Rumelhart *et al.* (1986) give a proof that this technique will find an optimal fit. The network is allowed to run until this optimum, as measured by the root mean square error (RMSE), is attained. Feedforward networks trained with the BP algorithm have been applied successfully in a wide range of problems such as classification, pattern recognition, control applications, and optimisation (Haykin, 1999). Additionally, there has been a steady increase in the number of published papers reporting the use of neural networks in marketing (Decker and Monien, 2003; Corney, 2002; Boone and Roehm, 2002; Moutinho and Phillips, 2002; Kuo, 2001; Phillips *et al.*, 2001; Thieme *et al.*, 2000; Li, 2000). As expected, the range of NN applications in the business world is continually expanding as researchers explore the potential of this approach.

3.2. *Structural equation modelling*

SEM is a technique that combines a measurement model with confirmatory factor analysis (CFA) and a structural model, in a simultaneous test (Hoe, 2008). Byrne (2010) suggests that the term SEM expresses two important aspects of the procedure: (i) that the causal processes under study are represented by a series of structural equations (i.e., regressions), and (ii) that these structural relations can be modelled allowing a clear conceptualisation of the theory under study.

Unlike the first generation statistical tools such as regression, canonical correlation or analysis of variance (Gerbing and Anderson, 1988), SEM enables researchers to estimate simultaneously a set of interrelated multiple equations (Hair *et al.*, 2006). It allows, as well, the analysis of the relationships between multiple constructs (observable or latent) independent and dependent. The combined analysis of the measurement model and the structural model allows the analysis of the measurement errors of the observed variables, as a part of the model, and the combination of factor analysis with the test of hypotheses. The final result is a more reliable analysis of the proposed research model and, very often, a better tool for evaluating the methodology adopted (Bollen, 1989; Jöreskog and Sörbom, 1989, Bullock *et al.*, 1994).

It is necessary to secure a better understanding of SEM to consider some key elements. SEM requires a substantial understanding of the metrics used, and in addition, it should be emphasised that the SEM process is based on covariance. In this sense, the basic proposition for the SEM process is that the covariance matrix of observed variables is a function of a set of parameters. If, for example, the model is correct and at least the parameters are known, the population covariance matrix is exactly reproduced (Bollen, 1989). This proposition is given by:

$$\sum = \sum (\theta),$$

where Σ is the population of the variance and covariance matrix of observed variables, θ is the vector containing the free parameters and constraints, and $\Sigma(\theta)$ is the variance and covariance matrix written as a function of θ.

At the same time, SEM requires that the investigator think in terms of investigation models, which must be specified and identified to carry out analysis, and it must be possible to obtain estimates for each parameter. The specification reflects the assumptions of the researcher and should, therefore, have a basis whether theoretical, results of previous studies, or an area of research and experience of the investigator.

The measurement model, or simply the CFA, specifies the relationship between the observable indicators and their non-observable constructs, whether independent or dependent (Bollen, 1989). Additionally, it allows us to evaluate the properties of the observed variables in terms of internal consistency and validity, according to the concepts they wish to measure (Anderson and Gerbing, 1988; Byrne, 1998). The structural model, known also as the 'path model', defines the causal relationships between independent and dependent latent variables, which are supported by the theoretical framework. In addition, flexibility in defining the direction of the relationship allows the analysis of direct and indirect effects between the latent variables in the model.

Using LISREL notation, developed by Keesling (1972) and Jöreskog and Sörbom (1984), Eqs. (3.1), (3.2) and (3.3) describe the measurement and the structural models:

$$\eta = \beta_\eta + \Gamma_\xi + \zeta, \tag{3.1}$$

$$Y = \Lambda_y \eta + \varepsilon, \tag{3.2}$$

$$X = \Lambda_x \xi + \delta. \tag{3.3}$$

Equation 3.1 represents the model of latent variables, the structural model, where η is an $m \times 1$ vector of the endogenous latent variables and ξ is a vector $n \times 1$ of the exogenous latent variables. The coefficients matrices are β and Γ. β is an $m \times m$ matrix that represents the effect of η on η, Γ is an $m \times n$ matrix for the effects of ξ on η, and ζ is an $m \times 1$ vector of random disturbances in the equation. The other two components of the structural model are the two covariance matrices. The covariance matrix is a non-standardised correlation matrix, where the variance of a variable is below the main diagonal and covariance of all pairs of variables off the diagonal. The $n \times n$ covariance matrix of exogenous latent variables (ξ 0s) is Φ (Phi), with elements $\varphi\, i, j$.

The measurement model is represented by Eqs. (3.2) and (3.3), where Y is a vector of $p \times 1$ indicators of η and X is a vector $q \times 1$ indicators of ξ. Λ_yeΛ_x are the matrices of the regression coefficients of the factors. These coefficients indicate the relationships between indicators and latent variables, assuming that each indicator is perfectly linked with its latent variable to be measured. The matrix is $p \times m$, where m indicates the number of η's and Λ_x is a matrix $q \times n$ where n represents the number of ξ's. Whereas the measures are imperfect, the measurement model includes a vector of error terms for Y^i which is ($\varepsilon\, i$), where ε is $p \times 1$. The error vector to X^i is (δ_i), where δ is $q \times 1$. However, ε and δ contain vectors of random variables. These terms represent the disturbances that affect the relationship between latent and observed variables. The measurement model also presents the variance and covariance matrices Y and X.

A critical issue in SEM is to retain control over the complexity of the model. A complex model composed of many variables and many parameters would tend to show poorer fit and increased measurement error, especially when the sample size is small or moderate (Bentler and Chou, 1987). A strategy recommended to minimise model complexity is the use of a partial disaggregation model (Bagozzi and Heatherton, 1994), applied in this study. Subsets of items are combined into several composites and these composites are treated as multiple indicators of a given construct (Baumgartner and Homburg, 1996).

4. Comparisons

The techniques such as Neural Networks and SEM derive from and encapsulate many other statistical techniques. NNs are related to predictive models, logical discriminant models, and generalised linear models (GLM). SEM is related to path analysis, multiple regression models, principal components analysis (PCA), correlations analysis and also GLM. Both NN and SEM subsume several multivariate statistical techniques described above.

ANNs seem to be performing well where other techniques can present difficulties or perform less well. Gronholt and Martensen (2005) state that ANNs present three main advantages: They are able to deal with both linear and non-linear relationships; they do not need very strict specifications and hence, are not subject to model mis-specifications; and they can estimate the effects of the interaction of several variables of the input layer, on the output.

The methodological framework used in this research, which was designed to compare the modelling, measurability and effectiveness of data analysis, relies on five major statistical criteria: (1) Latency effects (i.e., *etas* and hidden layer nodes); (2) Causal interactions; (3) Learned association properties; (4) Interconnectivity (i.e., neurons and indicators); and (5) Predictability.

4.1. *Latent variables*

SEM has the ability to model a construct as latent variables (variables which are not measured directly, but are estimated in the model) from measured variables which are assumed to 'tap into' the latent variables. This allows the modeller to explicitly capture the non-reliability of measurement in the model, which theoretically allows the structural relations between latent variables to be accurately estimated.

In the case of neural networks, each node in the hidden layers can be considered as a latent (that is, unobserved) random variable. A continuous latent variable may represent a location on a subspace or a manifold. The minimisation of the error in the replication gives auto-associative mapping, and the latent variables (hidden layer nodes) can be used as compressed versions of inputs.

4.2. Causal interactions

SEM is a powerful tool to explore and contrast hypotheses or causal relationships pathways among variables using continuous data. Although the presence of a correlation between two variables does not necessarily imply the existence of a causal relationship between them, the existence of a causal relationship between two variables does imply the existence of a correlation between them. This is in essence the basis for the SEM approach.

Causal connectivity of a neural system represents the dynamic interactions among elements of a neural system, reflecting a causal (pathway and weight patterns) influence between two nodes. Causal interactions can also be seen as a novel indicator of collective behaviour in neural systems. Analysis of networks of interactions built on the basis of causal interactions can lead to the individualisation of functional communities of neurons.

4.3. Learned associative properties

Advances in computational analysis of parallel-processing networks have made computer simulation of learning systems an increasingly useful tool for understanding complex aggregate functional effects of changes in neural systems (Gluck and Grangen, 1993). SEM of an event time series can be used to characterise learning-related changes in effective connectivity. Specific learning-related changes in effective connectivity can be found.

4.4. Interconnectivity — neurons and indicators

Unfully interconnected neural networks (UINNs) were proposed by Gan and Wei (1990) as associative memory. The basic idea is to form compact internal representations of patterns in order to increase the storage efficiency of the interconnections. Several effective methods for designing UINNs as associative memory include monolayered and multilayered neural networks. Multilayered neural networks are of relatively high storage capacity.

Concepts are latent variables that are measured by one or more indicators using SEM. The measures are often imperfect and contain measurement error. Consequences of measurement error include: (1) attenuation of effect — the estimated effect is weaker than the real effect; and (2) inconsistency — consistency is a property of an estimator wherein as the sample size increases the estimate converges to the true value. A perhaps surprising consequence of measurement error is that error in any variable can adversely affect estimated parameters throughout the model. In practice, researchers use reliable multiple indicators to try to overcome these problems.

4.5. Predictability

NNs are non-parametric universal function approximators that can learn from data, without assumptions, and as such, they can be used for surrogate predictability. SEM is an extremely flexible linear (within parameters) multivariate statistical modelling technique. The maximum likelihood (ML) solution maximises the probability that the observed covariances are drawn from a population that has its variances — covariances generated by the process implied by the model, assuming a multivariate normal distribution. The theory of partially determinate processes (Kratsov, 1989) is based on identifying randomness with unpredictability and establishes the interrelation between the real physical processes X(F), the observed process Y(F), and the model (predictive, hypothetical) process T(F) in this theory. The degree of determinateness, which is the correlation coefficient between observed process prediction, can be employed as a measure of the quality of predictability.

5. Results

5.1. Results from the SEM

The two-step approach was adopted. Using AMOS 19.0, a CFA was conducted and the measurement model showed good psychometric characteristics. Reliability and validity of the scales used was assessed. The measures of adequacy of measurement were, in general, above the accepted levels according to Hair *et al.* (2005) and Fornell and Lacker (1981).

The structural model, using the ML method, presents the relations shown below:

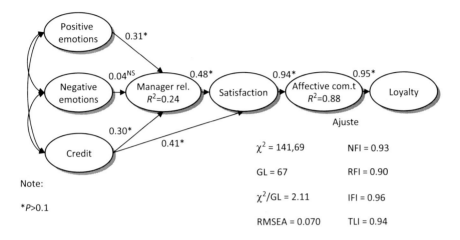

Note:

*P>0.1

Ajuste	
χ^2 = 141,69	NFI = 0.93
GL = 67	RFI = 0.90
χ^2/GL = 2.11	IFI = 0.96
RMSEA = 0.070	TLI = 0.94

To evaluate the overall performance of the structural model, the adjustment measures are presented. Absolute measures of adjustment χ^2, RMSEA and AGFI (which determine the degree to which the model predicts the observed absolute covariance matrix) was adequate, although the value of RMSEA of 0.07 is very close to the acceptable 0.08 limit suggested by Hair *et al.* (2005). As for comparative measures of adjustment NFI, TLI and CFI (comparing the proposed model with the null model), the model performed well, with values above 0.90 as recommended in the literature (Hair *et al.*, 2005).

However, the AGFI index of 0.88 is below 0.90, although values greater than or equal to 0.80 are considered acceptable for this index, when it comes to complex models (Cote, 2001).

DEPENDENT		INDEPENDENT	*Estimate*	S.E.	C.R.	Standard
RELGER	<—	EMOC_P	0.56	0.16	3.59	0.31
RELGER	<—	EMOC_N	0.04	0.15	0.30	0.02
RELGER	<—	CRED	0.54	0.14	4.01	0.30
SATSF	<—	CRED	0.63	0.10	6.13	0.41
SATSF	<—	RELGER	0.40	0.06	6.52	0.48
CAFET	<—	SATSF	0.75	0.05	13.64	0.94
LEALD	<—	CAFET	1.21	0.09	13.44	0.95

In the hypothetical model, among the seven proposed hypotheses, six were confirmed. The assumptions related to the relations credit -> quality of the relationship with the manager, credit -> satisfaction, quality of the relationship with the manager -> satisfaction, satisfaction -> affective commitment, affective commitment -> loyalty and positive emotions -> satisfaction were confirmed as stated by the literature. But the hypothesis concerning the relationship between negative emotions -> satisfaction was not confirmed, given that the *t*-value was above 3.29. This result was not expected as this relationship is commonly supported by the literature in this field. The importance of emotions in consumption experiences and, consequently, its influence on post-consumer judgments are usually assumed as relevant (Mano and Oliver, 1993; Richins, 1997; Espinoza, 2004).

In the context of services in Brazil, emotional factors independent of other influences, explain about 30% of the variation in customer satisfaction (Prado, 1997; Farias Santos, 2000; Costa and Farias, 2004).

Additionally, in concept, satisfaction is considered by some authors as an emotional response from consumers (Westbrook and Reilly, 1983; Giese and Cote, 2000; Oliver, 1997). This impact is partially confirmed by these results even if there are no impacts of negative emotions on the manager's relationship.

These results allow us to confirm a set of hypotheses while others remain unconfirmed. From those that are confirmed we can see the direct relationships between variables and mediating effects of some of them. The loyalty determinants emerging from this investigation seem to be aligned with the loyalty literature. However, any interactions between these variables can be extracted. The results presented and the final conclusions depend exactly on the model specifications previously determined.

5.2. *Results from ANN*

The feedforward with different training configurations provided by the multiple BP algorithm was run several times until it appeared that no further improvement could be made to the RMSE defined by:

$$\text{RMSE} = \frac{1}{2}\sqrt{\frac{1}{N_p N_o}\sum_{p=1}^{N_p}\sum_{o=1}^{N_o}(d_o^p - y_o^p)^2,}$$

where N_p represents the number of patterns.

The parameters of this supervised learning rule were properly tuned. The learning rate and the momentum term were initialised to 0.01 and 0.001 respectively and were updated automatically. Concerning the weights and taking into account the minimisation of the error function, different random initialisations were also considered. Then, we verified that the interval $[-1, 1]$ provides the best result. In addition, to reach robustness, the learning rate was further reduced by a factor of 0.5 each time the RMSE increased more than 0.1%. The contributory and inhibitory weights resulted within a range of between $[-2, +2]$ and the RMSE obtained for the test data was 0.0558. Finally, a goodness-of-fit coefficient, R^2, was computed to evaluate the performance of the NN model. This R^2 value, similar to R^2 provided in multiple regression analysis, was 0.9977 for the output variable. Therefore, the model proposed explains over 99% of the perceived performance of the loyalty variable.

The relationships between the input variables and the output variables are mediated by the hidden layers. The modelling outputs are presented in the following tables:

The Tables 1, 2 and 3 presented, show the impacts of the input variables on the hidden layer, the effects of the hidden layer on the output variables, and the labels given to the hidden nodes. The links between the input variables and the hidden layers are both contributory and inhibitory. The salient contributory and inhibitory weights attached to the input variables of the model, affecting hidden node 1 (HN1), demonstrate a more positive impact overall than a negative one. Customers' satisfaction (+1.13) and their affective commitment (+1.02) with the main bank are stressed in the neural network. The positive emotions show the most significant inhibitory effect on HN1 (-0.70). So, positive emotions do not seem to be

Table 1.   Impacts of the nodes of the input layer on the neurons of the hidden layer from the hidden layer.

From input layer

To hidden layer	Relations. closeness	Positive emotion	Negative emotion	Imag	Cred	Monet. sacrifice	Non-monet. sacrifice
1° node	−0.25	−0.70	0.06	0.37	0.20	−0.15	−0.31
2° node	−0.00	−0.47	−0.26	−0.04	−0.70	−0.51	−0.10
3° node	−0.13	0.10	−0.55	−0.53	−0.87	−0.54	−0.79
4° node	−1.16	0.31	0.17	0.74	0.57	0.05	0.26
5° node	0.59	1.12	0.38	0.54	−0.55	0.93	0.66
Total Contribution	2.16	2.72	1.45	2.24	2.91	2.20	2.14

From input layer

To hidden layer	Relation quality with the manag.	Perceiv. Value	Switching costs	Dependence	Satisfaction	Trust	Affective commitm.
1° node	0.36	0.07	−0.03	0.21	1.13	0.11	1.01
2° node	−0.41	−0.27	0.03	−0.65	−0.21	0.15	−0.98
3° node	−0.15	0.50	0.55	0.46	1.15	−0.33	1.13
4° node	−0.30	0.20	0.35	−0.67	0.22	1.00	0.86
5° node	−0.55	0.81	−0.00	−0.69	0.38	0.10	−0.46
Total Contribution	1.79	1.87	0.97	2.70	3.11	1.70	4.47

Table 2.   Impacts of the hidden neurons on loyalty.

To the output layer	1st neuron	2nd neuron	3rd neuron	4th neuron	5th neuron
Loyalty	1.24	−0.97	0.47	1.12	0.35

Table 3.   Labels given to the hidden neurons.

Hidden neurons	Labels
HN1	Relationship quality
HN2	Transactional factors
HN3	Loyalty potential
HN4	Reliability
HN5	Emotional content and value

a vital pre-requisite for micro, small and medium enterprises' loyalty to their main bank. Based on all contributory and inhibitory weights derived from the input measures, it was decided to label hidden node 1 'relationship quality', which means 'the degree of appropriateness of a relationship to fulfil the needs of the consumer associated to that relationship' (Hennig-Thurau and Klee, 1997: 751).

Twelve factors have a negative impact on hidden node 2. The highest negative impact is derived from affective commitment (−0.99) with the main bank, followed by credit (−0.70), dependence (−0.65), monetary sacrifice (−0.52), positive emotions (−0.47) and relationship quality with the manager (−0.42). After assessing all salient inhibitory weights, it was decided to label HN2 as 'transactional factors'. The negative connections stress relational factors that do not seem to influence micro, small and medium enterprises' loyalty to their main bank.

The most important input factor affecting HN3 is satisfaction with the main bank (+1.16). Satisfaction has both a cognitive character via disconfirmation and an affective character, similar to an affective nature. It is a hybrid answer, with knowledge data and emotional content (Oliver, 1997). This node also showed a positive link with affective commitment with the main bank, with a value similar to satisfaction (+1.14). The nodes switching costs (+0.55), perceived value (+0.51) and dependence (+0.47) have positive weights, albeit small. In respect of the input nodes with inhibitory weights on hidden node 3, the most salient impact is derived from credit (−0.87) and non-monetary sacrifice (−0.80), these being variables with a transactional content. Loyalty is perceived as an emotional phenomenon (Mattila, 2001) so HN3 is labelled 'loyalty potential'.

Eleven input factors have positive contributory weights and three have inhibitory weights on hidden node 4. The most important input factor positively affecting HN4 is trust (+1.00), followed by affective commitment (+0.87). The other positive (contributory) weights are derived from image (+0.75), credit (+0.57), switching costs (+0.35), and positive emotions (+0.31). The salient negative (inhibitory) weight is derived from relational closeness (−1.17), a higher level than the positive effect derived from trust (+1.00). The aspects related to reliability in respect of the main bank are stressed (trust, affective commitment, and image). Reliability means 'the ability to perform the promised service dependably and accurately' (Parasuraman *et al.*, 1991: 41). So, HN4 is labelled as 'reliability'.

Nine factors have positive contributory weights on HN5. The most positive contributory weight is derived from positive emotions (+1.12). The other contributory weights are derived from monetary sacrifice (+0.93) and perceived value (+0.82), followed by non-monetary sacrifice (+0.67), relational closeness (+0.59), image (+0.54), negative emotions (+0.39), and satisfaction (+0.39). The salient inhibitory weights are derived from dependence (−0.70), credit (−0.56), relationship quality with the manager (−0.56), and affective commitment (−0.47). Assessing all weights of hidden node 5, HN5 is labelled 'emotional content and value' because positive emotions have the highest contributory weight.

These results lead us to the conclusions that:

1. The perceived quality of the relationship is increasingly evolving around a number of intangible dimensions, namely within an 'emotional corridor'. The quality of the relationship is fuzzy and contradictory. There is no visible 'dependence' on the banks'

support to SMEs and the issue of relational closeness is not, apparently, a crucial determinant for institutional loyalty. A good relationship quality still rests upon some traditional 'building blocks' such as commitment, trust, and satisfaction

2. Positive emotions as a general input and mediating factor have only a low level of effect on corporate banking loyalty. This same low level of impact also seems to mediate the link between the relationship with the manager and the perceptions and acceptance of bank loyalty. The bank industry is based on rationality and there appears to be no room for an emotional approach. Personal bonds may be the least rational variable present in the loyalty process.

3. The relational closeness is still preponderant but is based on trust and functionality of benefits. One direct impact on loyalty is not relying on transactional factors but on the perceived reliability of the quality of the relationship. De facto, the final positive contribution to the formation and/or sustainability of bank loyalty, as measured from the impacts of the hidden layers (nodes) to the output node in the neural network topology, is derived from the whole issue of reliability and the overall perceived value.

The results found in this study, in general terms, contribute to support the statement presented in the literature review about the influence of relationship quality on positive behavioural outcomes (Dorsch *et al.*, 1998; Hennig-Thurau *et al.*, 2002). These findings may appear similar to others, based on different modelling approaches like SEM. However, the interpretations that can be extracted from them are more open and allow a different approach which is not simply concerned with confirming hypotheses but also with exploring the results. Furthermore, these results may be seen as a new departure to redefine and investigate new links between loyalty and its determinants.

6. Comparing Modelling Performance

The data presented in Table 4 show the main features that allow good modelling performance in respect of both NNs and SEM.

Table 4.   Comparative framework of NNs and SEM.

	Neural Networks	Structural Equations Modelling
Latency Effects	5 hidden layer nodes	3 etas and thetas
Causal Interactions	(I-HL)14*5 = 70	6 + 2 + 2 = 10
	(HL-O)5*1 = 5	Xs ME ME-Y
	T = 70/5 = 15	T = 10
Learned Associative Properties	$R^2 = 0.952$	$R^2 = 0.95$
	4 + 1 = 5	
	HLN = 5	5 pathwways confirmed
Interconnectivity	14 + 5 + 1 = 20	3 + 2 + 1 + 1 = 7
	I HL O	X Thetas eta Y
Predictability	RMSE = 0.0558	RMSEA = 0.076

According to the criteria used in the comparative framework to assess the effectiveness of NNs and SEM, the following conclusions can be derived. The NN topology has a 'deeper' psychological and non-direct nature, compared with the three latent constructs of SEM. Nevertheless, the two *thetas* and the one *eta* possess a high degree of mediating effect within their analytical structure. The intricate nature of the NN topology generated 15 causal interactions, a much higher number of underpinnings and indicators of causality, albeit one-way causation, as opposed to the reduced number (10) of interactions denoting causality of SEM. The *a priori* theoretical model behind the SEM analysis postulated only one-way causation and the lack of non-recursivity, which is an unusual premise when conducting research modelling under the structural equations approach.

In terms of learned associative properties, there is a balanced outcome in the overall effectiveness of both statistical techniques. In the NN solution, there are five resulting weight impacts (four positive, one negative) on the output factor. Likewise, in the SEM model, there are five causal pathways that have been confirmed by the data analysis.

With regard to the issue of interconnectivity, and as a result of the more complex structure of the NN model, when compared with the more parsimonious design of the structural equations model, one can find almost three times the number of network/model interconnections in the NN topology as compared to SEM. This higher degree of model complexity usually has a positive effect upon the performance and the goodness-of-fit of the modelling approach.

Finally, in terms of the overall predictability of both models, a single measure is applied (RMSEA), the results of which demonstrate that the NN model performs and predicts slightly better than the SEM model. Overall, and taking into account the five criteria used in this comparative framework, it can be said that the NN performed better than SEM in terms of structural accuracy (latency effects, causal interactions, and interconnectivity) as well as in the sense of estimated predictability (although in this case only marginally). It can be deducted that in the area of learned associative properties, both models (NN and SEM) performed well.

7. Comparing Results

The overall results achieved with both modelling approaches seem to support the general literature on loyalty. Several differences can be found, especially because the conclusions relying on SEM are 'prisoners' of the specified model and of the linear relationships established.

At the same time, ANNs have the ability to deal with both linear and non-linear relationships. Consequently, the findings can go far beyond the simple confirmatory character of the SEM approach. We can say that ANNs, more than confirming theory allow for the development of theory. The present investigation highlighted the role of this 'emotional corridor' based on a set of variables like commitment, trust and satisfaction that can become the departure for new investigations in search of a novel approach to relationship quality or for the definition of a new concept based on these variables.

Similarly, even if emotions seem to have an impact on bank loyalty, ANNs show that this role can be a very low one, perhaps mediating the relation or linking the relationship with the manager with loyalty. Emotions do not seem to be a crucial determinant in a

Table 5.   Comparison between neural networks and structural equation modelling.

	Artificial Neural Networks	Structural Equations Modelling
Results/ Conclusions	Total contribution of the factors of the input layer to the network: 1st affective commitment 2nd satisfaction 3rd credit 4th positive emotions 5th dependence Impact of hidden neurons on loyalty (output layer): 1st relationship quality 2nd reliability 3rd transactional factors 4th loyalty potential 5th emotional content and value	Structural relationship and hypothesis testing — equivalent structural model: Positive emotions → relationship quality with the manager: confirmed Negative emotions → relationship quality with the manager: not confirmed Credit → relationship quality with the manager: confirmed Credit → satisfaction: confirmed relationship quality with the manager → satisfaction: confirmed satisfaction → affective commitment: confirmed affective commitment → loyalty: confirmed
	Positive impacts of hidden neurons on loyalty: 1st relationship quality 2nd reliability 4th loyalty potential 5th emotional content and value	Equivalent model: The strongest loading of the model is on following the structural relation: Satisfaction → affective commitment The second one is on the relation affective commitment → loyalty
	Negative impact of the hidden layer on loyalty comes from: 3rd transactional factors	Structural model: Credit is the only construct with a transactional nature, although the structural model has seven constructs

(Continued)

Table 5.   (*Continued*)

	Artificial Neural Networks	Structural Equations Modelling
Differences	Total contribution of input factors to the network:	Structural model:
	The dependence factor has the fifth highest loading of total contribution to the network	Dependence construct is neither included in the hypothesised model nor in the equivalent model
	Negative emotions and relationship quality with the manager are in the last positions in the total contribution ranking, 13th and 11th, respectively.	Negative emotions and relationship quality with the manager are included in the structural model. They are strongly related to two constructs in the banking services context: positive emotions and credit, respectively, according to banking industry literature (Barnes, 1997; Winstanley, 1997). (continued)
Differences	Positive impacts of hidden neurons on loyalty:	Structural model:
	The reliability neuron has the second strongest loading of contribution to loyalty	The trust construct is neither included in the hypothesised model nor in the equivalent model
Similarities	Total contribution of the factors of the input layer to the neural network:	Structural model:
	Five factors have the most significant loadings to the network	In the structural model are included four among five input factors with the most significant loadings, suggested by the neural network
	Affective commitment and satisfaction are the two input factors with most total contribution to the neural network	The relation between satisfaction and affective commitment is the most loading of the hypothesised model and equivalent model

(*Continued*)

Table 5.   (*Continued*)

Artificial Neural Networks	Structural Equations Modelling
Negative emotions are in the 13th position in the ranking of total contribution to the neural network that has 14 factors in the input layer	Negative emotions generate neither influence on satisfaction (hypothesised model) nor on relationship quality with the manager (equivalent model)
Positive impacts of hidden neurons on loyalty: The hidden neuron relationship quality has the most contributory weight on loyalty.	Equivalent model: The most loadings of the model are on the following structural relations:
There is similarity in the results of four neurons of the hidden layer that have positive contributions: Relationship quality and potential to loyalty hidden neurons have mutual factors.	Satisfaction → affective commitment and Affective commitment → loyalty
Trust factor of the reliability may be a measure of the relationship quality.	Satisfaction and affective commitment are measures of the relationship quality (Hennig-Thurau *et al.*, 2002)
Positive emotions integrate the emotional content of a relationship	
Negative impact of hidden layer loyalty: The hidden neuron transactional factor has inhibitory weight on loyalty	Structural model: In the hypothesised and equivalent models the constructs of relational nature are stressed

very rational industry and their presence is due to the involvement of people, in this case, the account manager.

These are some of the findings that, more than confirming a theory, present the opportunity for new developments in the loyalty field.

8. Conclusion

This chapter shows how ANN modelling can be useful in the marketing field, particularly in respect of loyalty. It also shows how ANNs can provide additional insights and go beyond the limited results gathered from a model completely specified. More than comparing the results achieved in this particular example, the chapter highlights the specificities, the limits and the potential of both modelling approaches. Furthermore, it reinforces the idea that these specific modelling techniques can be used in a complementary way: SEM with a more confirmatory approach and ANNs as a more exploratory tool.

Studies conducted in the loyalty field rely, excessively, on a set of assumptions perfectly determined. Consequently, advances on the study of the determinants and causes of loyalty are scarce. Using a tool like ANNs, will help to discover new links between variables, new ways of interpreting results, and new starting points from which to develop theory, rather than simply confirming the assumptions generally accepted. That means ANNs can be useful in different stages of theory development.

The main limitation of this study lies in the design of the sampling procedures, since a convenience (non-probabilistic sample) has been used. However, even if the impact on the results may limit their ability to be generalised, the comparison between the two modelling approaches is not affected by the nature of the sample used. Furthermore, the non-probabilistic character of a sample may affect the normality of the data collected. The ANNs' algorithms are particularly well prepared to deal with normality deviations and to normalise the data. The performance showed by ANNs can be compared to SEM or even exceed it, depending on the nature of the investigation's aims.

References

Adamson, I, C Kok-Mun and D Handford (2003). Relationship marketing: Customer commitment and trust as a strategy for the smaller Hong Kong corporate banking sector. *International Journal of Bank Marketing*, 21(6/7), 347–358.

Audrain, AF (2002). The–satisfaction link over time: A study on panel data. In *Proc. 21st EMAC Conf.*, pp. 28–31, University of Minho and European Marketing Academy, Braga.

Aydin, S and G Özer (2005). The analysis of antecedents of customer loyalty in the turkish mobile telecommunication market. *European Journal of Marketing*, 39(7/8), 910–925.

Bagozzi, RP and TF Heatherton (1994). A general approach to representing multi-faced personality application to state self-esteem. *Structural Equation Modelling*, 133, 35–67.

Ball, D, PS Coelho and A Machás (2004). The role of communication and trust in explaining customer loyalty: An eExtension to the ECSI model. *European Journal of Marketing*, 38(9/10), 1272–1293.

Barnes, JG (1997). Closeness, strength and satisfaction: Examining the nature of relationships between providers of financial services and their retail customers. *Journal of Psychology and Marketing*, 14(18), 765–790.

Baumgartner, H and C Homburg (1996). Applications of structural equation modelling in marketing and consumer research: A review. *International Journal of Research Marketing*, 13, 139–161.

Bentler, PM and C Chou (1987). Pratical issues in structural modelling. *Sociological Methods and Research*, 16, 78–117.

Berscheid, E, M Snyder and A Omoto (1989). The relationship closeness inventory: Assessing the closeness of interpersonal relationships. *Journal of Personality and Social Psychology*, 57(5), 792–807.

Boone, DS and M Roehm (2002). Evaluating the appropriateness of market segmentation solutions using artificial neural networks and the membership clustering criterion. *Marketing Letters*, 13(4), 317–333.

Corney, D (2002). Food bytes: Intelligent systems in the food industry. *British Food Journal*, 104(10/11), 787–805

Cronin Jr., JJ, MK Brady and GTM Hult (2000). Assessing the effects of quality, value, and customer satisfaction on consumer behavioral intentions in service environments. *Journal of Retailing*, 76(2), 193–218.

Decker, R and K Monien (2003). Market basket analysis with neural gas networks and self-organising maps. *Journal of Targeting, Measurement and Analysis for Marketing*, 11(4), 373–386.

Dick, AS and K Basu (1994). Customer loyalty: Toward an integrated conceptual framework. *Journal of the Academy of Marketing Science*, 22(Spring), 99–113.

Dorsch, MJ, SR Swanson and SW Kelley (1998). The Role of relationship quality in the stratification of vendors as perceived by customers. *Journal of the Academy of Marketing Science*, 26(2), 128–142.

Fadlalla, A and CH Lin (2001). An analysis of the application of neural networks in finance. *Interfaces*, 31(4)(July/August), 112–122.

Fornell, C (1992). A national customer satisfaction barometer: The swedish experi-ence. *Journal of Marketing*, 56(1), January, 6–21.

Fornell, C and DF Larcker (1981). Evaluating structural equation models with unobservable variables and measurement error. *Journal of Marketing Research*, 18, 39–50.

Fornell, C, MD Johnson, EW Anderson, J Cha and BE Bryant (1996). The american customer satisfaction index: Nature, purpose and findings. *Journal of Marketing*, 60(4), 7–18.

Francisco-Maffezzolli, EC (2007). Qualidade do relacionamento, lealdade e resultado financeiro dos usuários de telefonia celular: Uma possível contra regra. In *Anais do XXXI Encontro da Associação dos Programas de Pós-graduação em Administração-ENANPAD*. Rio de Janeiro.

Gan, Q and W Yu (1990). Unfully interconnected neural networks as associative memory, circuits and systems. *IEEEE International Symposium on Circuits and Systems*, 1–3 May, 468–470.

Gluck, MA and R G (1993). Computational models of the neural bases of learning and memory. *Annual Review of Neurosciences*, 16 (March), 661–706.

Gronholt, L and A Martensen (2005). Analyzing customer satisfaction data: A comparison of regression and artificial neural networks. *International Journal of Market Research*, 47(2), 121–130.

Guarita, CEI (2005). Percepções de qualidade, sacrifício e valor: uma investigação em serviços bancários. Tese de Doutoramento, Escola de Administração de Empresas da Fundação Getúlio Vargas, São Paulo.

Han, X, RJ Kwortnik, Jr. and C Wang (2008). Service loyalty: An integrative model and examination across service contexts. *Journal of Service Research*, 11(1), 22–42.

Haykin, SS (1999). *Neural Networks: A Comprehensive Foundation*. Upper Saddle River, NJ: Prentice Hall.

Hennig-Thurau, T, KP Gwinner and DD Gremler (2002). Understanding relationship marketing outcomes: An integration of relational benefits and relationship quality. *Journal of Service Research*, 4(3), 230–247.

Hennig-Thurau, T and A Klee (1997). The impact of customer satisfaction and relationship quality on customer retention: A critical reassessment and model development. *Psychology & Marketing*, 14(8), S. 737–764.

Hornik, K, M Stinchcombe and H White (1989). Multilayer feedforward networks are universal approximators. *Neural Networks*, 2(5), 359–366.

Ibbotson, P and L Moran (2003). E-Banking and the SME/Bank Relationship in Northern Ireland. *International Journal of Bank Marketing*, 21(2), 94–103.

Johnson, MD, A Gustafsson, TW Andreassen, L Lervik and J Cha (2001). The evaluation and future of national customer satisfaction index models. *Journal of Economic Psychology*, 22, 217–245.

Jones, TO and WE Sasser Jr (1995). Why satisfied customers defect. *Harvard Business Review*, 73(6), 88–99.

Jones, MA, KE Reynolds, DL Mothersbaugh and SE Beatty (2007). The positive and negative effects of switching costs on relational outcomes. *Journal of Service Research*, 9(4), 335–355.

Kratsov, YA (1989). Randomness, determinateness and predictability. *Soviet Physics USP*, 32, 434–449.

Kuo, RJ (2001). A sales forecasting system based on fuzzy neural network with initial weights generated by generic algorithm. *European Journal of Operational Research*, 129, 496–517.

Li, S (2000). The development of a hybrid intelligent system for developing marketing strategy. *Decision Support Systems*, 27, 395–409.

Mattila, AS (2001). Emotional bonding and restaurant loyalty. *Cornell Hotel and Restaurant Administration Quarterly*, 42(6), 73–79.

Marques, A and A Coelho (2004). Os determinates do compromisso nar relações empresariais. In *anais of the XXVIII ENANPAD*, Curitiba.

Minsky, ML and SA Papert (1969). *Perceptrons*. MIT Press: Cambridge.

Morgan, RM and SD Hunt (1994). The commitment-trust theory of relationship marketing. *Journal of Marketing*, 58(3), 20–38.

Moutinho, L and PA Phillips (2002). The impact of strategic planning on the competitiveness, performance and effectiveness of bank branches: A neural network analysis. *The International Journal of Bank Marketing*, 20(2/3), 102–110.

Nguyen, N and A Cripps (2001). Predicting housing value: A comparison of multiple regression analysis and artificial neural networks. *Journal of Real Estate Research*, 22(3), 313–336.

Nguyen, N and G Le Blanc (1998). The mediating role of corporate imae on customers retention decisions: An investigation in financial services. *International Journal of Bank Marketing*, 16(2), 56–65.

Newman, JW and RA Werbel (1973). Multivariate analysis of brand loyalty for major household appliances. *Journal of Marketing Research*, 10(November), 404–409.

Oliveira, PA da S and HF de O Dutra (2002). Percepção de qualidade e construção de relacionamentos: Uma investigação num serviço financeiro. In *Anais do XXVI Encontro da Associação dos Programas de Pós-graduação em Administração-ENANPAD*. Salvador.

Oliver, RL (1997). *Satisfaction: A Behavioral Perspective on the Consumer*. Irwin/McGraw-Hill: New York, NY.

Oliver, RL (1999). Whence consumer loyalty? *Journal of Marketing*, 63(Special Issue), 33–44.

Ostrom, AL, MJ Bitner, SW Brown, KA Burkhard, M Goul, V Smith-Daniels, H Demirkan and E Rabinovich (2010). Moving forward and making a difference: Research priorities for the science of service. *Journal of Service Research*, 13(1), 4–36.

Parasuraman, A, LL Berry and VA Zeithaml (1991). Understanding customer expectations of service. *Sloan Management Review*, 32(3), 39–48.

Patterson, PG and T Smith (2001). Relationship benefits in services industries: A replication in a southeast asian context. *Journal of Services Marketing*, 15(6), 425–443.

Phillips, PA, MD Fiona and L Moutinho (2001). The interactive effects of strategic marketing planning and performance: A neural network analysis. *Journal of Marketing Management*, 17, 1–2(February), 159–182.

Phlesco, LP and SM Baqer (2008). A preliminary study of the relationships among consumer satisfaction, loyalty, and market share in health club consumers. *Proceedings of the Academy of Marketing Studies*, 13(1), 46–54.

Prado, PHM (1997). Dimensões da resposta afetiva ao processo de compra e a satisfação do consumidor: O caso dos super mercados. Anais do 21 ENANPAD, p. 123. Brazil.

Prado, PHM and R da C RSantos, (2003). Comprometimento e Lealdade: Dois Conceitos ou Duas Dimensões de um único Conceito? In *Anais do XXVII Encontro da Associação dos Programas de Pós-graduação em Administração-ENANPAD*. Atibaia.

Pritchard, M, M Havitz and D Howard (1999). Analyzing the commitment loyalty link in service contexts. *Journal of the Academy of Marketing Science*, 27(3), 333–348.

Reichheld, FF, (1994). Loyalty and the renaissance of marketing. *Marketing Management*, 2(4), 10–17.

Reichheld, FF and P Schefter (2000). E-loyalty: Your secret weapon on the web. *Harvard Business Review*, 78(4), 105–113.

Roberts, K, S Varki and R Brodie (2003). Measuring the quality of relationships in consumer services: An empirical study. *European Journal of Marketing*, 37(1/2), 169–196.

Rosenblatt, F (1958). The perceptron: A probability model for information storage and organization in the brain. *Psychological Review*, 65(6).

Rumelhart, DE, GE Hinton and RJ Williams (1986). Learning internal representations by error propagation. In *Parallel Distributed Processing*, DE Rumelhart and JL McClland (eds.), Vol. 1, Chapter 8, pp. 318–362. MA: MIT Press.

Sierra, JJ and S McQuitty (2005). Service providers and customers: Social exchange theory and service loyalty. *Journal of Services Marketing*, 19(6), 392–400.

Sheth, JN (1996). Relationship marketing: Paradigm shift or shaft? *Paper presented at the Annual Meeting of the Academy of Marketing Science*. Miami, Flórida.

Thieme, RJ, M Song and RJ Calantone (2000). Artificial neural network decision support systems for new product development project selection. *Journal of Marketing Research*, 37(4), 499–507.

Thuy, PN and N Hau, Le. (2010). Service personal values and loyalty: A study os banking services in a transitional economy. *International Journal of Bank Marketing*, 28(6), 465–478.

Wilson, E and T Wragg (2001). We cannot diagnose the patients' illness … but experience tells us what treatment works. *International Journal of Market Research*, 43(2), 189–215.

Chapter 7

THE APPLICATION OF NN
TO MANAGEMENT PROBLEMS*

Arnaldo Coelho
Faculty of Economics, University of Coimbra
Av. Dias da Silva, 165, 3004–512, Coimbra, Portugal
acoelho@fe.uc.pt

Luiz Moutinho
Graeme D Hutcheson
Manchester University

Maria Manuela Santos Silva
Faculty of Economics, University of Coimbra
Av. Dias da Silva, 165, 3004–512, Coimbra, Portugal
nelinha@fe.uc.pt

This chapter attempts to make available to the reader the main insights into the world of artificial neural networks (ANNs), seen as a generalized mathematical models which emulate human cognition, as well as, highlights several contributions of this statistical methodology trained by the multiple backpropagation algorithm in the management field. Artificial neural networks are pattern recognition algorithms capable of capturing salient features from a set of inputs and map them to outputs without making *a priori* assumptions about the specific nature of the relationships. It was shown that ANN modelling demonstrates good capacity to provide additional explanations to the different investigation problems, namely, giving the opportunity to identify new and different linkages between the variables in the models. At the same time, this modelling can be faced

---
*The Chapter 7 was done with the support of our doctoral team research Jorge Gouveia, Sandra Maria Holanda, Afonso Clemente Zinga, Renato Pedro Mugnol, Gelso Pedrosi Filho and Anabela Maria Bello Marcos.

as a new departure in the search of new solutions, giving insights to the use of other modelling tools, like SEM and others, which have a more confirmatory naure.

Keywords: Artificial neural networks, multiple backpropagation; dynamic and managerial capabilities; entrepreneurship; customer behaviour; relationship marketing.

1. Artificial Neural Networks in the Management Field

There has been a steady increase in the number of published research papers reporting the use of Artificial Neural Networks (ANNs) in marketing. However, there is a need for an increase in awareness in other areas of marketing and in management to complement the limited work undertaken in retailing and direct marketing. Indeed, Hruschka (1991) and Krycha and Wagner (1999), drew attention to the scarcity of articles applying ANN techniques to marketing and management issues.

Furthermore, although many studies using this modelling strategy have appeared, as might be expected, many of them are comparing ANNs with other more established techniques such as regression, discriminant analysis, and cluster analysis (Venugopal and Baets, 1994a). Many application areas of ANNs in marketing have been suggested, including market response modelling, retail sales forecasting, direct marketing, and target marketing (Krycha and Wagner, 1999; Mazanec and Moutinho, 1999; Venugopal and Baets, 1994b; Zahavi and Levin, 1995). In fact, ANNs have been applied to numerous marketing problems, for example, new product development (Thieme *et al.*, 2000), sales forecasting (Kuo, 2001), market segmentation (Boone and Roehm, 2002; Hruschka and Natter, 1999), marketing strategy (Li, 2000) and market orientation (Silva *et al.*, 2009).

Despite such comparatively development in research into ANNs, this modelling approach remains wide and unexpectedly unknown. However, the possibilities it brings are almost remarkable, compared to the interest and use that investigators are giving to it. Regardless of its wide use, multiple regression or Structural Equations Modelling encourage confirmatory rather than exploratory modelling, and thus, it is more appropriate to test rather than develop a theory.

The problem is that the causal assumptions that underlie the investigation models often have falsifiable implications.

So, the major advantage of neural networks (NNs) lies in their ability to represent both linear and non-linear relationships and to learn these relationships directly from the data being modelled. The use of NN modelling can help researchers to obtain a better understanding and structuring of the problems. This framework is based on the utilisation of non-directly measured components, 'the hidden layers', as strong mediating entities, lying between the measured variables, deriving from an information-processing system whose structure presents certain characteristics observed in the nervous systems of humans and animals (Haykin, 1999). They have been developed as generalisations of mathematical models of human cognition or neural biology. An ANN is characterised by its pattern of connections between the neurons (called its architecture), its method of determining the weights on the connections (called its learning algorithm), and its activation function. Such a network consists of a large number of computing cells usually denominated neurons, nodes or processing units linked by weighted connections. Each unit receives inputs from other neurons and generates a single scalar output.

The main goal of this chapter is to show different fields where ANNs can successfully be used and how they can help researchers to better capture and understand management problems, as well as to provide different linkages between variables. Hopefully, they will lead to new explanations for most of the studied phenomena. There will be examples in the field of: New ICT adoption, loyalty in the banking industry, entrepreneurial orientation and small firm performance, the influence of external market orientation, entrepreneurial orientation, innovation and resources on export performance, and the determinants of the involvement of university researchers in spin-off creation.

2. Why use ANNs?

The technique has been applied in a wide range of industries, for example, the food industry (Corney, 2002), retailing (Decker and

Monien, 2003), and banking (Moutinho and Phillips, 2002). Lim and Brewer (1996) reviewed the application of ANNs in marketing; and Agrawal and Schorling (1996) conducted an empirical comparison of ANNs and a multinomial logit model to forecast market shape. Aiken and Bsat (1999) forecasted market trends with NNs. At the same time Ainscough and Aronson (1999) conducted an empirical investigation to compare NNs and regression for scanner data analysis. Hruschka (1993) compared NN modelling to economic techniques to determine market response functions. West *et al.* (1997) developed a comparative analysis of NNs with discriminant analysis and generalised linear modelling (logistic regression) for predicting consumer choice. Yao *et al.* (1998) used NNs to forecast and analyse marketing data. Baesens *et al.* (2002) used a Bayesian NN learning algorithm for repeat purchase modelling in direct marketing. Venugopal and Baets (1994b) designed a conceptual comparison between NNs and statistical techniques (multivariate statistical analysis) in marketing research. And a NN was used by Moutinho *et al.* (1996) for the analysis of the impact of gender on car buyer satisfaction and loyalty, with hidden layer models being labelled to represent respondents' easily articulated attitudes or beliefs.

Curry and Moutinho (1993) used NNs in marketing, in particular to model consumer responses to advertising stimuli. Dasgupta *et al.* (1994) compared the predictive performance of a NN model with some traditional market response models. Phillips *et al.* (2001) studied the interactive efforts of strategic marketing, planning and performance using a NN analysis. The same authors (Phillips *et al.*, 2002) assessed the impact of market-focused and price-based strategies on performance also using a NN topology. Davies *et al.* (1999) developed two comparison studies based on structural equations (SEM) and NNs modelling.

Recently, NN modelling has received increasing attention and has been applied to an array of marketing problems such as market response and segmentation. For example, Bentz and Merunka (2000) showed that a Feed Forward NN with softmax output units and shared weights can be viewed as a generalisation of the multinomial logit model. In their study, they applied a hybrid approach for brand choice modelling. Balakrishnan *et al.* (1996) also co-paned the performance of the FSCL NN and the *K*-means algorithm for market segmentation. Furthermore, Alom *et al.* (2001) forecasted aggregate retail sales by comparing ANNs to traditional methods (i.e., Winters Exponential Smoothing, Box-Jerkins, ARIMA model, and Multivariate Regression).

Considering the multi-faceted demands of the marketing domain and the myriad sets of available marketing data, it can be very difficult to draw anything relevant from the available data because of the unrelatedness and nonlinearity. Therefore, a study was carried out by Proctor (1992) on the role of NNs in marketing. The strength of a NN is its availability to obtain the relationships of nonlinearly dependent variables. Venugopal and Baets (1994b) proposed application of NNs in retail sales forecasting, direct marketing, and target marketing.

Compared with other traditional statistical methods, NNs require only minimum knowledge of a problem's structure. No prior knowledge of the statistical distribution of the data is required because the network develops an internal relationship between the variables. All these advantages make NNs particularly suitable to complex classification problems in which the mapping rationale is fuzzy, inconsistent, or completely unknown. And as most business and marketing applications can be considered as fuzzy classifications, this is an area in which NNs can be of service.

Several other reasons justify the use of this modelling strategy:

- The NN topology has a 'deeper' psychological and non-direct nature. The nature of the NN topology usually generates more causal interactions, a much higher number of underpinnings, and indicators of causality, compared to other statistical tools, like SEM. The *a priori* theoretical model behind the SEM analysis postulates only one-way causation and the lack of the non-recursivity, which is an unusual premise when conducting research modelling under the structural equations approach.
- With regard to the issue of interconnectivity, and as a result of the more complex structure of the NN model, when compared with the more parsimonious design of other techniques, one

can find almost three times the number of the network/model interconnections in the NN topology as compared to SEM. This higher degree of model complexity usually affects positively the performance and the goodness-of-fit of the modelling approach.

• It can be said that NN performs quite well in terms of structural accuracy (latency effects, causal interactions, and interconnectivity) as well as in the sense of estimated predictability.

The particular nature of ANNs makes them complementary to SEM, since whilst SEM and other techniques are confirmatory in outcome, ANNs can play a more exploratory role, helping in theory development. The true power and advantage of NNs lies in their ability to represent both linear and nonlinear relationships, whereas traditional linear models are simply inadequate when it comes to modelling data that contains nonlinear characteristics (Wilson and Wragg, 2001; Audrain, 2002). No prior knowledge of the statistical distribution of the data is required because the network develops an internal relationship between the variables. Most business and marketing applications can be considered as fuzzy classifications, and this is the area where NNs can be of service. Wray *et al.* (1994) point out that NN models are most robust to missing and inaccurate data and are not quite as influenced by non-standard conditions. Furthermore, their performance is not diminished by multicollinearity.

3. Artificial Neural Networks

ANNs, usually called neural networks, are massively parallel interconnected networks of simple processing units also designated by cells neurons or nodes, which are intended to interact with the objects of the real world in the same way as biological systems do. The NN reproduces the network of neurons, which carry out the lower level computational actions (as opposed to the high level cognitive operations) in the human brain. The NNs do not require a knowledge base to be constructed, nor do they need an explicit inference procedure to be developed and subsequently encoded. In each computing cell, we can identify three fundamental elements:

A set of connecting links, each one characterised by a weight w_{kj} where k and j indicate the receiving and the emitting neuron, respectively; an adder for summing the input signals $x_1, x_2, \ldots, x_n$ and an activation function f, in order to limit the amplitude range of the output of the neuron. Note that a neuron model can also include an external constant input $x_0 = 1$ known by bias. Each unit of NN performs a weighted sum on the inputs received from many other nodes and applies the function, f, to the resultant value of the previous operation, generating a single scalar output that depends only on locally-available information, either stored internally or arriving via the weighted connections. The output is distributed to, and acts as an input to, other processing nodes. The most simple artificial neuron is the McCulloch–Pitts shown in Fig. 1.

Activation functions can be classified into three basic types: Threshold or Heaviside function, piecewise linear function, and sigmoid function. Sigmoid function is by far the most common form of activation function used in the construction of NN. It is a bounded no decreasing and nonlinear function that exhibits smoothness and asymptotic properties. An example of sigmoid is the logistic function defined by:

$$f(x) = \frac{1}{1 + \exp(x)}.$$

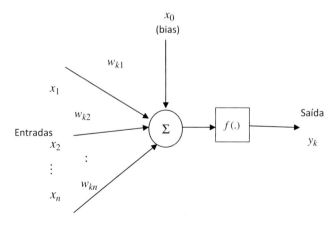

Fig. 1.   A McCulloch–Pitts neuron.

Furthermore, an ANN is also characterised by its architecture: The pattern of connections between neurons and its method of determining the weights on the connections, called a learning algorithm.

3.1. *Architecture of neural networks*

It can be observed that by itself, a single processing element is not very powerful. The power of the neural model emerges from the combination of many units in a network. So, in the design of a NN we must define its topology. A network can have an arbitrary structure but layered architectures are the most widely used.

In general, concerning the arrangement of neurons into layers and the connection patterns within and between layers, we can observe three different classes of network:

1. Single-layer networks or single-layer Perceptrons
2. Multi-layer networks or multi-layer Perceptrons (MLP)
3. Recurrent networks

The most elemental neural model, belonging to the first class, the Perceptron developed by Frank Rosenblatt, consists of a layer of input nodes, each of which is connected to each node in a layer of output nodes (Rosenblatt, 1958). Although the simple Perceptron model is of major significance, it suffers from some limitations. Indeed, in their book 'Perceptrons', Minsky and Papert (1969) pointed out that a single-layer Perceptron can only classify a special type of pattern said to be linearly separable. So the exlusive XOR function is a well-known example of a simple function that is not computable by it. Nevertheless, NNs have been liberated from these problems, by the addition of one or more hidden layers, as illustrated in Fig. 2.

These are interior layers of neurons, which are not directly observable from the inputs and outputs system. Each hidden node is linked to each input node and to each output node, with the network computing values for each processing unit as a weighted sum of the neurons in the preceding layer, according to the connection weights. The NNs with this architecture are usually designated by feedforward networks.

Input layer   Hidden layer   Output layer

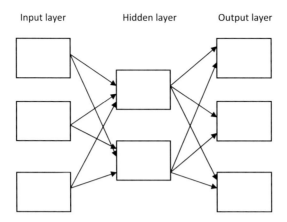

Fig. 2.   A neural network with one hidden layer.

Adding hidden layers, the network is enabled to extract high-order statistics because the network acquires a global perspective in spite of the extra set of links and the extra dimension of neural interactions. In fact, multilayer networks using arbitrary activation functions are universal approximators (Stinchcombe and White, 1989; Hornik *et al.*, 1989).

In the business world, hidden layer nodes play an interesting role: They can be assumed as latent or unobservable variables and the NN can be used to cast light on these variables through their links, identifying behavioural features or feelings which cannot directly be measured. The hidden layer nodes can be labelled taking into account the weights of the connections from the input nodes, which feed into them.

As mentioned previously, another important definition in the specification of a NN is its learning algorithm which is closely related to its architecture.

3.2.   *Learning algorithms*

A fundamental characteristic of the NN approach is that knowledge is acquired in the course of a learning process and the interneuron connection strengths or weights are used to store the knowledge. In NNs, learning refers to the method of modifying the weights and can be developed from training patterns or examples which consist either of inputs and desired outputs presented to the network — supervised learning, or through a sequence of only input vectors without specifying the correspondent target vectors — unsupervised learning, and can be derived from sources such as images, speech signals sensor data, financial data, and market data. Since NNs learn by examples, they have the potential for building computing systems that do not need to be programmed. This reflects a radically different approach to computing compared to traditional methods, which involve the development of computer programs. The ability to represent both linear and nonlinear relationships and to learn these interactions directly from patterns, as well as the capacity of generalisation, that is, to produce reasonable outputs for inputs not founded during training, allow modelling of complex systems whose behaviour rules are not known in detail or are difficult to analyse correctly, and consequently endow the network with sub-stantially increased representational power. Indeed, several studies have pointed out the superiority of NNs over traditional statistical techniques such as regression analysis, discriminate analysis, cluster analysis, and structural equations modelling. For example, some researchers have investigated the performance of NNs and found this new methodology outperforming multiple regression analysis (Spangler *et al.*, 1999; Uysal and Roubi, 1999; Johnson and Gustafson, 2000; Fadlalla and Lin, 2001; Nguyen and Cripps, 2001; Wilson and Wragg, 2001; Audrain, 2002; Gronholdt and Martensen, 2005).

For the single-layer Perceptron the most common scheme for supervised learning is an iterative procedure called the Delta rule, which cannot be applied to a network with hidden layers. It is impossible to compute prediction errors for hidden layer nodes since they do not have observed values. Feedforward networks, frequently referred to as MLP, have been applied successfully to resolve complex problems by training them in a supervised method with a highly popular algorithm known as the backpropagation (BP) algorithm. Indeed, there has been an enlargement in the number of published researched papers reporting the use of NNs trained with a BP algorithm in a broad range of areas such as pattern recognition, function approximation, signal processing, classification, time series prediction, control applications, optimisation, regression analysis. Many application areas of this methodology in marketing have been suggested, including market response modelling, retail sales forecasting, direct marketing, target marketing (Krycha and Wagner, 1999; Mazanec and Moutinho, 1999; Venugopal and Baets, 1994b; Zahavi and Levin, 1995), new product development (Thieme *et al.*, 2000), sales forecasting (Kuo, 2001), market segmentation (Boone and Roehm, 2002), marketing strategy (Li, 2000). The NNs have also been applied in a wide range of industries, such as, the food industry (Corney, 2002), retailing (Decker and Monien, 2003), and banking (Moutinho and Phillips, 2002). Bentz and Merunka (200) showed that a feedforward NN with softmax output units and shared weights can be viewed as a generalisation of the multinomial logit model, and applied a hybrid approach for brand choice modelling. Phillips *et al.* (2001), using NN analysis, studied the interactive efforts of strategic marketing, planning, and performance. The same authors (Phillips *et al.*, 2002) assessed the impact of market-focused and price-based strategies on performance also applying NN topology.

The range of NN applications in the business world is continually expanding as researchers and practitioners explore the potential of the approach. However, one of the common complaints about the BP algorithm is that it can be very slow. So, many variations of BP have been proposed in order to accelerate its speed of convergence as well as the capacity of generalisation of the resultant network. In Lopes and Ribeiro (2003), a new NN structure, multiple feedforward (MFF) network as well a new gradient-based algorithm called multiple backpropagation (MBP) were developed.

3.3. *Multiple feedforward networks*

MFF networks are obtained by integrating two feedforwards. The main network has selective neurons, whose activation role is detained through space localisation of input pattern data. In this sense, only those neurons fired by a particular data point turn out to be relevant while keeping the capacity to approximate closely, more general, nonlinear features in localised regions. The other, named

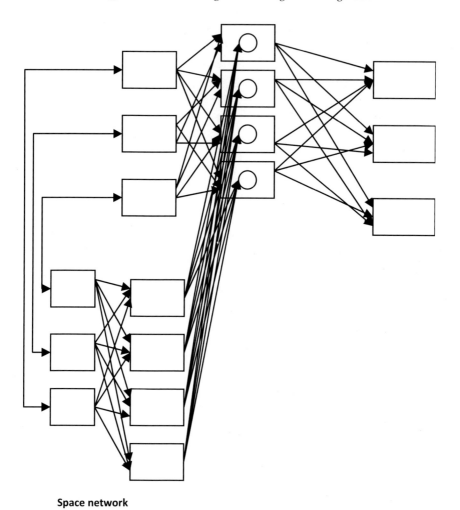

Space network

Fig. 3. A multiple feedforward network. The selective neuron contribution is represented by circles.

space network, is responsible for determining the importance factor of the main network neurons as far as each pattern is presented to the MFF network. Figure 3 shows the relationship between the networks that constitute this new class of NNs.

To identify if and how much a selective neuron k contributes to the network outputs when a pattern p is presented, a variable m_k^p is added in its output equation:

$$y_k^p = m_k^p f(a_k^p) = m_k^p f \left(\sum_{j=1}^{N} w_{jk} y_j^p + \theta_k \right), \qquad (1)$$

where N is the number of input connections of the neuron k, f is the activation function of the neuron k, a_k^p is the activation of the neuron k, w_{jk} represents the weight associated with the link between node j and node k, y_j^p is the output of neuron j, and θ_k is the bias of neuron k. The values of m_k^p are determined by the space network that receives the same inputs as the main network and generates the values m_k^p as outputs. From Eq. (1) we conclude how far from zero m_k^p is, as most relevant the k neuron contribution and a value of zero signifies that the neuron will not contribute to the network outputs. Besides, the main network outputs are computed after the space network outputs have been determined. In this way, the two networks will work jointly and must be trained as one.

3.4. *Multiple backpropagation algorithm*

In MFF networks, and regarding their output errors, we must consider two contributions: The first is concerned to the link weights of the main network and the second is relative to the importance assigned to each selective neuron by the space network. The main network weights are adjusted, applying the gradient descent method, in order to minimise the quadratic error function,

$$E^p = \frac{1}{2} \sum_{o=1}^{N_o} (d_o^p - y_o^p)^2,$$

where N_o is the number of outputs, and d_o^p and y_o^p are, respectively, the desired and the correspondent output of neuron o for pattern p. Therefore, the MBP updates the main network weights in agreement with:

$$\Delta_p w_{jk} = \gamma \delta_k^p y_j^p + \alpha \Delta_q w_{jk}, \qquad (2)$$

where γ is the learning rate, $\Delta_q w_{jk}$ is the weight change w_{jk} for last pattern q, α is the moment term and δ_k^p is the local gradient of neuron k given by:

$$\delta_o^p = (d_o^p - y_o^p)m_o^p f_o'(a_o^p) \quad \text{and} \quad \delta_h^p = m_h^p f_h'(a_h^p) \sum_{o=1}^{N_o} \delta_o^p w_{ho}, \tag{3}$$

for the output and hidden neurons, respectively. Since the relevance given to each selective neuron according to the pattern presented to the MFF contributes to the network output errors, the space network weights must be updated. This goal is attained using the gradient descent method, that is,

$$\Delta_p m_k^p = \frac{dE^p}{dm_k^p}.$$

Therefore, the corrections $\Delta_p m_o^p$ and $\Delta_p m_h^p$ applied to the importance of the output and hidden neurons are defined as follows:

$$\Delta_p m_o^p = (d_o^p - y_o^p)f_o(a_o^p) \quad \text{and} \quad \Delta_p m_h^p = \sum_{o=1}^{N_o} \delta_o^p w_{ho} f_h(a_h^p), \tag{4}$$

respectively.

Observe that the MBP algorithm can be implemented to train feedforward networks — the equations represented in (3), allow us to conclude that if all the neurons of the main network have the same importance regardless of the presented pattern, we can suppose, for example, $m_k^p = 1$ and so, they become equal to the corresponding BP equations. As a final point, the basic steps of the MBP algorithm can be reviewed:

1. Facing a pattern presented to the MFF network, the space network computes the relevance of each selective neuron and the main network will execute this input pattern and produce its outputs.
2. In the training phase, the variation of the importance of the neurons with selective actuation is computed and after the main network weights are adjusted by equations described by (2) and (3).
3. Through equations described in (4) and applying the BP algorithm, the space network weights can be updated.

4. ANNs Applied to the Adoption of New Information and Communication Technologies

The diffusion of innovations theory has been used, in the last two decades, in the investigation of the adoption of new information and communication technologies (ICT). Based on a data collection of 401 survey responses in Portugal, this investigation aims to give a contribution to the understanding of the consumer's decision on mobile Internet adoption.

The broadband internet access brought by the third generation of mobile telecommunications (3G) is allowing the mobile internet, defined in a broad sense as the wireless access to electronic services through mobile phones or other mobile devices (e.g., laptops, personal digital assistants), to assume an increasingly important role in modern societies.

The mobile internet and m-commerce may be one of the most profitable markets in the future with an unpredictable impact in the economic and social organisation (Kim *et al.*, 2007). As the mobile internet is an enabling technology for m-commerce, the study of the factors influencing the adoption of mobile internet is also important to understand m-commerce adoption.

For Everett Rogers (1985, 1992, 2003), whose work is considered as the main reference in the study of the diffusion of the innovations (known as innovation theory or diffusion theory), the adoption of an innovation can be defined as the mental process through which an individual passes from first hearing about an innovation to final adoption. Currently, it is consensual that the adoption of technologies is a complex process which goes beyond the technical superiority of a product (Rogers, 1992; Valente, 1995).

In spite of the important contributions of several authors to this investigation field, the model developed by Rogers (1983, 1995, 2003) is the main reference of diffusion theory regarding the analysis of the basic forces that affect the rate of adoption of innovations.

The first component of this model includes five attributes of the innovations, as perceived by individuals. Relative advantage is the degree to which an advantage is perceived as better than the ideas it supersedes, compatibility can be defined as the degree to which an innovation is perceived as being consistent with the existing values, past experiences and needs, complexity is seen as the degree to which an innovation is perceived as difficult to understand and use, trialability is used as the degree to which an innovation may be experimented with on a limited basis, and finally observability is the degree to which the results of an innovation are visible to others (Rogers, 1995, 2003).

The perceived attributes of innovations are universal concepts which allow comparisons not only between different innovations, but also, between diverse social and cultural contexts and historical moments. For this reason, they have been largely adopted in studies of different fields especially within the social sciences, and recently applied to the study of the adoption of new ICTs, a new field of investigation in considerable expansion (Moore and Benbasat, 1991; Corney, 2002; Mattila, 2003; Walczuch *et al.*, 2007).

In this field an important study was conducted by Moore and Benbasat (1991) based on Rogers' model, aiming to develop a valid instrument to measure its constructs. From this study, three main contributions were forthcoming. The model resulting from the investigation was built on the most consensual ideas of the innovation diffusion theory aggregated by Rogers and adds relevant contributions to its application to the study of the adoption of new ICTs.

Other investigation lines have been followed to better understand the factors influencing the adoption decision of new ICTs, namely the theory of reasoned action (Ajzen and Fishbein, 1975, 1980) the theory of planned behaviour (Anckar and D'Incau, 2002) and the technology acceptance model (Davis, 1989, 1993; Davis *et al.*, 1989).

The diffusion of innovations investigation has been studying different kinds of acceptance behaviour such as intention to use, current use and sustained use as other recent technology acceptance studies. In an initial approach two dependent variables were used, the factors influencing current use, as suggested by Moore and Benbasat (1991), and the intention to use or to increase use in the future, as proposed by Agarwal and Prasad (1997) for innovations in early stages of the diffusion process. This approach has been adopted

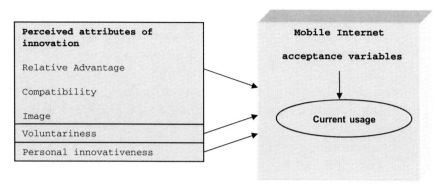

Fig. 4.   The proposed model.

recently by several technology adoption studies (Bouwman *et al.*, 2007; Hernandez and Mazzon, 2007, 2008).

In addition to the factors proposed in the model by Moore and Benbasat (1991), two additional research questions were tested in the present investigation.

It is proposed that there is a positive relation between current use and the intention to use the mobile internet in the future, bearing in mind the suggestions of Agarwal and Prasad (1997) who adapted the perceived characteristics of innovations model adding this new contribution.

It is proposed that there is a relationship between personal innovativeness and the intention to adopt the mobile internet (Fig. 4). The diffusion of innovation literature has recognised that individuals with higher levels of innovativeness tend to develop more positive perceptions of the innovation's characteristics and consequently have a higher propensity to adopt (Agarwal and Prasad, 1997; Rogers, 2003).

4.1.   *The modelling approach*

The scales used to measure the independent variables of the model were based on Moore and Benbasat (1991) and also used by several other investigators. The dependent variables were all based on technology acceptance investigations. The target population in this investigation field was the Portuguese population from 15 to 64 years old. A convenience sample was used and 401 valid questionnaires were collected from all age sets, all regions of the country, all education and income levels, and professional categories.

In order to look into the principal factors of the future use intentions of the mobile internet, several feedforward and MFF network architectures were trained with the MBP algorithm, online mode, on a Pentium IV at 782 Mhz. The dataset was comprises 401 input–output measurements of the factors determining the adoption of the mobile internet and future use intention. It was found that MFF network with a single hidden layer of five neurons, provided the smallest training time and the best generalisation capabilities. The space network had only one layer responsible for determining the relevance of the selective neurons that were placed in the hidden layer of the main network.

The activation function used for the hidden and output neurons of both networks, main and space, was the sigmoid function. The network had ten input nodes, corresponding to the following ten explanatory variables: Ease of use, image, innovation, visibility, voluntariness, relative advantage, results demonstrability, past experimentation, future experimentation, and current use. The output node corresponded to the future use intention. For the purpose of our study, the first 241 data items (60%) were used in the training set and the remaining 160 (40%) in the test set. Additionally, the data was pre-processed, rescaling the inputs and outputs at the intervals [0, 1]. The training examples were presented randomly. In the training setup the values of u (increment) and d (decrement) were set at 1 and 0.9 respectively. Moreover, to obtain robustness, the step sizes were further reduced by a factor of 0.5 each time the root mean square (RMSE) error, defined by:

$$\text{RMSE} = \frac{1}{2}\sqrt{\frac{1}{N_p N_o}\sum_{p=1}^{N_p}\sum_{o=1}^{N_o}(d_o^p - y_o^p)^2},$$

where N_p represents the number of patterns, increased more than 0.1%.

The MBP algorithm performed 30 runs, being the number of epochs constrained to a maximum of 10,000 because behold threshold level, any improvements were of an insignificant nature. This supervisioned learning rule presents a great diversity of training configurations, specifically an adaptive learning rate as well as an adaptive momentum term. In this framework, the learning rate and the momentum term of the main network were initialised to 0.1 and 0.3, decaying the latter, automatically, 1% every 1,000 epochs, whereas for the space network these values were 0.7 and 0.2. Furthermore, different random initialisations for the weights were tested. It was found that the interval $[-1, 1]$ provides better results regarding the error function.

Tables 1 and 2 show the weights of the network connections between the neurons and the contributions made by the different variables. The contributory and inhibitory weights resulted within a range of between $[-17, 21]$ and the root mean square error (RMSE) for the test data, was 0.0419. A goodness-of-fit coefficient, R^2, was computed to analyse the performance of the MFF network. The R^2 value obtained was 0.99801 for the future use intention. Hence, the neural model explains over 99% of the variance of perceived performance on the output variable.

4.2. Results

The NN resulting from this investigation is made up of ten input nodes linked to five hidden nodes which are finally connected to one output neuron, which behaviour it is intended to explain. In the present investigation, ANN modelling showed a good capacity for rendering some additional appreciation of a problem that seems not to be completely structured. The use of ANN as a methodological tool provided a higher interpretative capacity and dissection of the richness of the content. The ANN modelling showed an excellent fit with a RMSEA $= 0.0419$.

Additionally, the introduction of new variables (hidden layers) helped the comprehension of the relationship between initial constructs and mobile internet acceptance, a relationship that seems to be indirect rather than direct.

Table 1. The weights of the network connections and the contributions of the input variables.

From input layer

To the hidden layer	Img	RD	Visib	FExp	PExp	Innov	Volunt	Ease_U	RAdv_C	CUse
1st neuron	0.894091	2.86565	4.71819	3.415011	3.83777	0.763552	1.07711	2.52431	1.64285	1.98512
2nd neuron	11.7728	3.975	2.15422	9.62643	3.69834	−6.07462	3.79027	1.54195	−16.6326	−12.2502
3rd neuron	2.27141	20.5046	−5.47804	0.444323	4.45868	−16.3147	6.96744	1.91211	2.00658	0.333206
4th neuron	0.346576	3.49523	−2.20239	1.66157	1.34455	−3.07401	3.98096	0.559525	2.65845	6.5271
5th neuron	7.0383	3.7038	−6.38481	6.39408	3.13958	2.42131	1.079	3.06659	1.76873	7.19398
Total contribution	22.323177	34.54428	20.93765	21.541414	16.47892	28.648192	16.89478	9.604485	24.70921	28.289606

Notes: Img — Image RD — Results Demonstrability Visib — Visibility FExp — Fut_Exp. PExp — Past_Exp. Innov — Innovation Vol — Voluntariness Ease_U — Ease of use RAdv_C — Relative Advantage and Compatibility CUse — Current Usage.

Table 2.   The impacts of hidden nodes on future use intention.

From the hidden layer					
To the output layer	neuron				
	1st	2nd	3rd	4th	5th
Fut_Use Intention	−3.73735	−3.50282	1.80146	−4.80535	−4.80535

The hidden node 'projected image and use' (HN5) with the highest degree of impact underlines the importance of current usage, perceived image and perceived future experimentation opportunities in future use intentions. The significant positive effect of current usage in the intention to use the mobile Internet is consistent with other ICT studies (Agarwal and Prasad, 1997), and supports our first additional research question. Regarding the importance of perceived image, our results are also consistent with several mobile internet adoption studies (Lu *et al.*, 2003) which indicate that wireless internet technology is mostly used when the individual is socially exposed and, therefore, it can particularly influence and be influenced by, that individual's projected social image. Moreover, these results indicate that current usage and image have a direct relationship and together influence in a positive way, mobile internet future use intentions.

The rational aspects of the adoption decision process seem to be summarised in the hidden node 'concerted decision making' (HN3) with a positive effect in the intention to use the mobile internet. This result can be interpreted as that more effective and balanced decision-making processes seem to affect and maximise future adoption and future use of the mobile internet. In particular, the hidden node results showed that demonstrability had the strongest influence in this hidden node (and also in the entire network), and hence was found to have a strong explanatory power in internet acceptance investigations (Hernandez and Mazzon, 2007). Regarding the strong negative influence of personal innovativeness in the hidden node 'concerted decision making' (which revealed a positive contribution to the intention to use the mobile internet), even if it is not possible to clearly reject the idea of a positive linkage between personal innovativeness and technology acceptance (as assumed in additional proposition number 2), the importance of the rational aspects of the decision process in this hidden node rejects personal characteristics as innovativeness and, therefore, does not give support to this proposition.

The combination of the influences of current use and voluntariness (HN4) has the highest negative impact in the output layer. This result supports the position of Moore and Benbasat (1991) that individuals may have different degrees of freedom to implement personal adoption or rejection decisions. It also suggests that the mobile internet is viewed mainly in the professional or enterprise context where the decision to adopt is strongly influenced or determined by external factors which affect the individual freedom of choice (e.g., company policy, superior determination, customer demands).

The negative link-up between 'technology all around' (HN1) and the intention to use the mobile internet should be related with the fact that individuals with higher educational and economic levels and technology experience tend not to be influenced by their perception of visibility and ease of use especially regarding technological innovations (Agarwal and Prasad, 1997; Carter and Belanger, 2004; Davis, 1993). This result does not contradict the importance of these factors in the adoption decision which gathers a large consensus in the diffusion theory, but calls attention to the fact that the role of some innovation characteristics is particularly dependent upon the kind of innovation and potential adopter.

The fact that NNs attempt to reproduce the brain system means that the model developed can be a simplified representation of the associations and link-ups in an innovation potential adopter's mind which might be particularly relevant in the managerial point of view.

In this context, managerial strategies to promote ICT innovations and particularly mobile internet adoption, should be aware of the importance of 'projected image and use' which summarises the positive effects of current usage, perceived image and perceived future experimentation opportunities in future use intentions. The desire to gain social status may not be assumed by most people but is certainly a key trigger to adopt the mobile internet and should be explored using commercial messages associating its use with values like social recognition and both personal and professional success. These messages may also suggest that this technology should be widely used in the future and guarantee the possibility of experimentation without risks or commitments.

However, the results obtained suggest that the importance of perceived image and future experimentation tends to fade out when the perception of relative advantage and compatibility associated with the current usage increases. Relative advantage and compatibility are broadly referred to as strong contributors to the adoption of the mobile internet (Lee *et al.*, 2003; Kim *et al.*, 2007) and other services supported on it such as mobile payments (Chen, 2008).

In the development of new products and services for the mobile internet, the previous technological experience and background of the potential adopters should be considered in order to increase the perceived compatibility with existing experiences, values and lifestyle, all of which are seen as enablers in realising the relative advantages of an innovation. According to Rogers (2003), the main relative advantages compared to other alternatives are the economic benefits, low initial cost, effort or time savings, and the immediate and certain reward. These elements should be taken into account not only in the development but also in the promotion of mobile internet services. Anckar and D'Incau (2002) suggest that the main relative advantage of the mobile internet in comparison to other technologies, such as the fixed internet, is that it can be used independently of time and space which assures a 'new freedom' and a sense of ubiquity that should also be explored by the change agents.

Another outcome of this investigation that could be used in the managerial field is the importance of rational aspects and tangible results in the mobile internet future use intentions. In our view, the development and promotion of this ICT should focus on proving that there is a positive economic impact to be gained by its use, and should especially target the enterprise market. Simple ROI — return on investment — tools can include productivity gains such as reduction of travel needs (e.g., commercial forces do not need to go to the office so often), productive time gains (e.g., use of time in travelling or waiting for customers), and workflow gains (e.g., greater information speed flow within the organisation reduces time to market) that can easily provide a good return in a short pay-back period.

The results found in this study, in general terms, support the most common conclusions found in the diffusion of ICT innovations field but also provide a new model with a significant explanation power of the process of adopting the mobile internet including five hidden nodes which aggregate different aspects of the initial constructs.

In our view, among the results of this study, discussed above, the main contributions for the research in this field are the emergence of HN4 'use and voluntariness' as the strongest inhibitor of adoption and the convergence of current usage, image and future experimentation in HN5 'projected image and use' as the major contributor for adoption.

The inverse relation found between relative advantage and compatibility with image is also an interesting outcome which suggests that the more an innovation is perceived as being better than other alternatives and the more compatible with one's beliefs and lifestyle it is, the less is the importance of the perception that using an innovation will contribute to one's social status. This relationship has not been much explored and, therefore, should be addressed in future studies.

5.   The use of ANNs and Loyalty in the Banking Industry

This investigation uses NN modelling to evaluate loyalty in the banking industry, and takes as its research population, 229 customers of small- and medium-sized banks in Brazil. The key objective of this study is to investigate the contribution of NNs in explaining the main drivers of customer loyalty in the banking industry. Particularly, special attention has been given to the impact of emotions, in its two-dimensional view, positive and negative, on the relationship between customers and banks, and on customer loyalty.

In banking and financial services, the search for customer relationships is crucial, due to the great changes introduced in the last decades, within an increasingly competitive environment (Barnes, 1997). Banks have to deal with customer turnover (Ibbotson and Moran, 2003), as well as with customers, both individuals and companies, who simultaneously use the services of other different banks (Adamson *et al.*, 2003; Guarita, 2005). Relationship marketing seems to be the main tool of the banks' differentiation strategy (Oliveira and Dutra, 2002), and loyalty seems to be essential for service business survival (Reichheld, 1994).

In business markets, there is an assumption that purchasing managers' decision-making process is mainly guided by cognitive factors and not by affective ones (Gross, 1997), but this assertion is contested by empirical research (Eggert and Ulaga, 2002) that provides evidence of the stronger predictive power of satisfaction, an affective construct, on behavioural outcomes, compared to customer perceived value, a cognitive variable. Reichheld and Schefter (2000) show how loyalty drivers are changing and vary according to each situation, context and industry.

The behavioural approach to loyalty, based on repeated buying, has been presented since the 1970s. However, researchers came to realise that re-purchase is not enough evidence of brand loyalty or company loyalty (Newman and Werbel, 1973). Behavioural measures seem to present serious limitations and have been criticised for their lack of a conceptual basis. They are founded on a narrow perspective of loyalty, which ignores the dynamics of the underlying process (Day, 1969, in Bloemer *et al.*, 1999). Behavioural measures are not capable of distinguishing between true loyalty and spurious loyalty: That is true of all the situations where alternatives are not available for customers. As an example, Morgan and Hunt (1994) argue that in relational exchange, brand attitude becomes central to the repurchase decision.

Several researchers are now focusing on the importance of introducing both dimensions, behavioural and attitudinal, to achieve a reliable measure for loyalty (Dick and Basu, 1994; Jones and Sasser, 1995; Han *et al.*, 2008), capable of being widely accepted by marketing scholars. These two types of loyalty seem to be closely interconnected: Repeated buying leads to the development of a positive effect which precipitates an emotional commitment and, consequently, promotes a high level of connection and the intention to continue buying (Oliver, 1999).

This study then contributes to the literature by proposing an integrative loyalty model that links cognitive and affective loyalty determinants, related to the corporate sector of the Brazilian banking industry. And even if it is impossible to find a study that has examined the effects of all antecedents affecting loyalty (Aydin and Özer, 2005), the focus of this study is on the set of best potential antecedents of loyalty in this industry according to what is considered in consumer and business markets studies. The variables proposed in this model are classified by affective antecedents/variables (positive emotions, negative emotions, satisfaction, and affective commitment), and cognitive antecedents/ones (relationship closeness, image, monetary sacrifice, non-monetary sacrifice, perceived value, trust, switching costs, and dependence. Relationship quality with the manager, and credit were added as two new constructs in loyalty models).

5.1. *The modelling approach*

The aim of this study was to evaluate the antecedents of business customers' loyalty to their main bank. Data was gathered from 229 small and medium companies (SMEs) in Brazil, via questionnaire. The survey on banking relationships was conducted using personal interviews. The SME key informant was the first responsible person for the firm's financial and banking decisions. To select respondents, convenience sampling was used. This resulted in 254 enterprises being contacted, 229 of which agreed to participate, representing a 90% response rate. Due to the fact that 95% of the companies of this survey had 99 employees or less, the findings of this study will reflect the views of the small business segment of SMEs in the North-east of Brazil. As business customers may have accounts in more than one bank, the interviewees were asked to indicate their main bank, and answer the questions based on their interactions with this bank. All enterprises had at least one year as customer of their main banks, and 75% had held a relationship of four years or more.

To achieve the goal identified, feedforward networks trained by the MBP were proposed. Then, different network architectures were tested on a Pentium IV, at 782 Mhz and we verified that the optimal fit between inputs and outputs was obtained using a network with a single hidden layer of five neurons. To convert multiple-items constructs into the 14 single inputs, the items of every construct were calculated by mean. Then the NN had 14 input nodes corresponding to the 14 explanatory variables: Relationship closeness, positive emotions, negative emotions, image, credit, relationship quality with the manager, perceived value, monetary sacrifice, non-monetary sacrifice, satisfaction, trust, affective commitment, switching costs, and dependence. The single output node corresponded to loyalty. The activation function chosen for the hidden and output neurons was the sigmoid function. For the purpose of this study, the training set was composed of 137 data (60%), and the other 92 (40%) were used in the test set. The training examples were presented on line mode and randomly.

The contributory and inhibitory weights were found to be within a range of $[-2, +2]$ as illustrated in Tables 3 and 4. The RMSE obtained for the test data was 0.0588. Finally, to measure the performance of the network model, a goodness-of-fit coefficient, R^2, was computed. This R^2 value, similar to R^2 provided in multiple regression analysis, measures the amount of variance of output variable, and was shown to be 0.9965 by the NN model. Therefore, the proposed model explains over 99% of the variance of perceived performance on loyalty.

5.2. Results

The perceived quality of the relationship is increasingly evolving around a number of intangible dimensions, namely within an 'emotional corridor'. The quality of the relationship is fuzzy and contradictory. There is no visible 'dependence' on the banks' support to SMEs and the issue of relationship closeness is not, apparently, a crucial determinant for institutional loyalty. Good relationship quality still rests upon some traditional building blocks such as commitment, trust, and satisfaction.

Table 3.   Impacts of input nodes on hidden nodes.

From the Input Layer

To the hidden layer	Relations closeness	Positive emotion	Negative emotion	Imag.	Cred.	Monet. sacrifice	Non-Monet. sacrifice
First node	−0.25	−0.70	0.06	0.37	0.20	−0.15	−0.31
Second node	−0.00	−0.47	−0.26	−0.04	−0.70	−0.51	−0.10
Third node	−0.13	0.10	−0.55	−0.53	−0.87	−0.54	−0.79
Fourth node	−1.16	0.31	0.17	0.74	0.57	0.05	0.26
Fifth node	0.59	1.12	0.38	0.54	−0.55	0.93	0.66
Total Contribution	2.16	2.72	1.45	2.24	2.91	2.20	2.14

To the hidden layer	Relation quality with the manag.	Perceiv. Value	Switching costs	Dependence	Satisfaction	Trust	Affective Commitm.
First node	0.36	0.07	−0.03	0.21	1.13	0.11	1.01
Second node	−0.41	−0.27	0.03	−0.65	−0.21	0.15	−0.98
Third node	−0.15	0.50	0.55	0.46	1.15	−0.33	1.13
Fourth node	−0.30	0.20	0.35	−0.67	0.22	1.00	0.86
Fifth node	−0.55	0.81	−0.00	−0.69	0.38	0.10	−0.46
Total Contribution	1.79	1.87	0.97	2.70	3.11	1.70	4.47

Table 4. Impacts of hidden nodes on loyalty.

From the hidden layer

To the output layer	Relationship Quality	Transactional factors	Loyalty potential	Reliability	Emotional Content & value
Loyalty	1.24	−0.97	0.47	1.12	0.35

Nonetheless, an interesting finding is that positive emotion as a general input and mediating factor only has a low effect on corporate banking loyalty. This same low level of impact also seems to mediate the link between the relationship with the manager and the perceptions and acceptance of bank loyalty. The availability of credit is surely an inhibitory factor for loyalty development. The mediation of affective commitment on loyalty, as measured by the type of human treatment, bank policies and procedures is, in general terms, negative. Positive emotions are not major triggers *per se*; what is important is emotional content and value. Therefore, affective commitment is something more than just the overall image and the relationships with the managers.

Loyalty is not dependent upon transactional factors, but on relational factors based on competence, which subsequently establish a transaction bond with the customers. The relationship closeness is still preponderant but is based on trust and functionality of benefits. Consequently, loyalty seems not to be relying on transactional factors but on the perceived reliability of the quality of the relationship. De facto, the final positive contribution to the formation and/or sustainability of bank loyalty, as measured by the impacts of the hidden layers (nodes) to the output node in the NN topology, is derived from the whole issue of reliability and the overall perceived value.

The results found in this study, in general terms, support the statement presented in the literature about the influence of relationship quality on positive behavioural outcomes (Dorsch *et al.*, 1998; Hennig-Thurau *et al.*, 2002). But they do not support what is expected to occur in business markets: The purchasing manager's decision-making process is mainly guided by cognitive factors (Gross, 1997).

The results suggest that antecedents of loyalty, represented by five hidden nodes, have similarities with characteristics related to the intangible aspects of a relationship. Bank service reliability and perceived value will oversee any goal and stage of business development ranging from survival to sustainability, and clearly, they can both deliver long-term sustainable preference.

6.   The use of ANNs and Entrepreneurial Orientation and Small Firm Performance

The aim of the study was to investigate in detail, the contribution made by: Entrepreneurial orientation dimensions (innovativeness, risk-taking, proactiveness, internal locus of control, and competitive aggressiveness), access to financial capital (self-financing, bank loan, government funds, and non-governmental organisations' endowments), personal networks (family, business, government, and acquaintance ties), cultural values (vertical collectivism, horizontal collectivism, vertical individualism, and horizontal individualism), and environmental variables (dynamism and hostility) to small firm performance. This study analyses data collected from 144 small Angolan firms.

The existing entrepreneurship literature is deeply rooted in the seminal work of Schumpeter (1934), in whose view, entrepreneurial actions entail creating new resources or combining existing resources in innovative ways to develop and commercialise new products, move into new markets, and/or service new customers, thereby stimulating economic activity. The key assumption underpinning the notion of entrepreneurship is that it is a behavioural phenomenon that can be described as new entry, which is highlighted by entrepreneurial management (Stevenson and Jarillo, 1990) as it reflects the organisational 'methods, practices, and decision-making styles firms use to act entrepreneurially' (Lumpkin and Dess, 1996: 139), and thus to gain competitive advantage. The extensive body of literature has suggested that entrepreneurial behaviour has positive implications for small firms' performance (e.g., Wiklund and Shepherd, 2005; Zahra and Covin, 1995), but these prominent empirical studies have not analysed this relationship in a nonlinear manner.

The availability of financial resources seems to be the most basic factor needed by small ventures to foster entrepreneurial activities (Cooper *et al.*, 1994; Zahra, 1991, 1993). Young and small ventures are often resource-constrained, thus being considered as less attractive investments whose financial prospects, if not their longevity, are uncertain (Lee *et al.*, 2001), and they need to gain access to external financing for technology development, marketing research, and advertising in order to exploit new opportunities (Evans and Leighton, 1989). Financial capital access becomes central to the process of exploiting and bringing into existence entrepreneurial opportunities (Evans and Leighton, 1989; Shane and Venkataraman, 2000). Access to financial capital has been found to be relevant to small business performance (Lee *et al.*, 2001; Wiklund and Shepherd, 2005).

In general, the success of young and small ventures depends on the networks established by the entrepreneur (Steier and Greenwood, 2000). These networks may include relationships with family members, government and political entities, customers, suppliers, investors, and competitors among others, and they often extend across industry, geographic, and cultural boundaries (Hitt *et al.*, 2001). Arguably, small firm performance can be enhanced through the entrepreneur's ability to develop social capital. From this standpoint, we argue that networks can enhance small firm survival and success.

Following Hofstede's seminal research on cultural values, many studies have examined the association between cultural dimensions and entrepreneurial activities (Morris *et al.*, 1994; Mueller and Thomas, 2000; Shane *et al.*, 1995). The most studied dimensions are individualism–collectivism, uncertainty avoidance, power-distance, and masculinity–femininity (Shane *et al.*, 1995). In an attempt to improve our understanding of how cultural values may affect firm performance, we focus on the role of horizontal and vertical individualism, and collectivism, on firm performance.

A distinguishing characteristic of the entrepreneurship and strategic management discipline is the emphasis placed on the firm's competitive environment (Dess *et al.*, 1997; Miller, 1983; Porter, 1980). Clearly, environmental factors are relevant, not only because they open up opportunities to exploit market inefficiencies, as in the economic approach, but also in the sense that different environments are more or less conducive to entrepreneurial activities, and can be more favourable to the success of new and small ventures (Stevenson and Jarillo, 1990). In this regard, Lumpkin and Dess in their alternative independent-effects model, illustrate that the external environment has a direct and independent effect on firm performance (Lumpkin and Dess, 1996).

6.1. The modelling approach

The sample for this research study was identified using a list of firms obtained from the Angolan business associations. To achieve the sampling goal, we contacted business owners/managers from a set of randomly-selected firms. These individuals were considered to be key informants whose position qualified them to comment on their enterprise. This procedure resulted in viable responses from 144 firms, more than 70% of which were new entrants, while 26.4% were established enterprises with more than seven years experience. The average firm age was 5.21 years.

All variables were measured on a five-point scale. Entrepreneurial orientation dimensions (innovativeness, risk-taking, proactiveness, competitive aggressiveness, and internal locus of control) were measured using scales developed and tested for reliability by Covin and Slevin (1986, 1989). Items from Rotter's (1966) scale were also used to measure internal locus of control. Personal networks were measured using scales developed and tested for reliability by Peng and Luo (2000), and Zhao (2005). These scales were also slightly modified and supplemented by items developed from the literature review to capture aspects of the sub-constructs that were not included in the previously-used scales. Firm performance was measured using perceptual measures of performance, which is, therefore, consistent with the previous studies (Dess and Robinson,

1984; Venkatraman and Ramanujan, 1987). Therefore, in this study, firm performance was measured as the business owner's assessment of the firm's profit and sales growth in relation to that of competitors. Motivation and business goals were also used as firm performance measures. In this regard, respondents were asked questions regarding the extent to which they were motivated to achieve better performance and the extent to which business goals were achieved.

A factor analysis was conducted in order to determine the dimensionality of the construct used. In the next step, we applied the ANN approach to model the relationships. Given the purpose of our study, the analysis of factors influencing firm performance, we used feedforward networks trained by MBP. In that way, different network architectures were tried. It was decided that the network with a hidden layer of five hidden neurons provided the best fit between inputs and outputs; this was thought to be a reasonable number of intermediate variables that could be identified and labelled, and the network did not give significantly better results by increasing the number. The network had 19 nodes, corresponding to the 19 explanatory variables: innovativeness (INNOV), risk-taking (RTK), proactiveness (PRO), competitive aggressiveness (CAGG), internal locus of control (ILOC), self-financing (SELF-FIN), bank loans (BL), government funds (GF), Non-Governmental Organisations endowments (NGOEND), government network (GN), business network (BN), family network (FN), acquaintance network (ACQN), vertical and horizontal individualism and collectivism (VI, HI, VC, HC), environmental dynamism (ENVD), and hostility (ENVH).The four output nodes used to represent firm performance measures were: Net profit, sales growth, business goals, and motivation. The sigmoid function was employed for the hidden and output nodes.

In an attempt to minimise the RMSE, this is defined by:

$$\text{RMSE} = \frac{1}{2} \sqrt{\frac{1}{N_p N_o} \sum_{p=1}^{N_p} \sum_{o=1}^{N_o} (d_o^p - y_o^p)^2},$$

where N_p represents the number of patterns. Several training configurations were tested with the MBP algorithm. Indeed, this supervised learning rule makes available an adaptive learning rate and a momentum term. In this particular study, these parameters were initialised to 0.01 and 0.1 respectively, decaying the latter, automatically, 1% after each 100 epochs. Different random initialisations for the weights were also tested. The interval [−1, 1] was considered to provide better results concerning the error function. To attain robustness, learning rate was further reduced by a factor of 0.5 each time the RMSE increased more than 0.1%. The MBP algorithm performed 30 runs being the number of epochs confined to a maximum of 10,000 since beyond the threshold level no further improvement could be made to the quality of the network predictions. The contributory and inhibitory weights were within a range of [−2, +2] and the final RMSE obtained for the test data was 0.088. Moreover, to measure the performance of the network model, a goodness-of-fit coefficient R^2 was computed. The R^2 values, similar to the R^2 coefficients provided in multiple regression analysis, were 0.962, 0.976, 0.989, and 0.986 for the output variables: Business goals, motivations, net profit, and sales growth respectively.

6.2. *Results*

The overall contribution of the input variables in the model reveals, however, that personal network attributes have the major significant contribution to the hidden neurons. Looking at individual input factors in the NN topology depicted in Table 5, it is worthwhile to note that business networking has the highest significant contribution (4.17) to the five hidden neurodes, followed by family (3.63) and acquaintance ties (3.27), government funds (3.09), bank loans (3.08), NGO endowments (2.96), environmental dynamism (2.85), vertical collectivism (2.84), government network (2.82), risk-taking (2.76), innovativeness (2.66), horizontal individualism (2.54), and horizontal collectivism (2.52). Moreover, other input factors also have meaningful contribution weights, but much lower than those achieved by the previous ones.

With regard to the output layer, it is interesting to note the mixed level of impacts, which are derived from the input hidden nodes, with the exception of 'self-reliant orientation' that presents

Table 5. Neural network weights.

(a) From input node

To hidden node	GN	FN	BN	ACQ	NGO	BL	GF	SELF-FIN	ENV	ENVH	HC	VC	HI	VI	RTK	INNO	ILOC	PRO	CAGG
HN1	-0.97	-0.20	0.67	-1.03	0.16	-0.004	0.23	0.45	0.46	0.91	-0.17	-0.07	0.10	0.91	0.13	0.35	-0.53	0.76	0.39
HN2	-0.005	0.65	-0.88	-0.998	0.45	0.06	0.63	0.69	0.35	0.02	0.23	0.87	0.35	-0.7	0.63	-1.07	-1.19	-0.94	-0.82
HN3	-0.86	-0.65	-1.09	0.26	-0.94	-0.89	-0.78	0.24	-0.80	-0.83	0.51	-0.33	-1.1	-0.28	-0.77	-0.22	0.1	0.43	0.27
HN4	-0.32	1.26	0.44	0.76	0.75	-1.35	0.65	-0.38	0.75	0.04	-0.23	-0.93	0.94	-0.36	-0.51	0.33	0.37	-0.06	0.35
HN5	-0.67	0.87	1.08	0.22	-0.67	-0.77	0.80	0.05	-0.49	-0.06	1.38	-0.64	-0.05	-0.2	-0.72	0.69	0.27	0.27	-0.15
Total contribution of input nodes	2.82	3.63	4.17	3.27	2.96	3.08	3.09	1.80	2.85	1.86	2.53	2.84	2.54	2.43	2.76	2.66	2.46	2.46	1.98

(b) From hidden node

To the output	HN1	HN2	HN3	HN4	HN5
Business goals	-0.62	-0.36	-0.57	-0.08	1.56
Motivation	0.685	0.31	-0.02	0.41	1.34
Net profit	-0.37	-0.33	-0.18	1.04	0.02
Sales growth	0.09	-0.68	-0.58	0.96	0.50
Total contribution of hidden nodes	1.76	1.68	1.36	2.49	3.42

inhibitory weights on all individual firm performance measures. However, it is also relevant to highlight the fact that both 'capabilities and input resources' and 'social capital' have the highest contributory weights on firm performance, even in terms of the individual neurons of the output layer. The other result worthy of particular attention refers to 'in-group orientation', which reflects the overwhelming importance of focusing attention on co-operation and collaboration among organisational members, because this cross-functioning manner not only enhances knowledge-sharing, but may also promote firm commitment on such projects that require new knowledge development. However, our results are also consistent with previous research (Lumpkin and Dess, 2001; Miller, 1983; Zahra and Covin, 1995) that reveal certain 'contextual factors' to influence not only the firm's ability to reframe the environment, but the way it recombines its resources to achieve superior value.

The resulting hidden layers construct highlights the importance of having mediating effects in the relationship between firm performance and its determinants. The mediating effects are often left behind and are largely untapped variables in the models of many previous empirical studies. However, our results reveal that these hidden layer nodes (mediating effects) generally have positive implications for firm performance, a finding which is consistent with many of the prominent studies in the entrepreneurship and strategic management fields that state that contextual factors (Dess and Beard, 1984; Miller, 1983), in-group and self-orientations (Bandura, 2002; Shane *et al.*, 1995; Zahra *et al.*, 2004), and social capital (Hitt *et al.*, 2001), input resources and capabilities, all influence firm performance.

In addition, this study provides some managerial implications for the facilitation of improved performance. Organisations fostering entrepreneurial activities have recognised the importance of identifying and [re]-combining firm-specific resources and capabilities in achieving competitive advantage in a very rapidly-changing environment. Our results reinforce this belief in that they suggest that managers must create an organisational climate which promotes co-operation and collaboration with co-workers, because the cross-functioning manner not only enhances knowledge-sharing but can also promote commitment to projects requiring new knowledge development, and this is, therefore, an appropriate way of allocating firm-specific resources. Moreover, managers must capitalise, first, their efforts on the firm capabilities and input resources as well as on the social capital in the marketplace. These tacit resources are of particular relevance in achieving small firm performance.

Our findings also suggest that an appropriate identification of certain firm-specific capabilities is of particular importance in supporting organisations to fulfil their missions. Therefore, a proper programme of empowering co-workers at all levels in the organisation would in fact contribute to the success and survival of firm.

7. The Use of ANNs in the Analysis of the Influence of External Market Orientation, Entrepreneurial Orientation, Innovation and Resources on Export Performance

The aim of this study was to explain the export performance of a sample of 406 Brazilian companies, exporting to over 100 countries. This explanation is based on the intensity of the relationship between the foreign market orientation, international entrepreneurial orientation, innovation and the resources, on the companies' export performance.

The internationalisation of companies has been the object of many academic investigations for a long time. Such research efforts started with the economic approach (Hymer, 1960, 1968; Vernon, 1966, 1979; Buckley and Casson, 1976; Dunning, 1988), moved to the organisational approach, with models like the U-model (Johanson and Wiedersheim-Paul, 1975; Johanson and Vahlne, 1977, 1990, 1992, 2003), developed into the Imodel — Innovation-related internationalisation model (Bilkey and Tesar, 1977; Cavusgil, 1980; Reid, 1981), and culminated in the Nordic School of International Business.

Studies about internationalisation have highlighted the role of several variables on the decisions and performance of the operations in the foreign markets. Internationalising means not only reaching new markets, but also strengthening the brand, leveraging knowledge acquisition, and defending a competitive position. The success or failure of a company in the 21st century will depend on the ability to compete effectively in global markets (Zou and Cavusgil, 1996). Clearly, when a company starts to operate in the international market, the level and source of uncertainty increase (Pipkin, 2000), but, on the other hand, the existing risks are mitigated, making the company less dependent on local market fluctuations.

External market orientation studies began with Cadogan and Diamantopoulos (1995) who synthesised and adapted the models of Kohli and Jaworski (1990) and Narver and Slater models (1990) to the international environment. Francis and Collins-Dodd (2000) found a positive relationship between international market orientation and export performance among Canadian high-tech companies. And a little later, Cadogan *et al.* (2002) developed a scale to assess the degree of international market orientation in exporting companies.

Pursuing internationalisation is also associated with individual challenges, especially when the focus turns to the entrepreneur's role in identifying and exploiting opportunities that arise from the international market. The literature on international entrepreneurship has stated that the entrepreneurial human capital is a key element for a company to obtain advantages exploring international opportunities (Dimitratos and Plakoyiannaki, 2003; Zahra *et al.*, 2004). Consequently, Dornelas (2001: 21) believes that we have reached 'the era of entrepreneurship'. According to Dornelas (2001), 'entrepreneurs are eliminating trade and cultural barriers, shortening distances, globalising and renewing economic concepts, creating new working relationships and new jobs, breaking paradigms and generating wealth for society'. International entrepreneurship and its drivers is now the object of a wide range of investigations (Wright and Ricks, 1994; Oviatt and McDougall, 1995; Andersson, 2000; Simões and Dominguinhos, 2001; Zahra and George, 2002; McDougall *et al.*, 2003; Karra and Phillips, 2004; Georgiou *et al.*, 2005).

Some authors describe the manner in which societies and markets adopt changes in their behaviour, lifestyle or consumption (e.g., Mahajan *et al.*, 1990; Venkatraman, 1991; Parasuraman and Colby, 2001). Other authors exploit the organisational aspects of innovation, i.e., they try to explain how it is set up, how it develops, and what results occur within organisations. Among these studies of organisational innovation, several authors showed a direct and positive relationship between innovation and organisational performance (e.g., Kotabe *et al.*, 1997; Han *et al.*, 1998; Calantone *et al.*, 2002). Other authors also consider the importance of innovation capacity as a means for the company to obtain and sustain a lasting competitive advantage in the international market. Lukas and Ferrell (2000), for example, emphasised the importance of marketing and innovation to increase performance and competitive advantage, especially in global markets.

Many studies point out that performance and success achieved in the export activity are key factors in the decision to increase export involvement (Cavusgil, 1980; Leonidou *et al.*, 1996; Shoham, 1998; Aulakh *et al.*, 2000; Gencturk and Kotabe, 2001). The measurement model of export performance 'EXPERF' created by Zou *et al.* (1998) is widely accepted by the academic community. However, empirical studies in international entrepreneurship still produce inconclusive results concerning the connection between export performance and international entrepreneurship (Zahra and George, 2002). Nonetheless, some studies have shown a link between export activity and performance. Kim *et al.* (2002) found that international diversification promotes a superior performance in large enterprises; and Georgiou *et al.* (2005) show that, despite limited financial and human resources, international diversification can promote better performance in small businesses.

7.1. *The modelling approach*

This investigation is based on a sample of 406 Brazilian export companies, located in the states of the south. Initially a basic statistical procedure has been developed applying an Exploratory Factorial Analysis and Cronbach Alpha, to assess measures of unidimensionality and reliability.

Given the purpose of our research, the analysis of the principal factors influencing export performance, several topologies of MFF networks were trained by the MBP algorithm. It was found that

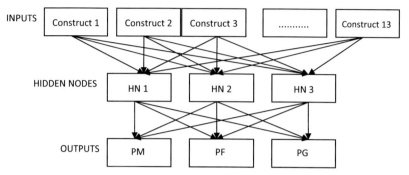

Fig. 5.   Main neural network applied to marketing, financial and overall performance.
Source: Data Analysis.

the optimal fit between inputs and outputs was obtained using a main network with a single hidden layer with three neurons as illustrated in Fig. 5. The 13 nodes of the main network correspond to the explanatory variables: Export intelligence generation, export intelligence dissemination, responsiveness, entrepreneurial orientation — innovation, proactiveness and risk-taking, organisational innovation, and resources. The three outputs used to represent export performance measures were performance, market performance financial performance, and overall performance. The space network had only one layer responsible for evaluating the importance factor of each neuron with selective actuation. Furthermore the activation function employed for the hidden and output neurons of the main and space networks was the sigmoid function.

In this study, the first 324 of sampling data were used in the training set and the remaining 82 in the test set. Note also that the presentation of the training patterns were in the on-line mode and randomly.

The MBP algorithm executes 30 runs being the number of the epochs of 308, since beyond the threshold level no improvement to the generalisability of the network was observed. This learning rule allows a great variety of training configurations, namely an adaptive learning rate as well as an adaptive *momentum* term. In the training set up, the values of the increment u and decrement d were set to 1.01 and 0.7, respectively.

A robust training method is also available such that, in this study, the step size was decreased by a reducing factor of 0.5 each time the RMSE, defined by:

$$\text{RMSE} = \frac{1}{2}\sqrt{\frac{1}{N_p N_o}\sum_{p=1}^{N_p}\sum_{o=1}^{N_o}(d_o^p - y_o^p)^2},$$

increased more than 0.1%.

In both networks, main and space, the learning rate and *momentum* term were initialised to 0.7 and 0.1, respectively.

Taking into account the minimisation of the error function, different random initialisations for the weights were tested. Nevertheless, we concluded that the interval $[-1, 1]$ provides better results.

The contributory and inhibitory weights, shown in Tables 6 and 7, were found to be within a range $[-3, 2.5]$ and the RMSE obtained for the test set was 0.0583.

To evaluate the performance of the network, a goodness-of-fit coefficient R^2, similar to R^2 provided in multiple regression analysis, was calculated through:

$$R^2 = 1 - \frac{(\text{RMSE})^2}{s_y^2},$$

where s_y^2 represents the variance of the desired output. The R^2 values were 0.9902, 0.989 and 0.991 for the three outputs market performance, financial performance and general performance, respectively, which allows us to say that the neural model explains over 99% of the variance of each dependent variable.

To conclude this section we remember that the values and the signals $+$ or $-$ of the network connection weights between the input nodes and hidden neurons were used to infer suitable intermediate attributes with which we label processing units. This technique is usually denominated by *labelling*.

The final results are presented in Tables 6 and 7.

From the input layer

Table 6. Impact of input nodes on hidden neurons.

To the hidden layer	Export intelligence generation	Intelligence dissemination	Respon-siveness	Innovation entrepreneurial orientation	Proactiv-entrepreneurial orientation	Risk-entrepreneurial orientation	Organisational innovation
1st neuron	1.508	0.29	1.821	−0.233	−0.15	0.082	0.797
2nd neuron	−0.026	−1.11	0.63	0.61	−0.453	−0.08	2.4
3rd neuron	−0.088	1.41	−0.5	1.41	−0.850	−0.03	0.37
Total Contribution	1.622	2.810	2.951	2.253	1.453	0.192	3.567

To the hidden layer	Product innovation	Technological innovation	Administrative resources	Financial resources	Organisational resources	Relationship resources
1st neuron	−0.72	0.255	−2.53	0.082	0.587	0.513
2nd neuron	−0.01	−1.42	−0.43	0.36	1.341	−0.06
3rd neuron	0.085	0.10	0.123	−0.22	0.57	−0.19
Total Contribution	0.815	1.775	3.083	0.662	2.498	0.763

Table 7. Impact of hidden neurons on output neurons.

From the hidden layer

To the output layer	Marketing performance	Financial performance	Overall performance
1st neuron	1.30	1.27	1.99
2nd neuron	1.10	0.40	1.83
3rd neuron	0.98	0.70	1.41
Total Contribution	3.38	2.37	5.23

7.2. Results

Analysing the results of the input layer nodes impact on the hidden layer neurons, the factors with higher positive weights in the first neuron (HN1) are export intelligence generation (1.508), response action (1.821), and organisational innovation (0.797), and the highest negative factors (inhibitors) are administrative resources (−2.53) and product innovation (−0.72). In the second neuron (HN2), the factors with the greatest positive contributions are organisational innovation (2.4) and organisational resources (1.341), and the major inhibiting factors are technological innovation (−1.42) and intelligence dissemination (−1.11). In the third neuron (HN3), the factors with higher positive weights are intelligence dissemination and innovation-entrepreneurial orientation (both 1.41), and the major inhibiting factors are proactiveness-entrepreneurial orientation (−0850) and response action (−0.5).

Considering the results gathered from the 406 companies that took part in this survey, one can conclude that the factors that more significantly influenced export performance (marketing, financial, and overall performance), were organisational innovation, organisational resources, response action, innovation-entrepreneurial orientation and export intelligence generation. Overall performance and, according to the main drivers found, marketing performance, received the largest contributions from the three neurons in the hidden layer. On the other hand, resources did not appear to impact significantly on the export performance.

These results show how export performance can depend more on the immaterial factors like entrepreneurial proclivity, creativity and innovation, commitment to internationalisation and knowledge. Therefore, these variables deserve greater attention from companies' managers when formulating strategies and implementing new actions to enhance their strategic, marketing, operational, and financial outcomes.

8. The use of ANNs in the Study of the Determinants of the Involvement of University Researchers in Spin-off Creation

The aim of this investigation was to identify the determinants of the involvement of academic researchers with entrepreneurial activities by creating spin-off. It is based on a sample of 587 researchers who agreed to answer the on-line questionnaire.

Several factors at micro and macro level influence the decision to create a new company to exploit an academic invention (Djokovic and Souitaris, 2008; O'Shea *et al.*, 2008, 2004; Hindle and Yencken, 2004).

At a micro level, studies have focused on businesses and individual entrepreneurs, and observed networks of spin-offs and their founders, as well as human relations and interactions during the process of creating spin-off. Research has shown that motivational factors (Shane, 2004; Steffensen *et al.*, 1999; Roberts, 1991), attributes specific to the technological invention (Shane, 2001a), the researcher's experience (Levin and Stephan, 1991), psychological traits (Roberts, 1991) and skills as a researcher (Zucker *et al.*, 1998) all influence the creation of academic spin-offs.

Meso level studies have focused on the university and the technology transfer office. These studies seek to identify the support mechanisms that may be employed by academic institutions to encourage the creation of spin-off, and to explore the effectiveness of spin-offs as a mechanism for technology transfer. Research has shown that characteristics of the parent organisation (Powers and McDougall, 2005; Rogers *et al.*, 2001; Shane, 2001b), the size of the technology transfer office — TTO (O'Shea *et al.*, 2005), experience of the TTO (Powers and McDougall, 2005; Roberts and Malone, 1996), level of business funding for science and engineering (Powers and McDougall, 2005; Shane, 2004), conflict between the spin-off and parent organisation (Steffensen *et al.*, 1999), the university's reward system, which is mainly based on publications and citations (Goldfarb and Henrekson, 2003, Franklin *et al.*, 2001), quality of the university (O'Shea *et al.*, 2005), intellectual property policies of universities (Goldfarb *et al.*, 2001), official policy on university spin-offs (Chiesa and Piccaluga, 1998; Roberts and Malone, 1996) all impact upon the process of creating an academic spin-off.

At the macro level, studies have focused on the macroeconomic environment of the spin-offs and analysed the role of government and enterprises in the process of spin-off. At this level of analysis the researchers observed the policies and support mechanisms related to the spin-offs, the impact of spin-offs on the regional economy as well as the favourable conditions in the business environment and market. Research has shown that the process of creation of academic spin-off is also influenced by attributes of the technological regime (Powers and McDougall, 2005, Rogers *et al.*, 2001; Shane, 2001b), availability of venture capital (Powers and McDougall, 2005; Druilhe and Garnsey, 2004), strength of patent protection in the industrial sector (Shane, 2002; Lowe, 1993), and government policies (Shane, 2004; Liu and Jiang, 2001).

The research model shown in Fig. 6 relates variables that influence the involvement of academic researchers with entrepreneurial activities by creating spin-off. Variables that influence the creation of academic spin-off were identified in the literature and grouped into attributes of individual researchers, university structures and policies, resources and capabilities of the university, and external environmental factors. The proposed model integrates into one comprehensive structure, prospects of different streams of research on factors influencing the decision of academic researchers to create spin-offs. Thus, we seek to test theoretical models of the activity of academic spin-off and assess the relative influence of variables previously identified on the spin-off activity.

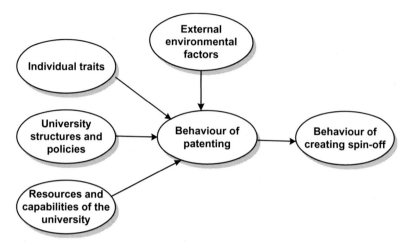

Fig. 6.   Research model.

Besides the creation of academic spin-off one of the manifestations of entrepreneurial orientation may be found in increasing the awareness and activity level of patent applications by academic researchers as a precondition for the commercialisation of academic research. In this study, therefore, the patenting behaviour is modelled as an activity that precedes the behaviour of creating spin-off.

In the research model the relationship between the factors that influence the involvement of academic researchers in entrepreneurial activities to patent their inventions and create spin-offs is explicit.

8.1. *The modelling approach*

Aiming to analyse the relationship between the explanatory variables of this investigation and the dependent variable — number of patent applications, the MBP algorithm was used to train a MFF network. To achieve this objective, the main NN model had 26 input nodes corresponding to the 26 variables of the explanatory model, and one neuron in the output layer corresponding to the amount of patent applications. We tested various network architectures and it was found that the best fit between the input units and output was obtained with a hidden layer with four neurons.

The parameters u (increase) d(decrease) were respectively 1.01 and 0.6. For the main network as well as for the spatial network, the speed of learning and the momentum term were initiated with a value of 0.7. In addition, the learning speed was reduced by a factor of 0.3 every time the RMSE increased more than 0.1%. Furthermore, training the network was performed with different ranges of initialisation for the weights and it was found that the interval $[-1, +1]$ showed better results for the error function. The weights of contribution and inhibition detailed in Table 8 were found to be in the range $[-2, +2]$ and the RMSE obtained for the test data was 0.0517.

8.2. Results

The weights of the NN connection between the input nodes and the hidden neurons, and the contributions made by different variables are shown in Table 8. It is worth noting that the factor 'removing barriers to technology commercialisation' with a value of $+2.9440$ has the largest total contribution to the four hidden neurons. The second largest total contribution with a value of $+2.9100$ is the factor 'ease of access to infrastructure of the university', the third is caused by factor 'the existence of policy on payment of royalties to researchers' with a contribution of $+2.6020$; the fourth is represented by the factor 'involvement in the commercialisation of technology increases the reputation in the scientific milieu' with a contribution of $+2.4610$, and the fifth is caused by the factor 'researcher's experience' with a contribution of $+2.4000$.

The weights of the most significant contribution and inhibitors linked with model variables that affect the first hidden neuron (HN1), show an overall more positive impact than negative. Thus, based on the evaluation of all weights of significant contribution and inhibitors, the HN1 has been designated by 'institutional support'. This concept means the institutional commitment to encourage and support the patenting of academic research results. Previous studies demonstrate the importance of institutional support for patenting activity (Baldini *et al.*, 2005; DiGregorio and Shane, 2003; AUTM, 2003).

Table 8.　Impact of input nodes on hidden neurons.

From input layer

To the hidden Layer	Venture Capital	Clustering of high technology firms	Flexibility of employment	Technol. transfer takes time	Free access to research results	Commercialisation of technol common	Reputation in the scientific milieu	Importance of private funding	Existence of a S&T park
HN1	-0.0260	-0.2700	-0.0520	-0.1000	0.0850	-0.4240	-0.2710	-0.2000	-0.3000
HN2	-0.0250	0.0400	0.4870	-0.2100	-1.000	1.6200	-0.5500	-0.2100	0.1100
HN3	-0.6050	-0.5980	0.9460	0.5390	0.9230	-0.2950	-0.6500	0.7000	0.4470
HN4	0.8580	-0.1050	0.0540	-0.0430	0.1330	-0.0005	-0.9900	-0.9000	0.4760
Total Contribution	1.5140	1.0130	1.5390	0.8920	2.1410	2.3395	2.4610	2.0100	1.3270

To the hidden layer	Sex	Effect of peers	Effort to protect intellectual property	Experience	Scientific production	Sources of public funding	Sources of private funding	Access to the university infrastructure	Social capital
HN1	0.263	-0.115	-0.3200	0.7810	-0.4740	-0.7700	0.2500	0.7900	0.1000
HN2	0.0256	-1.184	-1.1160	1.0710	1.2200	-0.4600	0.8000	-0.7200	0.1100
HN3	0.232	0.064	-0.3230	0.1500	-0.1300	0.0990	-0.5600	-0.8000	0.6100
HN4	0.940	0.242	-0.1880	-0.3980	0.2400	-0.4500	-0.2500	0.6000	0.3210
Total Contribution	1.4606	1.605	1.9470	2.4000	2.0640	1.7790	1.8600	2.9100	1.1410

(Continued)

Table 8. (Continued)

To the hidden Layer	Existence of policy on distri-bution of royalties	Support for the promotion of research results.	Entrepreneurial culture	Skills of the TTO	Newness of research results	Removal of restrictions for collabo-ration with business	Removal of barriers for commercial-isation of technology	Support for spin-off creation
HN1	−0.4300	−0.6400	0.3330	0.5740	0.0100	−0.3420	−0.7550	0.5460
HN2	0.8320	0.1100	−0.340	0.1500	0.1900	0.3040	−0.3970	0.6550
HN3	0.4500	−0.6200	−0.5620	−0.380	−0.6430	0.5770	0.7600	0.2540
HN4	−0.8900	−0.0700	0.1400	0.5100	−0.1890	0.7880	1.0320	−0.1040
Total Contribution	2.6020	1.4400	1.3750	1.6140	1.0320	2.0110	2.9440	1.5590

Source: Research data.

The weights of the most significant contribution and inhibitors linked with model variables that affect the second hidden neuron (HN2), also show an overall impact which is more positive than negative. Six input factors have a positive impact on this neuron, while five input factors show a negative impact on that processing unit. Considering all the weights of contribution and relevant inhibitors, the HN2 has been designated by the 'individual orientation of research'. In view of the most significant positive loadings, this result may be grounded in the perception that the individual orientation of research is a researcher's option for research projects, that lead more often to results potentially patentable (Baldini, 2009; Colyvas *et al.*, 2002).

The weights of the most significant contribution and inhibitors linked with model variables that affect the third hidden neuron (HN3), show an overall impact which is more negative than positive. Eight input factors have inhibitors weights, while seven have positive contribution weights on this neuron. Assessing weights of significant contribution and inhibitors, the third neuron is called 'relationships with the external environment'. This concept means the network of relationships with the external environment, i.e., companies, universities, research institutes, and public and private institutions supporting and nurturing the academic research. This result is consistent with the view of exploiting additional means of improving the economic value of knowledge to move it along the development process closer to the market, hoping to increase its value (Baldini, 2006). Networks with the external environment are important for the formalisation of collaboration agreements and a way to manage and commercialise the knowledge produced in university, in connecting the university to external problems, with sources of knowledge and with companies in search of academic resources (Coutinho *et al.*, 2003; Etzkowitz, 1998, 2003).

For the latter neuron of the inner layer (HN4), the results show an overall impact which is more positive than negative; six input factors have positive contribution weights and four have inhibitors weights. Analysing the weights of the most significant contributions and

Table 9. Designation of the hidden neurons.

Hidden neurons	Designation
HN1	Institutional support
HN2	Individual orientation of research
HN3	Relationships with the external environment
HN4	Resources and skills of the research context

Table 10. Impact of hidden neurons on the number of patent applications.

From hidden layer				
To the output layer	HN1	HN2	HN3	HN4
Number of Patent Applications	−0.073	+3.162	−1.333	−1.850

Source: Research data.

inhibitors the HN4 was named 'resources and skills of the research context'. This concept describes the resources and skills available at the research unit or laboratory to conduct research. This result is consistent with the perception that the resources of interest are not related to the size of the assets of the university, but with the resources available directly in the researcher's laboratory (Landry *et al.*, 2006; Kenney and Goe, 2004).

The Table 9 presents the labels proposed for the neurons that make up the single hidden layer of the model used to identify the variables that best explained the number of patent applications by researchers from public universities.

As shown in Table 10, the neuron number of patent applications of the output layer has a positive contribution weight in a neuron of the hidden layer and negative contribution weights in three neurons. As expected, considering the results of empirical studies (Baldini, 2009; Azoulay *et al.*, 2007), the individual orientation of research has a positive and direct effect, showing the greatest impact (+3.162) on the patenting activity. In this study, three hidden layers are inhibitory to the number of patent applications: institutional support (−0.073), relationships with the external environment (−1.333), and resources

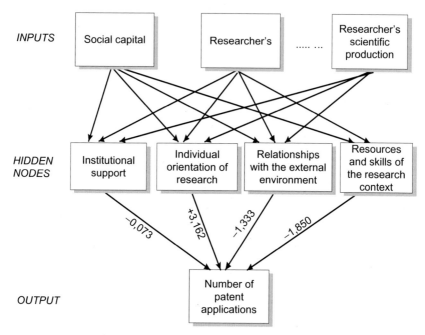

Fig. 7. Neural model with the contributions of the hidden neurons to patent applications.

and skills of the research context (−1.850), suggesting that these factors do not exert influence on the number of patent applications.

In summary, the contribution of the input nodes and of the hidden neurons to the network output suggests the NN model shown in Fig. 7:

The inhibitory contributions from the hidden layer come from resources and skills of the research context, relationships with external environment and finally, from institutional support. These results conflict with those from Baldini (2009), Baldini *et al.* (2005) Stuart and Ding (2006), DiGregorio and Shane (2003), and Colyvas *et al.* (2002). They show that for Brazilian researchers, overall resources which include all these variables, are not that important as drivers of the decision to involve in spin-offs. The researcher's individual perceptions and his/her investigation area may be crucial for the potential of patent applications.

9. The use of ANNs in the Investigation of Customer Loyalty in the Insurance Industry

Based on a sample of 744 insurance companies' customers this investigation aims to identify the loyalty drivers and the relationship behaviours in this industry.

Customer loyalty has become a key factor in company success, allowing a sustainable competitive advantage. Priorities are focused on the relationship with customers, and trades are made with the objective of establishing and preserving those relationships in the long term (Berry, 1995; Bitner, 1995; Grönroos, 1990). Over decades have passed since Berry (1983) first used the expression relationship marketing. However, there is a kind of agreement underlining the notion that the conceptual antecedents of this new proposal can be found in the contributions that emerged since the 1960s. We can find two main directions in the investigations developed in Scandinavia and Northern Europe, with the work of the Nordic Service School (Grönroos and Gummesson, 1985) and the Industrial Marketing and Purchasing Group (Hakansson, 1982; Johansson and Mattsson, 1985; Kock, 1991), respectively. These mainstreams are based on the same foundations regarding the relationships and their management. For these academicians, marketing should be taken as an interactive process of management, and not an organisational function or department.

According to Fornell (1992) most of the companies combine an offensive strategy (attracting new customers) with a defensive strategy (customer retention). However, in a situation of slow economic growth, customer loyalty became a priority, almost an obsession and the basis for a sustainable competitive advantage. The growth of the services industry created the perfect ground for the development of a consolidated investigation area, focused on relationships and loyalty.

All the theoretical contributions to relationship marketing have shown how loyalty and customer retention are the main goals of the process. Literature highlights the benefits that come from a portfolio of loyal customers. Loyal customers can increase sales income (Reichheld, 1993, 1996; Schlesinger and and Heskett, 1991), the opportunities for cross selling (Reichheld, 1996), and the positive word-to-mouth (Reichheld, 1996; Reichheld and Sasser, 1990; Schlesinger and Heskett, 1991). Loyal customers can also contribute to more cost effective company management, while the costs of attracting and keeping customers can be absorbed during the lifelong relationship.

Consequently, customer loyalty leads to a profit increase (Reichheld, 1993; Reichheld and Sasser, 1990; Edvardsson *et al.*, 2000; Hallowell, 1996; Naidu, *et al.*, 1999; Noone *et al.*, 2003). Moreover, loyal customers are less price sensitive and more oriented to relationship benefits (Berry and Parasuraman, 1991; Dowling and Uncle, 1997; Bowen and Shoemaker, 1998; Noone *et al.*, 2003).

The goal of this study was, therefore, to attempt to identify the main drivers of the relationship between insurance companies and their customers, and of their customers' loyalty.

9.1. *The modelling approach*

Data was gathered through a structured questionnaire, and 744 insurance company customers responded. The data was first submitted to an exploratory factorial analysis and the reliability of the constructs was measured using the Alpha coefficient, using Statistical Package for the Social Sciences (SPSS). Fifteen constructs were identified as input factors or loyalty drivers: front-office employees' expertise, communication, reputation, perceived value, customer orientation of contact employees, facilities quality, interactive service quality, customers' satisfaction, trust, commitment, loyalty, social benefits, switch costs, loyalty tendency, and justice.

In order to investigate the influence of the independent variables above-mentioned in the customer loyalty to insurance companies, the MBP algorithm was applied to train a MFF network. It was proposed a main network with four input nodes corresponding to the explanatory variables be used to achieve this aim. The neuron in the output layer represents the dependent variable — loyalty of the insurance companies' customers. Concerning the space network, that had only one layer responsible for determining the relevance of

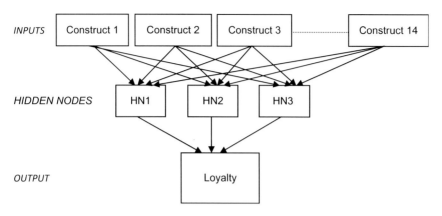

Fig. 8.   Main network applied to the loyalty of the insured persons.

the selective neurons that were placed in the hidden layer of the main network. On the other hand, the activation function used for the hidden and output neurons of the feedforward networks that integrate the MFF was the sigmoid function.

Several architecture networks were tested and we verified that the best fit between input nodes and the output neuron was obtained with a single hidden layer of three neurons as illustrated in Fig. 8.

Taking into account the minimisation of the error function, RMSE, defined by:

$$\text{RMSE} = \frac{1}{2}\sqrt{\frac{1}{N_p N_o}\sum_{p=1}^{N_p}\sum_{o=1}^{N_o}(d_o^p - y_o^p)^2}, \tag{5}$$

the MFF did not provide better results by varying the number of hidden layers and/or the number of hidden neurons.

In this study the first 521 data were used in the training set and the other 223 in the test set. Additionally, the patterns were presented on-line mode and randomly.

The MBP algorithm provides a great variety of training configurations, namely an adaptive learning rate as well as an adaptive *momentum* term. In the set training the parameters u (increment) and d (decrement) were initialised to 1 and 0.6, respectively. In both networks, the learning rate and the momentum term were initialised to 0.7. Additionally, to obtain robustness, the learning rate was further reduced by a factor of 0.5 each time the RMSE increased more than 0.1%.

Different random initialisations for the weights were also tested. The interval $[-1, +1]$ was considered to provide better results regarding the error function defined by (5). The contributory and inhibitory weights were within a range of $[-18, +2]$ as illustrated by Tables 11 and 12. The RMSE achieved for the data test was 0.044.

The values and the signals $+$ or $-$ of the network connection weights between the input nodes and the three hidden neurons were used to identify variables that are not directly observable, associated to these processing units. This procedure, similar to the factorial analysis, is designated by *labelling* and has subjective characteristics.

9.2. Results

Taking into account the NN weights we verify that the third factor of the input layer — communication — shows the greatest contribution, 3.691, to the hidden layer. The second more expressive total contribution comes from the factor commitment (3.172), the third comes from the factor justice (2.692) and the fourth results from social costs with a score of 2.423. Finally, trust and satisfaction present the last representative contributions.

The HN1 in the hidden layer has been named 'weak personal relationship' because the most significant inhibitory weights come from social switch costs (-2.361), communication (-2.349) and commitment (-2.116). Justice and trust are also inhibitory factors into a neuron that only receives inhibitory impacts.

The HN2 has been labelled 'relationship dissatisfaction' since its main impacts are mainly inhibitory and come from satisfaction, commitment and trust. Several authors refer to the concept of relationship quality or satisfaction as the sum of the satisfaction, commitment and trust. Even if these variables have been treated individually, the way they grouped in this neuron justifies this label.

The HN3, opposite to both of the other neurons, received mainly positive impacts. Communication, loyalty tendency, facilities' quality, switch costs, and customer orientation of the contact employees

Table 11. Impact of input nodes on hidden neurons.

From the input layer

To the hidden layer	Expertise	Customer orientation	Communication	Reputation	Perceived value	Interactive quality	Facilities quality
First neuron	0	−0.00011	−2.349	0	0	0	0
Second neuron	0	0.00067	0	0	0	0.0002	−0.026
Third neuron	0.0351	0.168	1.342	−0.896	0	0.0006	0.455
Total contribution	0.0351	0.16878	3.691	0.896	0	0.0008	0.481

To the hidden layer	Satisf.	Trust	Commitment	Loyalty tendency	Social costs	Switch costs	Justice
First neuron	−0.189	−1.642	−2.116	0	−2.361	−0.163	−1.807
Second neuron	−0.616	−0.172	−0.382	0	0	−0.151	−0.003
Third neuron	−0.500	0.127	−0.674	0.688	−0.062	0.255	−0.882
Total contribution	1.305	1.941	3.172	0.688	2.423	0.569	2.692

Table 12.   Impact of hidden neurons on Loyalty.

From hidden layer

	HN1	HN2	HN3
To loyalty	−0.209	−17.205	1.999

Table 13.   Labels of the hidden neurons.

Hidden layer neurons	Label
HN1	Weak personal relationship
HN2	Quality dissatisfaction
HN3	Informative communication

presented the highest impacts. Inhibitory impacts come from justice, commitment, and satisfaction. Hence, this neuron has been labelled 'informative communication', because of the decisive weight of communication, which adopted an informative approach as proposed by Crosby and Stephens (1987). In the insurance industry, the nature of communication, especially information and its robustness, seems to be critical.

Table 13 summarises the labels given to the hidden neurons.

According to Table 12, loyalty, the output, receives inhibitory impacts from HN1 (−0.209) and HN2 (−17.205) but a positive impact from the third neuron (1.999). HN2 presents the greatest inhibitory impact and it is a neuron where satisfaction is weighting significantly as well as commitment and trust. It is called 'quality dissatisfaction'. This could be inferred as customer dissatisfaction with their insurance companies, customer, a lack of customer trust, and the way in which customers retain a distant and reticent relationship. The third neuron has the only positive impact and this is based on communication with an informative basis. When one does not trust the insurance company, the less he can expect is to be completely informed about its insurance packages and about its services.

Finally, even if most of the studies show, empirically, how the relationship quality, trust and commitment can contribute to loyalty, we can conclude that insurance companies are not giving priority to customer satisfaction, to customer trust and to customer loyalty. Apparently, this means that a transactional approach is prevailing instead of a relational one, among insurance companies, and disloyalty seems to be the best result they can get.

10. Conclusions

This study seeks to call the attention to the use of the NN modelling in the resolution of numerous problems belonging to a wide range of areas such as business management, marketing, entrepreneurship, just to name a few.

As we pointed out previously, several researchers showed that this powerful statistical method, NNs, outperformed some other traditional techniques like regression, multivariate analysis, discriminant analysis, clustering analysis or even SEM.

In fact, the strength of NNs is based on several advantages:

1. They store the information as an internal structure;
2. They can work with data they have never seen before and, therefore, can be used for extrapolation;
3. They require only a minimum knowledge of the problem's structure;
4. They have the capacity to obtain relationships of nonlinearly dependent variables;
5. They are robust to missing and inaccurate data and are not quite as influenced by non-standard conditions, violations of assumptions;
6. Their performance is not diminished by multicollinearity.

So, we can conclude that the use of NNs shows a good capacity for the depiction, and some additional appreciation of a problem that seems not to be completely structured and consequently, as a methodological tool, provides a higher interpretative capacity and dissection of the richness of the content. Additionally, the introduction of new variables — hidden layer neurons — helps the comprehension of the relationship between input and output variables.

The results of these studies, using SEM, would probably show the usual relations between the variables presented. For instance, in the loyalty studies, the tests using SEM show the usual relationship between loyalty and its main drivers. However, using ANNs we can go further and conclude how unsatisfied customers are, how disloyal they can be, how insurance companies are disregarding their customers' satisfaction, the quality of their relationships with customers, and the loyalty practices.

Furthermore, a more intensive use of ANNs would probably help to achieve results capable of providing new or richer interpretations instead of the usually expected outcomes. ANNs seem to have the potential to help theory development beyond the traditional and purely confirmatory approaches.

References

Adamson, I, C Kok-Mun and D Handford (2003). Relationship marketing: Customer commitment and trust as a strategy for the smaller Hong Kong corporate banking sector. *International Journal of Bank Marketing*, 21(6/7), 347–358.

Agrawal, D and C Schopling (1996). Market shape forecasting: An empirical comparison of artificial neural networks and multinomial logit model. *Journal of Retailing*, 72(4), 383–407.

Agarwal, R and J Prasad (1997). The role of innovation characteristics and perceived voluntariness in the acceptance of information technologies. *Decision Sciences*, 28(3), 557–582.

Aiken, M and M Bsat (1999). Forecasting market trends with neural networks. *Information Systems Management*, 16(4), 42–48.

Ainscough, TL and JE Aronson (1999). An empirical investigation and comparison of neural networks and regression for scanner data analysis. *Journal of Retailing and Consumer Services*, 6, 205–217.

Ajzen, I and M Fishbein (1980). *Understanding Attitudes and Predicting Social Behavior*. Englewood Cliffs, NJ: Prentice-Hall.

Alom, I, M Qi and RJ Sadowski (2001). Forecasting aggregate retail sales: A comparison of artificial neural networks and traditional methods. *Journal of Retailing and Consumer Services*, 8, 147–156.

Anckar, B and D D'Incau (2002). Value creation in mobile commerce: Findings from a consumer survey. *Journal of Information Technology Theory & Application*, 4(1), 43–64.

Andersson, S (2000). The internationalization of the firm from an entrepreneurial perspective. *International Studies of Management & Organisation*, 30/1, 63–92.

Audrain, AF (2002). The — satisfaction link over time: A study on panel data. In *Proc. 21st EMAC Conf.*, pp. 28–31, University of Minho and European Marketing Academy, Braga.

Aulakh, P, M Kotabe and H Teegen (2000). Export strategies and performance of firms from emerging economies: Evidence from Brazil, Chile, and Mexico. *Academy of Management Journal*, 43(3), 342–361.

Autm (2003). Autm Licensing Survey. Fiscal Year 2002, AUTM, Norwalk.

Aydin, S and G Özer (2005). The analysis of antecedents of customer loyalty in the urkish mobile telecommunication market. *European Journal of Marketing*, 39(7/8), 910–925.

Azoulay, P, W Ding and T Stuart (2007). The determinants of faculty patenting behavior: Demographics or opportunities? *Journal of Economic Behavior & Organization*, 63(4), 599–623.

Baesens, B, S Viaene, D Van den Poel, J Van Thiemen and G Dedene (2002). Bayesian neural networks learning for repeat purchase modelling in direct marketing. *European Journal of Operational Research*, 138(1), 191–211.

Balakrishnan, DV, MC Cooper, VS Jacob and PA Lewis (1996). Comparative performance of the FSCL neural net and K-means algorithm for market segmentation. *European Journal of Operational Research*, 93(2), 346–357.

Baldini, N, R Grimaldi and M Sobrero (2005). Motivations and incentives for patenting within universities. A survey of Italian inventors. Prepared for the 2005 Academy of Management Meeting, Honolulu, 5–10 August. TIM Division.

Baldini, N (2006). University patenting and licensing activity: A review of the literature. *Research Evaluation*, 15(3), 197–207.

Baldini, N (2009). University spin-offs and their environment. Technology Analysis & Strategic Management, Forthcoming. Available at SSRN http://ssrn.com/abstract=1314233.

Bandura, A (2002). Social cognitive theory in cultural context. *International Association for Applied Psychology*, 51(2), 269–290.

Barnes, JG (1997). Closeness, strength and satisfaction: Examining the nature of relationships between providers of financial services and their retail customers. *Journal of Psychology and Marketing*, 14(18), 765–790.

Bentz, Y and D Merunka (2000). Neural networks and the multinomial logit brand choice modelling: A hybrid approach. *Journal of Forecasting*, 19(3), 177–200.

Berry, LL (1983). Relationship marketing. In *Emerging Perspectives on Services Marketing*, L Berry, GL Shostack and GD Upah (eds.), pp. 25–28. Chicago: American Marketing Association.

Berry, LL (1995). Relationship marketing of services-growing interest, emerging perspectives. *Journal of the Academy of Marketing Science*, 23(4), 236–245.

Berry, LL and A Parasuraman (1991). *Marketing Services, Competing Through Quality*. New York: Free Press.

Bilkey, W and G Tesar (1977). The export behavior of smaller wisconsin manufacturing firms. *Journal of International Business Studies*, 9(1), 93–98.

Bitner, MJ (1995). Building service relationships: It's all about promises. *Journal of the Academy of Marketing Science*, 23(4), 246–251.

Bloemer, J, K Ruyter and W Martin (1999). Linking perceived service quality and service loyalty: A multidimensional perspective. *European Journal of Marketing*, 33(11/12), 1082–1106.

Boone, DS and M Roehm (2002). Evaluating the appropriateness of market segmentation solutions using artificial neural networks and the membership clustering criterion. *Marketing Letters*, 13(4), 317–333.

Bouwman, H Carlsson, CF Molina-Castillo and P Walden (2007). Barriers and drivers in the adoption of current and future mobile services in Finland. *Telematics and Informatics*, 24, 145–160.

Bowen, T and S Shoemaker (1998). Loyalty: A strategic commitment. *Cornel Hotel and Restaurant Administration Quarterly*, 39(1), 12–25.

Buckley, P and M Casson (1976). *The Future of the Multinational Enterprise*. London: Macmillan.

Calantone, RJ, ST Cavusgil and Y Zhao (2002). Learning orientation, firm innovation capability, and firm performance. *Industrial Marketing Management*, 31(6), 515–524.

Carter, L and F Belanger (2004). The influence of perceived characteristics of innovating on e-government adoption. *Electronic Journal of e-Government*, 2(1), 11–20.

Cadogan, JW and A Diamantopoulos (1995). Narver and Slater, Kohli and Jaworski and the market orientation construct: Integration and internalization. *Journal of Satrategic Marketing*, 3, 41–60.

Cadogan, JW, A Diamantopoulos and JA Siguaw (2002). Export market-oriented activities: Their antecedents and performance consequences. *Journal of International Business Studies*, 33(3), Third Quarter.

Cavusgil, S (1980). On the internationalization process of firms. *European Research*, 8/6, 273–281.

Chen, L (2008). A model of consumer acceptance of mobile payment. *International Journal of Mobile Communications*, 6(1), 32–52.

Chiesa, V and A Piccaluga (1998). Transforming rather than transferring scientific and technological knowledge-the contribution of academic spin-out companies: The Italian way. In *New technology-based firms in the 1990s*, R Oakey and W During (eds.), Vol. 4., pp. 639–658. London: Paul Chapman.

Corney, D (2002). Food bytes: Intelligent systems in the food industry. *British Food Journal*, 104(10/11), 787–805.

Cooper, AC, FJ Gimeno-Gascon and CY Woo (1994). Initial human and financial capital as predictors of new venture performance. *Journal of Business Venturing*, 9(3), 371–396.

Colyvas, J, M Crow, A Gelijns, R Mazzoleni, RR Nelson, N Rosenberg and BN Sampat (2002). How do university inventions get into practice. *Management Science*, 48(1), 61–72.

Coutinho, M, E Balbachevsky, DO Holzhacker *et al.* (2003). Intellectual property and public research in biotechnology: The scientists opinion. *Scientometrics*, 58(3), 641–656.

Covin, JG and DP Slevin (1986). The development and testing of an organizational-level entrepreneurship scale. In *Frontiers of Entrepreneurship Research*, R Ronstadt, J A Hornaday, R Peterson and KH Vesper (eds.), Wellesley, MA: Babson College

Covin, JG and DP Slevin (1989). Strategic management of small firms in hostile and benign environments. *Strategic Management Journal*, 10(1), 75–87.

Crosby, L and N Stevens (1987). Effects of relationship marketing on satisfaction retention, and prices in the life assurance industry. *Journal of Marketing Research*, 24, 404–411.

Curry, B and M Luiz (1993). Neural networks in marketing: Modelling consumer responses to advertising stimuli. *European Journal of Marketing*, 27(7), 5–20.

Dasgupta, CG, GS Dispensa and DS Ghose (1994). Comparing the predictive performance of a neural network model with some traditional market response models. *International Journal of Forecasting*, 10(2), 235–244.

Davis, FD (1989). Perceived usefulness, perceived ease of use, and user acceptance of information technology. *MIS Quarterly*, 13(3), 319–340.

Davis, FD (1993). User acceptance of information technology: System characteristics, user perceptions and behavioral impacts. *International Journal of Man-Machine Studies*, 38, 475–487.

Davis,FD, RP Bagozzi and PR Warshaw (1989). User acceptance of computer technology: A comparison of two theoretical models. *Management Science*, 35(8), 982–1003.

Davies, F, G Mark, AM Josef and M Luiz (1999). LISREL and neural network modelling: Two comparison studies. *Journal of Retailing and Consumer Studies*: *Special Issue on Market Applications of Neural Networks*, 6(4), 249–261.

Decker, R and K Monien (2003). Market basket analysis with neural gas networks and self-organising maps. *Journal of Targeting, Measurement and Analysis for Marketing*, 11(4), 373–386.

Dess, GG and DW Beard (1984). Dimensions of organizational task environments. *Administrative Science Quarterly*, 29, 52–73.

Dess, GG, GT Lumpkin and JG Covin (1997). Entrepreneurial strategy making and firm performance: Tests of contingency and configurational models. *Strategic Management Journal*, 18(9), 677–695.

Dess, GG and RB Robinson (1984). Measuring organizational performance in the absence of objective measures: The case of the privately held firm and conglomerate business unit. *Strategic Management Journal*, 5(3), 265–273.

Diário da República, I SÉRIE, N.° 58 (2008). Lei Sobre os Incentivos Fiscais e Aduaneiros ao Investimento Privado (Lei 17 de 25 de Julho de 2003), Assembleia Nacional de Angola, pp. 1509–1513. Available at http://www. angoladigital.net/negocios/ PDF/incent_fisc_aduaneiros.pdf.

Dick, AS and K Basu (1994). Customer loyalty: Toward an integrated conceptual framework. *Journal of the Academy of Marketing Science*, 22, 99–113.

DiGregorio, D and S Shane (2003). Why do some universities generate more start-ups than others? *Research Policy*, 32, 209–227.

Dimitratos, P and E Plakoyiannaki (2003). Theoretical foundations of an international entrepreneurial culture. *Journal of International Entrepreneurship*, 1, 187–215.

Djokovic, D and V Soutaris (2008). Spinouts from academic institutions: A literature review with suggestions for further research. *Journal of Technology Transfer*, 33, 225–247.

Dornelas, JCA (2001). *Empreendedorismo: Transformando idéias em negócios*. Rio de Janeiro: Campus.

Dorsch, MJ, SR Swanson and SW Kelley (1998). The role of relationship quality in the stratification of vendors as perceived by customers. *Journal of the Academy of Marketing Science*, 26(2), 128–142.

Dowling, GR and M Uncles (1997). Do customer loyalty programs really work. *Sloan Management Review*, 38(4), 71–82.

Druilhe, C and E Garnsey (2004). Do academic spin-outs differ and does it matter? *The Journal of Technology Transfer*, 29(3–4), 269–285.

Dunning, J (1988). The eclectic paradigm of international production: A restatement and some possible extensions. *Journal of International Business Studies*, 19/1, 1–31.

Edvardsson, B, Johnson, D Michael, A Gustafsson and T Strandvik (2000). The effects of satisfaction and loyalty on profits and growth: Products versus services. *Total Quality Management*, 11(7), S917–S927.

Eggert, A and W Ulaga (2002). Customer perceived value: A substitute for satisfaction in business markets? *Journal of Business & Industrial Marketing*, 17(2/3), 107–118.

Etzkowitz, H (1998). The norm of entrepreneurial science: Cognitive effects of the new university-industry linkages. *Research Policy*, 27(8), 823–833.

Etzkowitz, H (2003). Research group as 'quasi-firms': The invention of the entrepreneurial university. *Research Policy*, 32(1), 109–121.

Evans, DS and LS Leighton (1989). Some empirical aspects of entrepreneurship. *American Economic Review*, 79(3), 519–535.

Fadlalla, A and CH Lin (2001). An analysis of the application of neural networks in finance. *Interfaces*, 31(4)(July/August), 112–122.

Fornell, C (1992). A national customer satisfaction barometer: The swedish experience. *Journal of Marketing*, 56(1), January, 6–21.

Francis, J and C Collins-Dood (2000). The impact of firms. export orientation on the export performance of high-tech small and medium-sized enterprises. *Journal of International Marketing*, 8(3), 84–103.

Franklin, SJ, M Wright and A Lockett (2001). Academic and surrogate entrepreneurs in university spin-out companies. *Journal of Technology Transfer*, 26(1–2), 127–141.

Georgiou, M, S Freeman and R Edwards (2005). International entrepreneurship: Antecedents and outcomes. *Working Paper*, Nonash University, Victoria.

Gençturk, E and M Kotabe (2001). The effect of export assistance program usage on export performance: A contingency explanation. *Journal of International Marketing*, 9(2), 51–72.

Goldfarb, B, M Henrekson and N Rosenberg (2001). Demand vs. supply driven innovations: US and Swedish experiences in academic entrepreneurship. *Working Paper Series* in Economics and Finance 0436, Stockholm School of Economics.

Goldfarb, B and M Henrekson (2003). Bottom-up versus top-down policies towards the commercialization of university intellectual property. *Research Policy*, 32(4), 639–658.

Guarita, CEI (2005). Percepções de qualidade, sacrifício e valor: uma investigação em serviços bancários. Tese de Doutorado, Escola de Administração de Empresas da Fundação Getúlio Vargas, São Paulo.

Gronholdt, L and A Martensen (2005). Analysing customer satisfaction data: A comparison of regression and artificial neural networks. *International Journal of Market Research*, 47(2), 121–130.

Grönroos, C (1990). *Service Management and Marketing. Managing the Moments of Truth in Service Competion*. Lexington, MA: Lexington Books y Macmillan Inc.

Grönroos, C and E Gummesson (1985). The nordic school of service marketing. In *Service Marketing–Nordic School Perspectives*, C Grönroos and E Gummesson (eds.), pp. 6–11. Sweden: Stockholm University, Department of Business Administration.

Gross, I (1997). Evolution in customer value: The gross perspective. In *Customer Value: New Directions in Theory and Practice*, B Donath (ed.). Thousand Oaks, CA: Sage Publication.

Hallowell, R (1996). The relationships of customer satisfaction, customer loyalty and profitability: An empirical study. *International Journal of Service Industry Management*, 7(4), 27–42.

Hakansson, H (ed.). (1982). *International Marketing and Purchasing of Industrial Goods. An Interaction Approach*. Chichester: Wiley.

Han, JK, N Kim and RK Srivastava (1998). Market orientation and organizational performance: Is innovation a missing link? *Journal of Marketing*, 62(4), 30–45.

Han, X, RJ Kwortnik, Jr and C Wang (2008). Service loyalty: An integrative model and examination across service contexts. *Journal of Service Research*, 11(1), 22–42.

Haykin, SS (1999). *Neural Networks: A Comprehensive Foundation*. Upper Saddle River, NJ: Prentice Hall.

Hennig-Thurau, T, KP Gwinner and DD Gremler (2002). Understanding relationship marketing outcomes: An integration of relational benefits and relationship quality. *Journal of Service Research*, 4(3), 230–247.

Hernandez, JMC and JA Mazzon (2007). Adoption of internet banking: Proposition and implementation of an integrated methodology approach. *International Journal of Bank Marketing*, 25(2), 72–88.

Hernandez, JMC and JA Mazzon (2008). An empirical study of the determinants of Internet Banking adoption among Brazilians non-users. *Revista de Administração Contemporânea, Curitiba*, 12, n. spe, 9–39.

Hitt, MA, L Bierman, K Shimizu and R Kochhar (2001). Direct and moderating effects of human capital on strategy and performance in professional service firms: A resource-based view perspective. *Academy of Management Journal*, 44, 13–28.

Hindle, K and J Yencken (2004). Public research commercialisation, entrepreneurship and new technology based firms: An integrated model. *Technovation*, 24, 793–803.

Hornik, K, M Stinchcombe and H White (1989). Multilayer feedforward networks are universal approximators. *Neural Networks*, 2(5), 359–366.

Hruschka, H (1991). Einsatz Kunstlicher Neuronaler Netzwerke zur Datenanalyse. In *Marketing*, ZFP (ed.), 4, pp. 217–225. Berlin: Vahlen, Mchn.

Hruschka, H (1993). Determining market response functions by neural network modelling: A comparison to econometric techniques. *European Journal of Operational Research*, 66(1), 27–35.

Hruschka, H (1994). Determining market response functions by neural network modelling: A comparison to econometric techniques. *European Journal of Operational Research*, 27–35.

Hruschka, H and M Natter (1999). Comparing performance of feedforward neural nets and K-means for cluster-based market segregation. *European Journal of Operational Research*, 114, 346–353.

Hymer, SH (1960). *The International Operations of National Firms: A Study of Direct Foreign Investment*. Cambridge, Mass.: MIT Press.

Hymer, S (1968). The large multinational corporation: An analysis of some motives for the international integration of business. *Revue Economique*, 19(6), 949–973.

Ibbotson, P and L Moran (2003). E-banking and the SME/bank relationship in Northern Ireland. *International Journal of Bank Marketing*, 21(2), 94–103.

Johanson, J and LG Mattsson (1985). Marketing investments and market investments in industrial networks. *International Journal of Research in Marketing*, 2, 185–195.

Johanson, J and J Vahlne (1977). The internationalization process of the firm — a model of knowledge development and increasing foreign commitments. *Journal of international Business Studies*, Spring/Summer.

Johanson, J and JE Vahlne (1990). The mechanisms of internationalization. *Internationalization Marketing Review*, 7(4), 11–24.

Johanson, J and F Wiedersheim-Paul (1975). The internationalization of the firm-four swedish cases. *Journal of Management Studies*, 12(3), 305–322.

Johnson, M, D, A Gustafsson (2000). *Improving Customer Satisfaction, Loyalty and Profit*, University of Michigan Business School Management Series. San Francisco, CA: Jossey-Bass.

Jones, TO and WE Sasser Jr. (1995). Why satisfied customers defect. *Harvard Business Review*, 73(6), 88–99.

Karra, N and N Philips (2004). Entrepreneurship Goes Global. *Ivey Business Journal*, 69(2), 1–6.

Kenney, M and WR Goe (2004). The role of social embeddedness in professorial entrepreneurship: A comparison of electrical engineering and computer science at UC Berkeley and Stanford. *Research Policy*, 33, 691–707.

Landry, R, N Amara and I Rherrad (2006). Why are some university researchers more likely to create spin-offs than others? Evidence from Canadian universities. *Research Policy*, 35, 1599–1615.

Lowe, J (1993). Commercialization of university research: A policy perspective. *Technology Analysis and Strategic Management*, 5(1), 27–37.

Kim, H, HC Chan and S Gupta (2007). Value-based Adoption of Mobile Internet: An empirical investigation. *Decision Support Systems*, 43(1), 111–126.

Kim, B, H Kim and Y Lee (2002). Modes of foreign market entry by Korean SI firms. *Asia Pacific Journal of Marketing and Logistics*, 14(4), 13–35.

Kock, S (1991). A strategic process for gaining external resources through long-lasting relationships. *Examples from two Finnish and two Swedish Industrial Firms*. Doctoral Dissertation, Swedish School of Economics and Business Administration, Helsinki.

Kohli, AK and B Jaworski (1990). Market orientation: The construct, research propositions, and managerial implications. *Journal of Marketing*, 54, 1–18.

Kotabe, M, W Wu and M Minor (1997). Innovative behavior and firm performance: A comparative study of U.S., Japanese and Taiwanese firms. In *AMA 1997 Winter Educator's Conf.*, Vol. 8.

Krycha, KA and U Wagner (1999). Applications of artificial neural networks in management science: A survey. *Journal of Retailing and Consumer Services*, 6, 185–203.

Kuo, RJ (2001). A sales forecasting system based on fuzzy neural network with initial weights generated by generic algorithm. *European Journal of Operational Research*, 129, 496–517.

Lee, MP, McGoldrick, JKA Keeling and J Doherty (2003). Using ZMET to explore barriers to the adoption of 3G mobile banking services. *International Journal of Retail & Distribution Management*, 31(6), 340–348.

Lee, C, K Lee and JM Pennings (2001). Internal capabilities, external networks, and performance: Study on technology-based ventures. *Strategic Management Journal*, 22(6–7), 615–640.

Leonidou, L, CS Katsikeas and NF Piercy (1996). Identifying managerial influences on exporting: Past research and future directions. *Journal of International Marketing*, 6(2), 74–102.

Levin, SG, and PE Stephen (1991). Research productivity over the life cycle: Evidence for academic scientists. *American Economic Review*, 81(1), 114–132.

Li, S (2000). The development of a hybrid intelligent system for developing marketing strategy. *Decision Support Systems*, 27, 395–409.

Lim, B and J Brewer (1996). Neural network applications in marketing. *Journal of Computer Information Systems*, 36(2), 15–20.

Liu, H and Y Jiang (2001). Technology transfer from higher education institutions to industry in China: Nature and implications. *Technovation*, 21(3), 175–188.

Lopes, N and B Ribeiro (2003). An efficient gradient-based learning algorithm applied to neural networks with selective actuation neurons. *Neural, Parallel and Scientific Computations*, 11, 253–272.

Lu, J, C Yu, C Liu and J Yao (2003). Technology acceptance model for wireless internet. *Internet Research: Electronic Networking Applications and Policy*, 13(3), 206–222.

Lumpkin, GT and GG Dess (1996). Clarifying the entrepreneurial orientation construct and linking it to performance. *Academy Management Review*, 21(1), 135–172.

Lumpkin, GT and GG Dess (2001). Linking two dimensions of entrepreneurial orientation to firm performance: The moderating role of environment and industry life cycle. *Journal of Business Venturing*, 16(5), 429–451.

Mahajan, V, E Muller and FM Bass (1990). New product diffusion models in marketing: A review and directions for research. *Journal of Marketing*, 54, 1–26.

Mattila, M (2003). Factors affecting the adoption of Mobile Banking Services. European Union Banking & Finance Network. Available at http://www.eubfn. com/.

Mazanec, JA and L Moutinho (1999). Editorial: Whit it is timely to publish a JRCS special issue on neural networks. *Journal of Retailing and Consumer Services*, 6, 183–184.

McDougall, PP, BM Oviatt and RC Shrader (2003). A comparison of international and domestic new ventures. *Journal of International Entrepreneurship*, 1, 58–82.

Miller, D (1983). The correlates of entrepreneurship in three types of firms. *Management Science*, 29(7), 770–791.

Minsky, ML and SA Papert (1969). *Perceptrons*. Cambridge: MIT Press.

Moore, GC and I Benbasat (1991). Development of an instrument to measure the perceptions of adopting an information technology innovation. *Information Systems Research*, 2(3), 173–191.

Morgan, RM and SD Hunt (1994). The commitment-trust theory of relationship marketing. *Journal of Marketing*, 58(3), 20–38.

Morris, MH, DL Davis and JW Allen (1994). Fostering corporate entrepreneurship: Cross-cultural comparisons of the importance of individualism versus collectivism. *Journal of International Business Studies*, 25(1), 65–89.

Moutinho, L and PA Phillips (2002). The impact of strategic planning on the competitiveness, performance and effectiveness of bank branches: A neural network analysis. *The International Journal of Bank Marketing*, 20(2/3), 102–110.

Moutinho, L, D Fiona and C Bruce (1996). The impact of gender on car buyer satisfaction and loyalty. *Journal of Retailing and Consumer Services*, 3(3), 135–144.

Mueller, SL and AS Thomas (2000). Culture and entrepreneurial potential: A nine country study of locus of control and innovativeness. *Journal of Business Venturing*, 16(1), 51–75.

Naidu, GM, A Parvatiyar, JN Sheth and L Westgate (1999). Does relationship marketing pay? An empirical investigation of relationship marketing practices in hospitals. *Journal of Business Research*, 46, 207–218.

Narver, JC and SF Slater (1990). The effect of a market orientation on business profitability. *Journal of Marketing*, 54(4), 20–35.

Noone, BM, SE Kimes and LM Renaghan (2003). Integrating customer relationship management and revenue management: A hotel perspective. *Journal of Revenue and Pricing Management*, 2(1), 7–21.

Nguyen, N and A Cripps (2001). Predicting housing value: A comparison of multiple regression analysis and artificial neural networks. *Journal of Real Estate Research*, 22(3), 313–336.

Newman, JW and RA Werbel (1973). Multivariate analysis of brand loyalty for major household appliances. *Journal of Marketing Research*, 10, 404–409.

Oliveira, PAS and HFDEO Dutra (2002). Percepção de qualidade e construção de relacionamentos: Uma Investigação num sector Financeiro. In *Encontro Nacional da Associação Nacional dos Programas de Pós-Graduação e Pesquisa em Administração*, 26, Salvador. *Anais*. Salvador: Anpad.

Oliver, RL (1999). Whence consumer loyalty? *Journal of Marketing*, 63, 33–44.

O'Shea, RP, TJ Allen, C O'Gorman and F Roche (2004). Universities and technology transfer: A review of academic entrepreneurship literature. *Irish Journal of Management*, 26(2), 11–29.

O'Shea, RP, TJ Allen, A Chevalier and F Roche (2005). Entrepreneurial orientation, technology transfer and spinoff performance of U.S. universities. *Research Policy*, 34(7), 994–1009.

O'Shea, RP, H Chugh and TJ Allen (2008). Determinants and consequences of university spinoff activity: A conceptual framework. *The Journal of Technology Transfer*, 33(6), 653–666.

Osland, GE, Taylor, R Charles and S Zou (2001). Selecting international modes of entry and expansion. *Marketing Intelligence & Planning*, 19(3), 153–162.

Oviatt, B and P Mcdougall (1995). Global start-ups: Entrepreneurs on a worldwide stage. *Academy of Management Executive*, 9(2), 30–43.

Parasuraman, A and CL Colby (2001). *Techno-ready Marketing: How and Why Your Customers Adopt Technology*. New York: Free Press.

Peng, MW and Y Luo (2000). Managerial ties and firm performance in a transition economy: The nature of a micro-macro link. *Academy of Management Journal*, 43(3), 485–501.

Phillips, PA, MD Fiona and L Moutinho (2001). The interactive effects of strategic marketing planning and performance: A neural network analysis. *Journal of Marketing Management*, 17(1–2), 159–182.

Phillips, PA, MD Fiona and L Moutinho (2002). Assessing the impact of market-focused and price-based strategies on performance: A neural network topology. *Journal of Market-Focused Management*, 5(3), 219–238.

Pipkin, A (2000). *Marketing Internacional*. São Paulo: Aduaneiras.

Porter, ME (1980). *Competitive Strategy: Techniques for Analyzing Industries and Competitors*. New York: The Free Press.

Powers, JB and PP McDougall (2005). University start-up formation and technology licensing with firms that go public: A resource-based view of academic entrepreneurship. *Journal of Business Venturing*, 20(3), 291–311.

Proctor, RA (1992). Marketing decision support systems: A role for neural networking. *Market Intelligence & Planning*, 10(1), 21–26.

Reichheld, FF and WE Sasser (1990). Zero defections: Quality comes to services. *Harvard Business Review*, 68(5), 105–111.

Reichheld, FF (1993). Loyalty-based management. *Harvard Business Review*, 71(2), 64–73.

Reichheld, FF (1994). Loyalty and the renaissance of marketing. *Marketing Management*, 2(4), 10–17.

Reichheld, FF (1996a). Learning from customer defections. *Harvard Business Review*, 74(2), 56–69.

Reichheld, FF (1996b). *The Loyalty Effect, The hidden Force Behind Growth, Profits, and Lasting Value*. Boston: Harvard Business School Press.

Reichheld, FF and P Schefter (2000). E-loyalty: Your secret weapon on the web. *Harvard Business Review*, 78(4), 105–113.

Reid, S (1981). The decision-maker and export entry and expansion. *Journal of International Business Studies*, 12, 101–112.

Roberts, EB (1991). *Entrepreneurs in High Technology: Lessons from MIT and Beyond*. Oxford: Oxford University Press.

Roberts, EB and DE Malone (1996). Policies and structures for spinning off new companies from research and development organizations. *R&D Management*, 26(1), 17–48.

Rogers, EM (1983). *Diffusion of Innovations*, 3rd edn. New York: Free Press.

Rogers, EM (1995). *Diffusion of Innovations*, 4th edn. New York: Free Press

Rogers, EM (2003). *Diffusion of Innovations*, 5th edn. New York: Free Press.

Rogers, EM, S Takegami and J Yin (2001). Lessons learned about technology transfer. *Technovation*, 21(4), 253–261.

Rotter, JB (1966). Generalized expectancies for internal versus external control of reinforcement. *Psychological Monographs: General and Applied*, 80(1), 1–28.

Rosenblatt, F (1958). The perceptron: a probability model for information storage and organization in the brain. *Psychological Review*, 65(6), 386–408.

Schlesinger, LA and JL Heskett (1991). Breaking the cycle of failure in services. *Management Review*, 32(3), 17–28.

Schumpeter, JA (1934). *The Theory of Economic Development*. Cambridge MA: Harvard University Press.

Shane, S (2001a). Technological opportunities and new firm creation. *Management Science*, 47(2), 205–220.

Shane, S (2001b). Technology regimes and new firm formation. *Management Science*, 47(9), 1173–1190.

Shane, S (2002). Selling university technology: patterns from MIT. *Management Science*, 48(1), 122–138.

Shane, S (2004). *Academic Entrepreneurship: University Spinoffs and Wealth Creation*. Cheltenham: Edward Elgar Publishing.

Shane, S and S Venkataraman (2000). The promise of entrepreneurship as a field of research. *Academy of Management Review*, 25(1), 217–226.

Shane, S, S Venkataraman and I MacMillan (1995). Cultural differences in innovation championing strategies. *Journal of Management*, 21(5), 931–952.

Shoham, A (1998). Export performance: A conceptualization and empirical assessment. *Journal of International Marketing*, 6(3), 59–81.

Simões, VC and PM Dominguinhos (2001). Portuguese Born Globals: An exploratory study. In *27th EIBA Conf. at ESCP-EAP*. Paris: EIBA.

Spangler, WE, JH May and LG Vargas (1999). Choosing data-mining methods for multiple classification: Representational and performance measurement implication for decision support. *Journal of Management Information System*, 16(1), 37–62.

Steier, L and R Greenwood (2000). Entrepreneurship and the evolution of angel financial networks. *Organization Studies*, 21(1), 163–192.

Stevenson, HH and JC Jarillo (1990). A paradigm of entrepreneurship: Entrepreneurial management. *Strategic Management Journal*, 11(4), 17–27.

Steffensen, M, EM Rogers and K Speakman (1999). Spin-offs from research centers at a research university. *Journal of Business Venturing*, 15(1), 93–111.

Silva, M, L Moutinho, A Coelho and A Marques (2009). Market orientation and performance: Modelling a neural network. *European Journal of Marketing*, 43(3/4), 421–437.

Stinchcombe, M and H White (1989). Universal approximation using feedforward networks with non-sigmoid hidden layer activation functions. In *Proc. Int. Joint Conf. Neural Networks*, IEEE, New York, Vol. 1(5), 613–617.

Thieme, RJ, M Song and RJ Calantone (2000). Artificial neural network decision support systems for new product development project selection. *Journal of Marketing Research*, 37(4), 499–507.

Uysal, M and SE Roubi (1999). Artificial neural networks versus multiple regression in tourism demand analysis. *Journal of Travel Research*, 38, 111–118.

Valente, TW (1995). *Network Models of the Diffusion of Innovations*. Cresskill, N.J: Hampton Press.

Venkatraman, M (1991). The impact of innovativeness and innovation type on adoption. *Journal of Retailing*, 67(1), 51–67.

Venkatraman, N and V Ramanujan (1987). Measurement of business economic performance: An examination of method convergence. *Journal of Management*, 13(1), 109–122.

Venugopal, V and W Baets (1994a). Neural networks and statistical techniques in marketing research: A conceptual comparison. *Marketing Intelligence and Planning*, 12(7), 30–38.

Venugopal, V and W Baets (1994b). Neural networks and their applications in marketing management. *Journal of Systems Management*, 45(9), 16–21.

Vernon, R (1966). International investment and international trade in the product cycle. *Quartely Journal of Economics*, 80/2, 190–207.

Vernon, R (1979). The location of economic activity. In *Economic analysis and the multinational enterprise*, J DUNNING (ed.). London: George Allen and Unwin.

Walczuch, R, J Lemmink and S Streukens (2007). The effect of service employees' technology readiness on technology acceptance. *Information & Management*, 44(2), 206–215.

West, PM, PL Brockett and LL Golden (1997). A comparative analysis of neural networks and statistical methods for predicting consumer choice. *Marketing Science*, 16(4), 370–391.

Wiklund, J and D Shepherd (2005). Entrepreneurial orientation and small business performance: A configuration approach. *Journal of Business Venturing*, 20(5), 71–91.

Wilson, E and T Wragg (2001). We cannot diagnose the patients' illness ... but experience tells us what treatment works. *International Journal of Market Research*, 43(2), 189–215.

Wray, B, A Palmer and D Bejou (1994). Using neural network analysis to evaluate buyer–seller relationship. *European Journal of Marketing*, 28(10), 32–48.

Wright, RW and DA RICKS (1994). Trends in international business research; Twenty-five years later. *Journal of International Business Studies*, 25(4), 687–701.

Yao, J, T Nicholas, H Poh and CL Tan (1998). Forecasting and analysis of marketing data using neural networks. *Journal of Information Science and Engineering*, 14, 843–862.

Zahavi, J and N Levin (1995). Issues and problems in applying neural computing to target marketing. *Journal of Direct Marketing*, 9(3), 33–45.

Zhao, X (2005). Active development of social networks and relationships to chinese small and micro business owners' success. Ph.D. thesis, Universität GieBen, GieBen, Germany.

Zahra, SA (1991). Predictors and financial outcomes of corporate entrepreneurship: An exploratory study. *Journal of Business Venturing*, 6(4), 259–285.

Zahra, SA and JG Covin (1995). Contextual influences on corporate entrepreneurship performance relationship: A longitudinal analysis. *Journal of Business Venturing*, 10(1), 43–58.

Zahra, SA and G George (2002). International entrepreneurship: The current status of the field and future research agenda. In *Strategic Entrepreneurship: Creating an Integrated Mindset*, MA Hitt, RD Ireland, SM Camp and DL Sexton (eds.), pp. 255–288. Oxford: Blackwell Publishers. Available at http://instruction.bus.wisc.edu/ggeorge/research/IE.pdf.

Zahra, SA, JC Hayton and C Salvato (2004). Entrepreneurship in family vs. non-family firms: A resource-based analysis of the effect of organizational culture. *Entrepreneurship Theory and Practice*, 28(4), 363–381.

Zahra, SA, JS Corrí and J Yu (2004). Cognition and entrepreneurship: Implications for research on international opportunity recognition and exploitation. *International Business Review*, 20, 1–18.

Zou, S and ST Cavusgil (1996). Global strategy: A review and an integrated conceptual framework. *European Journal of Marketing*, 30(1), 52–69.

Zucker, LG, MR Darby and MB Brewer (1998). Intellectual human capital and the birth of U.S. biotechnology enterprises. *American Economic Review*, 88(1), 290–306.

Chapter 8

LOGICAL DISCRIMINANT MODELS

Margarida G. M. S. Cardoso

BRU-UNIDE, ISCTE-IUL

Discriminant analysis aims to classify multivariate observations into *a priori* defined classes and explain the differences between them. Logical discriminant type models — trees and rules — emerge in this context and within the data mining framework as powerful predictive tools that generate very easy to interpret results. Moreover, they generally provide means to deal with explantory variables of different measurement levels (quantitative and qualitative), good handling of missing data and robustness. These characteristics are particularly appreciated in management decision support.

Discriminant analysis basic concepts and trees and rules algorithms are presented in this chapter. General issues concerning the evaluation of discriminant analysis and the key concept of diversity are outlined first. Tree algorithms, successively dividing a set of observations to conquer less diversity and increase accuracy, are described next. The induction of propositional rules, whether based on trees or yielded by a set covering approach, is also described. An application in retail and specific algorithms (e.g., CART, C5, CN2 and LEM) ilusrate the logical discriminant methodologies. Final remarks provide a contextualisation of the diversity of contributions in this domain.

Keywords: Decision trees; decision rule; classification; discriminant analysis.

The notion of a true model is nowadays regarded as a weak one. Rather, it is assumed that all models are approximations to whatever is going on in nature, and our aim is to find a model that is close enough for the purpose to hand.

Hand *et al.* (2001). Principles of Data Mining: The MIT Press. p. 231

1. Introduction

Discriminant or classification analysis is a supervised learning or dependence analysis that studies the association between a set of entities' attributes (predictors) and a categorical target attribute imposing classes to those entities — the *teacher* that supervises learning. For example, consider the customers of a wholesale divided into two classes — Retail and Horeca (Hotel/Restaurant/Café) — and the customers' information concerning diverse product categories purchases (amounts spent on grocery or fresh products, for example). Are there different spending patterns for the two groups of customers? If so, maybe the wholesale could differentiate its marketing actions directed to these groups. The discriminant analysis between Retail and Horeca customers could be used to answer the wholesale question.

The purpose of classification is twofold: to clarify and try to explain the differences between classes of observed entities, based on a set of predictors, and to build rules to classify the entities into classes, based on the same predictors (see the general diagram on Fig. 1). For the Horeca versus Retail customers' task, discriminant analysis results will then, yield a better understanding of the segments and enable the classification of customers into these classes.

Discriminant analysis can be viewed as a data analysis task that may be accomplished by statistical, data mining, or statistical

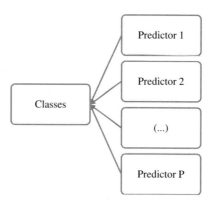

Fig. 1.   Discriminant analysis diagram with P predictors.

learning techniques. It may rely on functional, graphical, or logical type models.

Commonly used functional approaches are based on linear functions of predictors. They are generally built within the scope of the statistical inference paradigm which usually requires some assumptions to infer the model from the sample to the population, quantifying the correspondent degree of (un)certainty. Linear discriminant analysis is the best known discriminant method. In this analysis, the discriminant scores are a weighted sum of predictors and the derivation of classification rules requires Gaussian data and a common predictors covariances matrix (for all classes) which, often, may not be the case for real data. Logistic regression stands as the second next best known classification technique — it models the log-odds or logit transformations of classes probabilities as linear combinations of predictors and it makes less assumptions regarding data when compared to linear discriminant analysis (Hair *et al.*, 2005).

Some alternative discriminant functional approaches are built using data mining techniques — see (Hastie *et al.*, 2001) for an overview. Such techniques include neural networks (NN) — e.g., learning a multilayer perceptron with a backpropagation algorithm — or support vector machines (SVM) — see (Bennett and Campbell, 2000), for example. As opposed to statistical approaches, these methods do not generally require distributional assumptions on the data to infer the models to the population, establishing a degree of uncertainty. However, they generally have to rely on large datasets that can provide a holdout set (data not used for model estimation) in order to obtain alternative estimates of models' uncertainty.

Results' interpretability differs between the diverse discriminant techniques and it is certainly not a priority for some of them (e.g., NN or SVM). Logical type discriminant models (LDM) emerge in the context of discriminant techniques, within the data mining framework, as providing results that are very easy to interpret — trees and rules — making them very appealing, namely in management decision support. The LDM (also referred as symbolic learning systems), have some additional advantages when compared to other techniques, namely the capacity to deal with explanatory variables of different measurement levels (quantitative and qualitative), good handling of missing data and robustness.

2. On the Customers of a Wholesale Distributor

In the present chapter, logical discriminant models are illustrated based on data referring to 440 customers of a wholesale distributor: 298 from the Horeca (Hotel/Restaurant/Café) channel and 142 from the Retail channel.

The wholesale customers are grouped according to frequency-spending degrees into four groups: (1) low frequency-low spending; (2) high frequency-low spending; (3) regular frequency-regular spending; (4) high frequency-high spending. The corresponding distribution is illustrated in Table 1.

The wholesale data concerning the customers includes the annual spending in monetary units (m.u.) on diverse product categories, namely: fresh products, milk products, grocery, frozen products, detergents and paper products and delicatessen. The main related descriptive measures are presented in Table 2.

Data available also includes responses to a questionnaire where the wholesale tried to evaluate possible actions with potential impact on sales:

1. Offer free samples or tastings.
2. Offer discount tickets.
3. Improve the quality of products.
4. Improve packaging.

Table 1.   Wholesale customers groups distribution.

Group of customers	Count	Percentage
1. Low frequency-low spending	224	50.9%
2. High frequency-low spending	161	36.6%
3. Regular frequency-regular spending	45	10.2%
4. High frequency-high spending	10	2.3%
Total	440	100.0%

Table 2. Product categories sales (m.u.).

	Mean	Median	Std. Deviation	Minimum	Maximum
Fresh products	120,00	8,504	12,647	3	112,151
Milk products	5,796	3,627	7380	55	73,498
Grocery	7,951	4,756	9,503	3	92,780
Frozen	3,072	1,526	4,855	25	60,869
Detergents and Paper	2,881	817	4,768	3	40,827
Delicassen	1,525	966	2,820	3	47,943

5. Improve the store layout.
6. Prevent shortages.
7. Offer more competitive prices.
8. Offer better selection of products and brands.
9. Offer more diversity of products and brands.
10. Present more in-store highlights and leaflets.
11. Extend products assortment.

Customers' answers to these possible actions were registered in the scale: 1 — Certainly no; 2 — Probably no; 3 — Probably yes; 4 — Certainly yes (answers to "would you increase purchase if").

The wholesale data provide simple examples that help to clarify the use of trees and rules.

3. Logical Discriminant Models, an Overview

LDM are based on rules similar to logical implications, conjunctive statements known as propositional rules, e.g., consider the customers of the wholesale distributor referred in Sec. 2 and the rules:

1. **If** Group = high frequency-low spending **then** Horeca.
2. **If** Group = low frequency-low spending **then** Horeca.
3. **If** Group = regular frequency-regular spending **then** Retail.
4. **If** Group = high frequency-high spending **then** Retail.

In the above rule 1, the probability of obtaining the correct prediction for the 161 customers that match the rule's condition — Group = high frequency-low spending — is 77.3%; similarly, the percentage of correctly classified customers by the second rule is 69.9%. The

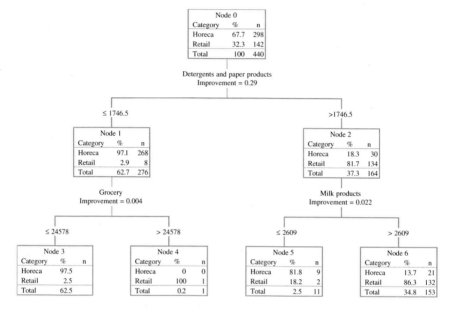

Fig. 2.   Classification tree for channels based on product category spending.

propositional rules logical value is not exactly true or false as in common logical statements, each rule having associated a probability of being true, i.e., a certain degree of uncertainty.

Rules may have a hierarchical order and constitute a tree logical discriminant model, its representation seeming like an upside-down tree, where the root is on the top and the leaves on the bottom (see Fig. 2). A tree illustrates a hierarchical divide-and-conquer process. It starts with a sample of observations (in the root node) and successively divides nodes based on the predictors' values. This process attempts to decrease diversity in each new descendent node of the tree, in order to decrease the risk of classification.

For example, consider the task of classifying Horeca versus Retail customers (database referred in Sec. 2) based on the amounts of annual spending on product categories and a tree model which attempts to perform this task — Fig. 2. In the root node, the use of modal classification yields Horeca as the predicted target for all customers (it is the prevailing or modal class), resulting in a 32.3% percentage of incorrect classification (the percentage of customers which are actually Retail customers). A risk reduction — as measured by percentage of correctly classified observations — can be observed in node 1, constituted in the first branching level. In fact, Horeca customers are much more concentrated on the node corresponding to customers *spending less than* 1746.5 *m.u. in detergents and paper products* (node 1), than in the root node, which favours correct classification in node 1. Each terminal tree nodes or leaf (nodes 3 to 6 in Fig. 2) represents a set of relatively homogeneous observations in what concerns classes' membership, the distribution tending to concentrate in one particular class. The higher the homogeneity in the leafs, the lower the risk of classification in the two customers channels: e.g., in node 6 of the tree in Fig. 2, 86.3% of the customers *spending more than* 1,746.5 *m.u. in detergents and paper products and more than* 2,609 *m.u. on milk products* are correctly classified as Retail customers. Note that in the root node there were no means to classify Retail customers, the mode being Horeca customers. The tree yields the classification in the Retail customers group in nodes 4 and 6.

The classification accuracy corresponding to the tree in Fig. 2 can be obtained considering all the tree leafs: they yield 97.5%, 100%, 81.8% and 86.3% of correctly classified elements in nodes 3, 4, 5 and 6, respectively. A weighted average — using the relative frequency of observations in these nodes — provides a final accuracy estimate: 93.2%.

The construction of LDM may recur to several techniques. Some of the most commonly used ones are referred in Sec. 5. All techniques aim to fit the best possible model for a specific classification task, maximising accuracy but also taking into account the model simplicity that favours interpretability.

4. The Models Evaluation

4.1. *Measures of accuracy*

Consider the results from classification that derive from the model in Fig. 2. They are summarised in Table 3 where the percentage of correctly classified observations — $Perc_c$ — is 93.2%, which seems to be a good result. It is, however, not necessarily so, since

Table 3.   Classification table for model in Fig. 2.

Observed	Predicted		
	Horeca	Retail	Percentage Correct
Horeca	277	21	93.0%
Retail	9	133	93.7%
Overall Percentage	65.0%	35.0%	93.2%

$Perc_c$ provides a limited perspective when evaluating the referred model.

First, one has to take into account the accuracy one would achieve with no model at all, e.g., by simply using modal allocation. In the original dataset, 67.7% is the percentage referred to the modal class (Horeca), which may be considered as the default percentage of correctly classified observations, $Perc_d$. Therefore, $Perc_c$ should be compared with $Perc_d$ to evaluate the model adequately. The Huberty index operationalises this comparison (Sharma, 1996), measuring the ratio between the relative increase in classification accuracy and the maximum possible increase (78.9% in the current case):

$$Huberty = \frac{Perc_c - Perc_d}{1 - Perc_d}.$$

Second, one has to distinguish the performance for each class which, in this particular case, is very similar: 93.7% for retail customers and 93.0% for Horeca customers.

So far, we focused on the percentage of correctly classified observations as a measure of accuracy for evaluating discriminant analysis results. This measure relates to the zero–one cost function, meaning that a unit cost is considered for each misclassified observation and a null cost for each correctly classified observation. In fact,

$$Perc_c = 1 - \frac{\sum_{n=1}^{N} e_n}{N},$$

where

$$e_n = \begin{cases} 1 & if \quad \hat{y}_n \neq y_n \\ 0 & if \quad \hat{y}_n = y_n \end{cases},$$

and y_n code the target classes.

Table 4. Binary classification results (counts).

Actual class	Predicted class	
	1	0
1	a	b
0	c	d

For binary problems in particular — y_n coded with one and zero, without loss of generality — one could also consider the difference between incorrectly classified cases related with counts b and c on Table 4.

Consider, for example, that the high-spending Retail customers are especially valuable for the wholesale and that they constitute a target in classification task (class 1) versus other Retail customers (class 0). Missing a correct classification on these customers could have a particular negative impact on the wholesale business. Therefore, it may be pertinent to distinguish between:

— Sensitivity, defined as $a/(a+b)$ and expressing the agreement between actual and predicted class 1 within this class, $P(\hat{y}_n = 1|y_n = 1)$; and
— Specificity, $d/(c+d)$, expressing the agreement between actual and predicted class within class O, $P(\hat{y}_n = 0|y_n = 0)$.

Using the implicit unit cost that relates to the use of the $Perc_c$ measure, one cannot favour sensitivity over specificity which could be a desirable action, taking into account the wholesale perspective. In order to favour sensitivity, the costs of incorrect classification within class 1 should be increased and conversely, for specificity (Table 5). However, it is not possible to simultaneously favour both specificity and sensitivity and, for practical applications, a trade-off must be equated.

The analysis of the trade-off sensitivity-specificity can be made using appropriate techniques that provide quantification and visualisation of this trade-off: The Kolmogorov–Smirnov statistic as well as the Receiver Operating Characteristic (ROC) curves may be used for this end (Hastie *et al.*, 2001).

Table 5. Classification costs: Sensitivity versus specificity.

	Unit cost			Costs that favour sensitivity			Costs that favour specificity	
	Predicted class			Predicted class			Predicted class	
Actual class	1	0	Actual class	1	0	Actual class	1	0
1	0	1	1	0	>1	1	0	1
0	1	0	0	1	0	0	>1	0

When using other than unit costs for incorrect classification, the final solution will then be evaluated by the quantification of the total cost of misclassification.

4.2. Fit and overfit

Table 3 results refer to the same observations that originated the model in Fig. 2. This fact raises some concerns — and what if the same model was applied to new data? Would it perform equally well? When using LDM procedures, some techniques may be used to address this issue:

1. LDM procedures may recur to the evaluation of performance on a set of independent data that enables to decide the next learning step — the evaluation set. For example, the decision of using *Detergent and paper products* for branching the root node in the first place (see Fig. 2) could have been evaluated for improvement on accuracy in new data.
2. The final evaluation of the model should rely on a all set of new data — the test set. That is to say that the matrix on Table 3 should, ideally, be complemented with a similar matrix referred to a test set.

When having trouble in gathering enough data to constitute the training set, the evaluation set and the test set — dealing with moderate or small sample sizes — the evaluation set is usually the first to be discarded.

When a test set is not available (original sample sizes may be moderate), one may recur to a cross-validation procedure. In cross-validation — V-Fold method — the original sample is partitioned into V subsamples of equal size and in which (hopefully) there is a similar distribution of the variables considered in modelling. V models are then estimated using each one of the subsamples as a holdout sample (excluding it from the modelling process) and the remaining V-1 subsamples for building the LDMs. The quality of the forecast is then averaged over the V subsamples used as holdout samples. Typical choices for V value are 5 or 10 — e.g. for the Retail versus Horeca classification problem, the percentage of correctly classified observations as estimated by 10-fold cross validation is 91.4%, slightly lower than the percentage based on the training sample 93.2%, but more realistic since holdout data is used to provide this estimate.

In addition to the use of holdout datasets — evaluation and/or test or subsamples for cross-validation — LDM generally implement preventive measures during the learning process intended to prevent overfit, i.e., fitting too much to training data. In fact, overfit may lead to missing the more general patterns that will appear in new data, impoverishing prediction accuracy related to these data.

When using LDM, specific procedures to avoid overfit include stopping rules and pruning procedures. Preventing one tree to grow too much (and overfit training data) may recur to stopping rules such as: fixing the minimum number of observations in parent and child nodes or the maximum number of tree levels. In addition, pruning procedures may be used to discard some tree branches, equating a trade-off between the tree complexity and its accuracy which may empower the likelihood of the model to apply to the population. In the current example, a limit of two levels was considered (a stopping rule) and no pruning was implemented.

Results presented in Table 6 illustrate the performance of two alternative models for classification of Horeca versus Retail customers. These are trees with unit misclassification costs, two and five levels limits imposed, pruning implemented and a training-test split of 50% observations considered. The tree with two levels is similar to the one in Fig. 2 with nodes 3 and 4 excluded by pruning, thus having five nodes. The tree with five levels has 17 nodes.

Table 6. Classification accuracy — $Perc_C$ — for two alternative models.

	Tree with two levels	Tree with five levels
Training set	92.7%	96.8%
Test set	90.9%	90.0%

The tree with five levels has a better performance on the training sample — again see Table 6. However, its additional complexity corresponds to a minor difference on the test set performance: 90.9% versus 90.0%. Furthermore, the two-levels tree has more consistent training–test results. Therefore, a trade-off complexity-accuracy and the consideration of consistency tend to favour the selection of the tree with two levels which is, certainly, more easy to interpret.

5. Techniques for Building Logical Discriminant Models

5.1. Decision trees and rules

5.1.1. The concept of diversity

Consider the task of building a classification or discriminant model having a target nominal variable — Y with possible categories $c = 1 \ldots C$ — with a uniform distribution in a set of observations O. Since the odds are equally distributed by its possible categories or classes, predicting in this situation is a particularly difficult task. Conversely, when all elements of the set O ($n = 1 \ldots N$) share the same category, this is the natural candidate value for forecasting when new data is considered.

A diversity measure for a nominal variable should clearly distinguish the two situations above, being minimum (e.g., zero) when all the observations share the same category and maximum when a uniform distribution is observed.

There are several diversity measures available. The Gini index, G, and the Entropy measure H can be presented as examples.

The Gini index (for the Y variable in the dataset O) is defined as follows:

$$G(Y; O) = \sum_{c=1}^{C} p(c; O)[1 - p(c; O)] = 1 - \sum_{c=1}^{C} p(c; O)^2.$$

This coefficient can be interpreted as the trace of the variance–covariance matrix of C variables which are binary indicators for the C categories of Y The empirical variance of these indicators (assuming a Bernoulli distribution) is given by $p(c; O)[1 - p(c; O)]$ where $p(c; O)$ quantifies the empirical probability of category c occurring in the dataset O Therefore, the Gini index can be interpreted as the corresponding total variance.

The Entropy measure can be defined by:

$$H(Y; O) = - \sum_{c=1}^{C} p(c; O) \log_2 p(c; O).$$

The rational for this measure relies on information theory. The amount of information contained in a message — for example, *the observation belongs to the class c of the target variable Y* — depends on its probability of occurrence, measured empirically by $p(c; O)$. This, in turn, can be measured in bits and quantified as $-\log_2 p(c; O)$. Entropy is the expected value of the amount of information needed to identify the Y class, given the set of possible messages (an element in O may be associated with any of the classes $c = 1 \ldots C$). If all observations are concentrated in only one category, this amount is zero and there is no uncertainty about the Y category (note that it is agreed that for a class with a zero probability, the corresponding entropy portion is also zero).

The construction of LDM relies on diversity measures to quantify the improvement in accuracy in the learning process. Naturally, conquering lower diversity favours misclassification error rates, i.e., the percentage of misclassified observations, $1 - Perc_c$.

5.1.2. *Decision trees*

Most logical discriminant models are derived from the construction of a tree model, using a Data Mining or Statistical Learning algorithm (e.g., see Fig. 2).

The trees' building process is based on a divide-and-conquer approach to prediction tasks, classification in particular. Dividing sets of observations into more homogeneous subsets enables the algorithm to conquer better predictions. In fact, when considering a constant target, the estimated predicted value naturally emerges as the same constant (class). On the contrary, the multiplicity and the dispersion of target classes in a given set of observations is an obstacle to a good prediction of this target variable.

The construction of a tree requires the definition of:

(1) A **branching criterion** for deciding on the best branching of a tree node;
(2) A procedure to deal with **missing values**;
(3) **Stopping rules** for deciding to stop the process of nodes branching and consider a node as a leaf node;
(4) **Pruning** using a cost-benefit criterion for the disposal of some branches;
(5) A function to use in each leaf node to estimate the target variable (usually the **mode**).

There are several algorithms to build trees: Classification and Regression Trees (CART) (Breiman *et al.*, 1984) and C5/See5 (based on C4.5 (Quinlan, 1993)) are, perhaps, the most popular. These algorithms adopt specific (1) to (5) criteria and also rely in some interaction with the analyst — as often occurs with other data mining techniques — to define some learning parameters, such as the ones related with stopping the tree construction (e.g., fixing the number of tree levels, the number of observations in a node or the minimum decrease in diversity that results from a node's branching).

Consider, for example, the **branching criterion**. Successive branching for building a tree can be seen as repeated attempts to minimise the diversity of the tree. The related problem is how to divide (branch) each set of observations in a node into subsets — descendant nodes — representing a partition of that node, in a way that favours prediction accuracy. Typically, in order to form this partition, all explanatory variables are considered as candidates.

Each explanatory variable can provide several alternative branches. In general, if a variable has K possible values, the number of possible ramifications, R, with C branches is:

(a) $R = \binom{K-1}{C-1}$ if the explanatory variable K values have order.

(b) $R = \sum_{c=0}^{C-1} (-1)^c \frac{(C-c)^K}{c!(C-c)!}$ if the explanatory variable is nominal (with K categories).

When considering binary branching in particular — branching of a node into two descendant nodes and thus setting $C = 2$ — one obtains: (a) $R = K - 1$; (b) $R = 2^{K-1} - 1$ (for the (a) and (b) situations referred above).

Since different partitions should provide different decreases in diversity, one selects the predictor and a specific related branching that yields the maximum decrease. This branching process is greedy, attempting to provide the maximum decrease in risk or diversity or the maximum improvement on prediction accuracy at each step. Note that a particular choice for branching establishes conditional subsequent choices, not accounting for the fact that a possible temporary increase of diversity may, in the end, turn into a better final solution. However, this algorithm simplicity favours computational efficiency and, in the end, for practical applications, the predictive accuracy of trees is widely recognised when compared to alternative approaches.

Several measures can be used for branching, namely the Entropy measure or the Gini index. Considering a general diversity or impurity measure I, the decrease in diversity yielded by branching is quantified by:

$$\Delta I(O|X) = \sum_{c=1}^{C} \frac{p(O_c)}{p(O)} I(O_c) - I(O),$$

where, commonly, $p(O_c)$ stands for the relative frequency of node O in the training set (costs of incorrect classification may eventually be incorporated in $p(O_c)$). The division of the observations by C descendant nodes O_c with $n(O_c)$ number of observations ($c = 1 \ldots C$) is, of course, such that $\sum_{c=1}^{C} n(O_c)$ equaling the number of training observations in O, $n(O)$.

Naturally, diverse algorithms have alternative options for branching — e.g., CART builds binary trees only allowing for branching a node into two descendant nodes and its assessment of candidate partitions may be based on the Gini index. The tree in Fig. 2 was built by CART. It exhibits an improvement of 0.290 for the first branching which is simply $-\Delta I(O|X)$ considering the Gini index for I. On the root node this diversity measure is $1 - (67.7\%^2 + 32.3\%^2) \cong 0.437$. For nodes 1 and 2, the Gini index values are 0.056 and 0.299, respectively. Considering $p(O_1) = 276/440$ and $p(O_2) = 164/440$, the referred improvement is obtained.

The branching criterion for the C5 algorithm is the Information Gain ratio. The Information Gain is a measure of relative entropy decrease of the dependent variable in the node O, implied by the knowledge of the categories of an explanatory variable X: $H(Y;O) - H(Y|X;O)$, where $H(Y|X;O)$ is a measure of conditional entropy, defined as the weighted average of entropies calculated on each of the descendant nodes associated with branching on X, $O_c \ c = 1 \ldots C$:

$$H(Y|X;O) = \sum_{c=1}^{C} p(O_c)H(Y;O_c).$$

The empirical finding of a bias in favour of explanatory attributes with more categories led Quinlan to adopt the Information gain ratio, a normalised Information Gain using the X entropy as denominator.

It is worthwhile to note that the choice of particular branching rules tends to have a minor impact on the predictive ability of a tree, according to (Breiman *et al.*, 1984).

A final remark regarding branching criteria concerns costs of incorrect classification: They may be considered in the divide-and-conquer process, integrated in the diversity measures (as well as in the evaluation of final results, as pointed in Sec. 4).

Tree procedures to deal with **missing values** — may be creative. When implementing tree branching consider where should an observation be assigned if it is missing for a branching predictor — e.g., for the tree Fig. 2 where goes an observation if the *Detergent and paper products* correspondent information is missing? This particular

Table 7. List of surrogate predictors for the root node in Fig. 2.

	Independent variable	Improvement	Association
Primary	Detergents and paper products	0.290	
Surrogate	Grocery	0.206	0.707
	Milk products	0.167	0.530
	Frozen	0.011	0.098
	Fresh products	0.010	0.073
	Delicatessen	0.007	0.049

tree was built with CART which selects the current most associated predictor to replace the missing information. For the example, CART provides a list of surrogate predictors — see Table 7. The referred association measure is based on the idea of maximising the intersection between node O actual descendants — nodes left (O_L) and right (O_R) — and the surrogate predictor referred descendants, O'_R and O'_L:

$$\frac{p(O_R \cap O'_R)}{p(O)} + \frac{p(O_L \cap O'_L)}{p(O)}.$$

This measure of association quantifies the relative reduction in error resulting from the use of a surrogate when compared to the majority rule (the observation following for the largest descendent node). If this reduction is negative, it is not worth introducing the predictor as a surrogate. For example in Table 7, all the surrogate predictors necessarily exhibit positive association with the partition provided by *Detergents and paper products*. The predictor *Grocery* (namely the specific partition provided by the condition *Grocery* $\leq$ 5726.5) is identified as the best surrogate partition for the root node.

C5 proposes missing cases to be split according to the descendant nodes' dimensions: e.g., if the branching predictor at node O generates descendant nodes O_1, O_2, O_3 which correspond to 20%, 35% and 45% of the number of observations in O, then similar portions of a missing case are forwarded by the descendant nodes of O. Therefore, in the final tree, the leaf nodes integrate numbers of observations which are not necessarily integers.

When a missing value occurs in C5 the calculation of the Information Gain is also corrected taking into account the missing observation: $H(Y; O) - H(Y|X; O)$ is multiplied by $[n(O) - 1]/n(O)$. Furthermore, for determining the normalising factor in the information gain ratio (the entropy of the branching predictor) C5 considers an extra category for this attribute — the category of missing values.

Pruning Trees is a procedure for cutting some branches without damaging the tree accuracy. The disposal of some branches may enhance the capacity of the tree to be generalised to new data and also improves its comprehension. However, some cost-benefit criterion must be considered to reason about the loss in its accuracy. In what concerns pruning decisions, again diverse algorithms make different options.

CART uses a cost-complexity criterion which takes into account the number of leaf nodes in a subtree candidate for pruning. Consider the subtree T_O descending from node O and the number of leafs on this subtree, $\#(T_O)$. Its error rate is $re(T_O) = 1 - Perc_c(T_O)$. An adjusted error rate is obtained introducing a penalisation factor δ such that:

$$re_\delta(T_O) = re(T_O) + \delta \times \#T_O).$$

The CART procedure increases δ successively to obtain a sequence of subtrees embedded in the entire tree T (with the same root node), among which the final model will be selected. As δ increases, the tree that minimises re_δ will have fewer leaf nodes. When δ is large enough this tree coincides with the root node. For a specific subtree T_O, prunning will not be worth making if $re_\delta(T_O) < re_\delta(O)$ where $re_\delta(O) = re(O) + \delta$ (considering node O with no descendant nodes).

Another pruning approach is provided by C5: It is based on a pessimistic estimate of misclassification error — $re_{pess}(O)$. In order to obtain estimates of the number of observations incorrectly classified with and without a subtree T_O descending of node O, C5 recurs to pessimistic error estimates using the upper limit of a $1 - \alpha$ confidence interval for the proportion of incorrectly classified observations (assuming that number of observations incorrectly classified in node O follows a binomial distribution). Usually, $\alpha = 25\%$ is used.

5.1.3. *Rules from trees*

Consider the task of classifying the wholesale 142 Retail customers into the four frequency-spending groups. The C5 algorithm can be used to accomplish this task. The C5 tree first two levels are illustrated on Fig. 3. This tree can be translated into a set of *propositional rules*, each rule corresponding to a leaf node. In the example in Fig. 3, the truncated tree (nodes 2 and 7 have descendants) resumes to four propositional rules, regarding nodes 2, 7, 21 and 22 — e.g., for node 2 the related rule is **If** *Grocery* ≤ 21203 and *Fresh products* ≤ 3996 **then** Group = Low Frequency − Low spending. In the tree all Retail customers are covered by exactly one rule condition. Sets of rules directly deriving from trees have a hierarchical structure which turns them complete and disjunctive.

There are, however, logical discriminant algorithms which provide non-hierarchical sets of rules. For example, the C5 algorithm provides the induction of sets of propositional rules starting its construction with a C5 tree.

C5 considers each subset of rules referred to each target class separately. Then it proceeds by simplifying the initial subset of rules trying to generalise rules by removing propositions from the rules' conditions, e.g., the rule **If** *Grocery* ≤ 21203 *and Fresh products* ≤ 3996 **then** *Group = Low Frequency-Low spending* may be simplified to **If** *Grocery* ≤ 21203 **then** *Group = Low Frequency-Low spending* (with some decrease in accuracy). In the end, C5 sorts the rules referred to each class or group by their precision (the ones that classify correctly higher percentages of individuals meeting the corresponding condition come first) and the groups are sorted according to a minimum of false positives criterion. As such, subsets that incorrectly classify the least number of cases are ranked in first place.

The C5 derived rules for the classification of frequency-spending groups are presented in Table 8. The corresponding classification table — Table 9 — depicts the performance on the training set: 83.1% of correctly classified cases. A cross-validation procedure, using 10-fold, provides a more realistic perspective of the rules'

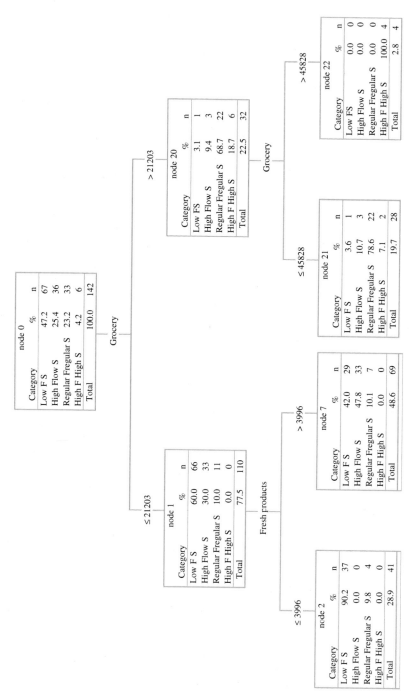

Fig. 3.   C5 tree for frequency-spending groups (first levels).

Table 8.   C5 rules for the frequency-spending groups.

Class	Rules	
1 — low frequency-low spending	Rule 1. 1: (110/44, lift 1.3) Grocery ≤ 21203 → class 1 [0.598]	
2 — high frequency-low spending	Rule 2.1: (8, lift 3.6) Fresh_prod > 19913 Grocery ≤ 12232 → class 2 [0.900] Rule 2.3: (69/36, lift 1.9) Fresh_prod > 3996 Grocery ≤ 21203 → class 2 [0.479]	Rule 2.2: (36/13, lift 2.5) Fresh_prod > 3996 Grocery ≤ 21203 Frozen > 1178 → class 2 [0.632]
3 — regular frequency-regular spending	Rule 3.1: (17/1, lift 3.9) Fresh_prod <= 11223 Milk_prod > 14069 Grocery > 12232 → class 3 [0.895] Rule 3.3: (28/6, lift 3.3) Grocery > 21203 Grocery ≤ 45828 →class 3 [0.767]	Rule 3.2: (3, lift 3.4) Fresh_prod > 19913 Grocery > 12232 Grocery ≤ 21203 → class 3 [0.800] Rule 3.4: (8/3, lift 2.6) Fresh_prod > 11223 Grocery > 12232 Grocery ≤ 21203 → class 3 [0.600]
4 — high frequency-high spending	Rule 4.1: (4, lift 19.7) → Grocery > 45828 → class 4 [0.833]	

Default class: 1 — low frequency-low spending

Table 9.   Classification table for C5 rules.

Classified as:				
Group	1	2	3	4
1	**56**	10	1	
2	6	**27**	3	
3	2		**31**	
4			2	**4**

performance (the dataset is too small to provide the constitution of a test set) — it yields 60.7% of correctly classified cases.

In order to build a set of rules, the first candidate rules C5 considers refer to the paths from the tree root to each leaf or terminal node. These initial rules are then be simplified by eliminating some attributes-propositions in the rules conditions, based on measures of classification accuracy.

Common indicators of rules' precision are:

— The ratio between the number of cases covered by the rule (n_{cov}) and the number of cases incorrectly classified by the rule (n_{inc}): n_{cov}/n_{inc}.

— Accuracy as estimated by the Laplace ratio: $\frac{n_{cov}-n_{inc}+1}{n_{cov}+2}$.

— The lift measure which is the result of dividing the rule's estimated accuracy by the relative frequency of the predicted class in the training set.

Table 8 presents (n_{cov}/n_{inc}, lift) after each rule identification and [accuracy] in the end. For example, Rule 1 on Table 8 covers 110 observations, incorrectly classifies 44 and, therefore, its accuracy is 0.598 and the lift is 1.3. Rule 4 only covers four cases but they are all correctly classified. In fact, it is the only rule that provides means for classification on class 4: The four high frequency-high spending customers are identified by the condition of spending more than 45,828 m.u. on Grocery per year.

Sets of propositional rules may not be disjunctive and/or complete. If an entity is classified differently by different rules, the rule having the higher precision wins the classification. If an entity is not classified by any rule, then a default class must be established by the algorithm — for the rules in Table 8 the default class is the '1 — low frequency-low spending'.

Following the general principles for evaluating LDM — see Sec. 4 — the evaluation of sets of rules should be based on an accuracy-complexity trade-off. For analysing rules complexity one takes into account not only the number of rules but also the average number of attributes per rule's condition.

5.2. *Other methods for rules*

Some algorithms are specifically designed for inducing rules without referring to any tree in the first place. In fact, in practical applications, trees can become very bushy and difficult to understand, whereas separate rules can be easily interpreted.

Michalski (1973) argued in favour of rule-based representations over tree structured representations, on the grounds of readability. He proposed building sets of rules without recurring to decision trees using the Algorithm Quasi-optimal, AQ. AQ uses a covering algorithm to build sets of rules, iteratively selecting the best rules that cover specific examples discarded in the next iterations. The AQ algorithm then randomly selects a new example or observation (seed) amongst the uncovered examples and a new iteration is generated.

The CN2 algorithm (Clark and Niblett, 1988) also proposed inducing rules from examples, inspired by the ideas from AQ and also from the ID3 — Iterative Dichotomiser algorithm which was used to generate decision trees. CN2 capitalised on the ID3 important idea of relaxing the requirement that the induced rules should be consistent with all training data. Clark and Niblett list some desirable characteristics their algorithm should have:

— Accurate classification, even in the presence of noise.
— Simple rules, for the sake of comprehension.
— Efficient rule generation — time should be linear in the size of the example set.

The CN2 implements a general-to-specific search extending the search space to rules that do not perform perfectly on the training set. Each iteration is dedicated to one class and the examples covered by each rule produced are excluded and the search proceeds. CN2 produces an ordered set of rules and tries each rule in sequence until it founds one that covers the example to be classified.

The CN2 rules' evaluation during the search process uses the entropy measure. Entropy can distinguish situations such as retail groups (1 — low frequency-low spending, 2 — high frequency-low spending, 3 — regular frequency-regular spending, 4 — high frequency-high spending) having corresponding frequencies (0.7, 0.1, 0.1, 0.1) from (0.7, 0.3, 0.0, 0.0). In fact, the entropy favours the later situation, while the percentage of correctly classified observations does not (it is equal for both). Therefore, when excluding observations from the modal class to proceed to the next iteration the first example yields (0, 0.33, 0.33, 0.33) while the later yields (0,1,0,0) which is clearly better for classification purposes.

To deal with **missing values,** CN2 recurs to imputation: average and mode are used for quantitative or qualitative attributes, respectively.

An alternative approach for the induction of propositional rules may be built within the framework of rough set theory introduced by Pawlak — see (Pawlak, 2002) for a review. Namely, the data system Learning from Examples based on Rough Sets (LERS) (Grzymala-Busse, 1997) may induce rules using several versions of the Learning from Examples Module (LEM) algorithm.

The LEM2 algorithm, in particular, is frequently used for rule induction. LEM2 explores the search space of attribute-value pairs. When inducing classification rules, the basic idea of LEM, is to use lower and upper approximation sets for observations in each target class, e.g., C. Rough sets enable to partition the objects considered, into elementary sets (states), the objects belonging to those elementary sets being indiscernible with regard to a given set of attributes A. The lower approximation $A_L(C)$ contains all objects, whose elementary set is completely contained in C (with regard to the set of attributes A). The upper approximation $A^U(C)$, in return, contains all those objects, for which at least one element of the associated elementary set is contained in C. Those objects are possible elements of C. The set C is called rough, if the lower approximation does not equal the upper approximation, otherwise C is called crisp [e.g., see (Decker and Kroll, 2006) for details and Marketing Research applications]. In general, LEM2 computes a local covering and then converts it into a rule set.

Consider, for example, the set of rules in Table 10, derived from a LEM2 based algorithm. They refer to the Horeca versus Retail classification problem based on annual spending in different product categories. In fact, spend amounts are previously discretised, using three to five intervals for coding — e.g., the first category of spending on fresh products refers to amounts lower than 2,438 m.u. Furthermore, there are some constraints considered when generating these rules: Rules with relative strength under 30% or

Table 10.   Rough sets based rules.

Class	Rules	
Horeca	Rule 1.1: (111, 108, 36.2%, 97.3%) Milk ≤ 1534 → class 1	Rule 1.2: (129, 114, 38.3%, 88.4%) Milk ∈] 1534, 3922] → class 1
	Rule 1.3: (171, 170, 57.1%, 99.4%) Grocery < 3204 → class 1	Rule 1.4: (276, 268, 89.9%, 97.1%) Detergents < 1716 → class 1
	Rule 1.5: (115, 98, 32.9%, 85.2%) Frozen > 1439 & Delicatessen ∈[222, 1333] → class 1	
Retail	Rule 2.1: (47,458, 31.7%, 95.7%) Grocery ∈]18622, 92780] → class 2	Rule 2.2: (95, 88, 61.9%, 92.6%) Detergents ∈]4508, 40827] → class 2

with minimum discrimination level under 80% are excluded (the analyst's prerogative). As a result few rules are produced but some cases remain uncovered.

Table 10 rules include information for support, strength, relative strength, discrimination level. For example, rule 1.1 covers 111 customers (support is 111), correctly classifies 108 customers (strength is 108), relative strength is $108/298 = 36.2\%$ (relative to the total of class members) and discrimination level is $108/111 = 97.3\%$ (the percentage of covered customers which are correctly classified).

The summary for accuracy in classification in Table 11 does not consider all 440 observations. In fact, the set of rules does not cover all training cases due to the learning constraints imposed on strength and discrimination level. In this specific case, a cross-validation 10-fold procedure is implemented using a stratified sampling procedure, aiming to replicate the classes' distribution in the original sample. Considering a default classification in the majority class this cross-classification result corresponds to a 71.6% percentage of correctly classified observations — the gain in parsimony implies a decrease in accuracy.

An alternative worth mentioning technique for generating sets of propositional rules is based on NN — (Setiono and Liu, 1996),

Table 11.   Classification table for Rough set based rules (results from cross-validation).

Class	Classified as	
	Horeca	Retail
Horeca	56	10
Retail	6	27

in an attempt to conjugate the NN predictive ability with the rules readability. First, the authors use the Backpropagation algorithm to estimate the weights of a multilayer perceptron neural network and implement network pruning. Afterwards, the hidden unit activation values are discretised and rules are extracted from the network using the referred discretised values.

6.   Predictors' Importance

In an attempt to differentiate actions to target the wholesale customers from the two different channels — Horeca and Retail — a tree is built generating discriminant views concerning diverse responses to possible marketing actions: The target classes are Horeca and Retail and the predictors are actions 1 to 11 in Sec. 2.

The CART algorithm is used with training-test sets of 50% of observations, pruning implemented and stopping rules allowing a parent node to have five observations and a child node to have a single observation while the tree can grow until five levels. Using this algorithm (similar attempts with similar results can be made with alternative techniques) the tree classification precision obtained hardly surpasses classification using the majority rule — the Huberty index values for training and test samples are 14.5% and 5%. While there is an evident difficulty in providing good classification results using the referred predictors, meaning that the customers from both channels tend to provide similar responses to most of the wholesale possible actions, additional useful insights can, however, be provided by the ranking of predictors (see Table 12).

Table 12 results suggest that, in what concerns Price and Quality actions, customers from both channels tend to have very similar

Table 12. Ranking of predictors.

Predictor	Importance (M)	Normalised importance (m)
Discount	0.026	100.0%
Assortment	0.017	62.6%
Package	0.009	35.3%
Layout	0.008	28.9%
Samples	0.007	28.1%
Highlights	0.007	27.1%
Diversity	0.007	24.8%
Selection	0.005	20.4%
Stocks	0.005	18.3%
Quality	0.004	15.5%
Price	0.004	13.3%

responses: The discriminant capacity of these two predictors is very low. On the opposite side of the ranking, one can observe that the Discount and Assortment actions tend to impact differently the two groups of customers. Note that the normalised importance values of predictors are obtained for all predictors and thus, different sets of independent variables may lead to alternative rankings. As a complement of the results provided in Table 12, a more detailed analysis of the attitudes towards the use of discount tickets and investment on assortment planning may bring added value to the wholesale.

Predictors' importance measures may, in general, offer useful insights to LDM results. Different measures of predictors importance can be considered. In what concerns the CART algorithm, the rationale behind this measure — $M(X_p)$ — is very simple: It is based on the diversity reduction provided by the X_p predictor's effective use as a node's branching predictor and its potential use as a surrogate branching variable (already defined for the purpose of handling missing values with CART).

The definition of the tree diversity decrease arising from a specific branching of node O, based on predictor X_p (and taking into account the tree nodes dimensions) is presented:

$$\Delta I(O|X_p; T) = \sum_{c=1}^{C} p(O_c)I(O_c) - p(O)I(O).$$

Then, the M measure is defined as:

$$M(X_p) = \sum_{O \in T} z^{pO} \Delta I(O|X_p; T),$$

where z^{pO} is a binary indicator of X_p being the actual branching predictor for node O or belonging to the set of surrogate predictors for the same node (unit value versus zero value when the predictor is neither the actual branching predictor nor a surrogate).

A normalised measure of importance — typically reported as a percentage — is then provided by:

$$m(X_p) = \frac{M(X_p)}{\max_p M(X_p)}.$$

Note that with $M(X_p)$ the degree of predictors importance is assessed globally, but resuming its local relevance in different regions of the input space corresponding to tree nodes. Furthermore, although an independent variable may not appear in the final tree as responsible for a branch, its measure of importance can be high, indicating that the potential contribution of this variable to the prediction may have been masked by others.

Diverse algorithms provide alternative measures of predictors' importance. The most common approach examines the relative importance of a given attribute for the classification of objects, by observing the changes in the quality of classification that originate from the exclusion of the same attribute.

7. Final Remarks

One of the most popular ways to acquire knowledge is based on learning from examples. LDM provide an accurate approach to do it, dealing with classification learning tasks, yielding results — propositional rules — that are particularly attractive due to their ease of interpretation.

The first LDM algorithms date back to the 1960s, namely the AID-Automatic Interaction Detector, (Morgan and Sonquist, 1963). Since then, they have been increasingly used in Management, particularly in the Marketing domain (Cardoso and Moutinho, 2003). Earlier versions of LDM algorithms have been successively improved and new algorithms continue to appear. The CART (*Breiman et al.*, 1984) or the C5 (Quinlan, 1993) algorithms, especially focused in this chapter, are amongst the most popular LDM (e.g., see (Wu *et al.*, 2008) list of Top 10 algorithms in data mining).

LDM algorithms typically employ divide-and-conquer or a set covering approach to induction. CART and C5 build trees using the divide-and-conquer approach. Specific algorithms to build sets of rules use a set covering approach: for example, CN2 (Clark and Niblett, 1988) or LEM2 (Decker and Kroll, 2006). The induction of trees is generally faster but the rules induction algorithms generate easier to interpret results. Therefore, a compromise is to use decision tree induction to build an initial tree and then derive rules from the tree, thus transforming an efficient representation into a clearer one (e.g., using the C5 rules approach).

Multiple LDM models enhance the accuracy of these predictive tools. Models ensembles may originate either from diverse subsamples drawn from an original dataset or from the consideration of various subsets of attributes. Furthermore, models of the same or of diverse types may be considered. In this context, the classification results may be provided by voting or by a combination of models (Friedman and Popescu, 2008).

The bagging strategy generates multiple models arising from multiple training sets — B random samples drawn with replacement from the original sample. In the end, the bagging prediction for an observation can consider the B votes for classification provided by the multiple models, the final classification being the one most often predicted by the different models. Note that some weighted combination of predictions (weighted vote taking into account the classifier accuracy) is also possible, and commonly used; an early example is (Breiman, 1996).

Boosting is an alternative learning strategy where the creation of multiple training sets is made conditionally: the formation of a new training set favours the integration of cases misclassified by a model based on a sample previously considered. In fact, this procedure assigns different weights to the training sample observations in successive learning iterations: in each iteration, the weights associated with incorrectly classified observations are increased and the weights associated with observations correctly classified decrease. In the end, predictions are based on the multiple models' votes; see (Friedman, 2001), for example.

Another source of randomisation relies on the selection of predictors — e.g., (Breiman, 2001) builds Random Forests — multiple trees — and introduces random selection of sets of predictors for branching.

LDM learning approaches also include incremental and constructive learning (Michalski *et al.*, 1986) and (Wnek and Michalski, 1994). When using incremental learning, the training set is progressively increased. Constructive learning generates new attributes in the process of learning and removes redundant or insignificant ones.

As commonly occurs in data mining, the final LDM results tend to rely heavily on the analyst's know-how and skills. Final results are generally influenced by the analyst's prior knowledge about the problem domain, but also by his selection of the algorithms' parameters (including stopping rules and pruning criteria) and also by his criteria for the evaluation of candidate solutions. Although Duin's note (Duin, 1996) rightly calls attention to this fact when comparing the performance of different classifiers, the means to overcome this issue may be controversial. In fact the use of a default parameterisation may introduce a significant handicap for techniques, such as LDM, that naturally rely on application related tuning.

When dealing with practical applications, multiple models should be definitely considered — whether individually or in combination — to perform the classification task at hand. When deciding upon the best solution, the domain expert's opinion must be taken into account. At this final stage, readability as well as predictive accuracy — the main advantages of LDM - will be fully appreciated by decision makers.

References

Bennett, KP and C Campbell (2000). Support vector machines: Hype or Hallelujah? *SIGKDD Explorations*, 2, 1–13.

Breiman, L (1996). Bagging Predictors. *Machine Learning*, 24, 123–140.

Breiman, L, JH Friedman, RA Olsen and C Stone (1984). *Classification and Regression Trees*. Pacific Grove: Wadsworth.

Cardoso, MG and L Moutinho (2003). A logical type discriminant model for profiling a segment structure. *Journal of Targeting, Measurement and Analysis for Marketing*, 12, 27–41.

Clark, P and T Niblett (1988). The Cn2 Induction Algorithm. *Machine Learning Journal*, 3, 261–283.

Decker, R and F Kroll (2006). Classification in marketing research by means of Lem2-generated rules. In *30th Annual Conf. Gesellschaft fur Klassifikation. Advances in Data Analysis–Studies in Classification, Data Analysis and Knowledge Organization*, pp. 425–432. Berlin: Springer.

Duin, RPW (1996). A note on comparing classifiers. *Pattern Recognition Letters*, 17, 529–536.

Friedman, JH and BE Popescu (2008). Predictive learning via rule ensembles. *The Annals of Applied Statistics*, 2, 916–954.

Friedman, JH (2001). Greedy function approximation: A gradient boosting machine. *Annals of Statistics*, 29, 1189–1232.

Grzymala-Busse, J (1997). A new version of the rule induction system lers. *Fundamenta Informaticae*, 31, 27–397.

Hair, JF, W Black, BJ Babin and RE Anderson (2005). *Multivariate Data Analysis — A Global Perspective*, 6th edn. New Jersey: Prentice Hall.

Hastie, T, R Tibshirani and JH Friedman (2001). *The Elements of Statistical Learning — Data Mining, Inference and Prediction*. New York: Springer-Verlag.

Michalski, RS (1973). Aqval/1 — computer implementation of a variable-valued logic system Vl1 and examples of its application to pattern recognition. In *Proc. First Int. Joint Conf. Pattern Recognition*, pp. 3–17. Washington, DC: College of Health and Human Services.

Michalski, RS, I Mozetic, J Hong and N Lavrac (1986). The multipurpose incremental learning system Aq15 and its testing application to three medical domains. In *AAAI-86 Proc.*, pp. 1041–1045. AAAI.

Morgan, JN and JA Sonquist (1963). Problems in the analysis of survey data and a proposal. *Journal of the American Statistical Association*, 58, 415–435.

Pawlak, Z (2002). Rough sets and intelligent data analysis. *Information Sciences*, 147, 1–12.

Quinlan, J (1993). *C4.5: Programs for Machine Learning*. California: Morgan Kaufmann Publishers.

Setiono, R and H Liu (1996). Symbolic representation of neural networks. *IEEE Computer*, 29, 71–77.

Wnek, J and RS Michalski (1994). Hypothesis-driven constructive induction. Aq17-Hci: A Method and Experiments. *Machine Learning*, 14, 139–168.

Wu, X, *et al.* (2008). Top 10 algorithms in data mining. *Knowledge Information Systems*, 14, 1–37.

Chapter 9

META-HEURISTICS IN MARKETING

Stephen Hurley
Cardiff University

Luiz Moutinho
University of Glasgow

In this chapter, we consider the application of mathematical optimisation algorithms to the field of marketing management. We describe the background and fundamentals of three techniques, simulated annealing, tabu search and genetic algorithms and give, following a literature review, worked examples of relevant marketing areas to whcih each of these techniques can be applied, in particular sales territory alignment, segmentation and site location analysis. These indicate how each optimisation technique can be applied beneficially to market management optimisation problems.

Keywords: Optimisation; market management; sales territory alignment; site location; segmentation.

1. Introduction

During the 1980s general interest in so-called meta-heuristic methods dramatically increased. This was due to their apparent widespread success in solving a variety of difficult problems in a wide range of disciplines. This chapter will describe three such meta-heuristics: *evolutionary algorithms* (EA), *simulated annealing* (SA) and *tabu search* (TS). Their development for discrete optimisation problems that arise in marketing will be discussed.

Meta-heuristics are a class of approximate methods that are designed to solve difficult combinatorial optimization problems.

They provide general frameworks that allow for the creation of new hybrids by combining different concepts derived from classical heuristics, artificial intelligence, statistical mechanics, biological systems, evolution and genetics. In particular, meta-heuristics use one or more of these concepts to drive some subordinate heuristic, such as local neighbourhood search.

Whereas specialised heuristics or optimisation procedures can usually only be applied to a narrow band of problems, meta-heuristics can be applied to a wide variety of problems. However, this robustness comes at the sacrifice of domain specificity. For example, if the function to be minimised is a quadratic bowl then Newton–Gauss optimisation will generate the optimal point in one iteration from any starting location; it would be unlikely that meta-heuristics could compete in this instance. On the other hand, Newton–Gauss will generally fail to find the optima of multimodal surfaces because it relies heavily on gradient and higher order statistics of the function to be optimised. Meta-heuristics would generally have a much more satisfactory performance on such problems.

2.   General Search Principles

Discrete optimisation problems can generally be modelled as a quadruple

$$(Z, D, C, g),$$

where

- $Z = \{t_1, t_2, \ldots, t_N\}$ is a finite set of objects to which some value needs to be assigned.
- $D = \{D_{t_1}, D_{t_2}, \ldots, D_{t_N}\}$ is a finite set of value domains for the objects in Z. Often each object has the same domain of possible values.
- $C = \{c_1, c_2, \ldots, c_m\}$ is a finite set of constraints on a subset of the objects in Z.
- g is the objective function, which associates with every possible assignment (solution) a numerical value, usually corresponding to some profit or utility measure.

Two approaches can be taken to solve this problem: Either design a specialised scheme, i.e., one that is specific to the problem instance, or adapt some general existing scheme. If the latter approach is used then it is convenient to consider the following three main ways of searching the combinatorial spaces involved (Costa *et al.*, 1995).

2.1. Constructive methods

This approach generates feasible solutions (assignments) by starting from an empty solution $s(0)$ and gradually assigning an object f_i to the current partial solution $s(i - 1) = (f_1, f_2, \ldots, f_{i-1})$. There is a progressive reduction in the size of the search space X_i at each iteration, i.e. $X_N \subset X_{N-1} \cdots X_1 \subset X$; see Fig. 1. The greedy method is an example of a constructive method. It simply takes the best choice at every iteration. Sequential assignment algorithms are greedy constructive methods which have been widely used in many discrete optimisation problems. They consist of three main steps or *modules*. First, the objects are listed in some specified order and the first object is assigned to the first available value. Second, the next object to be assigned is selected (which may differ in some way from that implied by the initial ordering). Finally, the selected object is assigned some value from the (ordered) domain of values. Several options are available for the ordering used in each module, and therefore by

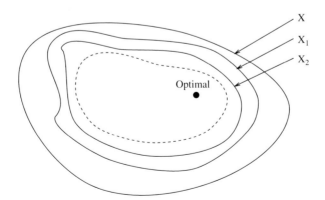

Fig. 1. Constructive methods process.

using different options in each module a large number of different sequential methods can be obtained.

The advantage of constructive methods is that they usually produce solutions quickly, but often as the expense of poor solution quality.

2.2. Improvement methods

Improvement methods start with some initial, not necessarily feasible, solution s, which could be randomly generated or obtained from a constructive method, and involve selecting a neighbouring solution from the neighbourhood $N(s)$ of s. The neighbourhood $N(s)$ is the set of candidate solutions that can be reached from s by a simple operation σ. For example, σ could be the removal of an object from, or the addition of an object to, a solution. Simple local neighbourhood search, outlined in Fig. 2, illustrates the overall structure of the improvement approach. Figure 3 illustrates the

---

generate starting solution $s \in X$
repeat
    select $s' \in N(s)$ such that $g(s')$ is minimal
    if $g(s) > g(s')$ **then** $s \leftarrow s'$
until $g(s) < g(s')$

Fig. 2.   Local neighbourhood search algorithm.

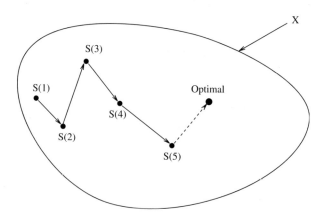

Fig. 3.   Improvement methods process.

operation of improvement methods. The starting point is $s(1)$, which is altered by some simple operation to give $s(2)$, i.e., $s(2)$ is within the neighbourhood of $s(1)$. In turn, $s(2)$ is then altered to give $s(3)$, which is within the neighbourhood of $s(2)$. This process is repeated until some termination criterion is satisfied.

This local search procedure will almost certainly terminate in a local minimum. Therefore, additional features are added in an endeavour to make further progress, giving rise to other improvement methods, such as simulated annealing and tabu search. The main difference between them is how they select the neighbouring solution at each iteration.

2.3. Evolutionary methods

Both the constructive and improvement approaches operate by considering one point in the search space (partial or complete). However, it seems reasonable to assume that performance could be improved by considering several such points in the search space, i.e., having a *population* of solutions, which can then be altered individually through *mutation* or in pairs through *recombination* or *crossover*. Each iteration or *generation* of an evolutionary algorithm usually involves both mutation and recombination. This is shown in Fig. 4, where the initial population consists of three candidate solutions

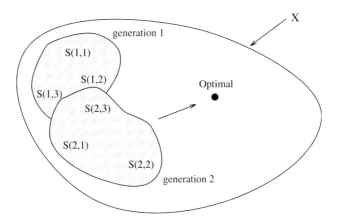

Fig. 4.   Evolutionary methods process.

(individuals), $s(1,1)$, $s(1,2)$, and $s(1,3)$. A new set of three individuals, $s(2,1)$, $s(2,2)$ and $s(2,3)$ is generated by mutating single individuals and by recombining certain pairs of individuals satisfying various conditions. This process proceeds until some termination criterion is reached. Such methods have the intuitive advantage that the search space is covered more widely at each iteration than in constructive or improvement methods. However, this can also be a drawback in that it often requires extra computational effort. Several different methods exist within this approach, for example, *evolutionary algorithms* (Back, 1996), *scatter search* (Glover, 1994) and *ant systems* (Costa and Hertz, 1997).

3. Overview of meta-heuristics

This section contains a brief overview of three types of meta-heuristics: evolutionary algorithms, simulated annealing, and tabu search. Comprehensive details of the methods can be found in Reeves (1995) and Aarts and Lenstra (1997). For a comprehensive account of application areas readers can consult Dell'Amico *et al.* (1997). Readers interested in the general principles of neural networks, which are not discussed here, can see Fausett (1994).

3.1. Evolutionary algorithms

Evolutionary algorithms are probabilistic optimisation algorithms based on the process of natural evolution and population genetics. They rely on the collective learning process within a population of individuals, where each individual represents a point in the search space, i.e., a candidate solution. After an initial starting population is set up (either randomly or using domain-specific information), the population evolves towards better regions of the search space by means of the selection, mutation and recombination (or crossover) processes. The optimisation problem under consideration gives a measure of an individual's quality, i.e., its fitness, and the selection process is biased towards individuals of higher fitness surviving for the next generation of the evolution process. Recombination exchanges information between parent individuals and mutation introduces new information into the population.

There are three main types of evolutionary algorithms following these principles: *genetic algorithms* (Holland, 1975; Goldberg, 1989), *evolutionary programming* (Fogel *et al.*, 1966; Fogel, 1991, 1992) and *evolution strategies* (Rechenberg, 1973; Schwefel, 1977, 1981). An excellent account of all three types can be found in Back (1996). The main differences between them are in:

- The representation used for individuals;
- The genetic operators used, i.e., recombination and/or mutation;
- The selection and reproduction scheme.

Evolutionary algorithms have the basic structure shown in Fig. 5 (with slight variations between types).

3.1.1. *Representation or encoding mechanism*

It is assumed that a candidate solution to a problem may be represented by a finite set of parameters. These parameters or *genes* are then joined to make a finite string or *chromosome*. The encoding mechanism depends on the nature of the problem variables. For example, when solving network flow problems the variables could assume continuous values, while the variables in a 0–1 decision problem may assume binary values. Evolution strategies are particularly suited to real-valued representations.

$k \leftarrow 0$
initialise starting population $P(k)$
evaluate fitness of $P(k)$
while *not finished*
    select individuals from $P(k)$ to generate offspring $P'(k)$
    generate offspring using recombination and/or mutation
    evaluate fitness of $P'(k)$
    select $P(k + 1)$ from $P(k) \cup P'(k)$
    $k \leftarrow k + 1$
end while

Fig. 5.   Genetic algorithm.

3.1.2.   The fitness function

A fitness function must be devised for each problem to be solved. Given a particular individual, the fitness function provides a single numerical value, which is a measure of the ability of the individual to solve the problem under consideration. For many problems, e.g., function optimisation, it is obvious what this function should be, but for other problems things are not so clear, particularly in multi-criteria optimisation problems.

3.1.3.   Selection and reproduction

To generate offspring, i.e., new candidate solutions, individuals are selected from the population and recombined. Parents are usually selected randomly, but biased towards fitter individuals. Good individuals will probably be selected several times, poor ones may not be selected at all.

Once individuals are selected for reproduction, recombination takes place. This usually involves *crossover* and/or *mutation*.

Crossover involves taking two selected individuals and combining them in some way to produce one or two new offspring. In the standard genetic algorithm, so-called one-point crossover is performed. A position in the chromosome is randomly determined as the crossover point, and an offspring is generated by concatenating the left substring of one parent with the right substring of the other parent. The second offspring is generated by concatenating the substrings not used to generate the first offspring. There are numerous extensions of this crossover operator, e.g., two-point crossover and uniform crossover, and also more general recombination operators.

Whereas crossover involves using two individuals to produce new offspring, mutation is applied to single individuals, usually after crossover has taken place. Mutation in genetic algorithms was originally introduced as a background operator of little importance (Holland, 1975). It works by changing gene values, e.g., by inverting bits in the case of binary alphabets, but with a very low probability, perhaps of the order of one altered gene in a thousand. Recent studies (Back, 1993) have shown that much larger mutation rates, decreasing as the algorithm progresses, are often beneficial in helping the convergence, reliability and speed of a genetic algorithm. Many other mutation operators, often problem specific, can also be defined.

3.2. Tabu search

Tabu search is an example of an improvement method as outlined in Sec. 2.2 It was first suggested by Glover (1977) and since then has become increasingly used. It has been successfully applied to obtain optimal or suboptimal solutions to such problems as scheduling, timetabling, travelling salesman and layout optimisation.

The basic idea, described by Glover *et al.* (1993), is to explore the search space of all feasible solutions by a sequence of *moves*. A move from one solution to another is the best available. However, to escape from locally optimal but not globally optimal solutions and to prevent cycling, at any iteration some moves are classified as forbidden or *tabu* (or *taboo*). Tabu moves are based on the *short-term* and *long-term* history of the sequence of moves. A simple implementation, for example, might classify a move as tabu if the reverse move has been made recently or frequently. Sometimes, when it is deemed favourable, a tabu move can be overridden. Such *aspiration criteria* might include the case where forgetting that a move is tabu leads to the best solution so far.

Formally, suppose g is the objective function on a search space X and it is required to find an $s \in X$ such that $g(s)$ has minimal value. For combinatorially hard (NP-complete) problems, this requirement is relaxed to finding an $s \in X$ such that $g(s)$ is close to the minimal value (a *suboptimal* value). This is because all known algorithms for determining the minimal solution require time which is exponential in the problem size. Suboptimal solutions may be found by halting when some threshold for an acceptable solution has been achieved or when a certain number of iterations has been completed.

A characterisation of the search space X for which tabu search can be applied is that there is a set of k moves $M = \{m_1, \dots, m_k\}$, the application of which to a feasible solution $s \in X$ leads to k (usually distinct) solutions $M(s) = \{m_1(s), \dots, m_k(s)\}$. The subset $N(s) \subseteq M(s)$ of *feasible* solutions is known as the neighbourhood of s.

The method commences with a (possibly random) solution $s_0 \in X$ and constructs a sequence of solutions $s_0, s_1, \ldots, s_n \in X$. At each iteration, s_{j+1} is selected from the neighbourhood $N(s_j)$. The process of selection is first to determine the tabu set $T(s_j) \subseteq N(s_j)$ of neighbours of s_j and the aspirant set $A(s_j) \subseteq T(s_j)$ of tabu neighbours. Then s_{j+1} is the neighbour of s_j which is either an aspirant or not tabu and for which $g(s_{j+1})$ is minimal; that is, $g(s_{j+1}) \leq g(s')$ for all $s' \in (N(s_j) \backslash T(s_j)) \cup A(s_j)$.

Convergence to a local minimum can be avoided since it is possible that $g(s_{j+1}) > g(s_j)$. The conditions for a neighbour to be tabu or an aspirant will be problem-specific. For example, a move m_r may be tabu if it leads to a solution which has already been considered in the last q iterations (*recency* or short-term condition) or which has been repeated many times before (*frequency* or long-term condition). A tabu move satisfies the aspiration criteria if, for example, the value of $g(s')$ for some $s' \in T(s_j)$ satisfies $g(s') < g(s_i)$ for all $0 \leq i \leq j$.

Example 1. Suppose for an positive integer B the search space is the discrete three-dimensional grid of B^3 vectors given by:

$$X = \{(u, v, w) : 0 \leq u, v, w < B\},$$

and the objective function is $g(u, v, w)$. Consider the set of six moves which increment or decrement a single coordinate by one unit. Thus:

$$M = \{m_1^+, m_1^-, m_2^+, m_2^-, m_3^+, m_3^-\},$$

with, for example, $m_1^+(u, v, w) = (u + 1, v, w)$. All moves are feasible moves except where s lies on the boundary of the grid. The inverse of move $m_j^\pm$ is $m_j^\mp$, for $1 \leq j \leq 3$.

A move is considered tabu if the inverse move has been made in the last q (e.g., three) iterations or accounts for a fraction of more than p (e.g., 25%) of all previous moves. The former condition prevents short-term cycling and the latter long-term cycling. Both allow the search to descend from a local minimum. The aspiration criterion will be that a tabu move will be overridden if the solution becomes a new minimum over the history of the search.

Suppose $B = 7$, the initial solution is $s_0 = (3, 5, 2)$ and there have been 10 iterations with moves:

$$m_2^+, m_3^+, m_1^-, m_2^+, m_1^-, m_3^-, m_1^-, m_2^-, m_2^-, m_3^+.$$

Successive solutions $s_1, \ldots, s_{10}$ are therefore:

$$(3, 6, 2), \quad (3, 6, 3), \quad (2, 6, 3), \quad (2, 7, 3), \quad (1, 7, 3)$$
$$(1, 7, 2), \quad (0, 7, 2), \quad (0, 6, 2), \quad (0, 5, 2), \quad (0, 5, 3).$$

The following table analyses the possible candidate solutions s', one of which will be chosen as s_{11}:

Move	m_1^+	m_1^-	m_2^+	m_2^-	m_3^+	m_3^-
s'	(1 ,5, 3)	(−1,5,3)	(0,6,3)	(0,4,3)	(0,5,4)	(0,5,2)
Comment		not feasible	tabu			tabu

Using the shorthand $g_i^\pm(s)$ for $g(m_i^\pm(s))$, the next move will correspond to the minimum of $g_1^+(s_{10})$, $g_2^\pm(s_{10})$ and $g_3^+(s_{10})$. Thus if $g_2^-(s_{10})$ is the minimum then $s_{11} = (0, 4, 3)$. However, if we also have $g_3^-(s_{10}) < g_2^-(s_{10})$ and $g_3^-(s_{10}) < g(s_j)$ for $j = 0, 1, \ldots, 10$, then the aspiration criterion forces the method to forget that move m_3^- is tabu and so $s_{11} = (0, 5, 2)$.

Example 2. In this example, the search space X is the set of all rooted binary trees with n terminal nodes (and therefore $n - 1$ internal nodes). The objective function g associates with each tree a real value and might, for example, involve the height of and the weighted distance between terminal nodes. The search commences with an initial tree whose nodes are labelled arbitrarily from 1 to $2n - 1$. A move m_{ij} consists of taking two nodes i and j and swapping the subtrees rooted at these nodes. Such a swap is valid only if i is not an ancestor or descendant of j. Figure 6 illustrates the move m_{26} applied to a tree with five terminal nodes. Note that the set of terminal nodes is left invariant by such a move.

In this example, a move m_{ij} is tabu if i or j has been one of the nodes involved in a recent move. This representation allows the exploration of the whole search space from any initial tree. It has

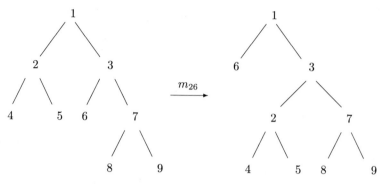

Fig. 6.   Tabu search move example.

similarities with the successful implementation of tabu search for the travelling salesman problem in Glover (1991).

To implement a simple tabu search procedure for a particular application generally involves making the following steps:

Step 1: Define a *representation* for the problem, so fixing the structure of each point in the search space X, i.e., s in the above description.

Step 2: Define an *objective function* $g(s)$, which is to be maximised or minimised.

Step 3: Define a *neighbourhood structure*, $N(s)$.

Step 4: Define the *tabu rules* (the short- and long-term memory). These can be the simple recency or frequency rules previously mentioned or much more complicated rules such as those in Reeves (1995). The choice of rules defines the set $T(s)$.

Step 5: Define the *aspiration criteria*. As for the tabu rules, they can be simple as in example 1 or more complex (again see Reeves (1995)). The choice of aspiration criteria defines the set $A(s)$.

Tabu search is a relatively simple technique. It can be applied in the basic form described above to a wide variety of problems. However, considerably improved results can be obtained by developing effective and efficient rules tailored to specific problems. Also, an apparent disadvantage of the method is that its efficiency can be dependent on fine-tuning a large collection of parameters. With tabu search, complexity is not only present in the application but also in the technique itself.

3.3. Simulated annealing

Simulated annealing (SA) is a stochastic computational technique derived from statistical mechanics for finding solutions of nearly minimum cost to large optimisation problems. It is an example of an improvement method, discussed in Sec. 2.2, and can handle objective functions with many local minima. A procedure for solving optimisation problems of this type should sample the search space in such a way that has a high probability of finding optimal or near-optimal solutions in a reasonable time. Over the past 15 years or so, simulated annealing has shown itself to be a technique which meets these requirements for a wide range of problems.

The method itself has a direct analogy with thermodynamics, specifically with the way that liquids freeze and crystallise, or metals cool and anneal. At high temperatures, the molecules of a liquid move freely with respect to one another. If the liquid is cooled slowly, thermal mobility is restricted. The atoms are often able to align themselves and form a pure crystal that is completely regular. This crystal is the state of minimum energy for the system, which would correspond to the optimal solution in a mathematical optimisation problem. However, if a liquid metal is cooled quickly (quenched), it does not reach a minimum energy state but instead a somewhat higher state corresponding, in the mathematical sense, to a suboptimal solution.

In order to make use of this analogy, one must first provide the following elements:

- A description of possible system *configurations*, i.e., some way of representing a solution to the problem; usually each configuration s may be written $s = (x_1, x_2, \ldots, x_N)$ for some variables x_i.
- A *generator* of random changes to a configuration; these changes are typically solutions in the neighbourhood of the current configuration, for example, a change in one of the parameters x_i.
- An *objective* or cost function $E(s)$ (the analogue of energy), whose minimisation is the goal of the procedure.

- A *control parameter* T (the analogue of temperature) and an *annealing schedule*, which indicates how T is lowered from high values to low values, e.g., after how many random changes in configuration is T reduced and by how much?

Metropolis *et al.* (1953) first introduced these principles into numerical minimisation. A succession of moves through neighbouring configurations is assumed to change its energy at each stage from E_{old} to energy E_{new} with probability:

$$P_{(E_{old}, E_{new})} = \begin{cases} e^{-(E_{new} - E_{old})/kT} & \text{if } E_{new} > E_{old} \\ 1 & \text{otherwise,} \end{cases}$$

where k is a constant known as the Boltzmann constant. The connection with the Boltzmann distribution in statistical mechanics should be apparent. If $E_{new} < E_{old}$, then the new configuration has a lower energy than the old one and such a move is always accepted. If $E_{new} > E_{old}$, then the new configuration has a higher energy than the old one; such a move may still be accepted, but with a reduced probability, thus helping the system jump out of local minima. This general scheme, of always taking a downhill step while sometimes taking a uphill step is known as the Metropolis Algorithm.

The simulated annealing procedure in Kirkpatrick *et al.* (1983) uses the Metropolis Algorithm but *varies* the temperature parameter T from a high value (the 'melting point', where most new configurations are accepted) to a low value (the 'freezing point', where no new configurations are accepted). The full SA procedure for minimisation is then as shown in Fig. 7 (for maximisation set $E = -E$).

The algorithm can be viewed as a Markov chain on the space of all configurations; N_c is the number of steps taken at each temperature T, and is chosen with the aim of reaching a state of minimum energy before moving to a lower temperature.

4. Using meta-heuristics for marketing problems

In this section, we will discuss three applications areas for the meta-heuristics described above.

```
initialise T
generate random configuration s_old
calculate E_old = E(s_old)
while T > T_min
    for u = 1 to N_c
        generate new configuration s_new
        calculate E_new = E(s_new)
        take r uniformly at random from [0,1]
        if E_new < E_old or r < P(E_old, E_new)
            s_old ← s_new
            E_old ← E_new
        end if
    end for
    reduce T (e.g., T ← 0.9T)
end while
```

Fig. 7.   Simulated annealing algorithm.

4.1.   Site location analysis using genetic algorithms

Site asquisition and retail outlet location is an important consideration in the enhancement of corporate profitability. For many types of markets, a multi-unit company will find that individual optimum locations do not necessarily result in a generally optimum network in a market area (Achabal *et al.*, 1982). In the situation where a large number of sites already exist, say 50 or more, and there is a choice of several proposed sites, the problem of finding the optimal network is difficult. We will consider the following problem: Find and identify how many of the proposed sites to use, to augment and improve the existing network in terms of profitabilty, attractiveness to potential customers or any other suitable metric. The existing network is assumed to be dynamic, i.e., existing sites may be removed from the network if this gives an improvement in overall network performance.

4.1.1.   *Chromosome representation*

Each chromosome represents a possible network consisting of existing sites and possible new sites. If there are S_e existing sites and S_p possible new sites, the length of the chromosome will be $S_e + S_p$.

The individual genes within each chromosome are represented by a binary alphabet, zero indicates a particular site is not used in the network, whereas a one would indicate that a site is used. The position within the chromosome is important as this indicates the site under consideration, e.g., bit position 4 (from left to right) represents site 4. To illustrate, if we have four existing outlets and three possible new sites then the chromosome {1111010} represents a network where sites 1, 2, 3, and 4 are used (the existing network) and site 6 is used; sites 5 and 7 remain unused.

4.1.2. Fitness function

The most important problem dependent aspect in applying genetic algorithms is finding a suitable function to determine the fitness or goodness of a chromosome in the genetic population. One possible fitness function involves a slight modification of the Penny and Broom spatial interaction model (Penny and Broom, 1988), and is given by:

$$\sum_i \sum_j EXP_{ij} = \sum_i \sum_j \left[\beta_0 \left(\sum_k E_k H_{ik} \right) \cdot \frac{W_j e^{-\beta_1 T_{ij}}}{\sum_m W_m e^{-\beta_1 T_{im}}} \right], \quad (1)$$

where, EXP_{ij} is the expenditure from zone i to site j; β_0 and β_1 are parameters; E_k is the mean expenditure on the product/service category by household category k; H_{ik} is the number of households of category k located in zone i; W_j is a subjective measure of attraction of the proposed store/outlet; T_{ij} is the travel time from zone i to the site at j; W_m is a subjective measure of attractiveness of competitor m or outlets from the same company (i.e., inter-company competition); T_{im} is the travel time from zone i to competitor m.

The genetic algorithm will then attempt to maximise this expression, i.e., find a network of sites which maximises customer expenditure.

4.1.3. Genetic operators

Each chromosome is represented by a binary string with an associated fitness. If two chromosomes are selected for reproduction by the selection procedure, the standard crossover operators (Goldberg, 1989) can be used to generate offspring. For example, if the two chromosomes:

$$1\ 1\ 1\ 1\ 0\ 1\ 0 \quad \text{(sites 5 and 7 unused)}$$
$$1\ 0\ 1\ 1\ 0\ 0\ 1 \quad \text{(sites 2, 5 and 6 unused)}$$

are selected for reproduction and one-point crossover is used (e.g., at position 3) then the following offspring are produced:

$$1\ 1\ 1\ 1\ 0\ 0\ 1 \quad \text{(sites 5 and 6 unused)}$$
$$1\ 0\ 1\ 1\ 0\ 1\ 0 \quad \text{(sites 2, 5, and 7 unused)}$$

Similarly, the standard mutation operator can be used, i.e., a bit is changed with a low probability e.g., 0.001.

4.1.4. *Simple illustration*

Given four existing sites and three possible new sites, consider a population of five chromosomes, consisting of the following:

$$
\begin{array}{lll}
C_1 & 1\ 0\ 1\ 1\ 0\ 1\ 1 & \text{fitness} = 1{,}562 \\
C_2 & 0\ 1\ 1\ 1\ 1\ 1\ 0 & \text{fitness} = 3{,}511 \\
C_3 & 1\ 0\ 1\ 0\ 0\ 0\ 1 & \text{fitness} = 4{,}756 \\
C_4 & 1\ 1\ 1\ 1\ 0\ 1\ 1 & \text{fitness} = 1{,}929 \\
C_5 & 1\ 0\ 0\ 1\ 1\ 1\ 1 & \text{fitness} = 756
\end{array}
$$

In this illustration the fitness values for each chromosome were randomly selected, whereas in actual site analysis using genetic algorithms the fitness would be calculated using Eq. (1).

Chromosomes C_2 and C_3 are the most fit so they would be more likely to be selected for crossover and mutation. If one-point crossover was used at a randomly choosen position, say position 2, the following offspring would be produced:

$$
\begin{array}{ll}
C_2 & 1\ 0\ 1\ 1\ 1\ 1\ 0, \\
C_3 & 0\ 1\ 1\ 0\ 0\ 0\ 1.
\end{array}
$$

If their respective fitness values, calculated using Eq. (1), were 4,212 and 5,681, then we have found a network of sites, represented by chromosome C_3, which is theoretically better than any network in the previous population. Full details of using genetic algorithms for site location problems, for example in tourism marketing, can be found in Hurley *et al.* (1998).

The advantages in using GA's are (1) they find an optimal or near-optimal site location in reasonable time; (2) the 'goodness' of alternative site networks can be easily accessed; (3) poor networks can be identified and, therefore, avoided and (4) it is relatively easy to solve different formulations of the site location problem. However, the limitation in using GA's is that the 'goodness' of any network is relative to the fitness function used.

4.2. Application of tabu search to segmentation

Ramaswamy and DeSarbo (1990) have proposed a new methodology for deriving hierarchical product-market structures from disaggregate purchase data. A hierarchical product-market tree was estimated from scanner panel purchase data in a maximum likelihood framework. The derived product-market representation portrays both products and market segments as terminal modes in a hierarchical tree where the 'closer' a product is to a particular segment the higher it revealed preference for that product. The hierarchical representation of products and segments as well as the composition of the market segments are derived simultaneously. Their new methodology called stochastic ultrametric purchase tree (SCULP-TRE) has been developed by formulating a stochastic choice model.

Given only scanner panel purchase data, we also consider the problem of deriving product-market structures by determining a hierarchical tree representation where terminal nodes are used for both products and segments. A segment's preference for a product is inversely related to d_{sj} the length of the unique path between the terminal nodes corresponding to the segment s and product j.

The raw data are the values x_{hj} which represent the number of choices of product j for household h. The objective is to determine the tree and the values of a_s, which are the proportion of households in the sample belonging to the segment s, by maximising the expression:

$$L(\mathbf{a}, \mathbf{x}, \mathbf{d}) = \prod_h \sum_s a_s \prod_j \left(\frac{\exp{(-d_{sj})}}{\sum_k \exp{(-d_{sk})}} \right)^{x_{hj}},$$

which measures the likelihood of the sample having this product-market structure.

In the application of tabu search to this multi-modal optimisation problem, a move will be either to change the vector **a** or to change the tree. These moves and the notion of tabu will be along the lines of the example in a previous section.

Thus, a solution of the search space t is represented by (1) a set of integer values y_s, one for each segment, with $\sum_s y_s = N$, for some fixed N, and (2) a binary tree each of whose terminal nodes corresponds either to a segment or a product. Such a solution is evaluated from the expression $L(\mathbf{a}, \mathbf{x}, \mathbf{d})$ by calculating the values of $a_s = y_s/N$ and d_{sj}, the length of the path between the terminal nodes representing the segment s and the product j. A move is either (1) to increment y_u and decrement y_v for two segments u, v, or (2) to swap the subtrees whose roots are at nodes i, j. Precise definition of a tabu move will be found by experimentation.

One of the advantages of this method of solving the optimisation problem is that the tabu search acts directly on the hierarchical tree rather than, as in Ramaswamy and DeSarbo (1990), the distances which are constrained to correspond to a tree. A second advantage is that the optimisation of the vector **a** and the tree are considered in parallel rather than as individual optimisation problems to be solved sequentially for each iteration. Full details of the background, modelling and use of tabu search in brand value segmentation is contained in Hurley and Mountinho (1998).

4.3. Sales territory design using simulated annealing

Here we indicate how the technique of simulated annealing can be applied to the problem of designing the territories for an organisation which wishes to deploy a sales force over a large geographical area. In the first subsection, we determine a mathematical model of the problem. This has been chosen to be simplistic for the purpose of descriptive ease yet it encorporates many of the criteria relevant to the design. In the second subsection, we descibe how such a model may be optimised.

We shall assume that the geographical area is presented as a number of small sales coverage units (SCUs) and that, for each unit, relevant statistical or factual information is available. For example, the SCUs might be zip codes (USA) or postcodes (UK) and the information might consist of volume of sales in a previous time period, the average time in contact with each customer per call, the contiguous SCUs and the travelling time between contiguous SCUs. The required properties of the territory design are: (1) **contiguity:** The SCUs in a territory form a connected cohesive block; (2) **equality of workload:** Each territory has equal sales workload; (3) **equality of sales potential:** Each territory has equal sales potential.

The problem of dividing the region into territories is seen as assigning each SCU to a single territory in such a way that, first, the constraints of contiguity, equal workload, equal sales potential are satisfied and, second, that the profit of the organisation is maximised. This model differs from those of Zoltners and Sinha (1983) and others by adding explicitly the maximisation of profit and allows extensions to models where profit is measured by a more complex formula. We have also added the constraint of equal sales potential as a desirable feature to ensure, for example, that commission potential is balanced among the SCUs. In the notion of Howick and Pidd (1990), the model we have chosen can be classified as multiple criteria using a travel measure and centre-seeking alignment.

We will suppose that the size of the sales force (i.e., the number of territories required) is fixed and also that the required number of calls to each customer in a time period has been predetermined. A package based on the algorithm to solve the sales territory design could be used on a 'what, if . . .' basis if these variables are unknown quantities.

4.3.1. *Information about a single SCU*

In a single SCU the sales force will devote its time between maintaining existing customers, prospecting for new customers and administering the SCU. We shall assume that the administration time is subsumed in the variables representing the contact time with the customer. For customer c, the workload, w_c, measured in hours, will depend on n_c, the number of calls, on t_c, the average time spent in contact with the customer and on s_c the average time spent in travelling to make a call:

$$w_c = n_c t_c + n_c s_c.$$

Summing over all customers in the SCU we get a total workload W given by:

$$W = \sum_c w_c = \sum_c n_c t_c + \sum_c n_c s_c.$$

For a sales force centred at a distance d from the centre of this SCU, the values s_c will all be approximately equal to $s = 2d/u$, where u is the average travelling speed. This assumes that separate calls require separate journeys from the centre of the territory.

For a particular SCU, let the workload for customer contact be $a = \sum_c n_c t_c$, and let $n = \sum_c n_c$ be the total number of calls. Then the total workload for the SCU is $W = a + ns$.

The sales potential depends on whether a customer is an existing or prospective one. For an existing customer, the sales potential q_c is measured using the sales q'_c for the previous time period and the holding rate h_c:

$$q_c = q'_c h_c.$$

For a prospective customer, the sales potential is measured by r_c, the estimated volume of sales if the customer is converted, and the probability, v_c, of the conversion:

$$q_c = r_c v_c.$$

Note that both h_c and v_c are influenced by the value of n_c, the number of calls that the customer receives and t_c, the average contact time. Summing over all customers in a SCU, we obtain a sales potential of $b = \sum_c q_c$.

The profit, p_c, associated with each customer is measured by the margin m on the sales q_c and the average cost z_c of servicing the customer:

$$p_c = mq_c - z_c.$$

For a customer c, two components of z_c are the cost of the time spent in contact with the customer and the cost of the sales calls. If these are the only components and f is the rate per hour for customer contact and g is the cost per unit distance for travelling then:

$$z_c = fw_c + gn_c s_c.$$

Summing over all customers, we obtain a profit for the SCU of p given by:

$$p = \sum_c p_c = m \sum_c q_c - f \sum_c w_c - g \sum_c n_c s_c = mb - f(a + ns) - 2ngd/u.$$

4.3.2. *The model*

Suppose there are J SCUs numbered from one to J and that for the jth SCU, $1 \leq j \leq J$, we have the following values derived in the last subsection: a_j denotes the workload for customer contact; b_j denotes the sales potential; n_j denotes the total number of calls required; s_j denotes the travelling distance from the centre of the SCU to the designated centre of the territory in which it lies; p_j denotes the profit.

In addition we suppose that, for each pair, j and k, of contiguous SCUs, the distance between their centres is the number d_{jk}. These values could be placed in a two-dimensional $J \times J$ array, H, where a zero entry indicates that the corresponding SCUs are not contiguous. Now suppose that I territories are required which are numbered from one to I. The value I will be significantly smaller than J. The problem of determining a territory design can be considered as the determination of an assignment function F which assigns to each

SCU j the territory $i = F(j)$. That is, for each j, $1 \leq j \leq J$,

$$F(j) = i \qquad (2)$$

for some i, $1 \leq i \leq I$. We now consider how the constraints and the maximisation of profit are affected by this assignment.

Contiguity. We will need to be able to ascertain for any design that all the territories are contiguous. For the other constraints we will also be required to determine a distance between two (not necessarily contiguous) SCUs in the same territory. Both can be accomplished by using Floyd's algorithm on subarrays of the array H as the distance matrix of a graph, (Sedgewick, 1990). Thus it is possible, using the representation described above, for a new territory design to be efficiently checked for contiguity.

Equal workload. The distance between two SCUs of a territory can be taken to be the shortest path between them using as intermediate junctions any other centres of the territory as are convenient to use. If j, k are the SCUs, then we denote by D_{jk} this distance. As mentioned in the paragraph above, these values can be simultaneously and efficiently determined using Floyd's algorithm. Suppose that the main office of territory i is placed at SCU c_i. From the expression for the workload of the SCU in the previous subsection, we have that the work of the territory is A_i given by:

$$A_i = \sum_{j, F(j)=i} (a_j + n_j s_j) = \sum_{j, F(j)=i} (a_j + n_j D_{j,c_i}).$$

The choice of the centre c_i of territory i may be chosen, for example, as that SCU in the territory which minimises the expression for A_i.

The constraint that the workload of each territory should be precisely the same will be impossible to achieve in practice. Instead, a margin of error, e_A, is accepted. Let A be the average of the workload taken over all territories:

$$A = (1/I) \sum_{i=1}^{I} A_i.$$

Then the equality of workload constraint can be expressed for each $i, 1 \leq i \leq I$: as

$$(1 - e_A)A \leq A_i \leq (1 + e_A)A. \tag{3}$$

Equality of sales potential. The sales potential for territory i is the aggregate of the sales potential for each SCU in that territory. If B_i denotes this total sales, then $B_i = \sum_{j,F(j)=i} b_j$. In a similar way for the discussion of the equality of workload, denoted by B the average sales potential, so that $B = (1/I) \sum_{i=1}^{I} B_i$, and let e_B denote error margin. Then the equality of sales potential constraint for each i, with $1 \leq i \leq I$, is given by:

$$(1 - e_B)B \leq B_i \leq (1 + e_B)B. \tag{4}$$

Profit. The overall profit, Q, of the organisation is given by the aggregate, P, of the expected profits from sales in each territory less the cost, R, of administering the sales force over all the territories. For territory i, the profit P_i is the sum of the profits from the SCUs in that territory. Thus,

$$P_i = \sum_{j,F(j)=i} p_j = mB_i - fA_i - (2g/u) \sum_{j,F(j)=i} n_j D_{j,c_i}.$$

Assuming R is independent of the territory design, the objective is to maximise P where:

$$P = \sum_{i=1}^{I} P_i = mIB - fIA - (2g/u) \sum_{i=1}^{I} \sum_{F(j)=i} n_j D_{j,c_i}. \tag{5}$$

To summarise, the formulation of the territory design problem is to determine an assignment function F defined by Eq. (2) which (1) makes the territories contiguous, (2) satisfies the equality of workload constraint given by Eq. (3), (3) satisfies the equality of sales potential constraint given by Eq. (4), and (4) maximises P given by Eq. (5).

4.3.3. *Applying simulated annealing*

An initial design is found for which the territories are contiguous. Values for e_A and e_B are computed so that equality of workload and sales potential constraints are satisfied. The profit P is computed. Denote this design by $\mathbf{X_{old}}$. Also initialised is the value of the temperature, T. After this initialisation the main iterative loop begins. The full procedure is as follows:

Initialise T and $\mathbf{X_{old}}$
Compute values e_A, e_B so that constraints 2,3 hold with equality
WHILE $T > T_{min}$ DO
   FOR $u = 1$ to N_c DO
      Make a random move by removing SCU j from territory i to k
      Call the new design $\mathbf{X_{new}}$
      IF territories i, k are contiguous and $\mathbf{X_{new}}$ satisfies constraints 2,3
      THEN
        compute P_{new} and $\Delta P = P_{old} - P_{new}$
        IF $\Delta P < 0$ or *random* $< prob = e^{-\Delta P/T}$ THEN
          $\mathbf{X_{old}}$ becomes $\mathbf{X_{new}}$
          update e_A, e_B so that equations 2,3 hold with equality
        END IF
      END IF
   END FOR
   reduce T
END WHILE

where N_c is the number of random changes in configuration at each temperature T and the variable *random* is a randomly generated number in the range $[0, 1]$. Precise details about the values of T and the annealing schedule will need to be determined by experimentation. Hurley and Mountinho (1997a, 1997b) contain full details of the use of simulated annealing in the design of sales territories.

5. Future Developments

Nature inspired search algorithms including genetic algorithms, tabu search and simulated annealing discussed above, are becoming ever more increasingly used in many problem domains. Within all of their individual algorithmic processes randomisation is an important and critical aspect. For example, mutation and crossover probabilities for genetic algorithms, move selection in tabu search and acceptance criteria in simulated annealing. In addition to these specific uses of random variables (usually uniformly distributed) there is current work which involves using different types of randomisation, in the form of so-called *Levy flights*, in alternative nature inspired global optimisation algorithms.

5.1. Levy flights

A Levy flight, named after the French mathematician Paul Levy is a mathematical concept that has been used to simulate many random or pseudo-random phenomena observed in nature such as the path of an animal, for example wandering albatrosses perform Levy flights when searching for prey on the ocean surface (Viswanathan, 1996). Levy flights are random walks, the step lengths of which come from probability distributions with heavy power law tails of the form $y = x^{-\alpha}(1 < \alpha < 3)$ (ben Avraham and Havlin, 2000), such that clusters of short steps are connected by rare long steps. An example of a Levy flight in two dimensions is given in Fig. 8, where the clusters of short steps and rare long steps can be clearly seen.

Recently, Levy flights have been incorporated into several optimisation algorithms in an attempt to produce more effective search processes. Two examples of this includes the incorporation of Levy processes into a simulated annealing framework (Pavlyukevich, 2007), and to direct the core random process into a Firefly algorithm, thereby creating a new meta-heuristic procedure (Yang, 2010).

In addition to the use of Levy flights in optimisation they are also being studied in other areas such as explaining complex human behaviour. For example internet use — when users discover an internet site they often browse around for a while (the short steps) and then move on to another site (the long step). Another example is in marketing and understanding consumer behaviour — supermarket sales to consumers seem to follow a Levy distribution

Fig. 8.   Two-dimensional Levy flight example.

with an exponent of $\alpha = 1.4$ similar to financial exchange markets and in stock markets.

References

Aarts, E and J Lenstra (eds) (1997). *Local Search in Combinatorial Optimization.* Chichester: Wiley.

Achabal, D, W Gorr and V Mahajan (1982). Multiloc: A multiple store location decision model. *Journal of Retailing*, 58, 5–25.

Back, T (1993). Optimal mutation rates in genetic search. In *Proc. 5th Int. Conf. Genetic Algorithms*, Morgan Kaufmann, pp. 2–8.

Back, T (1996). *Evolutionary Algorithms in Theory and Practice.* New York: Oxford University Press.

ben Avraham, D and S Havlin (2000). *Diffusion and Reactions in Fractals and Disordered Systems.* Cambridge: Cambridge University Press.

Costa, D and A Hertz (1997). Ants can colour graphs. *Journal of the Operational Research Society*, 48, 295–305.

Costa, D, A Hertz and O Dubois (1995). Embedding a sequential procedure within an evolutionary algorithm for coloring problems in graphs. *Journal of Heuristics*, 1, 105–128.

Dell'Amico, M, F Maffioli and S Martello (1997). *Annotated Bibliographies in Combinatorial Optimization*. Chichester: Wiley.

Fausett, L (1994). *Fundamentals of Neural Networks*. Englewood Cliffs: Prentice Hall.

Fogel, D (1991). *System Identification through Simulated Evolution: A Machine Learning Approach to Modelling*. Needham Heights: Ginn Press.

Fogel, D (1992). *Evolving Artificial Intelligence*. Ph.D. thesis, University of California, San Diego.

Fogel, L, A Owens and M Walsh (1966). *Artificial Intelligence through Simulated Evolution*. New York: Wiley.

Glover, F (1977). Heuristics for integer programming using surrogate constraints. *Decision Sciences*, 8, 156–166.

Glover, F (1991). Multilevel tabu search and embedded search neighbourhoods for the travelling salesman problem. *Technical report*, Graduate School of Business, University of Colorado at Boulder.

Glover, F (1994). Genetic algorithms and scatter search: Unsuspected potentials. *Statistics and Computing*, 4, 131–140.

Glover, F, E Taillard and D de Werra (1993). A user's guide to tabu search. *Annals of Operations Research*, 41, 3–28.

Goldberg, D (1989). *Genetic Algorithms in Search, Optimization and Machine Learning*. New York: Addison Wesley.

Holland, J (1975). *Adaption in Natural and Artificial Systems*. Ann Arbor: University of Michigan Press.

Howick, R and M Pidd (1990). Sales force deployment models. *European Journal of Operational Research* 48, 295–310.

Hurley, S and L Mountinho (1997a). A simulated annealing algorithm for sales territory alignment part I. *Journal of Targeting, Measurement and Analysis*, 5, 221–231.

Hurley, S and L Mountinho (1997b). A simulated annealing algorithm for sales territory alignment part II. *Journal of Targeting, Measurement and Analysis*, 5, 319–326.

Hurley, S and L Mountinho (1998). Brandval: A computational model for enhancing the measurement of brand value using scanner data. *Journal of Targeting, Measurement and Analysis*, 7, 46–58.

Hurley, S, L Mountinho and S Witt (1998). Genetic algorithms for tourism marketing. *Annals of Tourism Research*, 25, 498–514.

Kirkpatrick, S, CD Gelatt and MP Vecchi (1983). Optimization by simulated annealing. *Science* 220, 671–680.

Metropolis, N, A Rosenbluth, M Rosenbluth, A Teller and E Teller (1953). Equations of state calculations by fast computing machines. *Journal of Chemical Physics*, 21, 1087–1092.

Pavlyukevich, I (2007). Levy flights, non-local search and simulated annealing. *Journal of Compuational Physics*, 226, 1830–1844.

Penny, N and D Broom (1988). The tesco approach to store location. In *Store Location and Market Analysis*, N Wrigley (ed.), pp. 106–119. London: Routledge.

Ramaswamy, V and W DeSarbo (1990). Sculpture: A new methodology for deriving and analyzing hierarchical product-market structures from panel data. *Journal of Marketing Research*, 27, 418–427.

Rechenberg, I (1973). *Evolutionsstrategie: Optimierung Technischer Systeme Nach Prinzipies der Biologischen Evolution*. Stuttgart: Frommann-Holzborg.

Reeves, CR (ed.) (1995). *Modern Heuristic Techniques for Combinatorial Problems*. Advanced topics in computer science. New York: McGraw-Hill.

Schwefel, H-P (1977). *Numerische Optimierung von Computer Modellen Mittels der Evolutionsstrategie*, Vol. 26 of *Interdisciplinary Systems*. Basel: Birkhauser.

Schwefel, H-P (1981). *Numerical Optimization of Computer Models*. Chichester: Wiley.

Sedgewick, R (1990). *Algorithms in C*. New York: Addison Wesley.

Viswanathan, G (1996). Levy flight search patterns of wandering albatrosses. *Nature*, 381, 413–415.

Yang, X-S (2010). Firefly algorithm, Levy flights and global optimisation. In *Research and Development in Intelligent Systems*, M Bramer, R Ellis and M Petridis (eds.), pp. 209–218. London: Springer.

Zoltners, A and P Sinha (1983). Sales territory alignment: A review and model. *Management Science*, 29, 1237–1256.

Chapter 10

HOLD A MIRROR UP TO NATURE: A NEW APPROACH ON CORRELATION EVALUATION WITH FUZZY DATA AND ITS APPLICATIONS IN ECONOMETRICS

Chih Ching Yang
Department of Statistics
National Chengchi University, Taiwan
96354502@nccu.edu.tw

Yu-Ting Cheng
Department of Statistics
National Chengchi University, Taiwan
ting@nccu.edu.tw

Berlin Wu
Department of Math Sciences,
National Chengchi University, Taiwan
berlin@nccu.edu.tw

Songsak Sriboonchitta
Faculty of Economics
Chiangmai University, Thailand
songsak@econ.cmu.ac.th

How to evaluate an appropriate correlation with fuzzy data is an important topic in the economics. Especially when the data illustrated is an uncertain, inconsistent and incomplete type. Traditionally, we use Pearson's Correlation Coefficient to measure the correlation between data with real value. However, when the data are composed of fuzzy numbers, it is not feasible to use such a traditional approach to determine the fuzzy correlation coefficient. This study proposes the calculation of fuzzy correlation with fuzzy data: Interval, triangular and trapezoidal. Empirical studies are used to illustrate the application for evaluating fuzzy correlations. More related practical phenomena can be explained by this appropriate definition of fuzzy correlation.

Keywords: Fuzzy correlation; fuzzy data; evaluation; psychometrics.

1. Introduction

Traditional statistics reflects the results from a two-valued logic world, which often reduces the accuracy of inferential procedures. To investigate the population, people's opinions or the complexity of a subjective event more accurately, fuzzy logic should be utilised to account for the full range of possible values. Especially, when dealing with psychometric measures, fuzzy statistics provides a powerful research tool. Since Zadeh (1965) developed fuzzy set theory, its applications have been extended to traditional statistical inferences and methods in social sciences, including medical diagnosis or stock investment systems. For example, a successive series of studies demonstrated approximate reasoning methods for econometrics (Lowen, 1990; Ruspini, 1991; Dubois and Parde, 1991) and a fuzzy time series model to overcome the bias of stock markets was developed (Wu and Hsu, 2002).

Within the framework of classical statistical theory, observations should follow a specific probability distribution. However, in practice, the observations are sometimes described by linguistic terms such as *Very satisfactory, Satisfactory, Normal, Unsatisfactory, Very unsatisfactory*, or are only approximately known, rather than equating with randomness. How to measure the correlation between two variables involving fuzziness is a challenge to the classical statistical theory. The number of studies which focus on fuzzy correlation analysis and its application in the social science fields has been steadily increasing (Bustince and Burillo, 1995; Yu, 1993; Liu and Kao, 2002; Hong, 2006). For example, Hong and Hwang (1995) and Yu (1993) define a correlation formula to measure the interrelation of intuitionist fuzzy sets. However, the range of their defined correlation is from zero to one, which contradicts with the conventional awareness of correlation which should range from −1 to 1. Wang and Li (1999)'s article also has the same problems of lying the correlations between zero and one for the interval valued fuzzy numbers. In order to overcome this issue, Chiang and Lin (1999) take random sample from the fuzzy sets and treat the membership grades as the crisp observations. Their derived coefficient is between −1 and 1; however, the sense the fuzziness is gone. Liu and Kao (2002) calculated the fuzzy correlation coefficient based on Zadeh's extension principles. They used a mathematical programming approach to derive fuzzy measures based on the classical definition of the correlation coefficient. Their derivation is quite promising, but in order to employ their approach, the mathematical programming is required.

In addition, most previous studies deal with the interval fuzzy data, their definitions cannot deal with triangle or trapezoid data. In addition, formulas in these studies are quite complicated or required some mathematical programming which really limited the access of some researchers with no strong mathematical background. In this study, we give a simple solution of a fuzzy correlation coefficient without programming or the aid of computer resources. In addition, the provided solutions are based on the classical definition of Pearson correlation which should be quite easy and straightforward. The definitions provided in this study can also be used for interval-valued, triangular and trapezoid fuzzy data.

Traditionally, if one wishes to understand the relationship between the variables x and y, the most direct and simple way is to draw a scatter plot, which can approximately illustrate the relationship between these variables: Positive correlation, negative correlation, or zero correlation. In this study, we have proposed three kinds of fuzzy correlation which are based on the Neyman Person's correlation as well as the extension principle Definition 2.1, 2.2 and 2.3, the advantages are that we can compute various samples with fuzzy type, such as interval, triangle and trapezoid, the type for the continuous sample.

The issue at hand is how to measure the relationship in a rational way. Statistically, the simplest way to measure the linear relationship between two variables is by using Pearson's correlation coefficient, which expresses both the magnitude and the direction of the relationship between the two variables with a range of values from 1 to −1. However, Pearson correlations can only be applied to variables that are real numbers and is not suitable for a fuzzy dataset.

When considering the correlation for fuzzy data, two aspects should be considered: Centroid and data shape. If the two centroids of the two fuzzy dataset are close, the correlation should be high. In addition, if the data shape of the two fuzzy sets is similar, the correlation should also be high. An approach to dealing with these two aspects simultaneously will be presented later in this study. Before illustrating the approach of calculating fuzzy correlations, a review of fuzzy theory and fuzzy datasets are presented in the next section.

2. Fuzzy Correlation

The correlation coefficient is a commonly used statistics that presents a measure of how two random variables are linearly related in a sample. The population correlation coefficient, which is generally denoted by the symbol ρ is defined for two variables x and y by the formula:

$$\rho = \frac{\sigma_{X,Y}}{\sigma_X \sigma_Y} = \frac{Cov(X, Y)}{\sigma_X \sigma_Y}.$$

In this case, the more positive ρ is, the more positive is the association. This also indicates that when ρ is close to one, an individual with a high value for one variable will likely have a high value for the other, and an individual with a lower value for one variable will likely to have a low value for the other. On the other hand, the more negative ρ is, the more negative is the association, this also indicate that an individual with a high value for one variable will likely have a low value for the other when ρ is close to −1 and conversely. When ρ is close to zero, this means there is little linear association between two variables. In order to obtain the correlation coefficient, we need to obtain σ_X^2, σ_Y^2 and the covariance of x and y. In practice, these parameters for the population are unknown or difficult to obtain. Thus, we usually use r_{xy}, which can be obtained from a sample, to estimate the unknown population parameter. The sample correlation coefficient r_{xy} is expressed as:

$$r_{xy} = \frac{\sum_{i=1}^{n}(x_i - \bar{x})(y_i - \bar{y})}{\sqrt{\sum_{i=1}^{n}(x_i - \bar{x})^2}\sqrt{\sum_{i=1}^{n}(y_i - \bar{y})^2}}, \tag{1}$$

where (x_i, y_i) is the ith pair observation value, $i = 1, 2, 3 \ldots\ldots, n; \bar{x}, \bar{y}$ are sample mean for x and y respectively.

Pearson correlation is a straightforward approach to evaluate the relationship between two variables. However, if the variables considered are not real numbers, but fuzzy data, the formula above is problematic. For example, Mr. Smith is a new graduate from college; his expected annual income is 50,000 dollars. However, he can accept a lower salary if there is a promising offer. In his case, the annual income is not a definite number but more like a range. Mr. Smith's acceptable salary range is from 45,000 to 50,000. We can express his annual salary as an interval [45,000, 50,000]. In addition, when Mr. Smith has a job interview, the manager may ask how many hours he can work per day. In this case, Mr. Smith may not be able to provide a definite number since his everyday schedule is different. However, Mr. Smith may tell the manger that his expected working hours per day is an interval [8, 10].

We know Mr. Smith's expected salary ranges from [45,000, 50,000] and his expected working hours are [8, 10]. If we collect this kind of data from many new graduates, how can we use this data and calculate the correlation between expected salary and working hours? Suppose I_x is the expected salary for each new graduate, I_y is the working hours they desired, then the scatter plot for these two sets of fuzzy interval numbers would approximate as shown in Fig. 1.

For the interval valued fuzzy number, we need to take out samples from population X and Y. Each fuzzy interval data for sample X centroids has x_i, and for sample Y has centroids y_i. For the interval data, we also have to consider whether the length of

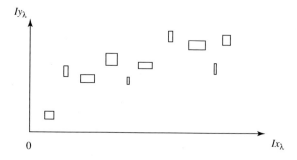

Fig. 1.   Fuzzy correlation with interval data.

interval fuzzy data are similar or not. In Mr. Smith's example, if the correlation between the expected salary and working hours are high, then we can expect two things: (1) The higher salary the new employee expects, the more working hours he can endure. (2) The wider the range of the expected salary, the wider the range of the working hours should be. However, how should one combine the information from both centroid and length? If they are combined with equal weight, it is possible that the combined correlation would exceed the boundaries of 1 or -1. In addition, the effect of length should not be greater than the impact of centroids. In order to get the rational fuzzy correlations, we used natural logarithms to make some adjustments.

Let $(X_i = [a_i, b_i], Y_i = [c_i, d_i]; i = 1, 2, \ldots n)$ be a sequence of paired trapezoid fuzzy sample on population Ω with its pair of center (cx_i, cy_i) and pair of area $(\|x_i\| = area(x_i), \|y_i\| = area(y_i))$. The adjust correlation for the pair of area will be

Definition 2.1. Let $(X_i = [a_i, b_i], Y_i = [c_i, d_i]; i = 1, 2, \ldots n)$ be a sequence of paired trapezoid fuzzy sample on population Ω with its pair of center (cx_i, cy_i) and pair of area $\|x_i\| = area(x_i), \|y_i\| = area(y_i)$:

$$cr_{xy} = \frac{\sum_{i=1}^{n} (cx_i - \overline{cx})(cy_i - \overline{cy})}{\sqrt{\sum_{i=1}^{n} (cx_i - \overline{cx})^2} \sqrt{\sum_{i=1}^{n} (cy_i - \overline{cy})^2}},$$

$$ar_{xy} = \frac{\sum_{i=1}^{n} (\|x_i\| - \|\bar{x}_i\|)(\|y_i\| - \|\bar{y}_i\|)}{\sqrt{\sum_{i=1}^{n} (\|x_i\| - \|\bar{x}_i\|)^2} \sqrt{\sum_{i=1}^{n} (\|y_i\| - \|\bar{y}_i\|)^2}}. \qquad (2)$$

Then fuzzy correlation is defined as:

$$FC = \beta_1 cr_{xy} + \beta_2 ar_{xy}, (\beta_1 + \beta_2 = 1).$$

We choose a pair of $(\beta_1\beta_2)$ that depend on the weight of practical use. For instance, if we think the location correlation is much more important than that of e scale, $\beta_1 = 0.7$, $\beta_2 = 0.3$ will be a good suggestion.

Example 1. Suppose we have the following data as shown in Table 1.

In this case, the correlation between the two centers is:

$$cr_{xy} = \frac{\sum_{i=1}^{n} (cx_i - 27.1)(cy_i - 1.7)}{\sqrt{\sum_{i=1}^{n} (cx_i - 27.1)^2}\sqrt{\sum_{i=1}^{n} (cy_i - 1.7)^2}} = -0.26,$$

and the correlation between the two length is:

$$ar_{xy} = \frac{\sum_{i=1}^{n} (\|x_i\| - 3.4)(\|y_i\| - 1.8)}{\sqrt{\sum_{i=1}^{n} (\|x_i\| - 3.4)^2}\sqrt{\sum_{i=1}^{n} (\|y_i\| - 1.8)^2}} = 0.05.$$

Table 2 is a list of combinations for choosing $\beta_1\beta_2$. The fuzzy correlation will be computed by cr_{xy} and ar_{xy} with $0 \leq \beta_1, \beta_2 \leq 1$. Such as, when $\beta_1 = 0.7$ and $\beta_2 = 0.3$ then $FC = 0.7 \times (-0.26) + 0.3 \times 0.05 = -0.17$.

Table 1. Numerical example for interval-valued fuzzy data.

Student	X Data	X Center	X Length	Y Data	Y Center	Y Length
A	[23,25]	24	2	[1, 2]	1.5	1
B	[21,26]	23.5	5	[0, 3]	1.5	3
C	[29,35]	32	6	[0, 1]	0.5	1
D	[28,30]	29	2	[1, 4]	2.5	3
E	[26,28]	27	2	[2, 3]	2.5	1
(fuzzy) mean		27.1	3.4		1.7	1.8

Table 2.   Different combinations of β_1, β_2.

	(1,0)	(0.9,0.1)	(0.8,0.2)	(0.7,0.3)	(0.6,4)	(0.5,0.5)	(0.4,0.6)	(0.3,0.7)	(0.2,0.8)	(0.1,0.9)	(0,1)
FC	−0.26	−0.23	−0.20	−0.17	−0.14	−0.11	−0.08	−0.05	−0.01	0.02	0.05

Considering the contribution of (area) length correlation to the fuzzy correlation, the idea of correlation interval is proposed. Suppose, we fix the (area) length correlation by the following adjusted values:

$$\lambda r_{xy} = 1 - \frac{\ln(1 + |ar_{xy}|)}{|ar_{xy}|};$$

where $\quad ar_{xy} = \dfrac{\sum_{i=1}^{n}(\|x_i\| - \|\bar{x}_i\|)(\|y_i\| - \|\bar{y}_i\|)}{\sqrt{\sum_{i=1}^{n}(\|x_i\| - \|\bar{x}_i\|)^2}\sqrt{\sum_{i=1}^{n}(\|y_i\| - \|\bar{y}_i\|)^2}},$ (3)

since $-1 \leq ar_{xy} \leq 1$, the range of λr_{xy} will be $0 < \lambda r_{xy} < 0.3069$. We will have the following definition for fuzzy correlation interval.

Definition 2.2. *Let* $(X_i = [a_i, b_i], Y_i = [c_i, d_i]; i = 1, 2, \ldots n)$ *be a sequence of paired trapezoid fuzzy sample on population* Ω *with its pair of center* (cx_i, cy_i) *and pair of area* $\|x_i\| = area(x_i), \|y_i\| = area(y_i)$:

$$cr_{xy} = \frac{\sum_{i=1}^{n}(cx_i - \overline{cx})(cy_i - \overline{cy})}{\sqrt{\sum_{i=1}^{n}(cx_i - \overline{cx})^2}\sqrt{\sum_{i=1}^{n}(cy_i - \overline{cy})^2}},$$

$$\lambda ar_{xy} = 1 - \frac{\ln(1 + |ar_{xy}|)}{|ar_{xy}|};$$

where $\quad ar_{xy} = \dfrac{\sum_{i=1}^{n}(\|x_i\| - \|\bar{x}_i\|)(\|y_i\| - \|\bar{y}_i\|)}{\sqrt{\sum_{i=1}^{n}(\|x_i\| - \|\bar{x}_i\|)^2}\sqrt{\sum_{i=1}^{n}(\|y_i\| - \|\bar{y}_i\|)^2}}.$ (4)

Then fuzzy correlation is defined as:

(i) *When* $cr_{xy} \geq 0$, $\lambda ar_{xy} \geq 0$, *fuzzy correlation* $= (cr_{xy}, min(1, cr_{xy} + \lambda ar_{xy}))$;

(ii) *When* $cr_{xy} \geq 0$, $\lambda ar_{xy} < 0$, *fuzzy correlation* $= (cr_{xy} - \lambda ar_{xy}, cr_{xy})$;

Table 3. Numerical example for interval-valued fuzzy data.

Student	X			Y		
	Data	Centroid	Area(length)	Data	Centroid	Area(length)
A	[23,25]	24	2	[1,2]	1.5	1
B	[21,26]	23.5	5	[0,3]	1.5	3
C	[29,35]	32	6	[0,1]	0.5	1
D	[28,30]	29	2	[1,4]	2.5	3
E	[26,28]	27	2	[2,3]	2.5	1
(fuzzy) mean		27.1	3.4		1.7	1.8

(iii) *When $cr_{xy} < 0, \lambda ar_{xy} \geq 0$, fuzzy correlation $= (cr_{xy}, cr_{xy} + \lambda ar_{xy})$;*
(iv) *When $cr_{xy} < 0, \lambda ar_{xy} < 0$, fuzzy correlation $= (\max(-1, c_{xy} - \lambda ar_{xy}), cr_{xy})$.*

Example 2. Suppose, we have the following data as shown in Table 3.

In this case, the correlation between the two centroids is:

$$cr_{xy} = \frac{\sum_{i=1}^{n} (cx_i - 27.2)(cy_i - 1.7)}{\sqrt{\sum_{i=1}^{n} (cx_i - 27.2)^2} \sqrt{\sum_{i=1}^{n} (cy_i - 1.7)^2}} = -0.26.$$

Similarly, the correlation between two lengths is:

$$ar_{xy} = \frac{\sum_{i=1}^{n} (\|x_i\| - 3.6)(\|y_i\| - 1.4)}{\sqrt{\sum_{i=1}^{n} (\|x_i\| - 3.6)^2} \sqrt{\sum_{i=1}^{n} (\|y_i\| - 1.4)^2}} = 0.05,$$

$$\lambda ar_{xy} = 1 - \frac{\ln(1 + 0.05)}{0.05} = 0.02.$$

Since the centers correlation $ar_{xy} \geq 0$, and the area(length) correlation $\lambda ar_{xy} \geq 0$, thus, fuzzy correlation $= (r, r + \lambda ar_{xy})) = (-0.26, -0.26 + 0.02) = (-0.26, -0.24)$. This implied that the relationship between the X and Y are quite small.

Another interesting idea is taking all possible correlations into consideration. That is we calculate the correlations for all endpoints of intervals. Then we take the mean of all possible correlations as our center of the fuzzy correlation. While the range is chosen by the three standard deviation, that is $\frac{3(r_{min} - r_{max})^2}{12}$. Here we apply the idea of three standard deviations from quality control.

Definition 2.3. *Let* $X_{ji} = [a_{1i}, a_{2i}]$ *and* $Y_{ji} = [b_{1i}, b_{2i}]$ *be a sequence of paired fuzzy sample on population* Ω. *Let*

$$r_{jk} = \frac{\sum_{i=1}^{n}(a_{ji} - \bar{a}_j)(b_{ki} - \bar{b}_k)}{\sqrt{\sum_{i=1}^{n}(a_{ji} - \bar{a}_j)^2}\sqrt{\sum_{i=1}^{n}(b_{ki} - \bar{b}_k)^2}}, \quad j = 1, 2, \quad k = 1, 2.$$

Then fuzzy correlation is $[-r_{low}, r_{up}]$ *with* $r_{low} = \bar{r} - s_r$ *and* $-r_{up} = \bar{r} + s_r$, *where*

$$\bar{r} = \frac{\sum_{j=1}^{2}\sum_{k=1}^{2} r_{jk}}{4} \quad and \quad s_r = \frac{\sum_{j=1}^{2}\sum_{k=1}^{2}(r_{jk} - \bar{r})^2}{4}.$$

Example 3. Suppose we have the following data as shown in Table 4.

Since *the mean and Standard Deviation of* r_{jk} *are* -0.14 and 0.12, thus, fuzzy correlation $= (-0.26, -0.2)$. This implied that the relationship between the X and Y are small.

Table 4.   Numerical example for interval-valued fuzzy data.

Student	X $[a_1, a_2]$	Y $[b_1, b_2]$	Correlation coefficient r_{a1b1}	r_{a1b2}	r_{a2b1}	r_{a2b2}
A	[23,25]	[1,2]	-0.07	-0.07	-0.32	-0.09
B	[21,26]	[0,3]				
C	[32,35]	[0,1]				
D	[28,30]	[1,4]				
E	[26,28]	[2,3]				
interval	$\bar{r} = -0.14, s_r = 0.12$					

A correlation coefficient is a number between −1 and 1 which measures the degree to which two variables are linearly related. If there is perfect linear relationship with positive slope between the two variables, we have a correlation coefficient of one; if there is positive correlation, whenever one variable has a high value. Thus, based on the measure of evaluation, the degree of the population correlation coefficient, we will be considered for the correlation of fuzzy interval. As the correlation of fuzzy interval, $[r_{low}, r_{up}]$, is computed then the value of fuzzy correlation can be evaluated that is defined as:

(1) When $[r_{low}, r_{up}] \in [-0.1, 0.10]$, *the fuzzy correlation is not significant.*
(2) When $[r_{low}, r_{up}] \in [-0.39, -0.11]$ or $[0.11, 0.39]$, *the fuzzy correlation is low value.*
(3) When $[r_{low}, r_{up}] \in [-0.69, -0.40]$ or $[0.40, 0.69]$, *the fuzzy correlation is middle value.*
(4) When $[r_{low}, r_{up}] \in [-0.99, -0.70]$ or $[0.70, 0.99]$, *the fuzzy correlation is high value.*

3. Empirical studies

In this section, two empirical examples will be considered to study the relationship with three schemes. In the first part, we employ the fuzzy interval data to investigate the relationship between climate and the price of vegetable from 2009 to 2011 in Taiwan. In the second part, we apply the exchange rate and the price of agriculture in Thailand.

3.1. *Correlation between climate and agriculture price in Taiwan*

A total of 33 samples are collected from the Central Weather Bureau and Agriculture and Food Agency Council of Agriculture Executive Yuan in Taiwan to study the factors impacting the relationship between climate (X) and the price of vegetable (Y). The result presents the correlation for fuzzy data and in comparison with the price of vegetable.

Table 5. Correlations interval based on temperature and the price of vegetable in Taiwan.

Scheme	Correlation coefficient
Fuzzy Correlation by Definition 1	0.212
Fuzzy Interval by Definition 2	(0.339, 0.489)
Fuzzy Interval by Definition 3	(0.348, 0.480)

Based on Table 5, we have the following findings. First, besides the correlation of temperature and vegetable price is positive, this result presents that as the temperature is increases, the price of vegetable also increases. Second, the correlation coefficient of both new method and length and center are close. This means that there is almost middle relationship between temperature and vegetable price in Taiwan.

3.2. *Correlation of both pair agriculture price in Thailand*

A total of 17 samples are collected from Thailand bank and Agriculture and Food Agency Council in Thailand. The results show the correlation for the exchanges rate and various price of agriculture with three approaches of evaluation of correlation coefficient. The results are listed in Table 6.

In the Table 6, we have the following findings. First, besides the correlation of exchange rate and the price of agriculture is negative, and this result denotes that the exchange rate decreases then the price of agriculture increases. Second, the correlation coefficient is considered to be the high level for exchange rate and the price of corn, wheat, this means the price of corn and wheat have a lot of effect on the exchange rate. In addition, the price of sugar will be slightly affected by exchange rate, and the price of race cannot be influenced by exchange rate. Third, any both price of agriculture are positive, and there are at least middle relationships for any pair price of agriculture. This result show that one price of agriculture will affect other price of agriculture, such as the price of wheat can be affected by the price of rice.

Table 6.   Correlations interval based on temperature and the price of agriculture in Thailand.

Fuzzy correlation	U$:TB	Sugar	Corn	Wheat	Rice
U$:TB	—	-0.373^1 $(-0.540,$ $-0.532)^2$ $(-0.560,$ $-0.500)^3$	-0.551^1 $(-0.850,$ $-0.783)^2$ $(-0.868,$ $-0.815)^3$	-0.545^1 $(-0.893,$ $-0.780)^2$ $(-0.902,$ $-0.868)^3$	-0.013^1 $(-0.019,$ $0.083)^2$ $(0.015,$ $0.143)^3$
Sugar		—	0.750^1 $(0.684,$ $0.972)^2$ $(0.578,$ $0.705)^3$	0.585^1 $(0.542,$ $0.781)^2$ $(0.468,$ $0.556)^3$	0.659^1 $(0.648,$ $0.886)^2$ $(0.567,$ $0.663)^3$
Corn			—	0.797^1 $(0.829,$ $1.000)^2$ $(0.744,$ $0.833)^3$	0.741^1 $(0.767,$ $1.000)^2$ $(0.683,$ $0.765)^3$
Wheat				—	0.518^1 $(0.561,$ $0.725)^2$ $(0.512,$ $0.554)^3$
Rice					—

Note: [1]Denote the value of Definition 1 under $\beta_1 = 0.7$, $\beta_2 = 0.3$.
[2]Denote the value of Definition 2.
[3]Denote the value of Definition 3.

4. Conclusions

Correlation between any two variables has wide applications in many applications. Previous studies have derived some solutions for calculating the correlation coefficient for fuzzy numbers. A common deficiency of those studies is that the correlation coefficients calculated are crisp values, instead of the intuitively believed fuzzy numbers. This chapter uses a simple way to derive fuzzy measures based on the classical definition of Pearson correlation coefficient which are easy and straightforward. Moreover, the range of the calculated fuzzy coefficient is a fuzzy number with domain $[-1, 1]$, which consist with the conventional range of Pearson correlation. In the formula we provided, when all observations are real numbers, the developed model becomes the classical Pearson correlation formula.

There are some suggestions for future studies. First, the main purpose of this study is to provide the formula of calculating fuzzy correlations. Only few samples are collected to illustrate how to employ the formula. Future interested researchers can use formula and collect large-scale fuzzy questionnaires to make this formula get implemented in practice. Second, when calculating the fuzzy correlation, we adopt λar_{xy} to adjust the correlations, but researchers can set up their own λar_{xy} values if there are defensible reasons. However, it is suggested that the impact of length correlation should not exceed the impact of centroid correlation. Third, this study only considered the fuzzy correlation for continuous data. Therefore, it would be interested to investigate the fuzzy correlation for discrete fuzzy data.

In practice, many applications are fuzzy in nature. We can absolutely ignore the fuzziness and make the existing methodology for crisp values. However, this will make the researcher over confident with their results. With the methodology developed in this chapter, a more realistic correlation is obtained, which provides the decision maker with more knowledge and confident to make better decisions.

References

Bustince, H and P Burillo (1995). Correlation of interval-valued intuitionistic fuzzy sets. *Fuzzy Sets and Systems*, 74, 237–244.

Chiang, DA and NP Lin (1999). Correlation of fuzzy sets. *Fuzzy Sets and Systems*, 102, 221–226.

Dubois, D and H Prade (1991). Fuzzy sets in approximate reasoning, Part 1: Inference with possibility distributions. *Fuzzy Sets and Systems*, 40, 143–202.

Hong, D and S Hwang (1995). Correlation of intuitionistic fuzzy sets in probability space. *Fuzzy Sets and Systems*, 75, 77–81.

Hong, D (2006). Fuzzy measures for a correlation coefficient of fuzzy numbers under Tw (the weakest t norm)-based fuzzy arithmetic operations. *Fuzzy Sets and Systems*, 176, 150–160.

Liu, S and C Kao (2002). Fuzzy measures for correlation coefficient of fuzzy numbers. *Fuzzy Sets and Systems*, 128, 267–275.

Lowen, R (1990). A fuzzy language interpolation theorem. *Fuzzy Sets and Systems*, 34, 33–38.

Ruspini, E (1991). Approximate reasoning: Past, present, future. *Information Sciences*, 57, 297–317.

Wu, B and Y Hsu (2002). The use of kernel set and sample memberships in the identification of nonlinear time series. *Soft Computing Journal*, 8(3), 207–216.

Zadeh, LA (1965). Fuzzy sets. *Information and Control*, 8, 338–353.

Yu, C (1993). Correlation of fuzzy numbers. *Fuzzy Sets and systems*, 55, 303–307.

Chapter 11

NON-PARAMETRIC TEST WITH FUZZY DATA AND ITS APPLICATIONS IN THE PERFORMANCE EVALUATION OF CUSTOMER CAPITAL

Yu-Lan Lee

Department of Educational Policy and Administration,
National Chi Nan University, Taiwan
aerylee@yahoo.com.tw

Ming-leih Wu

Graduate Institute of Adult and Continuing Education
National Chi Nan University, Taiwan
mlwu@ncnu.edu.tw

Chunti Su

Department of Educational Policy and Administration,
National Chi Nan University, Taiwan
voodoobiker@gmail.com

In such a globalised era accompanied with dramatically competitive waves, contemporary community colleges have drawn more and more attention on their performance management. This study aims to measure performance from customer capital and propose solutions that can effectively improve the performance measurement on community colleges. We utilise soft computing method to design a performance evaluation model. By fuzzy statistical methods, we retrieve the community college management features and build up performance indicators, such as enrollment, satisfaction, and attendance for customer capital. Community colleges can perform effective decision-making on performance evaluation by adapting the analysis of customer capital.

Keywords: Performance indicators; community colleges; customer capital.

1. Introduction

In recent years, international organisations have devoted themselves to promoting life-long learning and responding to the power of social change. The related measures have affected the development of community colleges all over the world. The community colleges need to deal with accountability in terms of educational goals, participants' needs, and internal curriculum design.

The establishment of community colleges has been viewed as the chance for reforming the civil society. Based on the belief of 'reconstruct the society', community colleges aim at promoting knowledge liberation and the formation of civil society. Huang (1999) categorises the curriculum into three dimensions: Exploring fundamental issues (academic programs), developing the public areas (club programs), and enriching the meaning of life (life skills programs).

By self-directed learning model (Knowles, 1980), the adult students enter the community college and take courses through the market mechanism. However, the community colleges have encountered three kinds of difficulties. First, the participants tend to have low interests in academic and public courses. Second, the participants prefer practical courses and lead some market-oriented community colleges to provide too many life skills courses. Third, academic and public welfare related courses are being crowed by too many life skills courses. The community colleges have faced the dilemma between maintaining its ideal core-value of developing civil society and meeting participants' recreational needs to survive. Hence, the community colleges become cram-school-liked. Further, the situation can be remedied as Tocqueville' mentioned, 'The electors trust their representative to be as eager in their private interests as in those of the country' (Tocqueville, 1840). We can combine private interests with the public good. By doing so, the participants will feel more meaningful with regard to community services. Fukuyama (1995) pointed out that being trusted in the group creates high individual and group performance. People join organisations out of an interest in cooperating with society, which adds meaning to life. Embedding concepts about public welfare, such as social participation, and social consideration in the life skills courses can not only suit personal need but also promote community participation. Above all, the community colleges might be approaching the goal of civil society.

2. Measuring the Performance of Community College

Performance indicators have gained support as the means for measuring institutional effectiveness in community colleges recently. However, only a few researches have examined performance management in community colleges from the perspective of customer capital. The purpose of this study is to explore the course performance in which factors have emerged and to assess the effects of performance indicators.

The so-called performance is a level where the individuals achieve their intended goals. Performance measurement should be taken by a multidimensional approach. Generally speaking, indicators to measure business performance can be divided into two categories — financial indicators and non-financial indicators. Hatten (1978) pointed out the level of business performance depends on the controllable and uncontrollable variables of a company. We can express the concepts as a function:

Performance $= f$ (factors of discussion domain, controllable variables, noise).

According to Venkatraman and Ramanujam (1986), there are three domains to measure the business performance: (1) financial performance; (2) business performance; (3) organisational effectiveness.

As the non-profit organisations, it is not suitable for community colleges to use business indicators for measuring the performance. The Gavilan College, located in California U.S., develops its indicators: (1) Course Success Rates; (2) Course Retention Rates; (3) Persistence Rates; (4) Award Rates (5) Transfer Rates (6) Population

Participation Rates (Gavilan College, 2010). Key Performance Indicators (KPI) is a province-wide accountability tool established by the Ontario government in 1998 to measure and reward College performance in meeting specific goals and objectives. The Ministry of Training, Colleges and Universities in collaboration with the Ontario Colleges identified five measurements to be used as the KPI: (1) Graduate Employment; (2) Graduate Satisfaction; (3) Employer Satisfaction; (4) Student Satisfaction; (5) Graduation Rate (Centennial College, 2010).

Kaplan and Norton (1996) co-developed Balanced Scorecard. Through four dimensions in terms of finance, customer, internal and learning process, and three time periods (past, current, and future), the BS help enterprises to examine their short-term operation and long-term foci and on the vision of the target (Olve *et al.*, 1999). As a policy framework for measurement and management system, it will combine performance evaluation systems and strategies to form a concrete action.

Among the indicators, knowledge or information from customers, the stakeholders of a certain organisation or institution, plays a critical role on performance evaluation. Edvinsson and Malone (1997) have indicated that customer capital has been viewed as a major source of competitive advantage in the knowledge economy. With regard to evaluating the customer capital, former researchers suggested some concepts, for instance, customer retention rate, customer attrition rate, customer loyalty, and customer profitability (Wayland and Cole, 1997).

Community colleges are different from general universities. The goal value is social participation instead of graduation rates. Hence, this study provides a customer-oriented model of performance measurement. The model includes three critical factors of customer capital, such as students' attendance, satisfaction and enrollment, to create indicators of performance measurement that are suitable for community colleges.

The purposes of this study are as follows: (1) To establish performance management indicators of community college. (2) To analyse the customer capital of community colleges.

3.   Fuzzy Methods

3.1.   *Research process*

This research establishes performance indicators and the value of the community college system to analysis the customer capital. Measure of weight is based on three dimensions: Student enrollment, satisfaction and attendance to explore performance management system.

Figure 1 represents a performance management dynamic process of community college. Through customer capital analysis in terms of the enrollment, customer satisfaction and student attendance, we analyses the course performance and examine whether the performance meet the goal orientation or not.

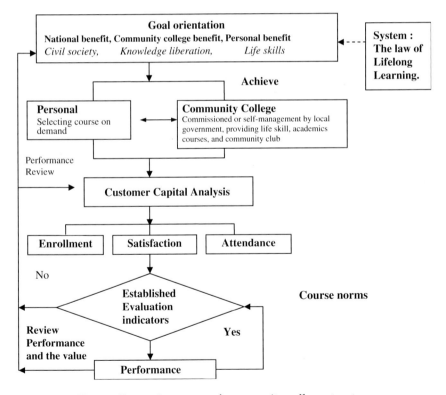

Fig. 1.   Dynamic process of community college structure.

3.2. Fuzzy statistics to analysis

Fuzzy statistics are becoming more important in measuring ambiguous concepts in social sciences. Why is it that the traditional numerical model cannot explain complex human and social phenomena? Manski (1990) reminded of the risk of too much demand for digital data and over-interpretation. Using fuzzy data, we may avoid such risks. However, ambiguous data are consistent with human logic during the computing process. Human thoughts and feelings are ambiguous and uncertain, and on the satisfaction scale, happiness, sadness, strength, weakness, optimism, pessimism, and so on are not easy to assess. Language and concepts are limited for analysis by traditional logic technology. The fuzzy sets concept, first proposed by Zadeh, uses the principle of fuzzy measure and classification to deal with the dynamic environment, to give a more reasonable description (Zadeh, 1965; Wu, 2010).

3.3. Determination about price fuzzy distribution

It is appropriate to apply the membership function, a more precise mathematical technique, in analysing the fuzzy information. The value of the membership function, between zero and one, is derived from the characteristic function, to express the membership grade of each element in a set. There are many types of membership functions, such as Z-type, Λ-type, Π-type, S-type, etc, (see Nguyen and Wu, 2006). In this research we use Λ-type membership functions. It assesses the fuzzy interval of various valuations, and then calculates the fuzzy value of an enterprise according to appraiser's fuzzy weighting.

We also use the Λ-type to reflect the value for a commercial house price distribution. That is, we will give the price of commercial houses into different linguistic terms, such as, high-level, intermediate and unfurnished. Each term will correspond to a real value, which will be determined by the sampling survey and fuzzy statistical analysis.

The highly correlated property for the discussion factors

After detailed discussion from the above sections, an integrated process of fuzzy valuation is started by fixing the crucial affection factors of the commercial house. We use the weighted arithmetic average instead of the geometric average. The reason is that the factors are highly correlated; any extreme value of a certain factor will influence the real price of the commercial house. Take evaluating the price of commodity house as an example.

Suppose the factors of the valuation price are {location, house type, community, quality}. If the factor location is valueless, no matter the community is high and/or the other factors are high too, the integrated valuation will be low.

Finally, we make weighted arithmetic average to get a more appropriate valuation. That is, suppose the factor set is $A = \{A_1, A_2, \ldots, A_l\}$ and which corresponding to the with a weight set $w = \{w_1, w_2, \ldots, w_l\}$, then the integrated Valuation Price will be Valuation Price $= \prod_{i=1}^{l} A_i^{w_i}$.

Definition 3.1. Fuzzy sample mode (data with multiple values): Let U be the universal set (a discussion domain), $L = \{L_1, L_2, \ldots, L_k\}$ a set of k-linguistic variables on U, and $\{FS_i, i = 1, 2, \ldots, n\}$ a sequence of random fuzzy sample on U. For each sample FS_i, assign a linguistic variable L_j a normalised membership m_{ij} ($\sum_{j=1}^{k} m_{ij} = 1$), let $S_j = \sum_{i=1}^{n} m_{ij}, j = 1, 2, \ldots, k$. Then, the maximum value of S_j (with respect to L_j) is called the fuzzy mode (*FM*) of this sample. That is $FM = \{L_j | S_j = \max_{1 \leq i \leq k} S_i\}$.

Note: A significant level α for fuzzy mode can be defined as follows: Let U be the universal set (a discussion domain), $L = \{L_1, L_2, \ldots, L_k\}$ a set of k-linguistic variables on U, and $\{FS_i, i = 1, 2, \ldots, n\}$ a sequence of random fuzzy sample on U. For each sample FS_i, assign a linguistic variable L_j a normalised membership m_{ij} ($\sum_{j=1}^{k} m_{ij} = 1$), let $S_j = \sum_{i=1}^{n} I_{ij}, j = 1, 2, \ldots, k$ $I_{ij} = 1$ if $m_{ij} \geq \alpha$, $I_{ij} = 0$ if $m_{ij} < \alpha$, α is the significant level. Then, the maximum value of S_j (with respect to L_j) is called the fuzzy mode (*FM*) of this sample. That is $FM = \{L_j | S_j = \max_{1 \leq i \leq k} S_i\}$. More than two sets of L_j that reach the conditions, assures that the fuzzy sample has multiple common agreement.

3.4. *Ranking fuzzy data*

Ranking method for continuous fuzzy numbers has so far not been defined uniquely semantically, and probably never will. Now we put our focus on two common methods. In order to solve the problems, we proposed that a method is not only relatively easy in computing but also has fewer limitations to fuzzy data types.

Definition 3.2. Defuzzification for a interval fuzzy number
Let $A = [a, b]$ be a interval on U with its centric $c = (a + b)/2$. Then the defuzzification number RA of $A = [a, b]$ is defined as:

$$RA = c + \left(1 - \frac{\ln(1 + r)}{r}\right),$$

where $r = |b - a|$ is the length of the interval.

3.5. *Non-parametric tests with fuzzy data*

Ranking data is an important concept on non-parametric tests. By using Ex. (3.2) above, we can rank continuous fuzzy numbers simultaneously and easily. Traditional non-parametric tests could not deal with fuzzy data. Therefore, ranking technique will be applied.

The use of non-parametric methods was introduced to test the hypotheses of (median) identical in the Wilcoxon rank sum test. That is to test if two random samples could have come from two populations with the same mean. The result of the two samples are combined and arranged in order of increasing size and given a rank number. This suggests the test statistics $W =$ the sum of the rank in the combined sample associated with X observations. If W is less than the critical value, the null hypothesis of the same median would be rejected.

Another interesting question is the issue of inconsistency of the scorer, which is thought to be the biggest barrier to reliable assessment. To answer this question, the use of non-parametric methods was introduced to test the hypotheses of (median) identical in the Kruskal–Wallis one-way analysis of variance. We let $N = \sum_{i=1}^{k} n_i$ be the total number of observations in the k treatments. We assigned the rank 1 to the smallest of pool scores, the rank 2 to the next, and so on to the largest, which was given the rank N. In case of ties we assigned the tied observations to the average of the ranks that would be assigned. The Kruskal–Wallis test statistics is defined as:

$$K = \frac{12}{N(N+1)} \sum_{i=1}^{k} \frac{R_i^2}{n_i} - 3(N+1).$$

Here R_i is the sum of the ranks assigned to observations in the k-th treatment. Since K follows a $\chi^2(k\text{-}1)$ distribution, the null hypothesis of equal means (median) is rejected when K exceeds the critical value.

Example 3.1. Taiwan researchers want to develop three kinds of new sleeping pills. They decide to test its effectiveness by measuring the time it takes for people to fall asleep after taking the pill. A random sample of 22 volunteers (was separated into three groups) who regularly suffer from insomnia is chosen. Each participant is fitted a device that measures the times sleep occurs until sleep ends. The data and calculations for obtaining the test statistics are summarised in Table 1. At the $\alpha = 0.05$ level of significance, can we say a difference in sleeping hours exists among these three new

Table 1.   Sleeping hours.

Obser- vations	1	2	3	4	5	6	7	8	9	R
Group 1	(2,4)	(3,4)	(2,3)	(3.5,4)	(5,6)	(5.5,7)	(3,3.5)	(1.5,2)	(2.5,4)	66
	4	7	3	8	14	18	6	1	5	
Group 2	(5,6.5)	(3.5,4.5)	(4.5,6.5)	(1.5,2.5)	(5,7)	(4.5,6)	(4,6)			84
	16	9	15	2	17	13	12			
Group 3	(3.5,4)	(6.5,7)	(3.5,6.0)	(6.5,8)	(6,8)	(6,7)				103
	10	20	11	22	21	19				

drugs?

$$K = \frac{12}{22(22+1)} \left(\frac{66^2}{9} + \frac{84^2}{7} + \frac{103^2}{6} \right)$$

$$- 3(22 + 1) = 8.32 > \chi^2_{0.05}(2) = 5.99.$$

Hence, we can say that there exists a difference in sleeping hours among these three new drugs.

4. An Empirical Study

4.1. *Fuzzy statistical analysis*

In this study, we focus on three major dimensions of customer capital that involves student satisfaction, registration numbers and student attendance as important factors. Moreover, we calculate the fuzzy-weighted values to reflect their real value. The testing statistic formula is as follows:

$EV_t = R_t^{0.2} \cdot A_t^{0.3} \cdot S_t^{0.5};$

$R_t = 0.8 + (x - 20)^*0.01,$ $x =$ *number of registered students* < 40

$A_t =$ *rate of attendants*;

$S_t =$ *degree of satisfaction*.

According to the significance of indicators, expert analysis and evaluation, we found that attendant rate would accounts for 0.3 powers; degree of satisfaction accounts for 0.5 power; number of registered students represents 0.3 powers.

4.2. *Performance analysis of community college courses*

As shown in Table 2, the chosen performance indicators must be applied to the community college courses for at least three consecutive years. The average score of community club is 0.9385 (The course name is 'Calligraphy Art'), whereas the average of academic class is 0.9373 (The course name is 'Life and Law'). As for life skill, the score is 0.90815 (The course name is ballroom dancing). With regard the minimum and maximum, there is no anomaly.

Table 2.   Descriptive statistics of performance indicators that community college courses have been for three consecutive years.

	Calligraphy (community club)	Life and Law (academic)	Ballroom Dancing (life skill)
Average	0.9385	0.9373	0.90815
Minimum	0.91	0.9036	0.8583
Max	0.9586	0.9534	0.9504
Variance	0.000347608	0.000326616	0.001028655

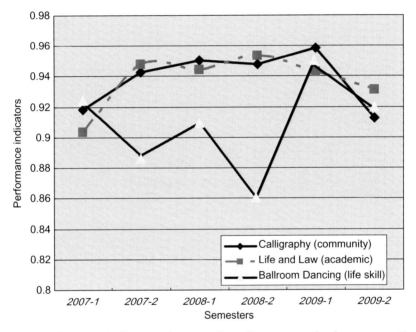

Fig. 2.   Performance indicators of community college courses for three consecutive years.

Among the three classes, community club that refers to Calligraphy Art possess the largest customer capital, while the second is academic courses (Life and Law). Life skill class is the least. The results display that variance of life skill class reached a maximum of 0.001, it implied that it has the largest differences between semesters in each performance indicator.

4.3. *Testing hypothesis with non-parametric methods*

We use Wilcoxon Rank-Sum Test and the Kruskal–Wallis (one-way ANOVA for non-parametric method) to see the differences of background variables on the study purposes among groups. We consider the variables, such as participants (gender, age, education), school location (city and country type), and three categories of courses (civil society, academics courses, and life skill) then we try to check the relationship with each other.

According to the result of Table 3 we find:

(1) Persons who study in city type community college accept civil society more.

Table 3.   Wilcoxon Rank-Sum Test and Kruskal–Wallis Test Ranks $N = 64$.

	Grouping variables	N	Testing statistics	Decision $\alpha = 0.05$
Civil society	City	35	Rank sum of W = 1327	Reject H_0
	Country	29	$Z = 2.56 > Z_{0.05} = 1.65$,	
			$p = 0.035$	
Knowledge liberation	Female	41	Rank sum of W = 1194	Reject H_0
	Male	23	$Z = -1.94 < Z_{0.05} = -1.65$,	
			$p = 0.047$	
Civil society	High school	27	Rank sum of W = 1002.5	Reject H_0
	College	37	$Z = 1.7 > Z_{0.05} = -1.65$,	
			$p = 0.0365$	
Life skill	High school	27	Rank sum of W = 724.5	Reject H_0
	College	37	$Z = -2.08 < Z_{0.05} - 1.65$,	
			$p = 0.0177$	
Life skill	20–40 years old	6	$K = 0.25 < \chi^2_{0.05}(2) = 5.991$,	Accept H_0
	41–60	49	$p = 0.88$	
	61~	9		
Diploma	20–40 years old	6	$K = 6.756 > \chi^2_{0.05}(2) = 5.991$,	Reject H_0
	41–60	49	$p = 0.034$	
	61~	9		
Vocational training	20–40 years old	6	$K = 10.166 > \chi^2_{0.05}(2) = 5.991$,	Reject H_0
	41–60	49	$p = 0.006$	
	61~	9		

(2) Persons with lower education background accept civil society more than the higher ones.

(3) Persons with higher education background like life skill course more.

(4) Men want to take academics courses that are a far greater status than women do.

(5) Students in their 20–40 years hope to obtain diploma.

(6) Students in their 41–60 years hope to obtain vocational training.

5. Conclusions

This study examines the performance of community college by fuzzy method from the perspective of customer capital. The evaluation model includes three major indicators: enrolment, satisfaction, and attendance. According to the function computing, community club possess the most customer capitals than academic and life skill. Although civil society courses are not the most favourite choice of students, teachers used the art of Calligraphy as the mediator to attract students to the class and made connection to a sense of community. It obtained a high degree of identity from the customers.

Based on the findings, this study makes the following suggestions: (1) Community clubs are the highest performance indicators. (2) By encouraging a sense of community, students can obtain a high degree of identity. (3) Life skill courses need to combine with civil society courses to attract higher education and female students to join the classes.

References

Centennial College (2010). *Key Performance Indicators*. Available at http://www.centennialcollege.ca/AboutUs/KPI [accessed on 6 November 2010].

Edvinsson, L and MS Malone (1997). *Intellectual Capital: Realizing Your Company's True Value by Finding its Hidden Brainpower*. New York: Harper Business.

Fukuyama, F (1995). *Trust: The Social Virtues and the Creation of Prosperity*. New York, NY: Free Press.

Gavilan College (2010). *Gavilan Community College-Performance Indicators and Goals*. Available at http://www.gavilan.edu/ce/index.html [accessed on 6 November 2010].

Hatten, KJ, DE Schendel and AC Cooper (1978). A strategic model of the U.S. brewing industry: 1952–1971. *Academy of Management Journal*, 21, 592–610.

Huang, WS (1999). A few questions, a dream, *National Association for the Promotion of Community Universities, NAPCU*. Available at http://apcu.taconet.com.tw/html/intro.htm [accessed on 29 April 2010].

Liu, H, B Wu and M Liu (2008). Investor's preference order of fuzzy numbers. *Computers and Mathematics with Applications*, 55, 2623–2630.

Lin, Y, M Yil and B Wu (2006). Fuzzy classification analysis of rules usage on probability reasoning test with multiple raw rule score. *Educational Technologies*, 2, 54–59.

Kaplan, RS and DP Norton (1996). *The Balanced Scorecard: Translating Strategy into Action*. Boston, Massachusetts: Harvard Business School Press.

Knowles, MS (1980). *The Modern Practice of Adult Education: From Pedagogy to Andragogy*, 2nd edn. New York: Cambridge Books.

Kreinovich, V, HN Guyen and B Wu (2007). On-line algorithms for computing mean and variance of interval data and their use in intelligent systems. *Journal of Information Science*, 177, 3228–3238.

Nguyen, H, V Kreinovich and B Wu (1999). Fuzzy/Probability~Fractal/Smooth. *International Journal of Uncertainty, Fuzziness and Knowledge-based Systems*, 7(4), 363–370.

Nguyen, H and B Wu (2006). *Fundamentals of Statistics with Fuzzy Data*. Heidelberg: Springer-Verlag.

Olve, N, J Roy and M Wetter (1999). *Performance Drivers: A Practical Guide to Using the Balanced Scorecard*. New York: Wiley.

Sun, CM and B Wu (2007). New statistical approaches for fuzzy data. *International Journal of Uncertainty, Fuzziness and Knowledge-based Systems*, 15(2), 89–106.

Tocqueville, AD (1840). *Democracy in America*. Available at http://www.tocqueville.org/ [accessed on 15 June 2010].

Venkatraman, N and V Ramanujam (1986). Measurement of business performance in strategy research: A comparison of approaches. *Academy of Management Review*, 11(4), 801–814.

Wayland, RE and PM Cole (1997). *Customer Connections: New Strategies for Growth*. USA: Harvard Business School Press.

Wu, B and L Kao (2007). New fuzzy dynamic evaluation for ERP benefits. *Journal of Applied Business Research*, 22(4), 89–102.

Wu, B and SK Chang (2007). On testing hypothesis of fuzzy mean. *Journal of Industrial and Applied Mathematics*, 242, 171–183.

Wu, B and SM Ho (2008). Evaluating intellectual capital with integrated fuzzy statistical analysis: A case study on the CD POB. *International Journal of Information and Management Sciences*, 19(2), 285–300.

Wu, B and YH Lin (2002). The introduction of fuzzy mode and its applications. *Information of Statistics with Measurement*, 47, 23–27

Xie, J, B Wu and S Scriboonchita (2010). Fuzzy estimation methods and their application in the real estate evaluation. *International Journal of Intelligent Technologies and Applied Statistics*, 3(2), 187–202.

Chapter 12

TOO MUCH ADO ABOUT NOTHING? FUZZY MEASUREMENT OF JOB STRESS FOR SCHOOL LEADERS

Berlin Wu

Department of Math Sciences,
National Chengchi University, Taiwan
berlin@nccu.edu.tw

Mei Fen Liu

Department of Education Policy and Ad,
National Chinan University, Taiwan
molly@mail.ksps.tcc.edu.tw

In such a globalised era that accompanied with dramatically competitive waves, schools leaders have drawn more and more stress on their jobs. This chapter is aimed at analysing and evaluating job stress factors of school leaders. We present the assessment program by using the Fuzzy Delphi method and fuzzy questionnaire sampling survey. We proposed the index of job stress of school leaders by the use of fuzzy evaluation methods as well as soft computation. From the empirical study, we can see that the three dimensions with eight indicators can explain the state of school leaders' pressure very well. The proposed index of job stress for school leaders shows an efficient index in the job stress research.

Keywords: Fuzzy evaluation; fuzzy set theory; job stress; school leaders.

1. Introduction

Measuring the stress indicator is a popular topic in the behaviour science. There is a lot of literature on the discoursing evaluation methods as well as the measurement process about school leaders' job stress.

Takao *et al.* (2006) indicated that as job stress now is one of the biggest health-related problems in the workplace, many education programs for supervisors have been conducted to decrease job stress. It stated a possible useful effect of supervisor education on the psychological problems and job performance of subordinates. This effect may be different according to specific groups.

Vetter (1977) argued that school leaders occupy vertex positions, and like all high level executives, they are subject to fierce pressures and stresses. As is the principal, so is the school (Valentine and Bowman, 1991). Esp (1981) addressed that recruitment of headmasters is hard, partly because the job is complex and involves pressures from different groups. Protheroe (2005) described the increasing pressures on principals to initiate rapid and significant change. Emery (2007) indicated that in the last 20 years, public education in the United States has been transformed under the pressures of high-stakes testing.

Stoelinga (2008) deemed that over time, new and experienced principals at both elementary and high schools have identified the same top challenges to improving their schools: Pressure to raise test scores quickly, recruiting and hiring teachers, social problems in the school community, difficulty removing ineffective teachers, and working with parents perceived to be apathetic. Overall, the report focuses on critical trends related to principal background and work issues, which includes time use and other challenges principals identify as most problematic.

Rooney (2003) discussed the role of principals in creating a caring community in schools. Characteristics of caring principals, information on the challenges are experienced by principals and role of principals in shielding schools from outside pressures. Auerbach (2009) stated that family and community engagement are increasingly seen as powerful tools for making schools more equitable, culturally responsive and collaborative. The commitment of school leaders is vital to school-community relations, yet is poorly documented in the literature and insufficiently addressed in training for administrators.

Hewitt *et al.* (2009) investigated why teachers, identified by their school principal as being leaders or having leadership potential, chose not to become school principals. The literature is reporting a shortage of qualified applicants for school administrative positions. The main reasons most cited by teacher leaders include testing/accountability pressures too great, job too stressful, too much time required, and societal problems make it hard to focus on instruction. The main factors for teachers choosing not to develop a career in school administration are categorised as stress and time demands are too great.

Pryor *et al.* (2004) represented that solving school problems and making policy decisions require that we anticipate how people will feel about an issue or how they will behave. School leaders must comprehend the values, attitudes, and beliefs brought to different situations.

Above all, we know in such a globalised era that accompanied with dramatically competitive waves, school leaders have paid more and more attention to their performance management and it will bring much job stress.

However, the main drawback in the conventional approach is that people use the true-false logic instead of linguistic logic to analyse human thought. In this chapter, we use interval value data and multiple concepts to measure the job stress.

There is a lack of systematic study about creating pressure indicators of school leaders. The purpose of this research is to examine the cause of relationship in three dimensions of school leaders' job-related stressors (personal dimension, campus dimension and social dimension) and eight factors(work load, role expectations, vision goal, use of resource, crisis management, policy plans, public relations, and parental expectation).

In this research, we use the concept of fuzzy statistic to explore and analyse school leaders' pressure indicators in an attempt to promote the work performance at schools. We will try to establish the school leaders' fuzzy statistical indicators of job stress. Major objectives of this research are listed as follows: (1) to understand the pressure distribution from personal, campus and social dimensions of the school leaders, (2) to establish stress indicators of school leaders, and (3) to explore the pressure index and stress factors of school leaders.

2.   Research Model and Hypothesis

2.1.   *Application with fuzzy set theory and soft method*

After the research of FGRS (Fuzzy Graphic Rating Scale) presented by Hesketh et al. (1988), Costas et al. (1994) furthered to choose 100 university students as a sample of the research, they found that FGRS really fits to the feature of human psychology.

Herrera *et al.* (2000) presented the steps of linguistic decision analysis under linguistic information. Their statements believe that there are certain degrees of possibilities to express linguistics based on fuzzy number, but it should be reconsidered if the response will produce the same fuzzy number.

Liu and Song (2001) developed one type of measurement whose linguistic is similar to semantic proximity. Based on the similarity of linguistic concept, they presented a formula of fuzzy association degree. They used the information of botany as an example to illustrate and analyse the categorical similarity of rare plant in the ecology. Carlsson and Fuller (2000a), Carlsson and Fuller (2000b), Chiang *et al.* (2000), Herrera *et al.* (2000), Dubois and Prade (1991) discussed many concepts about the computation of fuzzy linguistic and these concepts were worthy to broadcast.

Usually, more extensive sources of work stress come from the pressure content of school leaders through the literature review, pressure from three dimensions including individual, campus and social, and the weight to eight main factors. Fuzzy statistical model is built on the school leaders' pressure index. The dynamics of structure are shown in Fig. 1.

In this chapter, we will consider three dimensions of school leaders' job stress involving in indicators are: (1) Personal dimension: work load, role expectations; (2) Campus dimension: vision goal, use of resource, crisis management; (3) Social dimension: policy plans, public relations, and parental expectation.

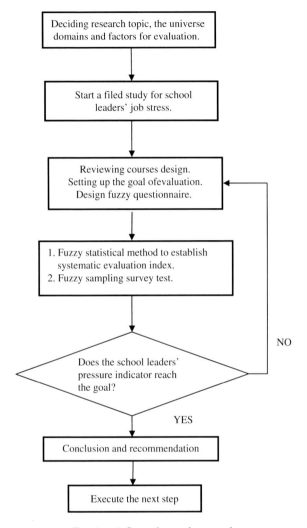

Fig. 1.   A flow chart of research.

2.2. *Statistical analysis with fuzzy data*

In the research on social sciences, the sampling survey is always used to evaluate and understand public opinions on certain issues. The traditional survey forces people to choose fixed answer from the survey, but it ignores the uncertainty of human thinking. For instance, when people need to choose the answer from the survey which lists five choices including 'Very satisfactory', 'Satisfactory', 'Normal', 'Unsatisfactory', 'Very unsatisfactory', despite of the fact that the answer to the question is continual type, we may be only allowed to choose one answer. It limits the flexibility of the answer and forces people to choose fixed answers. When the survey proposes to have the answer for sleeping hours of a person, it will be difficult to describe the feeling or understanding reasonably unless the fuzzy statistics are adopted.

Traditional statistics deal with single answer or certain range of the answer through sample survey, unable to sufficiently reflect the thought of an individual. If people can use the membership function to express the degree of their feelings based on their own choices, the answer presented will be closer to real human thinking. Therefore, to collect the information based on the fuzzy mode should be more reasonable. In the consideration for the question related with fuzzy property, the information itself had the uncertainty and fuzzy property.

Since many sampling survey is closely related to fuzzy thinking while the factor of set can be clearly grouped into many categories, it will be useful if we apply discrete fuzzy number to the public consensus. Social scientists want to study the internal motivation or feeling of personal behaviours, traditional quantifiable statistics almost require the subjects to express a single motivation or feeling and attempt to apply definitive quantified statistics to display irregular behaviours of human beings and analyse psychological measurements from a probability perspective, mathematical pattern actually simplified complex issue, nevertheless the complicated subjective point of view and thinking were usually overpass (Wu, 2005; Nguyen and Wu, 2006).

The purpose of this chapter is to develop an indicator system for the assessment of the school leaders' job stress. Using Fuzzy Theory through the Fuzzy Delphi method to form an expert questionnaire, Buckley (1985) mentioned that the fuzzy analysis does not use the exact value, but should adopt a vague message to conduct analysis, taking membership function to reflect the fuzzy messages of experts' answer, for the integration of experts' ambiguity of uncertainty levels for the indicators and to retain information and consensus that experts provided. The questionnaire data obtained in this way can more fully show the meaning and value of the study. Zimmermann (1991) proposed that the fuzzy message refers to the semantic variables and ambiguity when the experts determine things. Thence, this study utilises the fuzzy Delphi method to solve the problem of linguistic ambiguity and avoid the researchers getting too subjective in the integration of expert opinions.

Continuous fuzzy data can be classified into several types, such as interval-valued numbers, triangular numbers, trapezoid numbers and exponential numbers etc. Most fuzzy numbers get these names from the sharp of membership function. Even though there are various types of fuzzy numbers, but we limit the discussion to three usual types: Interval-valued numbers, triangular numbers, and trapezoid numbers here. The definitions of the three types of fuzzy data are given as follows.

Definition 2.1. *A fuzzy number $A = [a, b, c, d]$, defined on the universe set U of real number R with its vertex $a \leq b \leq c \leq d$, is said to be a trapezoidal fuzzy number if its membership function is given by:*

$$u_A(x) = \begin{cases} \dfrac{x-a}{b-a}, & a \leq x \leq b \\ 1, & b \leq x \leq c \\ \dfrac{d-x}{d-c}, & c \leq x \leq d \\ 0, & otherwise \end{cases}.$$

When $b = c$, A is called a triangular fuzzy number; when $a = b$ and $c = d$, A is called an interval-valued fuzzy number.

Definition 2.2. *Fuzzy expected values*

Let $A_i = [a_i, b_i, c_i, d_i]$ be a sequence of random trapezoid fuzzy sample on U. Then the fuzzy expected value is defined as $E(X) = \left[\frac{1}{n} \sum_{i=1}^{n} a_i, \frac{1}{n} \sum_{i=1}^{n} b_i, \frac{1}{n} \sum_{i=1}^{n} c_i, \frac{1}{n} \sum_{i=1}^{n} d_i \right].$

2.3. Correlation with fuzzy data

For the interval valued fuzzy number, we need to take out samples from population X and Y. Each fuzzy interval data for sample X centroids has x_i x_i and for sample Y has centroid y_i. For the interval data, we also have to consider whether the length of interval fuzzy data are similar or not. In Mr. Smith's example, if the correlation between the expected salary and working hours are high, then we can expect two things: (1) The higher salary the new employee expects, the more working hours he can endure; (2) The wider the range of the expected salary, the wider the range of the working hours should be. However, how should one combine the information from both centroid and length? If they are combined with equal weight, it is possible that the combined correlation would exceed the boundaries of 1 or −1. In addition, the effect of length should not be greater than the impact of centroids. In order to get the rational fuzzy correlations, we use natural logarithms to make some adjustments.

Definition 2.3. *Let* $(X_i = [a_i, b_i, c_i, d_i], Y_i = [e_i, f_i, g_i, h_i]; i = 1, 2, \ldots n)$ *be a sequence of paired trapezoid fuzzy sample on population Ω with its pair of centroid (cx_i, cy_i) and pair of area $\|x_i\| = area(x_i), \|y_i\| = area(y_i)$.*

$$cr_{xy} = \frac{\sum_{i=1}^{n} (cx_i - \overline{cx})(cy_i - \overline{cy})}{\sqrt{\sum_{i=1}^{n} (cx_i - \overline{cx})^2}\sqrt{\sum_{i=1}^{n} (cy_i - \overline{cy})^2}},$$

$$ar_{xy} = \frac{\sum_{i=1}^{n} (\|x_i\| - \|\overline{x}_i\|)(\|y_i\| - \|\overline{y}_i\|)}{\sqrt{\sum_{i=1}^{n} (\|x_i\| - \|\overline{x}_i\|)^2}\sqrt{\sum_{i=1}^{n} (\|y_i\| - \|\overline{y}_i\|)^2}},$$

(2)

Then fuzzy correlation is defined as:

$$FC = \beta_1 cr_{xy} + \beta_2 ar_{xy}, (\beta_1 + \beta_2 = 1).$$

We choose a pair of (β_1, β_2) depend on the weight of practical use. For instance, if we think the location correlation is much more important than that of e scale, $\beta_1 = 0.8, \beta_2 = 0.2$ will be an appropriate choice.

Example 2.1. Suppose we have the following data as shown in Table 1.

Table 1. Numerical example for interval-valued, triangular and trapezoidal fuzzy data.

	X			Y		
Student	Data	Centroid	Area (length)	Data	Centroid	Area (length)
A	[23,25]	24	2	[1,2]	1.5	1
B	[21,23,26]	23.3	2.5	[0,2,3]	1.7	1.5
C	[26,27,29,35]	28.3	5.5	[0,1]	0.5	1
D	[28,30]	29	2	[1,2,4]	2.3	1.5
E	[25,26,28,35]	28.5	6	[1,2,3,4]	2.5	2
(Fuzzy) Mean	[24.6, 25.2,27,30.2]	26.62	3.6	[0.6,1.4,2.2,2.8]	1.7	1.4

Table 2. Correlations with different combinations of β_1, β_2.

(β_1, β_2)	(1,0)	(0.9, 0.1)	(0.8, 0.2)	(0.7, 0.3)	(0.6, 0.4)	(0.5, 0.5)	(0.4, 0.6)	(0.3, 0.7)	(0.2, 0.8)	(0.1, 0.9)	(0,1)
	0.17	0.19	0.2	0.22	0.23	0.25	0.26	0.28	0.29	0.31	0.32

In this case, the correlation between the two centroids is:

$$cr_{xy} = \frac{\sum_{i=1}^{n} (cx_i - 26.62)(cy_i - 1.7)}{\sqrt{\sum_{i=1}^{n} (cx_i - 26.62)^2} \sqrt{\sum_{i=1}^{n} (cy_i - 1.7)^2}} = 0.17$$

$$ar_{xy} = \frac{\sum_{i=1}^{n} (\|x_i\| - 3.6)(\|y_i\| - 1.4)}{\sqrt{\sum_{i=1}^{n} (\|x_i\| - 3.6)^2} \sqrt{\sum_{i=1}^{n} (\|y_i\| - 1.4)^2}} = 0.32,$$

Table 2 is a list of correlations with various combinations of (β_1, β_2).

2.4. *Modelling stress index*

In order to get a more appropriate measure of the job stress, we evaluate the job stress of our subjects by fuzzy estimation method. The detailed valuation steps are as follows. The stress for school leaders come from three dimensions: Personal, campus, and society.

A trapezoid fuzzy set can be viewed as a continuous fuzzy set, which further represents uncertain events. When a sample of trapezoiddata is presented, we are interesting in scaling its value on the real line. In some practical applications, however, it is reasonable to consider, instead of the original class of all linear re-scalings, a more general class of nonlinear transformations between scales. For example, the energy of an earthquake can be described both in the usual energy units and in the logarithmic (Richter) scale. Similarly, the power of a signal and/or of a sound can be measured in watts and it can also be measured in the logarithmic scale, in decibels.

When we consider the reasonable and meaningful conditions to map trapezoid-data into the real line, we need to identify two conditions. This means that the transformation data should be (1) finite-dimensional, (2) the dependence on these parameters should be smooth (differentiable). In mathematical terms, this means that our transformation group is a Lie group.

Once such a transformation is selected, instead of the original trapezoid-data, we have a new value $y = f(x)$. In the ideal situation, this new quantity y is normally distributed. (In practice, a normal distribution for y may be a good first approximation.) When selecting the transformation, we must take into account that, due to the possibility of a rescaling, the numerical values of the quantity x is not uniquely determined.

Definition 2.4. *Scaling for a trapezoid fuzzy number on R.*

Let $A = [a, b, c, d]$ be a trapezoid fuzzy number on U with its centroid $(cx, cy) = (\frac{\int x u_A(x)dx}{\int u_A(x)dx}, \frac{\int \frac{1}{2}(u_A(x))^2 dx}{\int u_A(x)dx})$. *Then the defuzzification number RA of* $A = [a, b, c, d]$ *is defined as:*

$$RA = cx + \left(1 - \frac{\ln(1 + \|A\|)}{\|A\|}\right),$$

where $\|A\|$ is the area of the trapezoid.

Note that for convenience we will write $RA = \frac{a+b+c+d}{4}$, if A is a trapezoid; $RA = \frac{a+b+c}{3}$, if A is a triangle; $R(A) = \frac{b+c}{2}$, if A is an interval.

Example 2.2. Let $A_1 = [2, 2, 3, 3]$, $A_2 = [1, 1, 4, 4]$, $A_3 = [1, 2.5, 2.5, 4]$, $A_4 = [1, 2.5, 2.5, 8]$, $A_5 = [1, 2, 3, 4]$, $A_6 = [1, 2, 3, 8]$. Then:

$$RA_1 = 2.5 + \left(1 - \frac{\ln(1+1)}{1}\right) = 2.5 + 0.3069 = 2.8069,$$

$$RA_2 = 2.5 + \left(1 - \frac{\ln(1+3)}{3}\right) = 2.5 + 0.5379 = 3.0379$$

$$RA_3 = 2.5 + \left(1 - \frac{\ln(1+1.5)}{1.5}\right) = 2.5 + 0.3891 = 2.8891,$$

$$RA_4 = 3.83 + \left(1 - \frac{\ln(1+3.5)}{3.5}\right) = 3.83 + 0.5703 = 4.3,$$

$$RA_5 = 2.5 + \left(1 - \frac{\ln(1+2)}{2}\right) = 2.5 + 0.4507 = 2.9507,$$

$$RA_6 = 3.79 + \left(1 - \frac{\ln(1+4)}{4}\right) = 3.79 + 0.5976 = 4.3876.$$

In this chapter, we investigated the transaction pressure under the empirical studies in Taiwan. As is known to all, some of the schools are located in cities, and others are in village and even in mountains. Therefore, three typical cases in the district of Taiwan are selected by the rank of population.

Let:

$$S = P^{w_1} \cdot C^{w_2} \cdot O^{w_3},$$

where S = the total stress, P = stress comes from the personal reason, C = the stress comes from the campus, O = stress comes from the society; P, C, O are interval values between $(0,1)$; w_1, w_2, w_3 $(w_1 + w_2 + w_3 = 1)$, stand for the multiplicative weight.

Then we can get the assessment indicator system structure as Fig. 2.

3. Empirical Study

In this study, the Fuzzy Delphi method was used. First, we selected eight senior principals composed of the panel of expert judges.

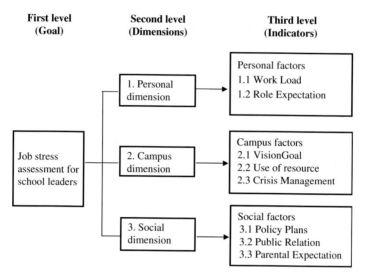

First level
(Goal)

Second level
(Dimensions)

Third level
(Indicators)

Fig. 2.   Index system structure of job stress for school leaders.

The consensus of the panel of expert judges confirmed the relatively fuzzy number for the fuzzy semantic measuring scales. The panel of expert judges expressed their views for the importance of the second level-dimensions and the third level-indicators of assessment system and decided the weight of the assessment dimensions and indicators, in order to construct and develop an assessment indicator system.

3.1. *Fuzzy questionnaires*

In the field of study, we collect 20 school leaders' responses to the information. Ages from 30 to 60, sex is male and female with a frequency 11 and 9 respectively. Most schools are around at the countryside. Descriptive statistics of the sample structure are given in Table 3.

Table 3 gives backgrounds information on the 20 respondents, including gender, age, years of service as a principal, highest level of education, and school size. Out of 20 participants, males were the majority, accounting for 55%, more than a half of the sample; 65% were in the 40–50 years old; 60% of the respondents have been elementary school principals for more than five years; the majority

Table 3. Descriptive statistics of samples.

Background variables		Frequency	Percentage (%)
Gender	Male	11	55
	Female	9	45
Age	< 40	2	10
	40–50	13	65
	> 50	5	25
Years as a principal	< 4	6	30
	5–8	9	45
	> 8	5	15
Highest level of education	University degree	3	15
	Master degree	15	75
	Doctorate degree	2	10
School size	< 12 classes	7	35
	13–24 classes	8	40
	> 24 classes	5	15

of them have master degree, accounting for 75%; 13–24 class school size was the majority of schools, accounting for 40%.

3.2. The experts' judgment opinion on assessment dimensions and indicators

This study established stress index for the school leaders, we accessed eight senior excellent principals in order to establish the content of the average fuzzy weight factors. Each expert has a different opinion on the point of view of the fuzzy linguistic concept. The measure of the fuzzy linguistic scale in this study converts an interval fuzzy number measurement into a fuzzy number representative value. The eight experts' judgment opinion on the weight of the three dimensions and the eight assessment indicators were illustrated in Table 4.

From Table 4, we can see the weights of job stress for school leaders, from personal dimension, campus dimension, and social dimension, has a little difference. For the eight factors, the weighted values exhibited type of uniform distribution among the interval 0.08 and 0.16. It can be said that the school leaders have general pressure from those eight factors.

Table 4.   School leader stress indicators of fuzzy weight.

Dimension	Indicators weight			Total
w_1 personal	*Work load* = 0.14	*Role expectation* = 0.13		0.27
w_2 campus	*Vision goal* = 0.16	*Use of resource* = 0.16	*Crisis management* = 0.11	0.43
w_3 social	*Policy plans* = 0.12	*Public relation* = 0.1	*Parental expectation* = 0.08	0.30

Table 5.   Fuzzy correlations of three factors for leaders' job stress.

	Personal versus campus	Personal versus social	Campus versus social
Centroid correlation	0.4	0.3	0.7
Area correlation	0.2	0.3	0.2
Correlation with $(\beta_1, \beta_2) = (0.9, 0.1)$	0.38	0.3	0.65
Correlation with $(\beta_1, \beta_2) = (0.7, 0.3)$	0.34	0.3	0.55
Correlation with $(\beta_1, \beta_2) = (0.5, 0.5)$	0.30	0.3	0.45

3.3.   The relatively fuzzy numbers of fuzzy linguistic measuring scale

Table 5 shows the fuzzy correlations of three dimensions for job stress.

From Table 5, we found that the correlations from centroid are higher than that of area correlation. Different combination of (β_1, β_2) will make a different correlation value. How to choose an appropriate pair of (β_1, β_2) can be decided from the empirical study.

3.4.   The average defuzzification values of various dimensions of assessment systems

Table 6 illustrates the index of job stress for 20 school leaders. It shows in the analysis results that the defuzzification value is between 0.41 and 0.57 for the three dimensions and eight indicators of the assessment system, indicating that each principal pressure index is medium. It represented that the principals' stress management is good.

Table 6.   Index of job stress for 20 school leaders.

Sample	Personal	Campus	Society	Index of stress
1	0.49	0.56	0.33	0.46
2	0.51	0.52	0.55	0.53
3	0.43	0.76	0.45	0.56
4	0.29	0.59	0.34	0.41
5	0.32	0.48	0.36	0.39
6	0.43	0.63	0.50	0.53
7	0.47	0.64	0.53	0.56
8	0.53	0.37	0.60	0.47
9	0.45	0.57	0.45	0.50
10	0.46	0.32	0.57	0.42
11	0.38	0.56	0.39	0.45
12	0.42	0.65	0.44	0.51
13	0.42	0.55	0.65	0.54
14	0.49	0.56	0.33	0.46
15	0.47	0.56	0.53	0.53
16	0.41	0.72	0.47	0.54
17	0.46	0.56	0.42	0.49
18	0.45	0.57	0.49	0.51
19	0.42	0.66	0.50	0.54
20	0.47	0.76	0.46	0.57

The whole results can first calculate the arithmetic mean of the indicators' values for each dimension, but avoids the value of a certain dimension being too low or equal to zero, influencing the overall results and generated errors, so the three dimensions should not use the arithmetic mean, but separately use the geometric mean of the three dimensions as the integrated stress value.

4.   Conclusions and Recommendations

In this chapter, we utilise fuzzy statistical analysis and fuzzy evaluation to measure the job stress for school leaders. The evaluation model constructed three pressure dimensions including: Personal, Campus and Social; composed of eight indicators of project on pressure scale including: Work load, role expectation, vision goal, use of resource, crisis management, policy plans, public relation, and parental expectation.

The questionnaire was divided into two phases to conduct the survey. The first stage of the Fuzzy Delphi method integrated the results of the panel of expert judges in converting the fuzzy linguistic variances into interval membership function value. The second stage developed the relative weight of assessment indicators. Table 4 shows in the analysis results that the defuzzification value is between 0.08 and 0.16 for the eight indicators of the assessment system, instruction that each of the assessment dimensions and indicators is of average importance. In the indicator weight of the assessment system, 'Vision goal (0.16)' and 'Use of resource (0.16)' attracted most experts' attention and showed the most importance, followed by the 'work load (0.14)'. The interval value of eight indicators was adopted to obtain discrete fuzzy data and established the defuzzification value for each indicator, thereby setting up the basic judgment standard of the assessment indicator system.

Table 6 shows the index defuzzification value of job stress is between 0.41 and 0.57 for the assessment system, indicating that each principal pressure index is medium. It represented that the principals' stress management is good.

The whole results can first calculate the arithmetic mean of the indicators' values for each dimension, but avoids the value of a certain dimension being too low or equal to zero, influencing the overall results and generated errors, so the three dimensions should not use the arithmetic mean, but separately use the geometric mean of the three dimensions as the integrated stress value. This study is only the first attempt to establish the assessment system for the school leaders' job pressure. For many school leaders, how to release the pressure from their jobs? It is worthy of further discussion.

We also found that interval fuzzy transformation is an interesting topic with great potential to interpret the fuzzy data. Because of vagueness and imprecision on human thinking so traditional statistics could not solve the problems in the field of social sciences. Soft computing with fuzzy theory is a reasonable statistical method for this kind of research.

References

Auerbach, S (2009). Walking the walk: Portraits in leadership for family engagement in urban schools. *School Community Journal,* 19(1), 9–32.

Buckley, JJ (1985). Fuzzy hierarchical analysis. *Fuzzy Set and System,* 17, 233–247.

Carlsson, C and R Fuller (2000a). Benchmarking in linguistic importance weighted aggregations. *Fuzzy Sets and Systems,* 114, 35–41.

Carlsson, C and R Fuller (2000b). Multiobjective linguistic optimization. *Fuzzy Sets and Systems,* 115, 5–10.

Chiang, DA, LR Chow and YF Wang (2000). Mining time series data by a fuzzy linguistic summary system. *Fuzzy Sets and Systems,* 112, 419–432.

Costas, CSL, PP Maranon and JAH Cabrera (1994). Application of diffuse measurement to the evaluation of psychological structures. *Quality and Quanty,* 28, 305–313.

Dubois, D and H Prade (1991). Fuzzy sets in approximate reasoning, Part 1: Inference with possibility distributions. *Fuzzy Sets and Systems,* 40, 143–202.

Emery, K (2007). Corporate control of public school goals: High-stakes testing in its historical perspective. *Teacher Education Quarterly,* 34(2), 25–44.

Esp, DG (1981). Report on the selection and training of headteachers in Sweden. pp. 22–73.

Herrera, F and E Herrera-Viedma (2000). Linguistic decision analysis: Steps for solving decision problems under linguistic information. *Fuzzy Sets and Systems,* 116, 67–82.

Hesketh, B, R Pryor, M Gleitzman and T Hesketh (1988). Practical applications and psychometric evaluation of a computerized fuzzy graphic ration scale. In *Fuzzy Sets in Psychology,* T Zetenyi (ed.), pp. 425–454. North-Holland: New York.

Hewitt, PM, JC Pijanowski and GS Denny (2009). Why teacher leaders don't want to be principals: Evidence from arkansas. *Education Working Paper Archive,* pp. 66–101.

Liu, MF, HT Yan and BL Wu (2010). Fuzzy evaluation on work assessment and time management for the school leaders. *International Symposium on Innovative Management, Information and Production IMIP2010,* pp. 343–357.

Liu, WY and N Song (2001). The fuzzy association degree in semantic data models. *Fuzzy Sets and Systems,* 117, 203–208.

Nguyen, HT and BL Wu (2006). *Fundamentals of Statistics with Fuzzy Data.* New York: Springer.

Protheroe, N (2005). Leadership for school improvement: With accountability pressures requiring rapid change, The burden falls on the principal to make it happen. *Principal,* 84(4), 54–56.

Pryor, BW and CR Pryor (2004). *The School Leader's Guide to Understanding Attitude and Influencing Behavior: Working with Teachers, Parents, Students, and the Community,* pp. 11–170. Thousand Oaks, CA: Corwin Press.

Rooney, J (2003). Principals who care: A personal reflection. *Educational Leadership,* 60(6), 55–130.

Takao, S, A Tsutsumi, K Nishiuchi, S Mineyama and N Kawakami (2006). Effects of the job stress education for supervisors on psychological distress and job performance among their immediate subordinates: A supervisor-based randomized controlled trial. *Journal of Occupational Health*, 48, 494–503. Available at http://www.jstage.jst.go.jp/article/joh/48/6/48_494/_article.

Stoelinga, SR (2008). The work of Chicago public schools principals. *Research report*, Consortium on Chicago School Research, pp. 33–80.

Valentine, JW and ML Bowman (1991). Effective principal, effective school: Does research support the assumption? *Nassp Bulletin*, 75, 1–7.

Vetter, WE (1977). Role pressure and the school principal. *NASSP Bulletin*, 76, 11–23.

Wu, BL (2005). *An Introduction to Fuzzy Statistics*. Taipei: Wu Nan.

Zimmermann, HJ (1991). *Fuzzy Set Theory and Its Applications*. Boston: Kluwer Academic.

Chapter 13

FUZZY COMPOSITE SCORE AND SITUATIONAL JUDGEMENT TEST: AN INTEGRATED OPERATION PERSPECTIVE OF SCORING

Hawjeng Chiou
College of Management
National Taiwan Normal University, Taiwan
hawjeng@ntnu.edu.tw
http://hawjeng.idv.tw

Tsung-Lin Ou
Department of Business Administration
National Central University, Taiwan

The aim of this chapter is to propose a mechanism based on Fuzzy Composite Score (FCS) to integrate multiple scoring methods for Situational Judgment Test (SJT). The proposed operating mechanism, besides dealing with various scale types, can also provide fuzzy space for linguistic judgment, allowing researchers to compare the difference of SJT score under different degrees of linguistic vagueness. Based on current SJT scoring method, this study simulated sample responses for four types of different scale to explain FCS operation. Also, the comparison between five different degrees of vagueness was executed in this fuzzy frame. Analysis of results concludes that: (1) Proposed FCS operation can integrate multiple scoring methods and provide subjects and experts advanced adjustment of linguistic vagueness to more closely match authentic cognition; (2) As the degree of linguistic vagueness increases, the diversity in FCS between high score and low score samples was reduced, but moderated by different SJT scoring methods. To conclude, practical and academic points of view about FCS of SJT were discussed for future study.

Keywords: Situational judgment test; fuzzy composite score; fuzzy measurement; linguistic modelling.

1. Introduction

Situational Judgment Test (SJT) has been one of the most valued assessment tools in recent years in the fields of management decision and personnel selection (Chan and Schmitt, 2005; Whetzel and McDanie, 2009). Favoured by practitioners for the last two decades, it has become not only widely utilised, but at the same time triggered scholarly interest of researchers. Empirical evidence suggests that SJT can predict a wide range of outcomes, such as job performance (McDaniel *et al.*, 2001) and can offer incremental validity over the predictions provided by cognitive ability, personality, and job experience (e.g., Chan and Schmitt, 2002). However, some theoretical and technical issues still exist in SJT (Weekley and Ployhart, 2006; Whetzel and McDanie, 2009).

Basically, SJT includes different kinds of situational problems found in authentic work fields, and requests subjects to response from different items, through which their knowledge, capability, personality, and attitude are reflected. A typical SJT example is as follows:

Question: You run unexpectedly into a business client at a restaurant on a holiday. Which of the following best describes your immediate habitual response?

1. *Approach and greet the client at once, and at the appropriate moment, invites the client to join your table.*
2. *Out of consideration for the client's privacy, wait until the client is closer to your seat before you approach and greet.*
3. *Stand up at your seat courteously and pay your compliments by waving and nodding to the client.*
4. *Observe the client for a while before making a decision whether or not to greet.*

The above example embodies a typical SJT stimulus component and response component pointed out by Kanning *et al.* (2006), which refers to a main item stem supplies situational cue and condition. Then, the subjects' responses are collected from a set of response options that comprises the scale (Motowildo *et al.*, 1990). A typical test procedure begins with familiarising the subjects with the situation described by the item stem, and then subjects execute judgment at the following response options.

To accommodate different SJT scoring methods and fuzzy space determination, this chapter intends to develop an integrated-operation mechanism, drawing on the advantage of Fuzzy Composite Score (FCS) to process fuzzy linguistic concepts directly; and by way of simulated data of different SJT scale types. Using a simple simulation example, this chapter also tries to illustrate the discrepancies of SJT scores under different linguistic fuzzy degrees.

This chapter first introduced the SJT format and scoring methods to generate common scoring principles. Furthermore, discussions extended to the frame of FCS, and proposed an integrated-operation mechanism for SJT scoring. By using example responses from four sets of different scale types, this chapter illustrates the parameter setting of FCS under different degrees of linguistic vagueness.

2. SJT and Scoring Issues

2.1. *Scoring issues in SJT*

In terms of the psychometric property, scoring is a major issue for the application of SJT (Weekley *et al.*, 2006; Whetzel and McDanie, 2009). Distinct from the self-report scale, scoring of SJT has to consider simultaneously items response effectiveness determination and scoring methods. But multiple types of response effectiveness determination and scoring methods create many issues in SJT scoring research. Consequently, different SJT scoring research performed by past scholars have fallen under two main categories. The first is mainly comparative studies of different SJT response effectiveness determination methods (e.g., Bergman *et al.*, 2006; Weekley and Ployhart, 2005; Such and Schmidt, 2004; Hunter, 2003; Sinar *et al.*, 2002); the second, empirical research related to each SJT scoring method (e.g., Muros, 2008; Weekley and Harding, 2004; Cucina and Vasilopoulos, 2003; McElreath and Vasilopoulos, 2002; McDaniel and Nguyen, 2001).

Despite having many varieties of SJT scoring approaches, current research is still unable to assert which is the optimal response effectiveness determination method or scoring method (Whetzel and McDanie, 2009). In other words, any designated scoring will always find its most befitting scale type and application domain. Furthermore, even though SJT scoring methods have been applied extensively in practical scale development, research in related issues still need to be continued in the future by related scholars. Therefore, based on multiple views of SJT scoring related research, this study does not attempt to compare the advantages and disadvantages of different SJT scoring methods, but instead focuses on developing scoring operation mechanism that can integrate current SJT scoring methods and, even more, accommodates flexibly other types of scoring method.

Neglecting to consider the uncertainty and vagueness of SJT is a severe matter in researching scoring issues. Whether the above discussed SJT scoring relates to response effectiveness determination or scoring method, calculation of scores still employ the principle of crisp scoring. However, whether it is Subject Matter Experts (SMEs) administering SJT response effectiveness determination, or subjects responding to SJT scale items, both behaviours fundamentally involve some kind of situational judgment; and the judgment itself is not a kind of precise response condition, but a kind of quasi-rational reaction that blends both intuition and analysis (Hammond, 1955); also, the characteristic of this perceptual process is covert (Hogarth, 2001). Applying the perspective of fuzzy theory, the concept of quasi-rationality coincides with human cognitive behaviour based on fuzzy theory; both take the perspectives of human complex cognition and behaviour into consideration. This explains fuzzy characteristics of human like, dislike, strength, and weaknesses toward things (Dounias *et al.*, 1998; Zimmermann *et al.*, 1984; Zopounidis and Documpos, 1998).

2.2.   Scoring approaches of SJT

SJT that relates to test scoring includes components of response effectiveness determination, scaling type of subject response and response effectiveness, and test scoring methods. Response effectiveness determination refers to the weight of responses.

Typically, response effectiveness determination has three strategies, (1) Rational scoring: utilising critical incident method to describe A-B-C set event-behaviour chain before SMEs assesses level of relevance in behavioural responses to prove weight of responses; (2) Empirical keying, obtains different correlation coefficients between behavioural orientation and validity criterion through measurable data in order to collect weighting information of each response; (3) Literature reasoning method, assesses quality level of responses directly based on theory, literature, or logical deduction.

After SJT designer completes response effectiveness scoring, the immediate problem would be finding a way to obtain test score. This can be achieved through test scoring methods to merge subject response and response effectiveness according to different scaling types. A simpler method is the forced-choice methods. 'i' stands for the best item determined by experts in the test; 'k' stands for the best response subjects are asked to select. The test score, $T_{\text{pick}-\text{best}}$, is calculated as follows:

$$T_{\text{pick}-\text{best}} = \begin{cases} 1, & i = k \\ 0, & i \neq k \end{cases}.$$

As test score is either zero or one, this method is also known as pick best. This kind of strategy has found to be effective in some empirical studies (Hunter, 2003; O'Connell *et al.*, 2001).

Partial credit score method extends from pick best method. i_b and i_w stand for the best item and worst item, respectively, determined by experts; k_b and k_w stand for the best response and worst response, respectively, determined by the subjects. The test score, $T_{\text{partial}-\text{credit}}$ is calculated as follows: (Motowidlo *et al.*, 1990):

$$T_{\text{partial}-\text{credit}} = \begin{cases} 2, & i_b = k_b \wedge i_w = k_w \\ 1, & (i_b = k_b \wedge i_w \neq k_w) \vee (i_w = k_w \wedge i_b \neq k_b) \\ 0, & i_b \neq k_b \wedge i_w \neq k_w \\ -1, & (i_w = k_b \wedge i_b \neq k_w) \vee (i_b = k_w \wedge i_w \neq k_b) \\ -2, & i_b = k_w \wedge i_w = k_b \end{cases}.$$

Rank ordering method was proposed by Weekly *et al.* (2004). n denotes items in the test and are required to be ranked from one to n by the subjects and SMEs, and d_i is assigned for the difference of ranking in i item between subjects and experts. Incorporating Spearman's rank correlation coefficient, the test score, $T_{\text{rank-ordering}}$ is calculated as follows:

$$T_{\text{rank-ordering}} = 1 - \frac{6 \sum_{i=1}^{n} d_i^2}{n(n^2 - 1)}.$$

The last kind of scoring strategy is Likert-type scale method (Chan and Schmitt, 2002; Sacco *et al.*, 2000; Wagner and Sternberg, 1985). This method leaves subjects or experts to assess responses in the test independently; it then calculates the test score based on the differences between subjects and experts scores on the Likert-type scale. With Wagner's (1987) SJT Likert-type scoring method as an example, n stands for the number of responses in test; and one to k stands for Likert-type scale measurement; and d_i is assigned for the difference of scale score in i item between subjects and experts. The test score $T_{li\,ker\,t-\text{type}}$ is calculated as follows:

$$T_{li\,ker\,t-\text{type}} = \left(\frac{\sum_{i=1}^{n} d_i^2}{n} \right)^{-1/2}.$$

The common principles exist between the above four kinds of SJT scoring methods, regardless differences in scale type. The first is the logic of test scoring. The value of test score is dependent on the difference between subject response and response effectiveness. From pick-best methods to Likert-type scale method, the more inconsistency between subject response and response effect are, the lower the test score becomes. Based on such a principle, a database of logical inference between SJT response pattern and test score can be constructed. Such a database constitutes an important foundation for developing FCS frame. Second, whether response effectiveness determination of SJT or scale type of subjects' response, it is the application of crisp scoring principle. However, it seems too arbitrary to express the subjects' behavioural response preference under a particular situation with a crisp numerical value. With a partial credit questions as example, answering one for a particular response in a test does not indicate that the subject completely does not consider answering zero or -1 for that response.

From another perspective, faced with complex, unpredictable situations, human thought and judgment can be better expressed through linguistic vagueness (Lo, 2002). Therefore, when subjects or experts employ quantitative method for situational judgment condition, authentic human cognition will be met only if the consideration for linguistic vagueness is incorporated. And an effective strategy for directly processing fuzzy linguistic concept is through applying FCS, which will be discussed in the following section.

2.3. Concept of fuzzy composite score

FCS, stemming from fuzzy theory development (Zadeh, 1965), was initially proposed for integrated determination of multiple learning assessment (Lo, 2002). FCS mainly uses fuzzy subsets to express linguistic vagueness and conducts logical inference. In practice, FCS, in the form of a function, is used to define the variables and its interpretations of degree of membership function. This multivalued function is termed membership function, while the variable is termed linguistic variable.

The fuzzy inference which FCS employs is classified as qualitative fuzzy reasoning. This kind of fuzzy approximate reasoning derives a specific proposition from a general proposition. Its basic process is a premise set deducing its own conclusion (Zadeb, 1975). The premise and conclusion belonging to this category of reasoning both involve membership function. Generally speaking, the inference method most frequently used in fuzzy approximate reasoning is Mamdani's minimum fuzzy implication rule (Mamdani, 1974), which this chapter explains using two sets of rule reasoning. Proposition of inference rule and conclusion are as follows:

If x is A_1 and y is B_1, THEN z is C_1 (proposition 1)
If x is A_2 and y is B_2, THEN z is C_2 (proposition 2)
Conclusion: z is C'

In the above two sets of proposition of inference rule, x and y are input variables, with corresponding linguistic variables A and B, respectively, each with two levels; z is the output variable, with corresponding linguistic variable levels C_1 and C_2. Their inference

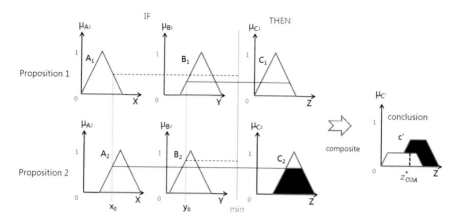

Fig. 1.　Mamdani fuzzy approximate reasoning.
Note: Edited from Neural fuzzy system: A Neurofuzzy synergism to intelligent systems (p. 155), by Lin and Lee (1996).

process is illustrated in Fig. 1: Under conditions of $x = x_0, y = y_0$, the value threshold of the membership function $\mu_{C_1}(z)$ belonging to the output linguistic variable level C_1 of the first proposition set lies between zero and $\mu_{B_1}(y_0)$ in accordance with inference rule. By the same reasoning, the value threshold of the membership function $\mu_{C_2}(z)$ belonging to the output linguistic variable level C_2 of the second proposition set lies between zero and $\mu_{A_2}(x_0)$. Therefore, the output results of the two sets of rule reasoning will form a composite linguistic variable c' whose membership function is $\mu_{C'}(z)$, with corresponding centralised output z^*_{COA}, which is also the so-called FCS.

The centroid point z^*_{COA} as the output of FCS could be obtained by the following stages:

First stage — Fuzzification: Transforming crisp input values, based on membership function of corresponding linguistic variable in database, to fuzzy linguistic values.

Second stage — Inference: Executing inference, based on IF-THEN Fuzzy Inference Rule (FIR), which is Mamdani's minimum fuzzy implication rule.

Third stage — Defuzzification: Execute the following operation with the most common Centre of Area Method (COA) (Berenji, 1992), in order to transform the composite output fuzzy linguistic to output crisp sets:

$$z^*_{COA} = \frac{\int z\mu_c(z)zdz}{\int z\mu_c(z)dz}.$$

As a result, FCS can integrate different kinds of SJT scoring because the frame of the three FCS stages can be flexibly set to conduct SJT response input, logical scoring rule, and output test score.

First, because a subject's item response is a kind of judgment (Hammond, 1955), based on authentic human cognition, adding crisp value to linguistic vagueness consideration is an appropriate strategy to combine intuition and analysis with judgment. And the different value types i of response input can be regarded as linguistic variable, or, fuzzy number $\tilde{i}$. Therefore, when either zero or one response type of pick best is selected, its linguistic variable's corresponding fuzzy number will be $\tilde{0}$ and $\tilde{1}$. By the same reasoning, fuzzy numbers of partial credit score would be $-\tilde{1}$, $\tilde{0}$, $\tilde{1}$; and fuzzy numbers of rank ordering and Likert-type scale would be, $\tilde{1}$, $\tilde{2}$, $\tilde{3}$, $\tilde{4}$, $\tilde{5}$. SJT responses, under FCS frame, can demonstrate vagueness because input variable can be transformed to fuzzy linguistic value, based on membership function.

In addition, because FCS frame allows more than two rule inferences to be set up simultaneously, several item responses within SJT can, based on SJT different scoring methods, produce different response arrangement and combination, as well as link output values to form multiple rule inferences. It should be carefully noted that the type of SJT output values is a combination of judgment of both subjects and experts, and therefore can be also regarded as a fuzzy subset of linguistic variables. In other words, through FCS frame, not only the judgment of subjects can be fuzzified, but outputs can set up fuzzy conditions as well. Finally, as SJT requires a crisp test score, the defuzzification in the third stage of FCS frame can also provide crisp FCS output values.

Such an operation mechanism, therefore, turns different types of original SJT scoring methods into an exceptional example of fuzzy

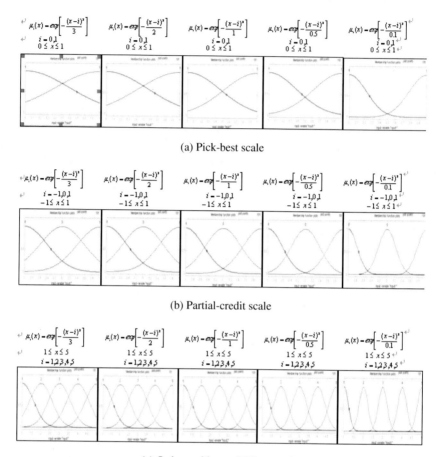

(a) Pick-best scale

(b) Partial-credit scale

(c) Order-ranking and Likert-scale

Fig. 2.   Input membership functions on four different scale types for five levels of linguistic vagueness.

membership equals to zero within FCS frame. As such, flexibility of FCS frame becomes an important feature in an integrated operation mechanism. This study constructs an FCS assessment operation mechanism, mainly by using Fuzzy Logic Controller (FLC) frame and based on the needs of research, FLC is adapted to become SJT scoring frame, as shown in Fig. 2. With its function primarily founded on three-stage process of FCS, it generates into a test score through the process of fuzzy inference with crisp item responses, which SJT users could employ.

All in all, FCS has the function to adjust degree of linguistic vagueness during the value input and output stage. In the meantime, because FCS is obtained through fuzzy inference, the results will not be completely similar to those results that are obtained from SJT crisp scoring. However, no matter what the results are, subjects under the same degree of linguistic vagueness must still produce the consistent judgment (for example, subjects with a higher score in SJT crisp scoring would also have higher FCS value).

3. Example Illustration

3.1. *Simulation design*

Limited by the scale type of each SJT scoring method, a same response set possibly could have been produced by several subjects, each with a different degree of linguistic vagueness. While SJT crisp scoring method can obtain the same test score results for the several subjects, employing FCS linguistic vagueness setting can distinguish more minute differences in test performance of the subjects. Therefore, according to each SJT scale type, this study first set up five response effects, incrementally from 'i1' to 'i5'. In order to give consideration to the factor of various degrees of vagueness, the sample design (1) allocated five levels (b1–b5) of linguistic vagueness of the input variable, representing five categories of subjects with different degrees of linguistic vagueness, and (2) compared the difference between crisp scoring and two kinds of output variable fuzzy scoring (FCS1, FCS2), the point made being that the same category of subjects has accepted the SMEs evaluative scoring of varying degrees of linguistic vagueness and the default crisp scoring of SJT. As above, the research produced random simulated responses of 30 subjects on each SJT scale type for a total of 60 trials as listed in Table 1.

3.2. *FCS parameters setting*

Based on the sample design, this section illustrates how to calculate composite fuzzy score of subjects under varying degrees of linguistic vagueness using parameters setting of FCS frame. In addition, as

Table 1.　Research design.

Degree of linguistic vagueness	Scroing type	Scale type of SJT			
		Pick best	Pattial credit	Order ranking	Likert scale
b1	crisp	t1	t16	t31	t46
	FCS1	t2	t17	t32	t47
	FCS2	t3	t18	t33	t48
b2	crisp	t4	t19	t34	t49
	FCS1	t5	t20	t35	t50
	FCS2	t6	t21	t36	t51
b3	crisp	t7	t22	t37	t52
	FCS1	t8	t23	t38	t53
	FCS2	t9	t24	t39	t54
b4	crisp	t10	t25	t40	t55
	FCS1	t11	t26	t41	t56
	FCS2	t12	t27	t42	t57
b5	crisp	t13	t28	t43	t58
	FCS1	t14	t29	t44	t59
	FCS2	t15	t30	t45	t60

there are many function forms used for determining membership functions, such as triangular functions, bell-shaped functions, trapezoidal functions, etc. Nevertheless, an objective method to determine a suitable membership function has still not been found (Bojadziev, 1995). Therefore, this study, with regard to membership function, employed normal fuzzy membership function to determine input and output for the purpose of this research.

The corresponding normal fuzzy number membership function $\mu_i(x)$ of the 'i' linguistic variable is:

$$\mu_i(x) = \exp\left[-\frac{(x-i)^2}{b}\right].$$

In the above formula, x stands for the value of FCS input or output, while b value is the degree of normal linguistic vagueness. While input membership function $\mu_i(x)$ is concerned, the scale range of four types measuring responses x of SJT is different, so the corresponding linguistic variable i is also different. By coordinating the setting of the five levels of degree of linguistic vagueness in the sample design ($b1_{input} = 0.1, b2_{input} = 0.5, b3_{input} = 1, b4_{input} = 2, b5_{input} = 3$), the research design's input membership functions on four different scale types (pick-best, partial-credit, order-ranking, and Likert-type) can be established, as presented in Fig. 2, respectively. Under each figure, as the value of linguistic vagueness increases, the overlapping area between input membership functions becomes large, which means subjects possess five levels of degree of linguistic vagueness on each scale type in the study.

While the output membership function $\mu_i(z)$ is concerned, the output value type of each SJT scoring method also can be presented as different linguistic variable i. By coordinating the two kinds of degree of linguistic vagueness output — with degree of linguistic vagueness output ($b1_{output} = 0; FCS1$) and degree of linguistic vagueness output ($b2_{output} = 1; FCS2$) — FCS output membership function on four different scale types can be produced, as presented in Fig. 3, respectively. This implies that SMEs have two levels of degree of output linguistic vagueness on each scale type in the study.

As output value is obtained from computing subject item response and response effect, based on each SJT scoring rule, therefore scoring rule can become the foundation of FCS frame inference structure. According to various SJT scoring methods, the inference structure of FCS in the research can be divided into four logical inference databases.

Where pick-best scoring is concerned, as it possesses two degrees of input linguistic variable ($\tilde{0}$ and $\tilde{1}$) and also five response inputs, there will be five possible fuzzy inference rules, as indicated in Table 2. According to the scoring rule of pick-best, the corresponding output result of each fuzzy inference rule are also two degrees of linguistic variables ($\tilde{0}$ and $\tilde{1}$). With the first fuzzy inference rule below as example, the full semantic meaning of the logical inference is:

When Subject Response 1 is Agree, Subject Response 2 is Disagree, Subject Response 3 is Disagree, Subject Response 4 is Disagree, Subject Response 5 is Disagree, experts determine that the test score of subjects is poor.

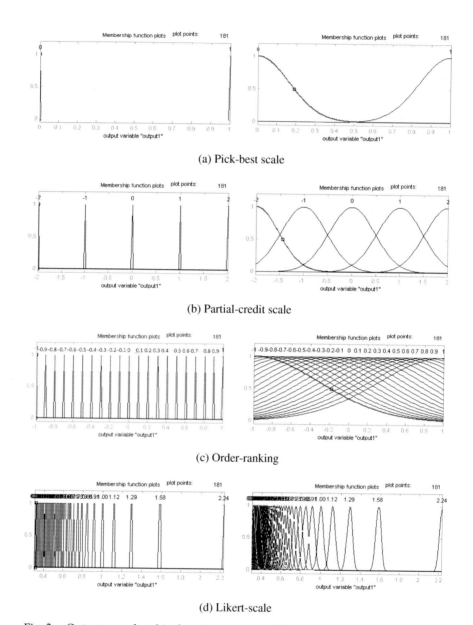

(a) Pick-best scale

(b) Partial-credit scale

(c) Order-ranking

(d) Likert-scale

Fig. 3.   Output membership functions on four different scale types for FCS1 and FCS2.

Table 2. Summary of sample's score and deviation from average on each trial.

Pick-best scale											
Group value	0.000	0.000	0.034	0.099	0.168	0.195	0.126	0.173	0.245	0.307	0.329
	1.000	1.000	0.966	0.901	0.832	0.805	0.874	0.827	0.755	0.693	0.671
Deviation	0.231	0.231	0.215	0.185	0.154	0.141	0.173	0.151	0.118	0.089	0.079
Partial-credit scale											
Group value	−1.000	−1.000	−0.936	−0.835	−0.746	−0.714	−0.981	−0.880	−0.677	−0.498	−0.439
	1.000	1.000	0.936	0.835	0.746	0.714	0.981	0.880	0.677	0.498	0.439
	2.000	2.000	1.902	1.729	1.562	1.496	1.633	1.426	1.153	0.959	0.899
Deviation	0.778	0.778	0.730	0.653	0.584	0.559	0.744	0.663	0.514	0.385	0.343
Rank-ordering scale											
Group value	−0.900	−0.900	−0.885	−0.862	−0.844	−0.837	−0.423	−0.422	−0.397	−0.370	−0.361
	−0.700	−0.700	−0.691	−0.679	−0.670	−0.667	−0.343	−0.343	−0.334	−0.303	−0.289
	−0.300	−0.425	−0.425	−0.425	−0.425	−0.424	−0.156	−0.156	−0.156	−0.155	−0.152
	0.300	0.350	0.350	0.349	0.341	0.335	0.156	0.156	0.156	0.155	0.152
	0.700	0.700	0.697	0.691	0.685	0.683	0.343	0.343	0.334	0.303	0.289
	0.900	0.833	0.833	0.833	0.832	0.832	0.423	0.422	0.397	0.370	0.361
	1.000	1.000	0.993	0.980	0.965	0.959	0.458	0.455	0.435	0.418	0.411
Deviation	0.468	0.469	0.466	0.461	0.458	0.457	0.222	0.221	0.212	0.196	0.189

(*Continued*)

Table 2. (Continued)

	Likert-type scale										
Group value	0.326	0.319	0.337	0.357	0.369	0.374	0.331	0.343	0.361	0.377	0.383
	0.358	0.377	0.399	0.422	0.435	0.440	0.359	0.372	0.391	0.407	0.415
	0.378	0.397	0.417	0.437	0.449	0.453	0.378	0.390	0.407	0.424	0.430
	0.389	0.416	0.434	0.452	0.461	0.465	0.389	0.404	0.423	0.441	0.448
	0.408	0.474	0.501	0.526	0.539	0.543	0.408	0.422	0.439	0.456	0.462
	0.477	0.493	0.514	0.533	0.544	0.547	0.477	0.495	0.521	0.541	0.548
	0.488	0.493	0.518	0.543	0.557	0.562	0.488	0.504	0.527	0.545	0.552
	0.513	0.512	0.537	0.560	0.574	0.578	0.488	0.506	0.532	0.552	0.560
	0.527	0.532	0.550	0.568	0.578	0.581	0.513	0.531	0.557	0.575	0.582
	0.645	0.647	0.664	0.678	0.684	0.687	0.527	0.542	0.564	0.580	0.586
	0.674	0.667	0.686	0.703	0.712	0.714	0.646	0.692	0.737	0.762	0.770
	0.745	0.744	0.778	0.807	0.820	0.824	0.674	0.716	0.757	0.781	0.788
	0.845	0.840	0.872	0.898	0.909	0.911	0.746	0.848	0.919	0.950	0.956
	1.000	0.995	1.045	1.105	1.141	1.150	0.845	0.948	1.010	1.034	1.038
Deviation	0.457	0.149	0.153	0.157	0.159	0.159	0.151	0.180	0.196	0.200	0.199

Taking a step further, only under the condition in which the responses for Response 1 to Response 4 are all 'Disagree' and the response for Response 5 is 'Agree' will the test output score be considered good (as in the fifth inference rule below).

1. If (input1 is 1) and (input2 is 0) and (input3 is 0) and (input4 is 0) and (input5 is 0) then (output1 is 0)(1)
2. If (input1 is 0) and (input2 is 1) and (input3 is 0) and (input4 is 0) and (input5 is 0) then (output1 is 0)(1)
3. If (input1 is 0) and (input2 is 0) and (input3 is 1) and (input4 is 0) and (input5 is 0) then (output1 is 0)(1)
4. If (input1 is 0) and (input2 is 0) and (input3 is 0) and (input4 is 1) and (input5 is 0) then (output1 is 0)(1)
5. If (input1 is 0) and (input2 is 0) and (input3 is 0) and (input4 is 0) and (input5 is 1) then (output1 is 1)(1)

As such, applying the same principle can obtain 20 fuzzy inference rules from partial credit response, 120 from ranking-ordering response, and 3,125 from Likert-type response.

Finally, after finishing the above FCS parameters setting, using Centre of Area Method (COA) to perform a defuzzification operation, the final FCS can be obtained.

3.3. *Result explanation*

This study used Fuzzy Logic Toolboxes developed by Math Works (USA) to complete the research program. Employing the main function, simulated response data were read into a sample response matrix; then, by applying sub function to call input sample responses into the Fuzzy Inference System (FIS), which has completed setting the related parameters, the FCS of the research design in this study can be obtained, as presented in Table 2.

In the Table 2, 30 samples can be separated into several groups. Ranging from pick-best method to Likert-type method, group values gradually increase in variety, which shows that the level of processing of sample variance by each scoring method was different. For FCS1, for example, when its degree of linguistic vagueness input is 0.1, and its degree of linguistic vagueness output is zero, its group value under each SJT scale type almost equals to the result of SJT crisp scoring method. This indicates that FCS frame, through degree of linguistic vagueness removed, can integrate crisp scoring method under each SJT scale type.

According to the results sorted out in Table 2, the FCS of sample groups under different trials is different. As the partial credit method demonstrates, before considering degree of linguistic vagueness, the crisp score for partial credit method of Subject A is one, and that of both Subject B and C is −1; however, after modifying their degree of linguistic vagueness input through FCS frame, the FCS of B has been adjusted to −0.75, but the score of A and C remain unchanged, reason inferred being the degree of linguistic vagueness of A and C is low, while that of B is high. This implies that even though the SJT partial credit item crisp score of B and C is the same, B demonstrates a difference with C after being modified through FCS degree of linguistic vagueness. However, within any kind of simulated trials, the group with the higher SJT crisp score tends to have an advantage in sample ranking under each degree of linguistic vagueness.

The variance of FCS in the pick best, partial credit, and ranking-ordering method sample group decreases as degree of linguistic vagueness input increases; but the variance of FCS of Likert-type method sample group increases significantly as degree of linguistic vagueness input increases; this indicates that the diversity of FCS varies with different SJT scoring methods.

Under each SJT scoring method, and when degree of output linguistic vagueness is zero, sample group's FCS mean deviation of pick best, partial credit, and ranking-order method is greater than the condition for degree of output linguistic vagueness as specific value. But the Likert-type method shows different results, as setting degree of output linguistic vagueness as specific value is also a kind of method for increasing the degree of linguistic vagueness. Therefore, the above results show that increasing degree of linguistic vagueness, according to different SJT scoring methods, has inconsistent impact on FCS diversity changes.

4. Discussions and Conclusions

4.1. *General findings*

From the results of this study, it is found that the SJT crisp scoring method is a kind of exceptional situation in which degree of linguistic vagueness is zero, indicating that through FCS frame operation mechanism; test scoring methods under each SJT scale type can be integrated.

FCS frame allows subjects and SMEs to reflect more authentic human responses by adjusting linguistic vagueness. Therefore, subjects with the same scores for SJT crisp scoring method will produce different FCS, due to difference in degree of linguistic vagueness input or difference in assessment of degree of linguistic vagueness by SMEs. Yet this discrepancy has been neglected in SJT crisp scoring method.

Even so, study results revealed that FCS sample ranking under each degree of linguistic vagueness does not change, which means the FCS sample ranking of groups with higher SJT crisp scores, under each degree of linguistic vagueness, tend to have an advantage. The above results concur with the expected hypothesis of this study.

Through comparative analysis of different degrees of vagueness, it can be observed that as degree of vagueness increases, the difference between two sample groups with extreme value gradually will decrease, but will be modified by different SJT scoring methods. The FCS variance of pick best, partial credit, and rank-ordering method sample groups significantly decreases as degree of linguistic vagueness input increases; but the FCS variance of Likert-type method sample group significantly increases as degree of linguistic vagueness input increases. Such a phenomenon can be discussed from two perspectives: (1) fuzzy inference principle; (2) type of SJT scoring method.

Based on fuzzy inference principle, the increase in degree of linguistic vagueness will cause the score of output linguistic function to centralise, in turn causing the scores of two sample groups with extreme value to gradually draw closer. Observing from each type of SJT scoring methods, what pick best, partial credit, order-ranking, and Likert-type method represent is the gradual increase in categories of scoring value. However, pertaining to the FCS of pick best, partial credit, and order-ranking method sample groups, the centralisation phenomenon on the score of output linguistic function will gradually slow down as categories of scoring value gradually increase.

The Likert-type is extraordinary. Besides having the most categories of scoring values, due to the additional factor of having a severely unequal interval on crisp output value, the Likert-type method even causes contrary FCS to the other three kinds of SJT scale types. Therefore, the special condition can generate some new topics for exploration: For example: What is the appropriate linguistic vagueness method for the unequal interval output value of Likert-type SJT?

The FCS frame developed in this study demonstrates an advantage of flexibility. For the purpose of highlighting issues in linguistic vagueness, this study processes SJT score under the setting that response options belonging to the same scale types, which is a considerably conservative strategy. From the viewpoint of extensive application, even if within SJT exist responses of different scale types, for example, that which are a combination of pick best and partial credit item, FCS frame theoretically would still be able to process them. In addition, even though this study is confined to only the calculation of SJT item-set score, the research scope of SJT scoring still includes the total test scores, which means that integrating several SJT item-set scores can similarly be explored using FCS frame. All the above fully explain the potential future development of applying FCS fuzzy integrated score to SJT scoring issues.

4.2. *Limitations and suggestions*

This study combines literature review with simulated research to explain the feasibility of integrating each SJT scoring method by using FCS operation mechanism. Still, in practical application, some technical issues remain to be overcome. First, administrators of SJT must have the ability to convert different kinds of scoring method to the settings of FIS. Related settings include input and output of linguistic membership function and also fuzzy inference rule database. Seemingly complicated settings can be overcome by developing related software in collaboration with a program designer.

A more frontend and important aspect regards the collection of subject or SMEs degree of linguistic vagueness data. Generally, the method of filling in percentage value on questionnaire response, called fuzzy linguistic questionnaire, reflects the individual subject's degree of cognition toward each item. However, an average subject's degree of acceptance toward fuzzy linguistic questionnaire may not be high, and, under fuzzy condition, it is not easy to express one's own cognition by means of filling in precise value. Therefore, a practicable fuzzy linguistic questionnaire which involves using interval value to express linguistic degree is also an alternative approach. Besides, special attention has to be paid to degree of linguistic vagueness setting of SMEs. Limited by FCS frame, degree of linguistic vagueness setting of SMEs should take into consideration the output value of SJT and not just the degree of linguistic vagueness of item weight.

This chapter reemphasises the importance of conducting empirical research. While simulated research based on related theories is able to propose the feasibility of applying SJT FCS frame, the potential problems in practical application may not have been fully considered within a simulated research process. Therefore, the results of empirical research can facilitate the process of effectively modifying FCS frame, and further contribute to related future study. After all, when we conduct SJTs, we can no longer ignore that inherent attributes of fuzzy judgment exist.

References

Berenji, HR (1992). An architecture for designing fuzzy controllers using neural networks. *International Journal of Approximate Reasoning*, 6(2), 267–292.

Bergman, M, F Drasgow, MA Donovan and SE Juraska (2003). *Scoring of Situational Judgment Tests*. Paper presented at the *18th Annual Conf. Society of Industrial and Organizational Psychology*, Orlando, FL.

Bojadziev, G and M Bojadziev (1995). *Fuzzy Sets, Fuzzy Logic, Applications. Advances in Fuzzy Systems — Applications and Theory*, Vol. 5. Singapore: World Scientific.

Chan, D and N Schmitt (2002). Situational judgment and job performance. *Human Performance*, 15, 233–254.

Chan, D and N Schmitt (2005). Situational judgment tests. In *Handbook of Personnel Selection*, A Evers, O Smit-Voskuijl and N Anderson (eds.). Oxford, England: Blackwell Publishers.

Cucina, JM, NL Vasilopoulos and JA Leaman (2003). The bandwidth-fidelity dilemma and situational judgment test validity. Paper presented at the 18th Annual Conf. Society for Industrial and Organizational Psychology, Orlando, FL.

Dounias, G, S Havellas and G Tselentis (1998). A fuzzy rule based approach for decision making in commercial food chains. *EUPIT'98*, Aachen, Germany, 7–10 September.

Gessner, TL and RJ Klimoski (2006). Making sense of situations. In *Situational Judgment Tests: Theory, Measurement, and Application*, JA Weekley and RE Ployhart (eds.), pp. 13–38. San Francisco: Jossey-Bass.

Hammond, KR (1955). Probabilistic functioning and the clinical method. *Psychological Review*, 62, 255–262.

Hogarth, RM (2001). *Educating Intuition*. Chicago, IL: The University of Chicago Press.

Hunter, DR (2003). Measuring general aviation pilot judgment using a situational judgment technique. *International Journal of Aviation Psychology*, 13(4), 373–386.

Kanning, UP, K Grewe S Hollenberg and M Hadouch (2006). From the subjects' point of view: Reactions to different types of situational judgment items. *European Journal of Psychological Assessment*, 22, 168–176.

Lin, CT and CS Lee (1996). *Neural Fuzzy System: A Neuro-fuzzy Synergism to Intelligent Systems*. New York: Prentice-Hall International Inc.

Lo, H-C (2002). A preliminary study of development of fuzzy composite score for multiple assessments. *Chinese Journal of Science Education*, 10(4), 407–421 (in Chinese).

Mamdani, EH (1974). Application of fuzzy algorithms for control of a simple dynamic plain. *Proc. IEEE Conf. Control Science*, 121, 1585–1588.

McDaniel, MA and NT Nguyen (2001). Situational judgment tests: A review of practice and constructs assessed. *International Journal of Selection and Assessment*, 9, 103–113.

McDaniel, MA, EB Bruhn-Finnegan, FP Morgeson, M Campion and EP Braverman (2001). Predicting job performance using situational judgment tests: A clarification of the literature. *Journal of Applied Psychology*, 86, 730–740.

McElreath, J and NL Vasilopoulos (2002, April). Situational judgment: Are most and least likely response the same? Paper presented at the 17th Annual Conf. Society for Industrial and Organizational Psychology. Toronto, Canada.

Muros, JP (2008). Know the score: An exploration of keying and scoring approaches for situational judgment tests. Doctoral dissertation, Minnesoda University. ProQuest Dissertations and Theses.

Motowidlo, SJ, MD Dunnette and G Carter (1990). An alternative selection procedure: The low-fidelity simulation. *Journal of Applied Psychology*, 75, 640–647.

Motowidlo, SJ, Hanson and JL Crafts (1997). Low-fidelity simulations. In *Applied Measurement Methods in Industrial Psychology*, DL Whetzel and GR Wheaton (eds.), pp. 241–260. Palo Alto, CA: Davies-Black Publishing.

O'Connell, MS, D Doverspike, C Norris-Watts and K Hattrup (2001). Predictors of organizational citizenship behavior among Mexican retail salespeople. *International Journal of Organizational Analysis*, 9, 272–280.

Sacco, JM, CR Scheu, AM Ryan, N Schmitt, DB Schmidt and KL Rogg (2000). Reading level and verbal test scores as predictors of subgroup differences and validities of Situational Judgment Tests. Paper presented at the *15th Annual Meeting of the Society for Industrial and Organizational Psychology*. New Orleans, LA.

Sinar, EF, SL Paquet and DR Scott (2002, April). Internet versus paper selection tests: Exploring comparability issues. Paper presented at the *17th Annual Conf. Society for Industrial and Organizational Psychology*, Toronto, Canada.

Such, MJ and DB Schmidt (2004). Examining the effectiveness of empirical keying: A cross-cultural perspective. Paper presented at the *19th Annual Conf. Society of Industrial and Organizational Psychology*, Chicago, IL.

Wagner, RK (1987). Tacit knowledge in everyday intelligent behavior. *Journal of Personality and Social Psychology*, 52, 1236–1247.

Wagner, RK and RJ Sternberg (1985). Practical intelligence in real world pursuits: The role of tacit knowledge. *Journal of Personality and Social Psychology*, 48, 436–458.

Weekley, JA and RE Ployhart (2005). Situational judgment: Antecedents and relationships with performance. *Human Performance*, 18, 81–104.

Weekley, JA and RE Ployhart (2006). *Situational Judgment Tests: Theory, Measurement, and Application*. Mahwah, NJ: Erlbaum.

Weekley, JA, RE Ployhart and BC Holtz (2006). On the development of situational judgment tests: Issues in item development, scaling, and scoring. In *Situational Judgment Tests: Theory, Measurement, and Application*, JA Weekley and RE Ployhart (eds.), pp. 157–182. San Francisco: Jossey-Bass.

Weekley, JA, R Harding, A Creglow and RE Ployhart (2004). Scoring situational judgment tests: Does the middle matter? Paper presented at the Annual Conf. Society for Industrial and Organizational Psychology, Chicago, IL.

Whetzel, DL and MA McDanie (2009). Situational judgment tests: An overview of current research. *Human Resource Management Review*, 19, 188–202.

Zadeh, LA (1965). Fuzzy set. *Information and Control*, 8, 338–353.

Zadeh, LA (1975). The concept of a linguistic variable and its application to approximate reasoning. *Information Science*, 8, 199–249.

Zimmermann, HJ, LA Zadeh and BR Gaines (1984). *Fuzzy Sets and Decision Analysis*. Netherland: Eiaevier Science Publishers.

Zopounidis, C and M Documpos (1998). Developing a mulyicriteria decision support system for financial classification problems: The finclas system. *Optimization Methods and Software*, 8, 277–304.

PART 3

MATHEMATICAL AND OTHER MODELS

Chapter 14

CLUSTER ANALYSIS: AN EXAMPLE ANALYSIS ON PERSONALITY AND DYSFUNCTIONAL CUSTOMER BEHAVIOUR

Malcolm J. Beynon

Cardiff Business School, Cardiff University
Colum Drive, Cardiff, CF10 3EU
beynonmj@cardiff.ac.uk

Kate L. Daunt

Cardiff Business School, Cardiff University
Colum Drive, Cardiff, CF10 3EU
dauntk@cardiff.ac.uk

Cluster analysis provides insights into data, such that objects in an identified cluster are more similar to each other that to objects in other clusters. This chapter offers a background to the general approach termed cluster analysis, including an illustrative cluster analysis of a real world problem. One feature of this chatper is the comparison approach to cluster analysis based research, with two different clustering techniques employed in a real application, namely Ward's method and K-means. The issue of cluster analysis is demonstrated here through the analysis of a pertinent marketing problem, namely the investigation of the relationship between personality and dysfunctional customer behaviour.

Keywords: Clustering; K-means; Ward's method.

1. Introduction

Cluster analysis provides insights into data, such that objects in an identified cluster are more similar to each other than to objects in other clusters (Duda *et al.*, 2001). The pertinence of the potential for cluster analysis in marketing and management, from its early development, is expressed in Franke *et al.* (2009), which stated (p. 273):

> *Developed in the 1930s (Tyron, 1939), cluster analysis has diffused quite successfully in marketing and management, as researchers in these areas often deal with large and complex populations such as customers, markets, employees, etc.*

The term cluster analysis does not identify a particular statistical method or model, as do discriminant analysis, factor analysis, and regression. The role of a clustering technique, to perform cluster analysis, is to facilitate the partitioning of the data into such clusters, based on specified cluster characteristics. This chapter offers a background to the general approach termed cluster analysis, including an illustrative cluster analysis of a real world problem.

At the technical level, one overriding issue when considering cluster analysis is the wide range of clustering techniques available to be employed. Kanungo *et al.* (2002) highlights this point, saying there are many techniques for finding clusters, subject to various criteria, both *ad hoc* and systematic. The availability of different clustering techniques to perform cluster analysis is not without its drawbacks, it is well understood that the accuracy of the final partition depends upon the method used to cluster the objects, so comparisons of results from different clustering techniques are often embedded in a clustering based investigation (Mingoti and Lima, 2006).

In the early 1980s, there were studies reviewing the impact of cluster analysis in marketing research (Punj and Stewart, 1983), they offer a pertinent cover for its employment, relevant today, stating (p. 134):

> *Cluster Analysis has become a common tool for the marketing research. Both the academic research and the marketing applications research rely on the technique for developing empirical groupings of persons, products, or occasions which may serve as the basis for further analysis.*

Some examples of its employment, in a marketing context, include; expositing configurations of marketing and sales (Homburg *et al.*, 2008) and consumer demand (Hu *et al.*, 2009), as well as more technical investigations in marketing (Dolmicar and Leisch, 2010).

Within the study by Dolmicar and Leisch (2010), they express a note of caution on clustering, when considering the market segmentation view of cluster analysis, stating (p. 84):

> ...*the quality of the market segmentation strategy depends on the quality of the segmentation solution informing it.*

The story is similar in the area of management, for example, Lorr (1983) describes the role of cluster analysis in social sciences, along with Ketchen and Shook (1996) describing its employment in strategic management as (p. 442):

> *Due to strategic management's emphasis on identifying groups of similar organisations, cluster analysis has been a popular methodology following its introduction into the field in a stream of research often referred to as the Purdue brewing studies. . . . Thus, cluster analysis can provide very rich descriptions of configurations without over-specifying the model.*

Examples of its employment in this area include; public sector management (Andrews and Beynon, 2010); strategic management (Harrigan, 1985); and human resource management (Janssens *et al.*, 2003).

One feature of this chapter, with the demonstration of the comparison approach to cluster analysis based research; two different clustering techniques are employed. Moreover, two of the most commonly applied clustering techniques are employed (Mingoti and Lima, 2006), namely; the hierarchical Ward's method (WM) (Ward, 1963; Janssens *et al.*, 2003) and the non-hierarchical k-means (KM) (MacQueen, 1967; Kanungo *et al.*, 2002). The hierarchical and non-hierarchical nature of these two techniques is one example of the variability prevalent in the different clustering techniques available to undertake cluster analysis. A further example of their variability is in their effectiveness when outliers are present in the investigated data, with the hierarchical techniques affected by their inclusion, while the non-hierarchical techniques are considered to be more robust (Mingoti and Lima, 2006).

Regardless of the technique adopted, the 'clustering' attained must be interpreted and validated, to ensure that it is theoretically and practically meaningful (Frayley and Raftery, 1998). Validation refers to procedures that evaluate the results of cluster analysis in a quantitative and objective fashion (Jain and Dubes, 1988). For Frayley and Raftery (1998), validity must also entail some form of supporting qualitative argument. Ketchen and Shook (1996) argue for validation based on statistical analysis, they state (p. 447):

> *Significance tests with external variables offer a powerful tool to establish validity of a cluster solution because the technique uses a test static (often an F-statistic), thereby avoiding having the researcher provide the meaning of results.*

The external variables mentioned in this statement are variables theoretically related to the clusters, but which have not been utilised in the *a priori* clustering process. The issue of validation is important, and moves the clustering process away from just the partitioning of the data into clusters to a form of hypothesis testing, so prevalent in marketing and management based research. Further, there is continued research on developing expressions for numerically validating cluster solutions (Halkidi *et al.*, 2001; Wang and Zhang, 2007).

Within this chapter, the issue of cluster analysis is demonstrated through the analysis of a pertinent marketing problem, namely the investigation of the relationship between personality and dysfunctional customer behaviour. While the magnitude of dysfunctional customer behaviour is evident in practice (Ariely, 2007), by comparison, academic understanding of the dynamics of this phenomenon is somewhat limited. Consequently, numerous calls for research into deviant customer motives have been raised (Fisk *et al.*, 2010; Daunt and Harris, 2012; Grove *et al.*, 2012).

The results presented include interpretations to the clustering performed, with respect to the different clustering techniques employed, on the types of personality traits that may be associated with customers. Validation of the undertaken clustering is performed using an external variable, namely a measure of dysfunctional customer behaviour. The intention of this accompanying analysis is not with the intent to offer or argue the most pertinent cluster technique based cluster analysis but rather to illustrate some of the concomitant issues in employing clustering techniques, in cluster analyses in marketing and management.

2. Rudiments of Cluster Analysis (Descriptions of Ward's Method and *K*-Means)

This section offers some exposition of the rudiments of cluster analysis, including the key issues in its application. Further, the technical details of two clustering techniques are also presented (not in any way an indication of preference to these clustering technique to other that exist and are often employed). Ketchen and Shook (1996) is one example of a well presented effort to describe such key issues, in the context of strategic management, pertinently when reading this section, they state (p. 443):

> *It is important to note that there is considerable variation in how unified methodological experts are regarding these issues. Specifically, experts tend to agree on what the important issues are, but often disagree about how to address them.*

The key issues discussed in Ketchen and Shook (1996) include: selection of clustering variables, standardisation of variables, multicollinearity among variables, selection of appropriate clustering algorithm, determining the number of clusters and validating cluster solution.

The availability of clustering algorithms is a pertinent to consider. While many developed clustering techniques are only available in bespoke form, a number of the more well-known techniques are available in statistical analysis software packages, such as SAS, SPSS and Stata (the internet site Wikipedia contains inventories and comparisons of exhaustive lists of statistical packages available). For example, the SPSS statistical analysis software has three different approaches that can be used to cluster data, hierarchical cluster analysis (including the WM as well as others like Centroid and Median methods), KM clustering (non-hierarchical), and two-step clustering, next briefly explained.

For hierarchical clustering, you choose a measure which determines the distance between two cases, subsequently intermittent clusters are formed (based on the measure), either by joining clusters (agglomerative) or splitting clusters (divisive). Determining how many clusters to construct depends on how similar clusters are when you join or split clusters. In non-hierarchical clustering, in terms of the KM type approach, given the number of clusters to construct, an iterative algorithm estimates the cluster means and assigns each object to the cluster for which its distance to the cluster mean is the smallest. Another non-hierarchical clustering approach is the *Self-Organisation Map* proposed by Kohonen (1995), following a neural network structure it is basically a competitive network with the rudiment of self-organisation providing a topology-preserving mapping from the input space (characteristics) to the clusters (Kohonen, 1995). In two-step clustering, particularly appropriate when considering large datasets, the first step assigns objects to pre-clusters, then the second step, clusters the pre-clusters using a hierarchical clustering algorithm (such as WM).

The first two of these approaches are considered in more depth (one hierarchical and one non-hierarchical clustering technique considered). For the purposes of describing two clustering techniques in this chapter, in general, n objects $X = \{x_1, x_2, \ldots, x_n\}$ are considered in a p-dimensional space ($\mathfrak{R}^p$), where $x_i = (x_{i1}, x_{i2}, \ldots, x_{ip})$, $i = 1, 2, \ldots, n$, represents the object vector (x_{ik} represents the kth characteristic (or trait) associated with the ith object), and c denotes a fixed and known number of clusters to be established.

2.1. Ward's method (WM)

Introduced in Ward (1963), this agglomerative hierarchical clustering technique starts out with n clusters of size one and continues until all the objects are included into one cluster (or a predefined c number of clusters). Based on the notion that clusters of multivariate objects should be approximately elliptical in shape, it (WM) assumes that the data from each of the clusters will be realised in a multivariate distribution.

Letting x_{ik}^j denote the value for characteristic k in object i belonging to cluster j, we have to define the following:

Error Sum of Squares: ESS $= \sum_j \sum_i \sum_k \left| x_{ik}^j - \overline{x_{\cdot k}^j} \right|^2$, when the ESS is small, it suggests that the data (objects) are close to their cluster means, implying that we have a cluster of like objects.

Total Sum of Squares: TSS $= \sum_j \sum_i \sum_k \left| x_{ik}^j - \overline{x_{\cdot k}^\cdot} \right|^2$, the TSS is defined in the same way.

R-Square: $r^2 = (\text{TSS} - \text{ESS})/\text{TSS}$, this r^2 value is interpreted as the proportion of variation explained by a particular clustering of the observations.

Using WM, we will start out with all sample units in n clusters of size one each. In the first step of the algorithm, $n - 1$ clusters are formed, one of size 2 and the remaining of size 1. The ESS and r^2 values are then computed. The pair of sample units that yield the smallest error sum of squares, or equivalently, the largest r^2 value will form the first cluster. Then, in the second step of the algorithm, $n - 2$ clusters are formed from that $n - 1$ clusters defined previously. These may include two clusters of size 2, or a single cluster of size 3 including the two items clustered in Step 1. Again, the value of r^2 is maximised. Thus, at each step of the algorithm clusters are combined in such a way as to minimise the results of error from the squares or alternatively maximise the r^2 value. The algorithm stops when all objects are combined into a single large cluster of size n. A graphical form of cluster membership visualisation in hierarchical clustering is available, called a *dendogram* it exposits the clustering results of each stage of the process (Johnson and Wichern, 2002).

2.2. K-means (KM)

The KM non-hierarchical clustering technique (MacQueen, 1967; Johnson and Wichern, 2002) starts with c initial cluster centroids $C^{(0)} = \{c_1^{(0)}, c_2^{(0)}, \ldots, c_c^{(0)}\}$ (seeds), one for each cluster to be established. All the n objects are then compared with each seed by means of the Euclidean distance and assigned to the closest cluster seed, generally given by the objective function (for the t-th iteration):

$$J_{KM}(U, C) = \sum_{i=1}^{n} \sum_{j=1}^{c} \left\| x_i - c_j^{(t)} \right\|.$$

The procedure is then repeated over and over again. In each stage, the seed of each cluster is recalculated by using the average vector of the objects assigned to the cluster. The algorithm stops when the changes in the cluster seeds from one stage to the next are close to zero or smaller than a pre-specified value ε, namely if $\|c_j^{(t)} - c_j^{(t-1)}\| < \varepsilon$, for $j = 1, \ldots, c$.

The accuracy of the KM method is very dependent upon the choice of the initial seeds (Milligan and Cooper, 1980). To obtain better performance the initial seeds should be very different among themselves, often by selecting different objects as initial centroids and then the results were compared until the minimum distance is found (Forero et al., 2004). A graphical aid to cluster membership visualisation in the KM type clustering approach is available, called a *silhouette plot*, it exposits how well objects lie within a cluster and which ones are somewhere in-between clusters (Rousseeuw, 1987).

One of the advantages of the KM method is that we do not have to calculate the distance measures between all pairs of subjects (such as in WM described earlier), it therefore seems much more efficient or practical when you have very large datasets. It is worth noting also that the WM is used to improve the performance of the KM clustering, whereby the WM is applied first to divide objects into a pre-defined number of clusters and then use the cluster means as the initial seeds to start the KM (Mingoti and Lima, 2006).

There has also been considerable research on the technical development of already well-known techniques, one reason being often observed counterintuitive results and a poor robustness against data within which inconsistencies may be apparent. One antecedent for these developments, as described here, is that the considered clustering methods involving hard partitioning objects are grouped in an exclusive way, so that if a certain object belongs to a cluster then it cannot be included in another cluster. The KM technique is one such clustering approach that demonstrates well the development direction of clustering. For the reader, this development is next described (see Masson and Denœux (2008) for further details), and should be read with an open mind for the kind of problems the developments of clustering techniques, like the KM, have tried to overcome.

An early development, with fuzzy partitioning, is the fuzzy c-means (FCM) method (Bezdek, 1981), where each object may belong to two or more clusters with different degrees of membership. Krishnapuram and Keller (1993) introduced the possibilistic (PCM) clustering algorithm, developing on the KM method, the cluster membership obtained by PCM is interpreted as a possibility degree that an object belongs to a particular cluster (relaxing the normalisation criteria in FCM). Using a different approach, Davé (1991) proposed to add a noise cluster, grouping objects badly represented by the clusters into their own cluster. A new concept of partition, the *credal* partition, based on the belief functions theory, has been introduced in Masson and Denœux (2008), extends the existing concepts of KM type partitioning, by allocating, for each object, a 'mass of belief', not only to single clusters, but also to any subsets of clusters. Beyond the details of the developments briefly mentioned here, the dates of the research studies expositing these developments demonstrates such developments are ongoing.

3. Description of Personality and Dysfunctional Behaviour

Research offers a number of interesting insights into dysfunctional customer behaviour (see Harris and Reynolds, 2004, Reynolds and Harris, 2009). Dysfunctional customer behaviour refers to 'behaviour in the exchange setting which violates the generally accepted norms of conduct in such situations and which is therefore held in disrepute by marketers and most customers' (Fullerton and Punj, 1993, p. 570). Researchers frequently use dimenions of personality to explore the antecedents of dysfunctional customer behaviour. Here studies acknowledge the role that personality traits and predispositions may play in obstructing normative behaviours by individuals. Eysenck (1964) proposed the notion that personality dimensions can be utilised in the explanation of individual criminality (Hollin, 2002).

Multi-faceted conceptions of personality are widely employed in the explanation of individual and context specific forms of deviant behaviour (see Gosling *et al.*, 2003; Özbaym, 2008). With the view to investigate the relationship between personality and dysfunctional customer behaviour, five personality traits and predispositions are considered here, known to be antecedents to dysfunctional behaviour (based on measures from factor analysis — with between four and six items used for each measure — where they are measured over the Likert scale of, one (disagree) to seven (agree)):

3.1. *Machiavellianism (MKVM)*

Individuals with high levels of the Machiavellianism are purported to exhibit a general detachment from others, an innate instinct to manipulate others and a general lack of concern for conventional morality, rules and regulations (Christie and Geis, 1970). With specific reference to consumers, Wirtz and Kum (2004) forward an association between Machiavellianism and consumer cheating behaviours.

3.2. *Aggressiveness (AGSV)*

'Aggressiveness' is commonly associated with criminal and deviant behaviours (see Andersson and Pearson, 1999), which can also be seen within the employee-specific (Lee *et al.*, 2005) and customer-specific (Rose and Neidermeyer, 1999) research.

3.3. *Sensation-seeking (SSKN)*

The personality trait of sensation-seeking and the propensity to seek simulation is forwarded as important in the perpetration of aberrant behaviours (for example, Crino, 1994). The sensation-seeking trait is linked to episodes of shoplifting (Krasnovsky and Lane, 1998) and also violent and antisocial behaviour (see Komarovskaya *et al.*, 2007).

3.4. *Consumer alienation (CSAN)*

Fullerton and Punj (1997) explore conceptually a link between the predisposition of consumer alienation and aberrant customer behaviour that is carried out for ego- and financial-related gains. Whereby, consumers experience a sense of powerlessness and subjection derived from a lack of perceived personal and/or financial life attainments.

3.5. *Self esteem (SFEM)*

Emphasising the role that self-esteem plays in generating deviant episodes, John and Klein (2003) argue an association between self-esteem and ego motivated boycotting behaviours. Cox *et al.* (1993) too stress the importance of self-esteem in the context of ego motivated acts of theft by adolescent shoplifters.

3.6. *Severity of Dysfunction Customer Behaviour (SEVC)*

The variable 'severity of dysfunctional customer behaviour' is considered with relation to the personality traits and predispositions of interest. Drawing on the concept of norm violation, Reynolds and Harris (2009, p. 322) define severity as 'the extent to which a customer deliberately behaves in a way that violates the norms and unwritten rules of an individual service setting in a negative fashion'. Manifestations of customer misbehaviours vary in terms of their severity ranging from making fraudulent complaints, to arguing with fellow customers, to thievery, to physically striking an employee or fellow patron. Support is also offered by the conceptual works of Fullerton and Punj (1993) and Lovelock (2001).

Throughout the cluster analyses next performed, the personality trait scores of between one to seven should be viewed as indicating the non-association (1) to association (7) of a customer to the concomitant trait, respectively.

4. Results of Cluster Analyses of Respondents towards their Psychological Contract

This section of the chapter presents results from the cluster analyses of the relationship between personality and dysfunctional behaviour. The personality traits and predispositions were analysed using the two cluster techniques previously described, namely the hierarchical WM and the non-hierarchical KM method. Since the considered traits are measured over the same scale (Likert scale one to seven), there was no reason to standardise the data (it may be necessary/worthwhile to in cases where variables are measured on different scales).

Two sets of clusters were found from using each of the methods, namely for when two (C_1 and C_2) and three (C_1, C_2 and C_3) clusters solutions were produced. Irrespective of the number of clusters produced, they represent groups of consumers which have within group personality trait similarity. While here there is no requirement to determine the appropriate number of clusters, when considered (see for example, Homburg *et al.*, 2008), the comparison work in Milligan and Cooper (1985) on procedure to identify appropriate cluster numbers offers pertinent suggestions, including the cubic clustering criterion (Sarle, 1983) and the pseudo-T2 index (Duda and Hart, 1973).

Comparison of the constituent factor cluster means enables us to evaluate the ability of the clustering process to discern perceived personality forms, see Fig. 1 and Table 1.

In Fig. 1 and Table 1, each set of established cluster solutions is represented by a graph and row group, respectively. A series of constituent cluster mean values are presented for each cluster (the mean of the trait values for the customers in the same cluster), over each of the domains of the five considered personality traits, MKVM, AGSV, SSKN, CSAN and SFEM (joined by lines labelled with lower case versions of the cluster labels C_1 and C_2, and C_1, C_2 and C_3). To aid in the discernment of these constituent cluster means, in Fig. 1 notched box plots are also presented showing the spread of the trait values over the respective domains.[1] In Table 1, the statistical background to the cluster solutions are presented, using ANOVA and post-hoc test results in the case of three cluster solutions (see Janssens *et al.*, 2003; Andrews and Beynon, 2010). Further, where two constituent cluster means were found to be not significantly different from each other (here in terms of Bonferroni post-hoc analysis tests and 5% significance level — see Table 1), they are

---

[1]Within a notched box plot, working from centre outward, the vertical line inside the box is the median, the notch away from the median is the median confidence interval (width 3.14 times the interquartile range divided by the square root of the total weight of the data), the left and right sides of the box are the first and third quartiles, and the left and right whiskers 1.5 the interquartile range (not extending past the range of the data), further points are potential outliers.

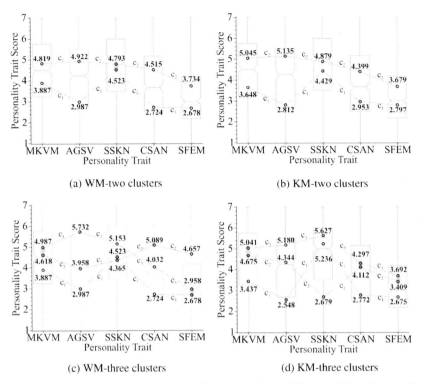

Fig. 1. Constituent cluster means details for two C_1 and C_2 (a and b) and three C_1, C_2 and C_3 (c and d) cluster solutions, found using, WM (a and c) and KM method (b and d).

enclosed in a shaded oval, signifying no significant difference in the values.

For the two cluster solutions (Figs. 1a and 1b), inspection of the graphs shows that a similar set of cluster means were found. Only in the WM based results (Fig. 1a), for the SSKN personality trait, are two points surrounded by a shaded oval, denoting no significant difference between the two mean values they represent (a 0.107 significance level shown in Table 1). With comparisons to the notched box plots shown, from both clustering methods, the two clusters C_1 and C_2 exhibit relatively 'low' and 'high' levels of presence of the five considered personality traits, respectively.

For the three cluster solutions there is variation in the cluster results, including a number of pairs of constituent cluster mean

Table 1. Statistical results describing the differences between factors across the different two C_1 and C_2 and three C_1, C_2 and C_3 cluster solutions using WM and KM (Frequency, ANOVA and post-hoc test results presented).

Cluster	Statistic		MKVM	AGSV	SSKN	CSAN	SFEM
WM 2 cluster							
C_1 — 161	ANOVA		39.989	180.203	2.610	164.015	62.307
C_2 — 219			(0.000)	(0.000)	(0.107)	(0.000)	(0.000)
KM 2 cluster							
C_1 — 169	ANOVA		105.163	336.106	7.425	94.289	41.936
C_2 — 211			(0.000)	(0.000)	(0.007)	(0.000)	(0.000)
WM 3 cluster	ANOVA		21.997	175.057	8.073	107.992	104.288
			(0.000)	(0.000)	(0.000)	(0.000)	(0.000)
C_1 — 161	Post-hoc	C_1 and C_2	**0.18 (0.00)**	**0.15 (0.00)**	0.20 (1.00)	**0.16 (0.00)**	**0.14 (0.00)**
C_2 — 100	Bonferroni	C_1 and C_3	**0.17 (0.00)**	**0.15 (0.00)**	**0.19 (0.00)**	**0.16 (0.00)**	0.14 (0.12)
C_3 — 119		C_2 and C_3	0.19 (0.16)	**0.17(0.00)**	**0.21(0.00)**	**0.17(0.00)**	**0.15(0.00)**
KM 3 cluster	ANOVA		52.521	150.271	289.962	41.121	20.683
			(0.000)	(0.000)	(0.000)	(0.000)	(0.000)
C_1 — 122	Post-hoc	C_1 and C_2	**0.18(0.00)**	**0.17(0.00)**	**0.13 (0.00)**	**0.19 (0.00)**	**0.18(0.00)**
C_2 — 106	Bonferroni	C_1 and C_3	**0.16 (0.00)**	**0.15 (0.00)**	**0.12 (0.01)**	**0.18 (0.00)**	**0.16(0.00)**
C_3 — 152		C_2 and C_3	0.17 (0.09)	**0.16(0.00)**	**0.13(0.00)**	0.19 (0.95)	0.17 (0.27)

Note: **In Bold** $p \leq 0.05$ (post-hoc Bonferroni two-tailed tests).

values which are not significantly different from each other (surrounded by shaded oval). The differences across the WM and KM cluster solutions are particularly in the personality dimensions SSKN, CSAN and SEFM, confirmed by inspection of Table 1. Concentrating on the clustering results, the three cluster solutions demonstrate the impact of choice of cluster technique employed. This is not apportioning preference to a cluster technique, simply that the mathematical rudiments underpinning a clustering technique define the concomitant cluster solution.

In terms of the clusters constructed in the three cluster solutions, the C_1, C_2 and C_3 labelled clusters generally describe 'low', 'medium' and 'high' associations with the personality traits, respectively, with notable exceptions. In the WM based analysis, the customers in the considered 'high' C_3 cluster are associated with medium CSAN and low SFEM, with the 'medium' C_2 cluster they are conversely associated with high CSAN and high SFEM. For the KM results, the 'medium' C_2 cluster has associated with it low SSKN, with the 'low' C_3 cluster conversely having medium SSKN.

Beyond the established cluster solutions found using the WM and *KM* methods of clustering, their relationship with severity of dysfunctional behaviour is next considered. Following Ketchen and Shook (1996), this exposition of the relationship between personality clusters and severity of dysfunctional behaviour serves a dual purpose. Theoretically, it offers insights into the relationship between two pertinent consumer concepts of significant pragmatic, as well as academic, interest — namely personality and severity of dysfunctional customer behaviour. Methodologically, the analysis validates the previously constructed clusters, by showing their relationship to a theoretically relevant external variable (severity of dysfunctional behaviour), not utilised in the clustering process. In this instance, the validation is both qualitative and statistical in nature. As a precursor to this analysis, the means, ANOVA and post-hoc tests for each set of established clusters are presented in Table 2.

In Table 2, the results from each cluster solution include a mean based ordering of the constituent SEVC cluster mean values, ANOVA tests across the clusters of employees, and for the three cluster

Table 2.　Statistical results describing the differences between the personality clusters' severity of dysfunctional behaviour (mean, ANOVA and post-hoc results reported).

Mean and Order	SEVC – WM 2 clusters				SEVC – KM 2 clusters			
	$C_1(4.0217) < C_2(4.8447)$				$C_1(4.0473) < C_2(4.8555)$			
ANOVA	Sum of squares	Mean square	F	Sig.	Sum of squares	Mean square	F	Sig.
Between Clusters	62.849	62.849	22.747*	0.000	61.282	61.282	22.147*	0.000
Within Clusters	1,044.395	2.763			1,045.963	2.767		
Total	1,107.244				1,107.244			

Mean and Order	SEVC – WM 3 clusters				SEVC – KM 3 clusters			
	$C_1(4.022) < C_2(4.733) < C_3(4.939)$				$C_1(3.910) < C_2(4.519) < C_3(4.951)$			
ANOVA	Sum of Squares	Mean Square	F	Sig.	Sum of Squares	Mean Square	F	Sig.
Between Clusters	65.167	32.584	11.788*	0.000	73.394	36.697	13.382*	0.000
Within Clusters	1,042.077	2.764			1,033.850	2.742		
Total	1,107.244				1,107.244			

Post-Hoc	Bonferroni's test			Bonferroni's test		
Between Clusters	Mean Diff.	St. Err.	Sig.	Mean Diff.	St. Err.	Sig.
C_1 and C_2	0.710*	0.212	0.003	0.609*	0.220	0.018
C_1 and C_3	0.917*	0.201	0.000	1.041*	0.201	0.000
C_2 and C_3	0.207	0.226	1.000	0.432	0.210	0.120

Note: $+p \leq 0.10$; $*p \leq 0.05$ (two-tailed tests) [Sig. — Significance, Mean Diff. — Mean Difference, St. Err. — Standard Error].

solutions Bonferroni post-hoc tests on pairs of clusters identified (see Janssens *et al.*, 2003; Andrews and Beynon, 2010).

In considering the ordering of the cluster means over the severity of dysfunctional customer behaviour (SEVC) personality trait, we note consistency in the ordering identified, namely for two cluster solutions, with 'low' C_1 and 'high' C_2 clusters have SEVC order $C_1 < C_2$ and for three cluster solutions, with 'low' C_1, 'medium' C_2 and 'high' C_3 clusters have SEVC order $C_1 < C_2 < C_3$. This suggests that the level of customer association with the personality dimensions, MKVM, AGSV, SSKN, CSAN and SFEM, increases, so does their association with SEVC. Comparison to theory serves as an affirmative qualitative measure of validation for all the clustering results. This qualitative support for the clustering achieved can be further strengthened by evaluating the statistical significances of the difference between the cluster means identified (and used to order the clusters) for each of the personality dimensions. Importantly, for this study, the statistical differences can also be used to gauge the pertinence of the different clustering techniques employed.

The ANOVA tests carried out on the different cluster results all show significance (at 5% level) for differences between the cluster means of customers to the SEVC measure. The worst and best results, in terms of F-statistic, were WM three clusters (F. 11.788, Sig. 0.000) and WM two clusters (F. 22.747, Sig. 0.000). The impact of these results is next considered through the post-hoc Bonferroni tests performed on pairs of clusters, for the three cluster solutions only. The post-hoc test results clearly show the presence of significant differences in SEVC trait between the C_1 and C_2 and C_1 and C_3 clusters, but not between C_2 and C_3 clusters.

5. Conclusions

This chapter has presented thoughts, details and examples of cluster analysis. It is hoped that this chapter offers insights and examples of the practical application of clustering techniques, and the practical benefit from their employment. Moreover, that it brings up many of the issues surrounding the employment of clustering techniques.

Clearly the future directions clustering analysis moves, both in terms of its development, and manner of application, will be diverse. The number of different clustering techniques available, and subsequent validation mechanisms to adopt, suggests fertile findings from such analysis will continue to be presented.

References

Andersson, LM and CM Pearson (1999). Tit for tat? The spiralling effect of incivility in the workplace. *The Academy of Management Review*, 24(3), 452–471.

Andrews, RA and MJ Beynon (2010). Organizational form and strategic alignment in a local authority: A preliminary exploration using fuzzy clustering. *Public Organization Review*, DOI 10.1007/s11115-010-0117-4.

Ariely, D (2007). The customers revenge. *Harvard Business Review*, December, 31–43.

Bezdek, JC (1981). *Pattern Recognition with Fuzzy Objective Function, Algorithms*. New York: Plenum Press.

Christie, R and FL Geis (1970). *Studies in Machiavellianism*. London: Academic Press.

Crino, MD (1994). Employee sabotage: A random or preventable phenomenon? *Journal of Managerial Issues*, 6(3), 311–331.

Daunt, KL and LC Harris (2012). Motives of dysfunctional customer behaviour: An empirical study. *Journal of Services Marketing*, 26(4), 293–308.

Davé, RN (1991). Clustering relational data containing noise and outliers. *Pattern Recognition Letters*, 12, 657–664.

Dolmicar, S and F Leisch (2010). Evaluation of structure and reproducibility of cluster solutions using the bootstrap. *Marketing Letters*, 21, 83–101.

Duda, RO and PE Hart (1973). *Pattern Classification and Scene Analysis*. New York: John Wiley & Sons.

Duda, R, P Hart and D Stork (2001). *Pattern Classification*. New York: Wiley.

Eysenck, HJ (1964). *Crime and Personality*. London: Routledge and Kegan Paul.

Fisk, R, S Grove, L Harris, D Keeffe, KL Daunt, R Russell-Bennett and J Wirtz (2010). Customers behaving badly: A state of the art review, research agenda and implications for practitioners. *Journal of Services Marketing*, 24(6), 417–429.

Forero, MG, F Sroubek and G Cristóbal (2004). Identification of tuberculosis bacteria based on shape and color. *Real-Time Imaging*, 10, 251–262.

Franke, N, H Reisinger and D Hoppe (2009). Remaining within-cluster heterogeneity: A meta-analysis of the "dark side" of clustering methods. *Journal of Marketing Management*, 25(3/4), 273–293.

Frayley, C and E Raftery (1998). How many clusters? Which clustering method? Answers via model-based cluster analysis. *The Computer Journal*, 41(8), 578–588.

Fullerton, RA and G Punj (1993). Choosing to misbehave: A structural model of aberrant consumer behavior. *Advances in Consumer Research*, 20, 570–574.

Fullerton, RA and G Punj (1997). What is consumer misbehavior. *Advances in Consumer Research*, 24, 336–339.

Gosling, SD, PJ Rentfrow and WB Swann Jr. (2003). A very brief measure of the big-five personality domains. *Journal of Research in Personality*, 37, 504–528.

Grove, SJ, GM Pickett, SA Jones and MJ Dorsch (2012). Spectator rage as the dark side of engaging sports fans: Implications for services marketers. *Journal of Service Research*, 15(1), 3–20.

Halkidi, M, Y Batistakis and M Vazirgiannis (2001). On clustering validation techniques. *Journal of Intelligent Information Systems*, 17(2/3), 107–145.

Harrigan, KR (1985). An application of clustering for strategic group analysis. *Strategic Management Journal*, 6(1), 55–73.

Harris, LC and KL Reynolds (2004). Jaycustomer behavior: An exploration into the types and motives in the hospitality industry. *Journal of Services Marketing*, 18, 339–357.

Hollin, CR (2002). Criminal psychology. In *The Oxford Handbook of Criminology*, M Maguire, R Morgan and R Reiner (eds.), pp. 144–175. Oxford: Oxford University Press.

Homburg, C, O Jensen and H Krohmer (2008). Configurations of marketing and sales: A taxonomy. *Journal of Marketing*, 72, 133–154.

Hu, W, T Woods and S Bastin (2009). Consumer cluster analysis and demand for blueberry jam attributes. *Journal of Food Products Marketing*, 15(4), 420–435.

Jain, A and R Dubes (1988). *Algorithms for Clustering Data*. Englewood Cliffs, NJ: Prentice Hall.

Janssens, M, L Sels and I Van Den Brande (2003). Multiple types of psychological contracts: A six-cluster solution. *Human Relations*, 56, 1349–1378.

John, A and J Klein (2003). The boycott puzzle: Consumer motivations for purchase sacrifice. *Management Science*, 49(9), 1196–1209.

Johnson RA, DW Wichern (2002). *Applied Multivariate Statistical Analysis*, 5th edn. Upper Saddle River: Prentice Hall.

Kanungo, T, DM Mount, NS Netanyahu, CD Piatko, R Silverman and AY Wu (2002). An efficient *k*-Means clustering algorithm: Analysis and implementation. *IEEE Transactions on Pattern Analysis and Machine Intelligence*, 24(7), 881–892.

Ketchen, DJ and CL Shook (1996). The application of cluster analysis in strategic management research: An analysis and critique. *Strategic Management Journal*, 17, 441–458.

Kohonen, T (1995). *Self-Organizing Maps*. Springer-Verlag: Berlin.

Komarovskaya, I, AB Loper and J Warren (2007). The role of impulsivity in antisocial and violent behavior and personality disorder among incarcerated women. *Criminal Justice and Behavior*, 34(11), 1499–1515.

Krasnovsky, T and RC Lane (1998). Shoplifting: A review of the literature. *Aggression and Violent Behavior*, 3(3), 219–235.

Krishnapuram, R and J Keller (1993). A possibilistic approach to clustering. *IEEE Transaction on Fuzzy Systems*, 1(2), 98–110.

Lee, K, MC Ashton and KH Shin (2005). Personality correlates of workplace anti-social behaviour. *Applied Psychology: An International Review*, 54(1), 81–98.

Lorr, M (1983). *Cluster Analysis for the Social Sciences*. San Francisco, CA: Jossey-Bass.

Lovelock, C (2001). *Services Marketing: People, Technology, Strategy*, 4th edn. New Jersey: Prentice Hall.

MacQueen, JB (1967). Some methods for classification and analysis of multivariate observations. In *Proc. 5th Berkeley Symp. Mathematical Statistics and Probability,* University of California Press, Berkele, pp. 281–297.

Masson, M-H and T Denœux (2008). ECM: An evidential version of the fuzzy *c*-means algorithm. *Pattern Recognition*, 41, 1384–1397.

Milligan, GW and MC Cooper (1980). An examination of the effect of six types of error perturbation on fifteen clustering algorithms. *Psychometrika*, 45(3), 159–179.

Milligan, GW and MC Cooper (1985). An examination of procedures for determining the number of clusters in a data set. *Psychometrika*, 50(2), 129–79.

Mingoti, SA and JO Lima (2006). Comparing SOM neural network with fuzzy *c*-means, K-means and traditional hierarchical clustering algorithms. *European Journal of Operational Research*, 174, 1742–1759.

Punj, G and DW Stewart (1983). Cluster analysis in marketing research: Review and suggestions for application. *Journal of Marketing Research*, 20, 134–148.

Özbay, Ö (2008). Self-control, gender, and deviance among Turkish university students. *Journal of Criminal Justice*, 36, 72–80.

Reynolds, KL and LC Harris (2005). When service failure is not service failure: An exploration of the types and motives of 'illegitimate' customer complaining. *Journal of Services Marketing*, 19(5), 321–335.

Reynolds, KL and LC Harris (2009). Dysfunctional customer behavior deverity: An empirical examination. *Journal of Retailing*, 85(3), 321–335.

Rose, RL and M Neidermeyer (1999). From rudeness to road rage: The antecedents and consequences of consumer aggression. *Advances in Consumer Research*, 26, 12–17.

Rousseeuw, PJ (1987). Silhouettes: A graphical aid to the interpretation and validation of cluster analysis. *Journal of Computational and Applied Mathematics*, 20, 53–65.

Sarle, WS (1983). *Cubic Clustering Criterion.* Cary, NC: SAS Institute Inc.

Tyron, RC (1939). *Cluster Analysis.* Ann Arbor (MI): Edward Brothers.

Wang, W and Y Zhang (2007). On fuzzy cluster validity indices. *Fuzzy Sets and Systems*, 158, 2095–2117.

Ward, JH (1963). Hierarchical grouping to optimize an objective function. *Journal of the American Statistical Association*, 58(301), 236–244.

Wirtz, J and D Kum (2004). Consumer cheating on service guarantees. *Journal of the Academy of Marketing Science*, 32(2), 112–126.

Chapter 15

ASSESSING THE PERCEPTION OF SUPERSTITIOUS NUMBERS AND ITS EFFECT ON PURCHASING INTENTIONS

Dina-Fu Chang
Graduate Institute of Educational Policy and Leadership,
Tamkang University, Taiwan
140626@mail.tku.edu.tw

Yi-Sheng Jiang
Department of Education Policy and Administration,
National Chi Nan University, Taiwan
ysjon@ncnu.edu.tw

Numerous studies have indicated that the use of membership functions and fuzzy interval data are more realistic and suitable for social science research. This chapter designed a fuzzy questionnaire to calculate how much Chinese people care about the superstitious number '4', and estimate their purchasing intentions and the price reduction that would induce them to purchase items featuring the number 4. The results from using fuzzy statistics and soft computing will more accurately reflect the intentions of consumers. In this chapter, the study found that Chinese respondents care about phone numbers containing the number four and fourth floors equally. Additionally, groups categorised according to age, ethnicity, religion, and education differed significantly in their perception of the superstitious number four.

Keywords: Fuzzy statistics; non-parametric test; superstitious number; purchasing intention.

1. Introduction

In social science research, many decisions, evaluations, or selections are conducted using surveys/questionnaires to obtain people's opinions. Traditional sampling surveys use questions with a single answer or a specified answer range, but this method is inadequate for reflecting the complexity of people's thoughts (Lin *et al.*, 2010). However, if people can use membership functions to express the degree of their feelings based on their own perceptions, the result will more accurately reflect their genuine thoughts. The commonly used method instructs people to use binary logic to consider a multiple-choice questionnaire. Empirical studies show that fuzzy statistics with soft computing are more realistic and suitable for social science research, and the results more accurately reflect their genuine thoughts (Wang *et al.*, 2010).

In our daily lives, people always hope for good luck and avoid bad luck (Jiang *et al.*, 2009). In the age of technology, Chinese people are still superstitious toward the number four. For example, when buying a new cell phone or car, people tend to select phone numbers or car license plates featuring the numbers six or eight. Additionally, when purchasing an apartment, the fourth floor is always the last choice. A significant proportion of purchasing intentions are similarly affected by these superstitions (Carlson *et al.*, 2009).

The reason why Chinese people dislike the number four is because it is a homograph of 'death' in Mandarin or Taiwanese. Thus, in Taiwanese society, we occasionally observe the absence of a fourth floor in department stores and hospitals. In hospitals, the fourth floor is typically renamed as the fifth floor (Jiang *et al.*, 2009; Vaidyanathan *et al.*, 2007). In this chapter, we explore whether differences in age, ethnicity, religion, and education result in varying levels of superstition and concern regarding the number four. Additionally, the case study aims to determine the price reduction that would induce consumers to purchase items featuring the number four.

2. Framework for analysis

In this chapter, the study designs a fuzzy questionnaire to calculate the degree of superstitious concern Chinese people have toward the number four (phone numbers featuring four, or the fourth floor) and estimates the price reduction necessary to induce customers to purchase items featuring the number four. The innovative evaluation of superstitious numbers and purchasing intentions in this study are shown in the flowchart as follows:

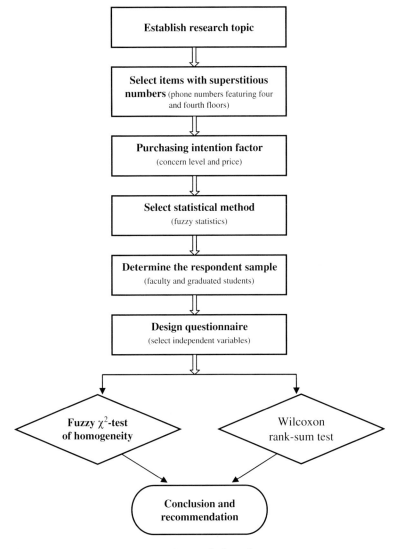

Fig. 1.   Research flowchart.

3.   Research Design

This case study focuses on respondents with a tertiary education to explore their superstitious concerns of the number four, and estimates their concern level and the price reduction necessary to induce them to purchase an item featuring the number four. Data collected using a fuzzy questionnaire and survey samples were obtained from one public and one private university in Central and southern Taiwan. Because we consider the influence of death education, the special course offered and limited students only in one of university. Data of the frequency distribution of respondents is shown in Table 1.

The mode for traditional statistics only involves a single number and cannot express human thought. However, numerous empirical studies indicate that the use of membership and interval data are more realistic and suitable for social science research. The self-designed fuzzy questionnaire was used to collect data; the fuzzy model was used to calculate the concern level Chinese people have for the number four, and to estimate their purchase intentions and the price reduction necessary to induce them to purchase. Using the precision of statistics, the fuzzy and soft computing results

Table 1.   The frequency distribution of respondents.

Category	Group	Number	Percentage
Gender	male	19	48%
	female	21	52%
Age	under 40	23	58%
	over 40	17	42%
Profession	faculty	17	42%
	non-Faculty	23	58%
Ethnicity	Taiwanese	28	70%
	non-Taiwanese	12	30%
Religion	no religious	25	62%
	religious	15	38%
Life and death education	not yet	20	50%
	major	20	50%

Table 2.   Using fuzzy membership function to express the respondents.

Care level Respondent	Very low (1)	Low (2)	Medium (3)	High (4)	Very high (5)
A	0	0	80%	20%	0
B	0	50%	50%	0	0

of the questionnaire can more accurately express the intentions of consumers.

The fuzzy questionnaire comprises two questions that the respondent can answer using membership and interval data (shown in Example 2.2). We transform the data into the fuzzy sample mean and its defuzzification value (D_f) and realisation value (RD_f) for discrete fuzzy data. Additionally, this study uses the fuzzy χ^2-test of homogeneity to examine whether phone numbers featuring the number four and fourth floors have the same distribution ratio. This case study aims to determine whether significant differences exist between the varying groups of age, ethnicity, religion, and education using the Wilcoxon rank-sum test. An example of fuzzy model analysis is shown below:

Example 1. Do you care to buy the fourth floor apartment? Respondents A and B might answer using membership as follows (see Table 1):

If the real estate company reduces price of the fourth floor apartment, how much of a price reduction would you require to purchase the apartment? (Suppose the floor space is 120 square yards, and the market price is US$100,000) Respondents might answer using interval data: 'Approximately US$5,000 to US$10,000'.

4.   Fuzzy analysis

Definition 1. *Fuzzy numbers*:

Let U be an universal set and $A = \{A_1, A_2, \ldots, A_n\}$ be the subset of discussion factors in U. For any term or statement of X on U, the membership corresponding to $\{A_1, A_2, \ldots, A_n\}$ is $\{\mu_1(X), \mu_2(X), \ldots, \mu_n(X)\}$, here

$u : U \rightarrow [0,1]$ is a real function. The fuzzy number of X can be written as follows:

$$\mu_U(X) = \sum_{i=1}^{n} \mu_i(X) I_{A_i}(X), \tag{1}$$

where $I_{A_i}(x) = 1$, if $x \in A_i$; $I_{A_i}(x) = 0$, if $x \notin A_i$.

If the domain of the universal set is continuous, the fuzzy number can be written as $\mu_U(X) = \int_{A_i \subseteq A} \mu_i(X) I_{A_i}(X)$.

Notably, in numerous writings people typically write a fuzzy number as:

$\mu_U(X) = \frac{\mu_1(X)}{A_1} + \frac{\mu_2(X)}{A_2} + \cdots + \frac{\mu_n(X)}{A_n}$ (where '+' stands for 'or', and ':' stands for the membership $\mu_i(X)$ on A_i) instead of $\mu_U(X) = \sum_{i=1}^{n} \mu_i(X) I_{A_i}(X)$ (Nguyen and Wu, 2006).

Example 2. How many hours do you spend exercising per day?

Let U be the universal set that can be regarded as an integer set and $A = \{0, 1, 2, 3, 4\}$ be the hours of exercise per day. Then a fuzzy number of X = hours of exercise can be expressed as:

$$\{\mu_0(X) = 0.25, \mu_1(X) = 0.6, \mu_2(X) = 0.1, \mu_3(X) = 0.05, \mu_4(X) = 0\}.$$

Then the fuzzy number for exercise hours per day can be expressed as:

$$\mu_A(X) = \frac{0.25}{0} + \frac{0.6}{1} + \frac{0.1}{2} + \frac{0.05}{3} + \frac{0}{4}.$$

Definition 2. *Fuzzy sample mean (data with multiple values):*

Let U be the universal set (a discussion domain), $L = \{L_1, L_2, \ldots, L_k\}$ be a set of k-linguistic variables on U, and $\{Fx_i = \frac{m_{i1}}{L_1} + \frac{m_{i2}}{L_2} + \cdots + \frac{m_{ik}}{L_k}, i = 1, 2, \ldots, n\}$ be a sequence of random fuzzy sample on U; $m_{ij} (\sum_{j=1}^{k} m_{ij} = 1)$ is the memberships with respect to L_j. Then the fuzzy sample mean is defined as follows:

$$F\bar{x} = \frac{\frac{1}{n}\sum_{i=1}^{n} m_{i1}}{L_1} + \frac{\frac{1}{n}\sum_{i=1}^{n} m_{i2}}{L_{i2}} + \cdots + \frac{\frac{1}{n}\sum_{i=1}^{n} m_{ik}}{L_k}. \tag{2}$$

Definition 3. *Fuzzy sample mean (data with interval values):*
Let U be the universal set and $\{Fx_i = [a_i, b_i], a_i, b_i \in R, i = 1, \ldots, n\}$ be a sequence of random fuzzy sample on U. Then the fuzzy sample mean value is defined as $F\bar{x} = \left[\frac{1}{n}\sum_{i=1}^{n} a_i, \frac{1}{n}\sum_{i=1}^{n} b_i\right]$.

Example 3. Let $x_1 = [2, 3]$, $x_2 = [3, 4]$, $x_3 = [4, 6]$, $x_4 = [5, 8]$, and $x_5 = [3, 7]$ be the beginning salary for five newly graduated Master's students. Then the fuzzy sample mean for the beginning salary of the graduated students is:

$$F\bar{x} = \left[\frac{2+3+4+5+3}{5}, \frac{3+4+6+8+7}{5}\right] = [3.4, 5.6].$$

Definition 4. *Defuzzification for discrete fuzzy data:*
Let D be a fuzzy sample on universe domain U with ordered linguistic variable $\{L_i; i = 1, \ldots, k\}$. $\mu_D(L_i) = m_i$ is the membership with respect to L_i, $\sum_{i=1}^{n} \mu_D(L_i) = 1$. We can consider $D_f = \sum_{i=1}^{k} m_i L_i$ the defuzzification value (D_f) for the discrete fuzzy sample D (Nguyen and Wu, 2006).

Definition 5. *Realisation for a fuzzy number on R (discrete type):*
Let D be a discrete fuzzy number on the universe domain U with the ordered linguistic variable $\{L_i; i = 1, \ldots, k\}$. $\mu_D(L_i) = m_i$ is the membership with respect to L_i, $\sum_{i=1}^{n} \mu_D(L_i) = 1$. $D_f = \sum_{i=1}^{k} m_i L_i$ is the defuzzification value for the discrete number D. The realisation is defined as:

$$RD_f = D_f + \frac{1}{n-1}\sum_{i=1}^{n} m_i |i - D_f|. \tag{3}$$

Example 4. Let $D = \frac{0}{1} + \frac{0.2}{2} + \frac{0.5}{3} + \frac{0.3}{4} + \frac{0}{5}$ be a discrete fuzzy sample on the ordered linguistic variable $\{L_1 = 1, L_2 = 2, L_3 = 3, L_4 = 4, L_5 = 5\}$. Then the defuzzification value for the fuzzy sample D is:

$$D_f = \sum_{i=1}^{k} m_i L_i = 0 \cdot 1 + 0.2 \cdot 2 + 0.5 \cdot 3 + 0.3 \cdot 4 + 0 \cdot 5 = 3.1$$

The realisation is:

$$RD_f = 3.1 + \frac{1}{4}(0 \cdot |1 - 3.1| + 0.2 \cdot |2 - 3.1| + 0.5 \cdot |3 - 3.1|$$
$$+ 0.3 \cdot |4 - 3.1| + 0 \cdot |5 - 3.1|) = 3.1 + 0.15 = 3.25 \tag{4}$$

5. Testing of fuzzy homogeneity

In this chapter, we attempt to determine whether respondents' concern for phone numbers featuring the number four and fourth floors have different ratios. The questionnaire was designed using fuzzy data; however, a relatively ambiguous question is whether (quantitative) discrete data can be considered categorical, and use the traditional χ^2-test. For example, suppose a respondent is asked the following question: 'How much do you care about phone numbers featuring the number four?' If the responses are a fuzzy number (for example, 70% of the time), the traditional χ^2-test for the analysis is clearly inappropriate. Therefore, we choose the fuzzy χ^2-test of homogeneity.

We present a χ^2-test for fuzzy data in this study as follows:

Procedures for testing the homogeneity hypothesis for discrete fuzzy samples:

(1) Sample: Let Ω be a domain, $\{L_j, j = 1, \ldots, k\}$ be ordered linguistic variables on Ω and $\{a_1, a_2, \ldots, a_m\}$ and $\{b_1, b_2, \ldots, b_n\}$ be random fuzzy samples from populations A and B with the standardised membership functions mA_{ij} and mB_{ij}.

(2) Hypothesis: The two populations A and B have the same distribution ratio:

$$H_0 : F\mu_A =_F F\mu_B,$$

where

$$F\mu_A = \frac{\frac{1}{m}MA_1}{L_1} + \frac{\frac{1}{m}MA_2}{L_2} + \cdots + \frac{\frac{1}{m}MA_k}{L_k}$$

$$F\mu_B = \frac{\frac{1}{n}MB_1}{L_1} + \frac{\frac{1}{n}MB_2}{L_2} + \cdots + \frac{\frac{1}{n}MB_k}{L_k},$$

$$MA_j = \sum_{i=1}^{m} mA_{ij}, \quad MB_j = \sum_{i=1}^{n} mB_{ij}.$$

(3) Statistics: $\chi^2 = \sum_{i \in A,B} \sum_{j=1}^{c} \frac{([Mi_j]-e_{ij})^2}{e_{ij}}$ (To perform the Chi-square test for fuzzy data, we transfer the decimal fractions of Mi_j in

each cell of the fuzzy category into the integer Mi_j, counting 0.5 or higher fractions as one and discarding the rest.)

(4) Decision rule: under significance level α, if $\chi^2 > \chi^2_\alpha(k-1)$, then H_0 is rejected (Nguyen and Wu, 2006).

Because the respondents' answers were fuzzy discrete data, we transformed the discrete data into a defuzzification value and, using the Wilcoxon rank–sum test, examined whether different groups of respondents show significant differences. The procedures for the Wilcoxon rank–sum test were as follows:

(1) Data: The two independent populations of X and Y and random samples $X_1,...X_m, Y_1,...Y_n, m+n = N$.

(2) Hypothesis: The two populations X and Y have the same median in their distribution.

$$H_0 : Mx = My, \quad H_1 : Mx \neq My.$$

(3) Statistics testing: $T = W_x = \sum_{i=1}^{m} R(X_i)$.

(4) Decision rule: Under significance level α, if $W_L \leq T \leq W_U \geq$, then H_0 is accepted.

However, when sample (m, n) size is large, for example $m \geq 10$, and $n \geq 10$, then the t-value of the Wilcoxon rank–sum test can be replaced by the z-value of a t-test. If $Z \leq Z_\alpha$, then H_0 is accepted (Wu and Shieh, 2010).

6. Empirical Case Studies

Using the fuzzy χ^2-test of homogeneity (shown in Table 3), the results show that the average concern level for phone numbers featuring the number four and fourth floors have the same distribution ratio among respondents, indicating that respondents primarily care about the number four, regardless of whether it features in phone numbers or floor numbers.

The statistical results of the Wilcoxon rank–sum test (shown in Table 4) reveal significant differences among groups categorised according to age and life and death education show significant differences. The realisation value (RD_f) shows that the group of 'aged

Table 3.   Results of fuzzy χ^2-test of homogeneity.

Care level item	Very low	Low	Medium	High	Very high
Phone number 4	46%	18%	16%	11%	8%
Floor fourth	45%	20%	13%	14%	9%

Notes: $\alpha = 0.05$, $\chi^2 = 0.826$, $p = 0.935$.

Table 4.   Results of the Wilcoxon rank–sum test for phone numbers featuring the number four.

Category	Z-test	
Gender	$Z = -0.071$	male (2.23) female (2.21)
Age	$Z = -1.752^*$	**under 40(2.44) > over 40(1.93)**
Profession	$Z = -0.331$	faculty (2.40) non-Faculty (2.19)
Ethnic	$Z = -0.824$	Taiwanese (2.23) non-Taiwanese (2.20)
Religion	$Z = -0.534$	no religious (2.32) religious (2.07)
Life and death education	$Z = -01.720^*$	**have not received (2.49) > have received (1.95)**

Notes: $^*p < 0.05$, $^{**}p < 0.01$, $^{***}p < 0.001$.

under 40' and 'have not received life and death education' care more about phone numbers featuring the number four.

The statistical results of the Wilcoxon rank–sum test (shown in Table 5) reveal that the different groups among age, ethnicity, religion, and education differ significantly. The realisation value shows that the groups of 'aged under 40', 'Taiwanese', 'no religion', and 'have not received life and death education' expressed a higher degree of concern regarding fourth floors.

The price reduction required for phone numbers featuring the number four and fourth floors differed (shown in Table 6). Statistical results show that the average price reduction for phone numbers featuring the number four was US$5.6, and the interval value was US$3.4 to US$7.9; this is cheaper than the market price of US$15 that allows consumers to select their phone number. In contrast, the average price reduction for fourth floor apartments was US$13,025,

Table 5.   Results of the Wilcoxon rank–sum test for fourth floors.

Category	Z-test	(RD_f)
Gender	$Z = -0.207$	male (2.41)
		female (2.17)
Age	$Z = -2.638^{**}$	**under 40(2.63) >**
		over 40(1.80)
Profession	$Z = -0.544$	faculty (2.31)
		non-Faculty(2.26)
Ethnicity	$Z = -2.040^{**}$	**Taiwanese (2.41) >**
		non-Taiwanese (1.99)
Religion	$Z = -2.480^{**}$	**no religious (2.68) >**
		religious (1.62)
Life and death education	$Z = -2.809^{**}$	**have not received (2.77) >** have received (1.79)

Notes: $^*p < 0.05$, $^{**}p < 0.01$, $^{***}p < 0.001$.

Table 6.   Statistical results of phone numbers featuring the number four and fourth floors Unit: USD.

Statistical value item	Min	Max	Average	Fuzzy sample mean [interval values]
Phone number four	0	$25	$ 5.6	($3.4, $7.9)
Floor fourth	0	$40,000	$13,025	($9,500, $16,550)

Note: Assume that the space of the fourth floor is 120 square yards, and the market price is $100,000.

and the interval value was US$9,500 to US$16,550. Though the average concern level of phone numbers featuring the number four and fourth floors have the same distribution ratio as obtained in the empirical studies, the reduced price between phone numbers featuring the number four and fourth floors differed, indicating that the acceptable price reduction depends on the total cost of the item.

7.   Conclusion

In this chapter, we selected an interesting topic about the superstition number and its influence on purchasing intentions in Chinese people of Taiwan. We addressed the application of fuzzy statistics models. This empirical study shows that the average concern level for phone numbers featuring the number four and fourth floors have the same distribution ratio, indicating that respondent care primarily about the number four, regardless of whether it is featured in phone numbers or floor numbers. We infer that most Chinese people have the same level of concern toward the number four. Therefore, companies developing new products should consider whether they relate to the number four.

Statistical results also show that the average price reduction of phone numbers featuring the number four is US$5.6; this is cheaper than the market price of US$15 that allows consumers to select their phone number. These results indicate that people with a tertiary education could be the major customers of telephone or cell phone companies selling phone numbers featuring the number four.

The various groups of age, ethnicity, religion, and education showed significant differences, and the groups of 'aged under 40', 'Taiwanese', 'no religion', and 'have not received life and death education' expressed a higher level of concern with the number four, particularly floors numbered four. According to the messages, we will suggest real estate companies could enhance their advertising or offer reasonable prices to maximise their profits.

References

Carlson, BD, JC Mowen and X Fang (2009). Trait superstition and consumer behavior Re-conceptualization, measurement, and initial investigations. *Psychology and Marketing*, 26(8), 689–713.

Jiang, Y, A Cho and R Adaval (2009). The unique consequences of feeling lucky: Implications for consumer behavior. *Journal of Consumer Psychology*, 19(2), 171–184.

Lin, PC, BL Wu and J Watada (2010). Kolmogorov–Smirnov two sample test with continuous fuzzy data. *Advances in soft computing*, 175–186; *Science and Statistical Decision*, 7(1), 122–130.

Nguyen, HT and BL Wu (2006). *Fundamentals of Statistics with Fuzzy Data*. Berlin Heidelberg, New York: Springer.

Vaidyanathan, R, P Aggarwal, T Cha and S Chun (2007). A need-satisfaction model of superstitious behavior. *Advances in Consumer Research*, 34, 355–357.

Wang, S, D Chang and B Wu (2010). Does the digital natives technologies really help? A fuzzy statistical analysis and evaluation on students learning achievement. *International Journal of Innovative Management, Information & Production*, 1, 18–30.

Wu, BL and MC Shieh (2010). *Modern Education & Psychological Statistics*. Taipei: Airiti.

Chapter 16

QUALITATIVE COMPARISON ANALYSIS: AN EXAMPLE ANALYSIS OF CLINICAL DIRECTORATES AND RESOURCE MANAGEMENT

Malcolm J. Beynon* and Aoife McDermott[†]
Cardiff Business School,
Cardiff University, Colum Drive
Cardiff, CF10 3EU
*BeynonMJ@cardiff.ac.uk
†McDermottA@cardiff.ac.uk

Mary A. Keating
School of Business, Trinity College of Dublin,
mkeating@tcd.ie

Qualitative Comparison Analysis (QCA) is an innovative analytical technique that bridges the gap between qualitative and quantitative approaches to research. Grounded in set theory, it allows the analyst to make causal about the structure of relationships between variables and outcomes. This is achieved through the identification of multiple configuration of causal conditions leading to an outcome of interest. QCA has typically been viewed as a small and medium-N approach although it is increasingly being applied to large-N datasets. This chapter describes the variants and rudiments of the QCA technique. These are illustrated with reference to a tutorial example and a real-world application that considers alternative configurations of causal conditions associated with clinician involvement in resource management in Irish hopitals.

Keywords: Causality; configurations; consistency; QCA; truth table; complex solution; parsimonious solution.

1. Introduction

This chapter offers a description of Qualitative Comparative Analysis (QCA). Introduced in Ragin (1987), QCA is an analytical tool grounded in set theory that allows the analyst to make causal claims about the structure of relationships between variables, attributes and outcomes (Rizova, 2011), in ways that account for multiple conjunctural causation. Although the name of the technique suggests an emphasis on the derivation of findings from qualitative data, the underlying mechanics of QCA are wholly quantitative. As a result, it is considered as an innovative technique for case-oriented research, that aims to *bridge the gap* between qualitative (case study oriented) and quantitative (variable oriented) approaches to social scientific research (Grofman and Schneider, 2009).

The underlying objective of QCA is to compare similar cases (as similar as possible) (Maggetti, 2009) that differ only in the causal conditions (independent variables), which should explain the variation in an outcome (dependent variable). The intention is to identify the necessary and sufficient causes leading to that outcome (*ibid.*). Causes are necessary when the outcome cannot occur without their presence. Causes are sufficient when the outcome always occurs when the causal condition is present although the outcome could also result from other conditions (Rihoux and Ragin, 2009). The key difference between QCA and traditional case-oriented methods is that QCA facilitates the extension of analysis beyond a small number of cases (Ragin and Rihoux, 2004). Further comparisons have been made with QCA and more traditional techniques, e.g., see comparison between QCA and cluster analysis (Cooper and Glaesser, 2011); and comparison between QCA and certain types of regression (Seawright, 2005; Grofman and Schneider, 2009).

Achen (2005) and Ragin (1987) summarise the contribution of QCA as follows:

1. The qualitative case-study method can provide in-depth and contextualised insights into social phenomena, which cannot be learned in other ways.

2. Many quantitative methods, and particularly linear statistical models, do not capture the contextual and conjunctural nature of causation evident in social reality.
3. In the light of Claims 1 and 2, conventional quantitative methods should be de-emphasised in favour of QCA, which aims to garner the best of both approaches. It replicates the logic of case study analysis in a mathematical framework that differs from statistical theory.

The second point above raises concern about the potential role and impact of quantitative research methods. Such arguments are prevalent. For example, Achen (p. 28) notes that:

Of course, powerful statistical methods are a good thing. I like them myself; they're fun. The point, however, is that substantively ill-informed use of them is not a good thing.

The core argument here is that many such concerns stem from 'perfunctory, slapdash, or otherwise unimpressive' applications and understanding of quantitative methods. He notes potential for similar issues to arise in the application of QCA.

To date, QCA has been applied in a wide range of domains, including many beyond the political science and historical sociology arenas for which it was developed (Schlosser *et al.*, 2009). For example, in marketing it has been used to construct micro-tipping point models for leisure destination behaviour (Woodside and Martin, 2008); to exposit market orientation (Ordanini and Maglio, 2009) and; to explore industrial marketing (Wagner *et al.*, 2010). More broadly, it has been applied to analyses of social policy development (Hicks, 1994); labour management practices in textile mills (Coverdill and Finlay, 1995) and; to managing barriers to the diffusion of the home and; to public sector and healthcare management (Kitchener *et al.*, 2002).

The purpose of this chapter is to give an overview of the theoretical and practical fundamentals of QCA. As a result, it combines theoretical discussion with worked examples. The first hypothetical example clearly illustrates the technical rudiments of QCA. A second real-world example is then utilised to more fully demonstrate the potential application of QCA. The example utilised is drawn from healthcare management. The problem considers whether the use of a clinical directorate management structure in hospitals is associated with the involvement of clinical staff in hospital decision-making.

2. Description of QCA

QCA aims to identify the causal conditions (independent variables) that associate cases (such as people or countries) to a considered outcome (dependent variable). However, unlike conventional statistical analysis, QCA does not ask about the independent effect of a variable on the likelihood of an outcome. Instead, it considers the effect of configurations of causal conditions on the outcome (known as conjunctural causation) (Ragin, 1987; Kitchener *et al.*, 2002). QCA has typically been viewed as a small-N approach. Schlosser *et al.* (2009) note that although binary comparison can be undertaken with two or more cases, QCA is typically associated with analyses of 10 to 15 cases. This focus on small-N emerged from the origins of the technique in disciplines with a macro focus — on countries, for example. However, the extension of the approach to meso and micro levels has led to its application to intermediate-N (15–100 cases) and large-N (100+) cases (*ibid.*). For ease of illustration, we provide examples with four and six cases, although the rudiments of the technique remain the same for small and large numbers of cases. Further details on the technique are available in Drass and Ragin (1992) and Ragin and Rihoux (2004).

Four forms of QCA have been developed (Rihoux and Ragin, 2009). The first, crisp set QCA (csQCA) is the most widely utilised technique to date. The csQCA is premised on the analysis of variables with only two potential values — typically denoting the presence or absence of a condition. The second, multi-value QCA (mvQCA) develops csQCA by allowing multi-value (rather than bi-value) variables. The mvQCA can be used with ordinal or interval data (poor, average or good performance, for example), or with nominal-scale conditions (Cronqvist and Schlosser, 2009; Cronqvist, 2005). The strengths and shortcomings of mvQCA are usefully assessed in Vink and van Vliet (2007). Third, in fuzzy set QCA (fsQCA) there is continuous measurement, with cases coded on a zero to one scale according to their degree of membership in a particular set (Ragin, 2000). Finally, Caren and Panofsky (2005) acknowledge that the temporal order in which variables occur might provide as much information as does the interaction of these variables. They present a modification of QCA which they call Temporal QCA. This allows the researcher to take account of the temporal nature of causal interactions. The values allocated for each causal condition are summarised in a data matrix, known as a truth table.

The operational rudiments of QCA are based on set-theoretic relations (Ragin, 2000, 2006). QCA uses Boolean algebra to implement a mode of logical comparison through which each case is represented as a combination of causal and outcome conditions (Ragin *et al.*, 1984). The method identifies different logical combinations of variables, using AND (*) or OR (+) expressions, which might be necessary and/or sufficient to produce the outcome. One feature of QCA analysis is the option to include the use of 'remainders', combinations of causal condition variables that are not represented by specific cases in the data, but which are theoretically possible (termed un-observed cases).

QCA uses the Quine–McCluskey method to minimise the equations formed from a truth table, as discussed in Ragin (1987). The Quine–McCluskey method has two components. First, additive terms that differ only by having opposite values of one multiplicative variable are combined — and the variable on which they differ is dropped. In more complicated equations, this process of combining terms that differ only by having opposite values of one multiplicative variable is repeated until no further simplifications are possible. The terms of the resulting equation are called prime implicants. The second component of the Quine–McCluskey method is to eliminate any redundant prime implicants, producing a minimal equation that is logically equivalent to the original. This minimal equation expresses the final inference drawn from a QCA analysis: Each equation is interpreted as a separate causal path to the outcome.

Table 1.   Truth table of raw data
for small hypothetical example.

C_i	V1	V2	D1
C1	0	0	0
C2	0	1	1
C3	1	0	0
C4	1	1	1

A small hypothetical example is next considered to exposit some aspects of the QCA approach. The example considers four cases (C1 to C4), each described by two causal condition variables (V1 and V2) and a single decision outcome (D1), see Table 1.

In Table 1, the four cases are described with reference to two causal variables. The four combinations of pairs of causal variable values shown are exhaustive. The implication is that there are no remainders (combinations of causal condition variables that would describe unobserved cases) associated with this truth table. There are also no contradictions to be resolved (no cases with same causal variable values but different outcomes values).

When the configurations with a positive outcome are considered (coded one in the D1 column in Table 1), it is clear that the cases C2 and C4 are described by the equations with conditions v1 * V2 and V1 * V2, respectively. This conventional representation requires brief explanation: The codes in upper case letters indicate the presence of a variable (coded one); while the codes in lower case letters indicate the absence of the variable (coded zero). It follows that the path of causality can be written as the *equation*, v1 * V2 + V1 * V2, to describe the positive outcome D1. The plus sign (OR) indicates multiple causation because each configuration of values on the causal variables is linked to the outcome (following the notation in Ragin (1987)).

Adhering to the Quine–McCluskey method, the separate v1 and V1 terms, by their representation are opposite in value, and can be dropped (i.e., it does not matter whether v1 or V1 are present), resulting in V2 describing the positive outcome D1 (D1 = 1). Thus there is a single prime implicant in this case. A similar result would be found in considering the outcome d1 (D1 = 0), which would identify v2 as the condition.

Although not utilised here, two key parameters for assessing the fit of QCA results to the underlying data are consistency and coverage (Ragin, 2006; Grofman and Schneider, 2009). Consistency refers to the proportion of the cases with the condition X that also have the outcome Y, relative to all cases with X. For any given dataset the maximum consistency value is 100%. The higher the consistency value of X, the closer it is to being a consistently sufficient condition for Y. For conditions that are 'consistent enough' to be regarded as sufficient for Y (Ragin, 2006) coverage refers to the proportion of cases with Y where we also find X, relative to all cases with Y. The higher the coverage score for X, the more cases displaying Y are covered by this sufficient condition.

As mentioned in the introduction, QCA attempts to identify necessary and sufficient causes leading to an outcome. Schneider and Wagemann (2006) offer an informative discourse on the relationship between causality and concomitant necessity and/or sufficiency. A cause is defined as necessary if it must be present for a certain outcome to occur. In contrast, a cause is sufficient if it by itself is sufficient to produce an outcome. Following these and other definitions, necessity and sufficiency statements lead to the use of set theoretic relations as indicated by the 'if … then …' structure.

For Ragin (2008) considerations of necessity and/or sufficiency must address set-theoretic relations. This makes it difficult for them to be established using conventional quantitative methods. Ragin's summary of when a cause is necessary but not sufficient or sufficient but not necessary is clearly demonstrated in Table 2.

To understand the details in Table 2, for the case of a cause being considered necessary but not sufficient, it means all cases must have that cause present in a configuration that describes it (as described in Schneider and Wagemann, 2006). With sufficiency, the presence of the cause will lead to the outcome — but alternative causes might also do the same.

Table 2.   Details of a cause's condition for necessary but not Sufficient and sufficient but not necessary.

	Cause absent	Cause present
Cause is Necessary but Not Sufficient		
Outcome present	No cases here	Cases here
Outcome absent	Not relevant	Not relevant
Cause is Sufficient but Not Necessary		
Outcome present	Not relevant	Cases here
Outcome absent	Not relevant	No cases here

3.   QCA Analysis of Clinical Directorates and Resource Management

Next an applied example from healthcare management is considered. A sustained theme in international policy change has been the notion that clinicians should become more integral to healthcare management (Montgomery and Oliver, 2007). In hospitals, clinical directorate (CD) structures have provided a structural vehicle to achieve this. Their primary purpose is to incorporate clinicians into hospital management. However, the literature lacks significant evidence regarding the impact of CDs on the primary objective they were designed to address, namely unifying resource decisions with financial responsibility (Llewellyn, 2001). In moving to explore the structural, management-process and cultural factors supporting clinician involvement in resource-management, six observed hospitals were considered, with the underlying premise being to include organisations pursuing similar ends through different means. This is a common qualitative research strategy. As Kitchener *et al.* (2002: 486) note:

> In public services research, as in other fields, a common strategy in comparative case-oriented studies is to analyse a small to moderate number of cases in which a focal event (outcome or process) has occurred, or is occurring.

The specific outcome considered here is *Clinician involvement in resource-management* (CIRM), which refers to when doctors, nurses and allied health professionals have input into resource-management decisions regarding service-delivery and improvement. Following Maggetti (2009), although similar, the six considered hospitals have a number of causal conditions in place which should explain the variation in the cases' association or non-association to the outcome CIRM. A total of six potential causal conditions influencing this outcome are considered. These pertain to structure, management-processes and culture. The causal conditions are described as follows:

1. *Clinical directorate structure in place* (CDP) — Hospitals with a tripartite CD structure, with a clinical director, a nurse manager and a business manager are coded one, others are coded zero;
2. *Budgetary devolution* (BDEV) — Hospitals with budgetary devolution, such that clinicians have authority and capacity to make and implement unit-level resource-allocation decisions are coded one, others are coded zero;
3. *Accountability* (ACC) — Hospitals which have feedback mechanisms in place, making clinicians accountable for unit financial performance are coded one, others are coded zero;
4. *Information* (INFO) — Hospitals that make high-quality, accurate and timely information available to clinicians are coded one, others are coded zero;
5. *Cross-professional decision-making forums* (CPF) — Hospitals that have formal management forums with cross-professional representation are coded one, others are coded zero;
6. *Cultural support* (CULT) — Hospitals with cultural support for clinician involvement in resource-management were, respectively, coded one, others were coded zero.

The subsequent coding of these causal conditions and the CIRM outcome across the six considered hospitals is reported in Table 3, in the form of a truth table.

The csQCA produced the following three minimised equations of hospitals' clinical involvement in resource-management (CIRM = 1):

$$H2, H5 : cdp * ACC * INFO * cpf * CULT + \qquad (1)$$

$$H1 : CDP * bdev * acc * INFO * CPF * CULT + \qquad (2)$$

$$H6 : CDP * BDEV * ACC * INFO * CPF * CULT \qquad (3)$$

Table 3.   Truth table of six case studies (hospitals), including six causal conditions (CDP, BDEV, ACC, INFO, CPF, CULT) and outcome (CIRM).

	CDP	BDEV	ACC	INFO	CPF	CULT	CIRM
H1	1	0	0	1	1	1	1
H2	0	1	1	1	0	1	1
H3	0	0	0	0	0	0	0
H4	1	0	0	1	1	0	0
H5	0	0	1	1	0	1	1
H6	1	1	1	1	1	1	1

These equations specify, in a logically minimal way, the different combinations of causal conditions that are linked with the outcome CIRM = 1, namely that there is a presence of clinical involvement in resource-management.

Two features of the QCA simplification process that derived these equations are worth reemphasising. First, the process of paired comparison, which requires that two configurations differ only in one respect, means that the importance of any given causal condition for CIRM = 1 cannot be evaluated in isolation. Second, the simplification process is context specific, meaning that a causal condition can be understood as unimportant in one context but critical in others (e.g., the inclusion and non-inclusion of budgetary devolution (BDEV) in the equations).

In reviewing the patterns of causal conditions across the sets of equations we note that 'INFO' referring to the availability of high-quality, accurate and timely information is the only factor present in all equations. This makes it a necessary condition for CIRM outcomes to occur (Kitchener *et al.*, 2002). In addition, we note that three configurations of causal conditions can facilitate CIRM. These are (1) a combination of financial accountability, availability of information and a supportive culture, without a CD (Eq. (1), observed in H2, H5); (2) having a clinical directorate structure, availability of information, cross-professional forums for decision-making and cultural support for clinician involvement (Eq. (2), observed in H1) and; (3) having a clinical directorate structure, budgetary devolution, financial accountability, availability of information, cross-professional forums for decision-making and a supportive culture (Eq. (3), observed in H6). Contrary to our expectation, Eq. (1) suggests that CIRM can be achieved without a CD structure. This has implications for theory and practice. The two observed hospitals from Eq. (1), H2 and H5, were private sector organisations, characterised by strong financial accountability, the availability of information to inform decision-making and strong cultural support for CIRM. Their experiences can be used to derive lessons for public sector organisations.

This example illustrates that QCA is useful in identifying systematic patterns in data. In general such patterns give rise to 'medium range' rather than grand and universal social theories, such as those of Habermas or Giddens (see Schlosser *et al.*, 2009).

4. A Summary of Best Practice in Undertaking QCA

The above examples provide insight into the mechanics and interpretation of simple QCA examples. However, Ragin and Rihoux (2004) identify technical and procedural best practices for undertaking QCA. Their recommendations are summarised below:

1. Select cases in a rigorous manner. The way cases are selected should be stated explicitly.
2. To the greatest extent possible, develop an in-depth knowledge of each case.
3. Select the causal condition variables in a rigorous, theoretically and empirically informed way. Try to be parsimonious and do not select too many variables. Focus on conditions that seem decisive from the perspective of either substantive or theoretical knowledge.
4. Where the raw data is quantitative and the N is not too large, display the data in tables so that colleagues can test other operationalisations of your conditions.
5. When using crisp set QCA, explain clearly how each causal condition is dichotomised. Justify the placement of the 0/1 threshold on empirical and/or theoretical grounds.

6. If possible, display the truth table and indicate which observed cases correspond to each combination of conditions.

7. If the truth table contains contradictory configurations, resolve them.

8. Proceed systematically to four analyses: Those for the configurations with a positive outcome (coded one), first without and then with the inclusion of remainders; and then analyse the configurations with a negative outcome (coded zero), first without and then with the inclusion of remainders. This process of analysis requires that cases with a '0' and with a '1' outcome should be included in the research.

9. The analysis should be done with software using the Quine–McCluskey algorithm and not by hand.

10. Resolve any 'contradictory simplifying assumptions' that may have been generated in the process of minimisation with the inclusion of remainders.

11. Provide some information (even in a shorthand manner) about the main iterations of the research (back to cases, back to theories, fine-tuning of the model, etc.).

12. At the end of each truth table analysis, report all combinations of conditions linked to the outcome.

13. Proceed to a real 'return to the cases' (and/or theory, depending on research goals) at the end of the analysis, using the truth table solution as a guide.

5. Conclusions

This chapter has considered QCA, a data analysis technique which is rising in prevalence and prestige across the social sciences. The chapter has provided a brief introduction to its focus on conjunctural causation, its capacity to bridge quantitative and qualitative approaches and its associated potential to facilitate the emergence of theoretical and generalisable insights. QCA is a particularly useful tool for researchers attempting to explore configurations, conjunctural or contextualised causation.

Those with an interest in adopting the technique may wish to visit www.compasss.org where they will find a network of researchers interested in comparative case research; details on software; and insights into theoretical, methodological and practical advancements in the QCA method.

References

Achen, CH (2005). Two cheers for charles ragin. *Studies in Comparative International Development*, 40(1), 27–32.

Caren, N and A Panofsky (2005). TQCA: A technique for adding temporality to qualitative comparative analysis. *Sociological Methods and Research*, 34(2), 147–172.

Cooper, B and J Glaesser (2011). Using case-based approaches to analyse large datasets: A comparison of ragin's fsQCA and fuzzy cluster analysis. *International Journal of Social Research Methodology*, 14(1), 31–48.

Coverdill, JE and W Finlay (1995). Understanding mills via mill-yype methods: An application of qualitative comparative analysis to a study of labor management in southern textile manufacturing. *Qualitative Sociology*, 18(4), 457–478.

Cronqvist, L (2005). TOSMANA–tool for small-N analysis [Version 1.25], Marburg. Available at http://www.tosmana.net [accessed on 16 May 2011].

Cronqvist, L and D Berg-Schlosser (2009). Multi-valued QCA (mvQCA). In: Rihoux, B and Ragin, CC (2009) Configurational Comparative Methods, *Applied Social Research Methods Series*, 1–19.

Drass, K and CC Ragin (1992). *QCA: Qualitative Comparative Analysis*. Evanston, IL: Institute for Policy Research, Northwestern University.

Grofman, B and CQ Schneider (2009). An introduction to crisp set QCA, with a comparison to binary logistic regression. *Political Research Quarterly*, 62, 662–672.

Hicks, A (1994). Qualitative comparative analysis and analytical induction: The case of the emergence of the social security state. *Sociological Methods and Research*, 23(1), 86–113.

Kitchener, M, M Beynon and C Harrington (2002). QCA and public management research: Lessons from an early application. *Public Management Review*, 4(4), 485–504.

Llewellyn, S (2001). Two way windows: Clinicians as medical managers. *Organization Studies*, 22(4), 593–623.

Maggetti, M (2009). The role of independent regulatory agencies in policy-making a comparative analysis. *Journal of European Public Policy*, 16(3), 450–470.

Montgomery, K and AL Oliver (2007). A fresh look at how professions take shape: Dual-directed networking dynamics and social boundaries. *Organization Studies*, 28(5), 661–687.

Ordanini, A and PP Maglio (2009). Market orientation, internal process, and external network: A qualitative comparative analysis of key decisional alternatives in the new service development. *Decision Sciences*, 40(3), 601–625.

Ragin, CC (1987). *The Comparative Method: Moving Beyond Qualitative and Quantitative Strategies*. Berkeley: University of California.

Ragin, CC (2000). *Fuzzy-Set Social Science*. Chicago, University of Chicago.

Ragin, CC (2006). Set relations in social research: Evaluating their consistency and coverage. *Political Analysis*, 14, 291–310.

Ragin, CC (2008). *Redesigning Social Inquiry*. NCRM Research Methods Festival 2008, 30th June–3rd July 2008, St Catherine's College, Oxford.

Ragin, CC, SE Mayer and KA Drass (1984). Assessing discrimination: A boolean approach. *American Sociological Review*, 49, 221–234.

Ragin, CC and B Rihoux (2004). Qualitative comparative analysis (QCA): State of the art and prospects. *Newsletter of the American Political Science Association Organized Section on Qualitative Methods*, 2(2), 3–13.

Rihoux, B and CC Ragin (2009). Configurational comparative methods. *Applied Social Research Methods Series*, 51. London, UK: Sage.

Rizova, PS (2011). Finding testable causal mechanisms to address critical public management issues. *Journal of Comparative Policy Analysis: Research and Practice*, 13(1), 105–114.

Schneider, CQ and C Wagemann (2006). Reducing complexity in qualitative comparative analysis (QCA): Remote and proximate factors and the consolidation of democracy. *European Journal of Political Research*, 45, 751–786.

Seawright, J (2005). Qualitative comparative analysis vis-à-vis regression. *Studies in Comparative International Development*, 40(1), 3–26.

Vink, M and O van Vliet (2007). Not quite crisp, not yet fuzzy assessing the potentials and pitfalls of multi-value QCA. *COMPASSS Working Paper WP 2007–52*, 1–29.

Wagner, SM, P Lukassen and M Mahlendorf (2010). Misused and missed use — grounded theory and objective hermeneutics as methods for research in industrial marketing. *Industrial Marketing Management*, 39, 5–15.

Woodside, AG and D Martin (2008). Applying ecological systems and micro-tipping point theory for understanding tourists leisure destination behaviour. *Journal of Travel Research*, 47, 14–24.

Chapter 17

DATA MINING PROCESS MODELS: A ROADMAP FOR KNOWLEDGE DISCOVERY

Armando B. Mendes
Universidade Açores, Portugal,
amendes@uac.pt

Luís Cavique
Universidade Aberta, Portugal,
lcavique@univ-ab.pt

Jorge M.A. Santos
Universidade Évora, Portugal,
jmas@uevora.pt

Data mining applications are common for quantitative modelling management problems resolution. As their learning curve has been very much simplified, is no surprise that many users try to apply data mining methods to data bases in a non-planned way. In this chapter, the CRISP-DM process model methodology is presented with the intention of avoiding common traps in data mining applications utilization. The use of this methodology is exemplified with serveral cases of application developed by the authors.

Keywords: Data mining; process model; CRISP-DM.

1. Introduction

Extracting knowledge from data is the major objective of any data analysis process, including the ones developed in several sciences as statistics and quantitative methods, database\data warehouse and data mining.

From the latter disciplines the data mining is the most ambitious because intends to analyse and extract knowledge from massive often badly structured data with many specific objectives. It is also used for relational database data, network data, text data, log file data, and data in many other forms.

In this way, is no surprise that a myriad of applications and methodologies have been and are being developed and applied for data analysis functions, where cross industry standard process for data mining (CRISP-DM) and sample, explore, modify, model, assessment (SEMMA) are two examples.

The need for a roadmap is, therefore, highly recognised in the field and almost every software company has established their own process model.

The data mining community and allied fields went through a long process of decomposing the tasks involved and many alternatives were developed in the process. These resources can be best utilised when we systematically analyse which of the tasks should be accomplished and which methods are best for each task and for each phase.

Traditional statistics companies tend to overvalue the analysis phase. This is obviously one of the core phases with a large number of methods developed to handle many search and model building tasks. But, hypothesis test and inference classification and forecast are only a part of the whole process of knowledge discovery, and often a short one of that. The entire process must include many more phases as is detailed in this chapter. We will walk through each phase, outlining typical tasks and methods involved and present cases of application.

Many of these methodologies recognise the iterative foundation of the process with many loops connecting the phases through the same application domain and feeds back on earlier findings. This adaptive development process is not new to data analysis literature. Keen (1980) describes continuous actions cycles that involved significant user participation. As each cycle is completed, the system gets closer to its established state like an evolution spiral (Lavrač *et al.*, 2004).

In this chapter we present in some detail the CRISP-DM process model. The CRISP-DM methodology, working over the successful results of those earlier experiences developed a very well specified process model where even the user intervention or domain knowledge was not forgotten. In fact, as Arnott and Pervan (2005) noticed, data warehouse and data mining development are dominated by IT departments. As IT professionals have little experience with quantitative modelling, some basic concepts of data models have recently being rediscovered like evolutionary development.

On the other hand, note that, compared to the traditional manual analysis, the process models supply a much higher degree of system autonomy, especially in processing large hypothesis spaces. However, at the current state of the art, a human analyst still makes many decisions in the course of a discovery process. Is also important to note that, using the decision support paradigm, the intention is not to automate the process but to help the analyst and decision maker to use their intuition in understanding the dynamic, using domain knowledge and knowledge extract from data for ultimately making decisions and manage problems.

The chapter is organiSed in the following sections. In Sec. 2, CRISP-DM Process Model is presented. In Sec. 3. we point some authors' studied cases. In Sec. 4, the Electricidade dos Açores (EDA) cases are developed. Finally, in Sec. 5, we draw some conclusions.

2. CRISP-DM Process Model

Several authors have been suggesting process models for knowledge extraction from databases (e.g., Klösgen and Żytkow, 2002; Hand *et al.*, 2001; Fayyad *et al.*, 1996). In spite of that, the CRISP-DM has been progressively becoming more visible, as the users recognise it as well structured and practical. It has also being validated by successful stories in projects of substantial dimension. The initiative that lead to CRISP-DM was conducted by companies in software development, consulting firms, as well as clients of data mining, with the objective of becoming independent of the business sector as well as of the software application (Clifton and Thuraisingham, 2001; Lavrač, 2004).

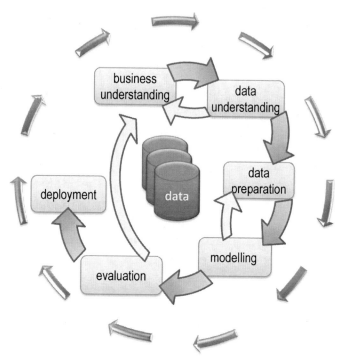

Fig. 1.   CRISP-DM v. 1.0 process model (reproduced with authorisation from www.crisp-dm.org).

In Fig. 1, are depicted the six phases of the CRISP-DM process model version 1.

1. Business Understanding
2. Data Understanding
3. Data Preparation
4. Modelling
5. Evaluation
6. Deployment

This process model is described in detail by the authors in Chapman *et al.* (2000) or by one of the companies involved in the development of the process model Shearer (2000). An explanation of each phase is expressed in the following paragraphs.

In the Business understanding phase the analyst should understand the business purposes, define and evaluate the problem, and establish purposes for the data mining project. The main output is a project plan.

Strong competitive pressure, the often saturated market, and maturity of products cause a higher demand for information and quantitative modelling of the behaviour of customers and competitors. These mean a big variety of problems to tackle in business. Some examples are market basket analysis, portfolio's return of investment, which determine the credit worthiness of a customer or identify fraudulent use of credit cards. Controlling and scheduling of production is another application field. Understanding of dynamic behaviour is another common business concern in many areas, such as identification of faults in telecommunications networks or analysing costumer interaction with a Website (Klösgen and Żytkow, 2002).

The problems can often be divided in two big sets. The classification and forecasting problems where an especial variable, often called decision, target or dependent variable has to be predicted by using the information contained in a set of explanatory or predictor variables. The intention in this type of problems is to set a model using data over both types of variables and use the model to make forecasts or classifications when the value of the dependent variable is unknown. These are called supervised problems.

In the case of unsupervised problems, there are no specially variables and all the data is treated equally. In that case the intention is to divide the data in previously unknown classes (clustering modelling) or construct association rules like in market basket analysis.

The Data understanding phase includes activities as data collection, exploration and data quality verification. The main purposes are to get familiar with the data, to detect especially interesting subsets and to discover first insights. Data screening is very relevant. If we seek predictors for one variable, we need this variable in the data as well as a number of potential predictor variables whose values are known before the value of the variable can be predicted. This means understanding very well the variables which are available and have a good insight over how they are associated. We must also be sure that data cover a broad range of values. In particular, data should be available for contrasting various generalisations.

Data preparation includes Extract, Transformation and Loading (ETL) and pre-processing activities, as selecting data, data cleansing, data fusion and integration, and all other activities needed to prepare data for modelling. It is an iterative process including feedback loops, as the modelling process may generate insights in the domain that require additional data preparations. New variables may be derived if they are more suited to the analytical tasks, like scale reduction as discretisation or dichotomisation. This process is usually called feature extraction in data mining literature. If the size of the data is too large for efficient analysis, data reduction techniques can be used, either by feature selection, which consists on selecting subsets of relevant variables, and sampling methods for selecting subsets of records or data table lines.

The necessary data commonly is spread over various relational tables, databases, or even information systems. Data fusion and integration is so a very relevant issue as we must find out how data from different sources can be pulled together, because the preponderance of quantitative modelling tools apply to single tables.

ETL, data cleaning, selection and reduction are some of the key steps in creating a data warehouse, which is a repository of data that summarises the history of business operations and is created for the purpose of analysis.

Several modelling techniques are applied to the dataset and modelling parameters are optimised. The models are built by searching in a combinatory space where many possibilities are explored (Klösgen and Żytkow, 2002). Huge heuristics for model construction have been developed in the latter years. When the explanatory variables and also the dependent variables are categorical the methods for classification trees and induction of rules are adequate. In the case of numerical variables, some examples are neural networks and linear regression, but rules and trees, namely regression and model trees, can also be used. Other methods like support vector machines and nearest neighbour method can also produce good results. Models can be expressed as equations, logical rules, visual trees or even sets of nearest neighbours. Choosing the set of right methods is not a simple task, and can be modelled as a multicriteria decision problem, so that the choice must include external judgment on the importance of the different criteria for the particular application. As is recognised, each heuristic method searches for the best model in a particular hypothesis space. So, is necessary to evaluate and compare models by applying the model to new data or dataset apart from the modelling data.

Before accepting the model or models resulting from the last phase, a thorough evaluation is imperative. Klösgen and Żytkow (2002) mention the case of survey analysis. Sometimes, some unexpected and not substantively explained results are apparent. Most of them led to the identification of some tricky behaviour of interviewers trying to speed up their interview efforts and other types of deficiencies or errors in data. This evaluation uses not only verification against new data, but mainly domain knowledge and knowledge generated by the process, especially in business and data understanding. A key task is to verify if the model solves the initial problem in a suitable way.

Another serious problem that requires knowledge refinement stems from the abundance of results normally easily obtained using data mining software. Such abundance is one of the main challenges in many business applications. Performance measures comparisons are the major technique to deal with the refinement of results. It is also relevant to ensure robustness of results according to several small data variations. Results from many instances of search process can be generalised, for example, by identifying the main influence and their conditions. Visualisation is also an important tool in this phase. Visualisation enhances understanding of data, models and knowledge, allowing the analyst to redirect and focus the search process.

The deployment are ways to spread the models and\or the knowledge generated by the project, and make sure that the appropriate decision maker or user who understands and uses it.

This process model recognises that users can only be in charge of knowledge applications if they understand the knowledge discovered. But users are often not familiar with tools and different data and knowledge formats that those tools use. The understandable presentation of results is critical. For that means everything from writing a report to implementing an application for model renewal whenever needed is possible. The process starts from business problem and data understanding, and ends with actionable conclusions from the discovered knowledge. After the action is deployed, practical evaluation of results is possible.

Authors like Adriaans and Zantinge (1996) note the difficulty in finding documented and detailed information about deployment of results in the corporate world. The same authors claim that KLM estimated that the implementation of projects including a substantial element of discovery from historical data, had a pay-back time less than one year and lead to a 2% reduction in total human resource costs.

This process model can be compared with the OR decision methodology (White, 1975) or general methodologies for solving problems and it is easy to show the high similitude between them being the latter mainly an evolution from the first with some adaptation of data rich environments.

Several authors, like Poon and Wagner (2001), recognise as a major critical factor the executive and operational sponsorship in the adoption of systems based in business models.

The following sections will present the application of this methodology. At the end, the results and conclusions will be presented.

3. Process Model Cases of Application

The authors have been applying CRISP-DM process model to quantitative modelling management problems, mainly problems tackled by data mining procedures. In the Table 1, two of the cases are summarised.

In the same table, for each application, the CRISP-DM handicaps, like customer disinterest in the implementation, no business

Table 1.   CRISP-DM process model and cases of application.

Business understanding	Understanding commercial market and the itemset bought by each customer.	The proverbs are a manifestation of traditional culture. Knowing a proverb is an indicator of the cultural reference region a person lived.
Data understanding	Big database with records of distribution of frozen food items throughout Portugal by the Nestle enterprise and bought together by customers.	In a series of interviews, it was collected a heterogeneous set of several million relations of positive and negative knowledge that a group of 1,000 people had regarding a set of about 22,000 Portuguese proverbs.
Data preparation	It was necessary to transform the data table extracted from the database to a table (transaction, item) with a set of all transactions where each transaction contains a subset of items.	The data had many faults and inconsistencies that were corrected using the knowledge gathered during the interviews. A data table was prepared using a query from the clean database.
Modelling	First, the input dataset is transformed into a graph-based structure and then the maximum-weighted clique problem is solved using a meta-heuristic approach in order to find the most frequent itemsets.	The problem was tackled by reduction of the dataset and rule covering algorithms. A new two-phase algorithm was presented. First, the problem is transformed by generating a matrix with the disjoint constraint. Second, the minimal subset of attributes is chosen using a well-known Set Covering Problem.
Evaluation	To validate the Similis algorithm a real dataset of frozen-food and other datasets from the Frequent Itemset Mining (FIM) Implementations Repository were used. Several measures were calculated to compare results.	Using Leave-One-Out cross-validation, several measures like area under ROC curve and k statistics were calculated. The dataset reduction results in a dozen of attributes and a 100 rules.

(*Continued*)

Table 1. (*Continued*)

Deployment	The algorithm was made available to modellers.	The new algorithm was made available to modellers.
Handicaps	Customer disinterest in the implementation.	The main difficulties were in data preparation, because of faults in database.
Reference	Cavique (2007)	Cavique *et al.* (2011)

understanding, or very long data preparation due to inconsistencies in data.

The following cases are described in more detail to serve as case study of CRISP-DM application.

3.1. *Business understanding*

In these cases, top EDA management was the client, being the users the IT specialists designed and developed the system with the authors. Those last ones were profoundly involved in the system development and were also responsible for all the communication with the client's project.

Following CRISP-DM process model, we first collected data over the company and main business. This was an easy phase, because the EDA collaborators collected all the data and answered all the questions. The following phases were trickier and so much more interesting for case study purposes.

Both decisions engaged in mentioned the projects which needed learning from data, as it is defined in knowledge management literature (see for instance Wijnhoven, 2003). For learning we used two main approaches: A business Intelligence project based on OLAP technologies (MS. SQL Server) and a data mining project which used statistics and machine learning models. The CRISP-DM was applied as a way to define methodological phases and to integrate business intelligence in a data mining framework.

This work reports on the methodological knowledge generated by several projects which intended to support decisions in the Electric Company of Azores Islands (Portugal), EDA. These are real life applications of business intelligence and data mining technologies.

All the projects meant to extract organisational knowledge from data records to support different kinds of decisions.

One strategic decision would be whether EDA communications, among the islands, should be moving to Voice over IP (VoIP) from present telephone lines and, if the feedback is positive, how to do it. This decision is not properly structured and must be based on technical and non-technical criteria. For the technical criteria, a Decision Support System (DSS) was developed based on data of an external telecommunications company, and MS SQL technologies. This project generated several others related to fraud detection in using telecommunications within EDA installations in all the nine islands. The detailed results were published, in a previous publication (Mendes *et al.*, 2009).

Another project intended to analyse the relation between the climatic factors and the consumption of electric power. This is, certainly, a different type of decision, more frequent and operational. But is not completely structured, since the climate influences direct and indirectly the consumption of electric power. With this project, we plan to develop models and knowledge to support consumption forecasts. These are critical decisions for a power producing energy, since this type of energy cannot be efficiently stocked, and so production must always be in phase with consumption.

Most papers on this subject focus on improving the prediction of electricity demand and on how to obtain forecasts as soon as possible, for better resemblance between production and consumption (see for instance: Smith, 1989; Troutt *et al.*, 1991; Engle *et al.*, 1992). All these papers mention the relevance of weather in electricity demand. In Smith (1989), the climate is considered as the major error factor in electricity demand forecasts. This problem can be even more complex when it comes to islands, subordinated to many weather variations, and where the investment in alternative renewable energies is higher. Decisions about how much energy to produce by flexible ways, like burning fuel, are especially relevant. In this context, we welcome any new knowledge.

The EDA Company (www.eda.pt) is responsible for the production, transportation and trade of electric power in all of the nine

Azores islands. Other companies can also produce electric power, but they must sell it to EDA, because this is the only one certified company to transport and resell electricity to consumers. Data of 2010 fiscal year indicate a turnover of 199 million euros and a total of 121.164 customers spread over the nine islands of the archipelago of Azores. EDA company has 687 employees, and it is the head of a group, which include six other companies, approaching 870 permanent employees. EDA has a particular complex communication system, because of the dispersion of clients spread over a wide discontinuous area of 66,000 square kilometres (see Fig. 2).

The EDA Company produces a mix of energy that is still largely dominated by thermoelectric power, although it also includes geothermic production (only in the biggest island), hydrologic and private production, mainly biogas. In recent years, the investment in renewable energy, such as geothermic, has been growing rapidly, for 43.5% of all energy consumed in São Miguel during 2010.

Most of the decisions were semi-structured. Since the seminal work of Keen and Morton (1978), it has been shown that data analysis systems are very useful in the screening of these types of decisions. As the major part of the work meant to analyse data, in regular basis or relating a decision taken in one specific moment in time, we suggested an approach based on OLAP and data mining. This was discussed with EDA specialists and decision makers, and was accepted for both projects. In this way, MS. SQL Server software was selected as the adequate, and, more decisively, accessible for the EDA specialists to manipulate, as well as to improve the system in order to come within reach of the user's needs, in an iterative and interactive process initiated by projects like these. In fact, any data mining and BI software could be used in this context. We used an opportunistic criterion to select SQL Server software.

3.2. *Data understanding and exploration: The OLAP phase*

In both projects, the contact with management to establish purposes and patronise the projects was easy. In both of them, the acknowledged purposes were to identify operational rules related to reducing costs and, in the case of the communications project, to also support

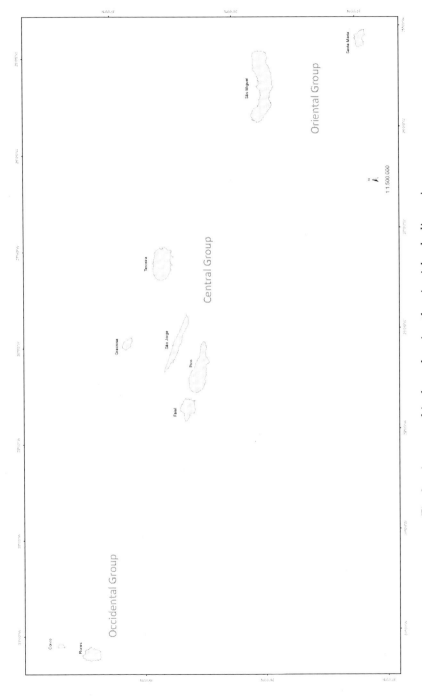

Fig. 2.   Azores archipelago showing the nine islands dispersion.

the decision about moving from external telephone service operators to VoIP, handled internally.

Also in both projects, a data warehouse was built from scratch, because there were not any data or information regarding both problems. The required data was, in both cases, external and for the communications decision it includes working patterns, number of calls, length, frequency and use in peak hours. In the forecast project: electricity consumption\production values by the hour and mainly climate data, such as temperature, humidity, rain quantity, visibility, wind direction and intensity, and a record of climatic events like exceptional winds or rain. Both projects benefitted greatly from inside experience on communication technology, data and models.

In spite of the fact that nowadays we live submerged in big data waves, it is still very tricky to capture, evaluate quality and explore data. These are the main purposes of the CRISP-DM phase of data understanding. This phase was done before the data warehouse construction, using small parts of data and easily accessible and simple software, like statistical packages and R-software for table and graphic data exploration and the discussion of the results with EDA professionals. In this phase, the initial purpose grew deeper and the knowledge generated from discussion was shared.

Some poor communication between information systems was also an obstacle in the case of communications data, as we needed pre-existing data, as the locations, phone numbers, and the identification of the user accountable for the phone terminal.

The outputs of this phase concern knowledge about data. Facts, like the three almost perfect direct linear relationships between costs and call duration, were almost completely explained by the three different time periods cost values. Obvious seasonalities on the number of calls, much higher during weekdays with strong reductions in weekends, were as well simple to explain, as only maintenance staff work on holidays and weekends. Similar seasonalities were easily identified in electric power consumption with much lower values during nights and week-ends. By graphing call duration in a histogram, a distribution similar to an exponential distribution was recognised, with almost all calls very short, tough some can be very long. Some long calls were specially noticed by EDA professionals. By graphing two years of daily costs in communications some other seasonalities were recognised as lower activity during the summer due to vacations and to a period during 2005, when EDA main building was transferred to a new location.

To make data exploration and dicing easy to any user, an OLAP application was implemented in both projects. This was a time consuming phase and comprehend pre-processing of the data, data exploration, data reduction and visualisation. The Software tools used were based on the Microsoft SQL Server technologies, already known and used by the EDA systems professionals. The main components included the Data Base Engine, Analysis Services and Integration Services from Business Intelligence (BI) Studio. This became a major measure in both cases. But in the case of the strategic decision about communications network, the OLAP project was considered more relevant and the application was extensively used by professionals. In the case of electric power forecast, the OLAP software was used mainly for data exploration.

In spite of all this tools, some actually helpful, the construction and management of data cubes was a long and hard phase. Process flows from Integration Services were identified as one of the most important tools for data preparation, such as the generation of new fields, tables' relational integration and populated fields. One example, for the transformation and preparation of the foreign keys in relational tables for new months, and establishing several relations with existing ones, is shown in the Fig. 3. The nodes in the process

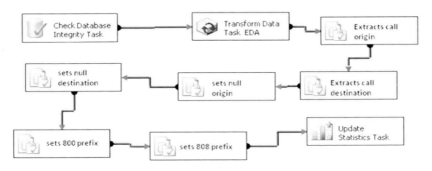

Fig. 3.   Process flow example for the communication network decision.

flow correspond to SQL coding and some other parameters. This is not uncommon in this kind of projects. Many other authors reported similar problems in supporting decisions in data rich (Chen, 2001).

This phase is also very important for data quality evaluation. In both projects many of the problems described in the book by Chen (2001) were actually identified. That was the case especially for electric power data and data collected from internet. Many missing values or non-conform values were identified and coded. Another important problem identified in both projects was the keys mismatch in related tables. This problem, often consequence of data fusion activities, is tackled in Chen (2001) and Saporta (2002). For instance in matching electric power consumption with climatic data, a process flow was programmed to extract the records that matched the year, month, day and hour.

In 1993, E.F. Codd (cited in Larson, 2006), one of the fathers of relational database and on-line transaction processing (OLTP) theory, proposed a different type of system that would be turned to the needs of data analysts. He called it an on-line analytical processing system (OLAP). The criteria Codd originally developed for an OLAP system were not widely accepted, but the acronym and the name are widely used today for systems designed to quickly access, aggregate and explore large data tables.

For the data mart design in the communications project, three measures were defined: Number of calls, simply the row counting of the data table, call duration, and call cost. These are numeric quantities easily obtained from the external phone company, noticeably linked with the project purposes. The first one was only included in a later stage of the project, as it was considered relevant by the EDA professionals.

Dimensions are discrete fields used to define the aggregation degree of the measures. A very useful concept of MS. SQL 2005 is a hierarchy which is a way to organise dimension in various levels. For instance, in Fig. 4 the time period is used in the following way: As the year dimension is above the trimester and this later one, above the month. Many other dimensions are used in the cube shown in Fig. 4, as the company, telephone equipment, island of origin and

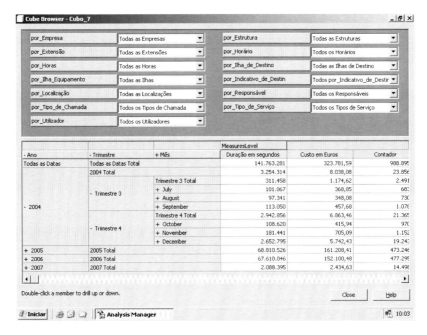

Fig. 4.   The final data cube for the communication network decision.

destination, type of call, equipment user, time of the day, etc. Other than new data, many are extracted from several OLTP databases already available in the EDA group.

As you can see in Fig. 4; the categorical fields can be used as aggregation dimensions (as the three dimensions of time period in the example above) or as filters as the other dimensions over the table. To interchange the dimensions used to filter and to aggregate data is only a necessary click and drag between both areas.

Several data cubes were constructed in an evolutionary process, as the discussion about data mart design went on and new data were integrated in the data warehouse. The star scheme was selected as it is known to have less performance problems in a ROLAP architecture (see Chen, 2001; de Ville, 2001).

3.3.   *Modelling: The data mining phase*

In fact, the OLAP project was much more than the data preparation and the exploration phase of CRISP-DM methodology. With the final data cube we answered many of the initial questions and actually generated knowledge and business intelligence, especially in the strategic decision.

In spite of this, it is also clear that the main data preparation necessary for an OLAP project is also required for the use of data mining algorithms. Many software houses recognise it by implementing both business intelligence technologies in the same framework. In the Microsoft case, the Business Intelligence Development Studio includes several tools for both OLAP analysis services and data mining. Both can use SQL server integration services to extract the data, cleanse it, and put it in an easily accessible form.

For modelling, we employed the same data as the one used in the cube of both projects, as data source, in order to generate data tables for learning and testing. This data was used in a twofold validation scheme: circa of 2/3 of older data (130,000 lines, years 2005 and 2006, in communications project and 16,000 lines, years 2006 and 2007, in forecast project) for model estimation (or learning), and most recent data for validation (or testing).

The Business Intelligence Development Studio in MS SQL Server 2005 includes seven mining algorithms, which perform the main tasks usually associated with data mining. These are: classification using a categorical target field, regression for a continuous target field, segmentation for defining clusters without a target field, association for rule induction, and sequence analysis for rules including a sequence of steeps.

In spite of the fact that data mining packages always have many algorithms for data model, is important to understand that they have different purposes and use different types of data. For instance, the forecast project had data which consists mostly on time series.

For the forecast purpose we need algorithms capable of identifying patterns in older data that can be extrapolated for future as well, as relations between the power consumption and other descriptive variables. For that propose, and also considering that the target variable has a continuous scale, the chosen algorithms were *Microsoft Decision Trees*, *Microsoft Linear Regression* and *Microsoft*

Neural Network. A brief description of these algorithms can be found in Larson (2006).

In the communications project the object was less restrict in terms of algorithms that can be used. As the intention was to produce knowledge about the way telephone lines were used, almost any algorithm could be tried in this exploratory approach. Therefore, several algorithms were tested and four were regarded useful, considering their results and the project point: *Microsoft Naïve Bayes*, *Microsoft Decision Trees*, *Microsoft Clustering*, and *Microsoft Association*.

Other algorithms were regarded as not suitable for the defined data mining goals, inappropriate for the available data types, or we just could not find any interesting result. One example was the *Microsoft Time Series algorithm*. Since the available data is chronological series, this could be regarded as one of the major algorithms in the use of forecasting continuous variables. In spite of this, the unique autoregressive tree model used in this software does not allow the estimation of parameters we needed as seasonal factors (see Meek *et al.*, 2002 for a complete description of the algorithm). For this reason we estimated regression models with dummy variables using statistical software for the calculation of the month seasonal factors.

One interesting feature of the software utilised was the dependency network which is a network where nodes represent attributes (or variables) and links represent causal relations or correlation dependencies between attributes. This is an interesting way to visualise algorithm results (Larson, 2006). Other uncommon feature we would like to distinguish is the possibility of generating data tables on the fly by selecting a key variable for aggregation purposes. This is very handy when dealing with lots of data, since the models are usually generated from aggregated data. This means that it is not necessary to maintain several tables with data aggregated for different keys in order to generate different models, but, as would be expected, the consequence is some delay in presenting algorithm results.

From these two projects and others in different contexts, we found that the data mining algorithms provided in the Business

Intelligence Development Studio, the *Microsoft Naïve Bayes* was found one of the most useful. This was the case because usually many of the variables used in these projects are categorical. For instance, in applying this algorithm to the call data and only having in consideration the more expensive ones, we found that 80% of this were originated from the main island, where the headquarters are located, 80% of this calls had duration between 3 and 10 minutes; 51% were made directly and 42% by human operator (the remaining 7% were for special numbers). This last figure was considered too high by the professionals and other models were built to understand what was happening.

This algorithm can, also, produce a ranking of the best predictors of a dependent variable. For example, from climatic data we found that the best predictors of electric power consumption were, in order, humidity, dew point and temperature. The last variables in the list were wind velocity and climatic conditions. Note that the Naïve Bayes algorithm used in SQL Server 2005 does not consider combinations of variables (Larson, 2006), which is unexpected in data mining software (see any data mining text book as Witten and Frank (2005)).

Microsoft Decision Trees is an algorithm that produces a tree structure defining logical rules for explaining a target variable, using several explaining categorical or categorised variables. In the MS implementation, it can be regarded as a generalisation of Naïve Bayes algorithm or a form of Bayesian network (de Ville, 2001). Analysing many trees built for the call data and suing the cost variable as a target and other many variables as keys, used to define the aggregation levels, it became simple to recognise the obvious relation between call duration and cost. Excluding duration from the explanatory variables it was possible to conclude that when the destination of the call is the island of São Miguel (the biggest one with half of the total archipelago population) the majority of the calls were not direct calls, especially the most expensive ones.

The *Microsoft Clustering* algorithm builds clusters of entities based on proximity measures calculated from the training dataset. Once the clusters are created, the algorithm describes each cluster, summarising the values of each variable in each cluster. This algorithm has the originality of displaying results not only in tabular form, but also in a network scheme, where links and colour codes relate clusters. From the many clusters defined in this way, cluster 6 represented an especial interest as it was characterised by long calls; it had a strange distribution far from peak hours, and also abnormal destination numbers. This cluster represents a significant amount of suspicious calls.

Using this algorithm on the climatic data and day as key attribute, we found 10 clusters, some of that could be used to confirm the results obtained from other algorithms like the Naïve Bayes. For instance, in one of the clusters high power consumption (bigger than 47 MW in 82% of the cases) corresponds to high temperatures (bigger than 19.7°C in 98.3% of the cases).

The *Microsoft Association* is an *a priori* algorithm type association for the induction of association rules. It produces an ordered list of item sets, rules with precision values and it results on a dependency network. This algorithm was considered very interesting and was one of the most used in the communications study. For example, it was possible to conclude that there was a high support for calls by human operator with origin and destination in the same island, which seems suspicious as these calls may easily be made by a direct call using the company network.

All that models were validated using the main tools in MS SQL server, the lift chart and classification (or confusion) matrix. These are charts that compare the precision of the classification (or forecast for continuous variables) for the different models used. These charts can take a long time to be built and were useful only to compare models with each other in the worst case scenario. They confirmed that rules induced by decision trees and Naïve Bayes were the best ones for call cost forecast.

In both projects, it was possible to find good validated models. In the communications study, the quality measures calculated over the test data were coefficient of determination of 87%, root mean square of error of 5.9, a mean absolute deviation of 5.0 and the mean absolute percentage error of 19%. For the climatic data identical procedure resulted in coefficient of determination of 94%, root mean square error of 3.52, a mean absolute deviation of 0.21, and the mean absolute percentage error of 2.92 %. We believe that these are fair good results which were corroborated with domain knowledge from EDA professionals.

3.4. *Results and decisions*

The model results were discussed with EDA experts in order to consolidate the knowledge captured. For instance, for more exploratory study, where this phase is especially relevant, the peak hours are between 9 to 11 and between 14 to 16 hour each weekday and there is very low use at night and during lunch time, and also at weekends and holidays. There were no seasonalities between the weekdays, as they have almost the same high use. On the other hand, the month seasonal factors indicate less use during summer and around the New Year's Eve. The most common call destination goes to the tree bigger towns in the region, as it was expected, and the calls' length is usually lower than three minutes. The special numbers, like the call centre number, are of low usage.

This kind of exploratory information is enormously important for the particular decision to support. Especially the strong seasonalities identified mean that the equipment capacities must be planned for peak periods. From the trends estimated by the regression models, there is no evidence of increasing total duration of calls, or even in peak periods, as trend lines were always non-significant for the two years of data.

As it was recognised by other authors (see for instance Cortes *et al.*, 2001) the key criteria for decisions relating a telecommunication investment is the cost of the different solutions. In this way, for a final decision, a cost analysis was also prepared using data collected from the previous analysis, comparing the costs for the existent communication system with two change scenarios. The three options defined in this phase are based in different technical solutions derived by the EDA experts.

Option A applies a minimum of investment using the existing lines and only buying the necessary equipment's. In spite of a reduced investment, there is a reduction in the annual operation costs by 15%, but there is no expected cost reduction for the new VoIP links between internal locations, due to low volume calls. This option maintains the two technologies presently used by the communication system until the end of equipment life: A PBx central for voice communication and VoIP, being this last one much more utilised than the one before as the connections between islands main stations would utilise this technology.

Option B emphasises on replacing progressively all equipment's resulting in a new telecommunications infrastructure based on VoIP Routers and Call Managers for voice and data communications. This option requires a big investment in new equipment's, seven times option A, but, when finished, it will decrease the annual operation costs by 165% from the present values.

The current situation has no capital but high operational costs. As it was a complex decision with a multicriteria structure, all the factors considered for that decision are summarised in Table 2. Our conclusion, from cost analysis and business intelligence, is that both new solutions look attractive as the benefits compensate the costs in the long run. The decision aid group recommended the adoption of option B, as in a strategic view it will benefit the company, relating not only money, but also a 'technological image' of the company and the simplification of operation activities. In spite of the fact that no numerical evaluation of criteria neither weight was calculated, as the decision seemed clear, the recommendation was adopted by decision makers executives and a project is now being implemented.

For the climatic data project, there were no decisions to been taken, but there was a need for better models and for the understanding of climatic effects on electricity consumption. For the model construction a simple to complex approach was adopted. Starting from simple regression models we ended by choosing a regression model tree as the final model. This model is a combination of regressions with a classification tree which divides the initial data in smaller sets. These smaller datasets are then used to obtain regression models. In Fig. 5, we present the results for a terminal node of the model tree.

Table 2.   Decision features of the two change alternatives.

Actions	Costs	Benefits	Critical factors

Option A — VoIP connections maintaining present WAN equipment's with minor changes

Actions	Costs	Benefits	Critical factors
Upgrade existing infrastructure; Upgrade circuits bandwidth; Provision of additional VoIP cards to existing equipment's; Configure all network.	High ongoing and support costs due to obsolete and mixed technologies; High cost with service operators; High operation costs if traffic increases.	Reduced investment on infrastructure; Low reduction on telephone service costs.	Age of telephonic equipment and end of life (presently with eight years); Cost of introduction of additional VoIP links exceed the actual costs.

Option B — VoIP connections replacing WAN equipment's

Actions	Costs	Benefits	Critical factors
Upgrade circuits bandwidth; Provision of Routers, Call-Manager's, Switching and terminal equipment; Change all WAN and LAN equipments supporting voice Configure all networks.	High cost of initial investment; Change management.	Reduced ongoing cost and high reduction on support costs; Fixed telephone service; Renewed WAN infrastructures; New services introduced by IP telephony.	Long-term benefits due to the reduction on ongoing costs and new services; Capability of existing service provider to implement and support the new infrastructures; Migration of existing services (Call Centre).

This model can be easily described. In every Thursday between 15 to 18 hours for one degree Celsius over the average temperature the power consumption is 0.293 MW higher, if we do not consider changes in all other variables. For the same expansion value of the dew point, the power is 0.344 MW. We can find, also, an improvement of the average annual power consumption of 1.783 MW and

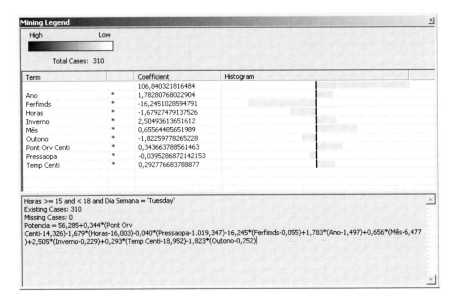

Fig. 5.   One terminal node of the model tree obtained with climatic data.

0.656 MW monthly. In winter, an improvement of 2.505*(1 − 0.229) or 1.93 MW is also expected and also a reduction in power consumption of 1.823*(1 − 0.252) or 1.36 MW is expected in autumn.

In other branches of the tree we can see that temperature, dew point and humidity are the more important climatic factors and we can find an improvement in power consumption every time these factors present higher values. This was rationalised by specialists for the need to use refrigerator and humidity control systems when temperatures and humidity are higher. On the other side, there is a known physical phenomenon that explains higher losses in electric energy transportation in these conditions. There is also a possibility of other indirect factors may be influencing power consumption, like sun exposure and higher population in summer due to tourism.

This model is considered a good representation, not only because of the good quality statistics and graphs, like the one in Fig. 6, but also because domain knowledge supports the fact that the very strong seasonalities identified make the division of data more adequate for regression models. This pattern in electrical power

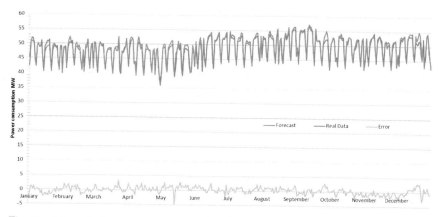

Fig. 6. Mean daily power consumption for year 2007, both recorded and fore-casted.

consumption is highly recognised in published work, being common the recommendation of modelling only particular periods of time like peak hours (see Engle *et al.*, 1992; Liu and Harris, 1993).

4. Conclusion

In this chapter, we explain the need for a process model in quantitative modelling of management problems supported by database management systems, data warehouses and OLAP technologies. The CRISP-DM Process Model is presented and two applications are described.

In each application the decisions to support were completely different, in structure and frequency as well as in data requirements, the technologies used were found very useful and resourceful. The component of data mining seems to have as main purposes the easiness to use and automation. SQL Server 2005 Data Mining Add-ins was found especially interesting for easily exploring relatively small datasets. Some algorithms are black boxes and not very clear for the user. In spite of that, it can be actually relevant in management context for quantitative model, especially with big data tables and using database management systems.

In addition to the fact that was possible to support the right decisions, and producing reports or models for future use, this technology also allowed to collect actually good knowledge. Examples of that is all the knowledge about seasonalities in the climatic data, and more relevantly the relative importance of climatic factors.

But, the most fundamental example of information collected is all the relevant faults and inefficient procedures identified in the communications project. A concrete example is the high number of long calls not related to business activities, for personal and shopping purposes. It was also possible to identify a miss configuration on automatic call distribution, resulting on additional external calls, which were more expensive, and terminal equipments not used but that had subscription costs. From these fault detection activities several terminal equipments have been eliminated and some ghost traffic reduced.

But the major and unexpected result was the high number of indirect calls, using human service operator, as a way around to the existing control system. Doing an indirect call, the link between the call origin and destination is much more difficult to establish. This fact led to new rules of operation, restricting calls by human operator. In the deployment phase applications (as the OLAP cube) were developed for use by several technicians and decision makers.

These successful projects are good examples of quantitative modelling in data mining supported by a comprehensive process model.

References

Adriaans, P and D Zantinge (1996). *Data Mining*. Massachusetts, USA: Addison-Wesley.

Arnott, D and G Pervan (2005). A critical analysis of decision support systems research. *Journal of Information Technology*, 20, 67–87.

Cavique, L, AB Mendes and M Funk (2011). Logical analysis of inconsistent data (LAID) for a paremiologic study. Proceedings in press, EPIA 2011.

Cavique, L (2007). A scalable algorithm for the market basket analysis. *Journal of Retailing and Consumer Services, Special Issue on Data Mining in Retailing and Consumer Services*, 14(6), 400–407.

Chapman, P, J Clinton, R Kerber, T Khabaza, T Reinartz, C Shearer and R Wirth (2000). CRISP-DM 1.0 — Step-by-step data mining guide. SPSS Inc.

Chen, Z (2001). *Intelligent Data Warehousing: From Data Preparation to Data Mining*. Boca Raton: CRC Press.

Clifton, C and B Thuraisingham (2001). Emerging standards for data mining. *Computer Standards & Interfaces*, 23, 187–193.

Cortes, P, L Onieva, J Larrañeta and JM Garcia (2001). Decision support system for planning telecommunication networks: A case study applied to the Andalusian region. *Journal of Operational Research Society*, 52, 283–290

Engle, RF, C Mustafa and J Rice (1992). Modelling peak electricity demand. *Journal of Forecasting*, 11, 241–251.

Fayyad, M, G Piatetsky-Shapiro and P Smyth (1996). From data mining to knowledge discovery: An overview. In *Advances in Knowledge Discovery and Data Mining*, UM Fayyad, G Piatetsky-Shapiro, P Smyth and R Uthurusamy (eds.), pp. 1–34. Menlo Park, USA: MIT Press.

Hand, DJ, H Mannila and P Smyth (2001). Principles of Data Mining. *Adaptive Computation and Machine Learning*. Cambridge, USA: MIT Press.

Keen, PGW (1980). Adaptive design for decision support system. *Data Base*, 12, 15–25.

Keen, PGW and MSS Morton (1978). *Decision Support Systems: An Organizational Perspective (Addison-Wesley Series on Decision Support)*. Reading, USA: Addison-Wesley.

Klösgen, W and JM Zytkow (2002). The knowledge discovery process. Inö *Handbook of Data Mining and Knowledge Discovery*, W Klösgen and JM Zytkow (eds.), pp. 10–21, 1st edn. New York, USA: Oxford University Press.

Larson, B (2006). *Delivering Business Intelligence with MS SQL Server 2005*. Emeryville: McGraw-Hill.

Lavrač, N, H Motoda, T Fawcett R Holte, P Langley and P Adriaans (2004). Introduction: Lessons learned from data mining applications and collaborative problem solving. *Machine Learning*, 57, 13–34.

Liu, L-M and JL Harris (1993). Dynamic structural analysis and forecasting of residential electricity consumption. *International Journal of Forecasting*, 9, 437–455.

Meek, C, DM Chickering and D Heckerman (2002). Autoregressive tree models for time-series analysis. In *Proc. 2nd ed. of the Int. SIAM Conference on Data Mining*, pp. 229–244. Arlington: SIAM.

Mendes, AB, A Ferreira and PJ Alfaro (2009). Supporting a telecommunications decision with OLAP and data mining: A case study in Azores. In *Proc. CENTERIS 2009*, MM Cruz-Cunha, JEQ Varajão and LAM Amaral (eds.), pp. 537–549. Ofir, Portugal: CENTERIS.

Poon, P and C Wagner (2001). Critical success factors revisited: Success and failure cases of information systems for senior executives. *Decision Support System*, 23, 149–159.

Saporta, G (2002). Data fusion and data grafting. *Computational Statistics & Data Analysis*, 38, 465–473.

Shearer, C (2000). The CRISP-DM model: The new blueprint for data mining. *Journal of Data Warehousing*, 5(5), 13–22.

Smith, DGC (1989). Combination of forecasts in electricity demand prediction. *Journal of Forecasting*, 8, 349–356.

Troutt, MD, LG Mumford and DE Schultz (1991). Using spreadsheet simulation to generate a distribution of forecasts for electric power demand. *Journal of the Operational Research Society*, 42, 931–939.

De Ville, B (2001). *Microsoft Data Mining: Integrated Business Intelligence for E-commerce and Knowledge Management*. Boston: Digital Press.

White, DJ (1975). *Decision Methodology*. London, UK: John Wiley & Sons.

Wijnhoven, F (2003). Operational knowledge management: Identification of knowledge objects, operation methods, and goals and means for the support function. *Journal of Operational Research Society*, 54, 194–203.

Witten, IH and E Frank (2005). Data mining: Practical machine learning tools and techniques. In *The Morgan Kaufmann Series in Data Management Systems*. San Francisco, USA: Morgan Kaufmann Pubs.

Chapter 18

GROWTH MODELS

Mladen Sokele
University of Zagreb
Mladen.Sokele@t.ht.hr

Growth models are widely used for time series data analysis and forecasting of a future growth which is important for optimal planning of
resources, investments, revenue, marketing and sales. This chapter deals
with models for S-shaped bounded growth giving the overview of the
most suitable ones for the first phase and later phases of product/service
life cycle, methods for model parameters determination and measures for
the forecasting accuracy. Presented models are mainly based on the logistic
and Bass model adapted in a way to accept judgementally determined
environmental variables and information from business operations as
explanatory model parameters. Moreover, auxiliary parameters are introduced into models to enable adjusting the model to the specific practical
requestments.

Keywords: S-shaped growth models; quantitative forecasting; explanatory
model parameters.

1. Introduction

Growth models represent similarities between growth in nature and
growth in economy. They are widely used in quantitative research for
time series data analysis and enable better understanding of forces
that influence growth in a sense of its dynamics, market capacities
as well as forecasting of a future growth. The growth models can
be unbounded or bounded assuming that limit or saturation level
of growth exists as the time increases. The diffusion of innovation and new technology, market adoption of consumer durables,

products/services that do not include repeat sales, subscription services (e.g., telecommunications services) and allocations of restricted resources are examples of the S-shaped bounded growth.

In the rest of the text, the focus will be on the models that describe such bounded growth and cumulative volume (sales) of market adopted products/services (or similar) at time t which will be denoted as $N(t)$.

In general, during its life cycle, after the design phase, every product/service passes through the following phases: introduction, growth, maturity and decline, resembling the profile of the technology life cycle and its associated market-growth profile. The understanding of each segment of the product/service life cycle (P/SLC) for the business planning purposes is especially important in highly competitive market environment and for products/services resulting from emerging technologies.

Only at the beginning of the P/SLC there is no interaction with other products/services regarding market adoption, therefore, its growth may be described with simple growth models presented in Table 2. During the later P/SLC phases, market capacity changes in hops and resembles a series of stairs. Immediately after the market capacity change occurs, product/service adoption starts to adjust to this new circumstance. Market adoption of a product/service during the entire P/SLC consists of several growth/decline segments encompassing interaction between different products/services or similar product/service offered from different providers. Therefore, growth may be described with a set of individual S shaped segments, as presented in Table 3.

The growth model in a form of differential equation is created as the result of analysis and understanding of growth for the specific product/service. In cases where differential equation has a solution, an analytical form of the growth model is used offering possibility to obtain value for $N(t)$ directly from the chosen time point t. Otherwise, differential equation is approximated with recursive equation that requires repetitive calculation of one or more preceding terms to obtain value for $N(t)$ at the chosen time point t.

The growth models with only one dependent variable are called univariate, and those with more than one as multivariate. The multivariate ones simultaneously model growth of more than one product/service.

2. Determination of Growth Model Parameters

For the time series growth model $f(t; a_1, a_2, \ldots, a_k)$ based on k parameters $a_1, \ldots, a_k$, at least k known data points $(t_i; N(t_i))$ are needed for full parameter determination. In cases when exact k data points are available, parameters a_i are solution of a system of equations (1):

$$N(t_i) - f(t_i; a_1, a_2, \ldots, a_k) = 0, \quad i = 1, \ldots, k. \tag{1}$$

The system (1) is usually nonlinear system, so iterative numerical methods have to be performed for its solution.

In cases when k or more data points are available, the Maximum-likelihood method or the Least squares method can be used for parameters determination to adjust the parameters of a model so as to best fit a dataset. Values obtained for parameters are statistically smoothed, i.e., the influence on parameter values is reduced due to particular measurement errors (such as unanticipated seasonal variation, uncertain measure, etc.).

The Maximum-likelihood method determines values of the model parameters that maximise the probability (likelihood) of the data points.

The Least squares method finds out the values of model parameters so that the sum of squared difference between data points and model evaluated points will be minimal. Commonly used subtypes of the Least squares method with their correspondent way of parameter determination are described in Table 1. Minimisation of sum of squared difference S can be done by software tools (e.g., Excel solver), or analytically by solving the system of equations (2):

$$\frac{\partial S}{\partial a_j} = 0, \quad j = 1, \ldots, k. \tag{2}$$

Table 1.   Commonly used sub-types of the Least squares method. (*Dots = known data points (measurements); curve = growth model through data points*).

Ordinary least squares method (OLS)   **Weighted least squares method (WLS)**

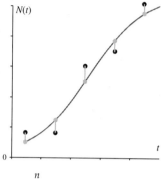 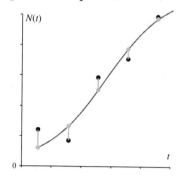

$$\min_{\{a_1 \ldots a_k\}} \sum_{i=1}^{n} [f(t_i; a_1, \ldots, a_k) - N(t_i)]^2$$

$$\min_{\{a_1 \ldots a_k\}} \sum_{i=1}^{n} w_i \cdot [f(t_i; a_1, \ldots, a_k) - N(t_i)]^2$$

Parameters are determined by minimisation of the sum of squares of the differences between observed and modelled values.

Introduction of weights w_i enables handling situations where data points are of varying quality or focusing on the specific time sub-interval (e.g., near the last observed data).

OLS with the fixed data point   **OLS with the fixed model parameter**

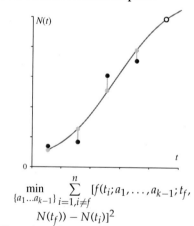 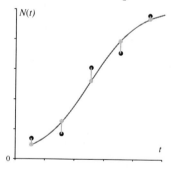

$$\min_{\{a_1 \ldots a_{k-1}\}} \sum_{i=1, i \neq f}^{n} [f(t_i; a_1, \ldots, a_{k-1}; t_f,$$
$$N(t_f)) - N(t_i)]^2$$

$$\min_{\{a_1 \ldots a_{k-1}\}} \sum_{i=1}^{n} [f(t_i; a_1, \ldots, a_k) - N(t_i)]^2$$

The value of a particular data point $(t_f, N(t_f))$ is embedded in the model. There is no difference between observed and modelled values at time t_f.

The value of a particular model parameter a_k is embedded in the model. The remaining set of parameters is determined by OLS method.

(Continued)

Table 1.   (*Continued*)

OLS applied on the inverse model	Total least squares method (TLS)
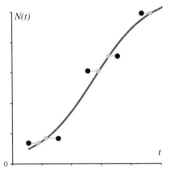	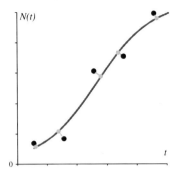

$$\min_{\{a_1 \dots a_k\}} \sum_{i=1}^{n} [f^{-1}(N(t_i); a_1, \dots, a_k) - t_i]^2$$

Parameters are determined by minimisation of the sum of the squares of the differences between observed and modelled independent (time) variable.

Method in which observational errors on both dependent and independent variables are taken into account. Deviations are measured perpendicular to the tangent of the curve. TLS is not scale invariant, which makes difficulties if the variables are not measured in the same units.

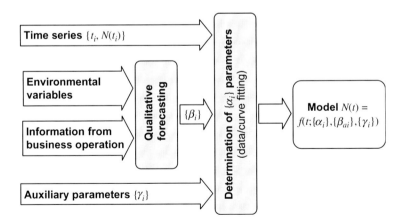

Fig. 1.   Flowchart of growth model for the growth forecasting purposes.

3. Growth Forecasting

Quantitative growth forecasting relies on the principle that a growth model will be valid in the perceivable future, and forecasting result could be obtainable by extrapolation of the observed values sequentially through time and supplementary information. In general, this principle is valid only for stable markets (e.g., same market segment boundaries, customer base, competition, cause-and-effect among similar products/services, etc.) without changes of external influences (e.g., technology, macroeconomics, purchasing power, regulation, etc.) and without changes of internal business operations (strategy, business plan, resources, ability of vendors and partners, etc.).

To encompass market changes that can be perceived only by the qualitative forecasting methods, the growth models should be able to accept environmental variables and information from business operations as explanatory model parameters. Moreover, the growth models should accept auxiliary parameters that do not make the model more complex but enable customisation of the model to the specific practical requirements.

The result is an optimal combination of qualitative and quantitative methods, which is presented as a flowchart in Fig. 1.

The above described growth model has the following general form:

$$N(t) = f(t; \{\alpha_i\}, \{\beta_i\}, \{\gamma_i\}),$$

where:

$\{\alpha_i\}$ Set of model parameters - resulting primarily from fit of time series data $\{t_i, N(t_i)\}, i = 1, \ldots, n$;

$\{\beta_i\}$ Set of explanatory parameters — resulting from qualitative forecasting, for example: t_s — time of launch; t_e, $N(t_e)$ — target point in the future; M — (current) market capacity of product/service; t_m — time of sales maximum, etc.;

$\{\gamma_i\}$ Set of auxiliary parameters in model which allows forecasting practitioner to customize model to her/his specific needs.

For the forecasting purposes, parameter determination is usually focused on the time interval near the last observed data point. Thus, weights in WLS can be set to a higher value for the most recent data points, than for data points in far history.

In some forecasting cases, model $f(t_i; a_1, a_2, \ldots, a_k)$ is modified to include the fixed value of the last data point $(t_f, N(t_f))$. Therefore, this model has one parameter less, because for example parameter a_k can be obtained from the equation:

$$N(t_f) - f(t_f; a_1, a_2, \ldots, a_k) = 0. \tag{3}$$

The above-mentioned simplification is used only when it is certain that the last data point is obtained with a negligible measurement error.

Furthermore, introduction of explanatory parameters, obtained by qualitative forecasting, reduces the number of unknown parameters in the growth model.

4. Models for First Phase of P/SLC

The growth models given in Table 2 are univariate S-shaped (sigmoidal) models commonly used for the first phase of P/SLC, that are suitable for forecasting growth of new product/service in their first phase of P/SLC or even prior to their launch.

5. Models for Later Phases of P/SLC

The growth models given in Table 3 are univariate models, consisting of a set of individual S shaped segments, that are suitable for forecasting growth of product/service in their later phases of P/SLC.

6. Forecasting Accuracy

In general, grouping of forecast results for specific market segments (e.g., separately for residential segment, for business segment and/or for segments related to specific life-styles, etc.) yields better forecasting accuracy than aggregate forecasting performed for the whole market.

Table 2.   S-shaped models for the first phase of product/service life cycle.

Model	Parameters	Comments
Logistic Model $$L(t; M, a, t_m) = \frac{M}{1 + e^{-a(t-t_m)}}$$	M — market capacity a — growth rate parameter t_m — time of sales maximum (time of inflexion point)	$M, t_m \in \{\beta_i\}; a \in \{\alpha_i\}$ For $a > 0$ growth, for $a < 0$ decline modelling. Limitations: Only for $t \to -\infty \Rightarrow L(t) = 0$, which makes it unsuitable for modelling of the beginning phase of P/SLC. Fixed point of sales maximum $I(t_m, M/2)$.
Logistic Model through Two Fixed Points $L(t; M, t_s, \Delta t, u)$ $$= \frac{M}{1 + \left(\frac{1}{u} - 1\right)^{1-2(t-t_s)/\Delta t}}$$	M — market capacity t_s — time when product/service has penetration level u, Δt — time period needed for penetration grows from the level u to the level $(1 - u)$ u — chosen level of penetration (e.g., 1%, 5% or 10%); $0 < u < 1$	$M, t_s, \Delta t \in \{\beta_i\}; u \in \{\gamma_i\}$ Useful for forecasting of new products/services adoption prior to launch assuming M, and two points (t_s, uM); $(t_s + \Delta t, (1 - u) \cdot M)$. If time of sales maximum t_m is known, Δt can be obtained from: $\Delta t = 2(t_m - t_s)$. Same limitations as for the Logistic model.
Logistic Model through One Fixed Point $L(t; M, t_m, t_f, N(t_f))$ $$= \frac{M}{1 + (M/N(t_f) - 1)^{\frac{t-t_m}{t_f-t_m}}}$$	M — market capacity t_m — time of sales maximum (time of inflexion point) $(t_f, N(t_f))$ — fixed point embedded in the model	$M, t_m \in \{\beta_i\}$ Useful for forecasting from the last observed point $t > t_f$. Same limitations as for the Logistic model.

(Continued)

Table 2. (*Continued*)

Model	Parameters	Comments
Bass Model $B(t; M, p, q, t_s)$ $= M \dfrac{1 - e^{-(p+q)(t-t_s)}}{1 + \dfrac{q}{p} e^{-(p+q)(t-t_s)}}$	M — market capacity p — coefficient of innovation, $p > 0$ q — coefficient of imitation, $q \geq 0$ t_s — time when product/service is introduced, $B(t_s) = 0$.	$M, t_s \in \{\beta_i\}; p, q \in \{\alpha_i\}$ Corrects deficiency of the Logistic model, $B(t_s) = 0$. For $q > p$ time of sales maximum t_m is identical to the time of inflexion point t_I; for $q \leq p$, $t_m = t_s$. Limitations: Cannot model decline; fixed inflexion point $I(t_I, B(t_I))$: $t_I = t_s + \dfrac{1}{p+q} \ln\left(\dfrac{q}{p}\right),$ $B(t_I) = M \dfrac{(q-p)}{2q}.$
Reparametrised Bass Model $B(t; M, t_s, \Delta t, t_m, v)$ — similar to the Bass model, but p and q are obtained from explanatory parameters Δt and t_m by solving the nonlinear system of equations in implicit form: $\Delta t = \frac{1}{p+q} \ln\left(\dfrac{1 + vq/p}{1 - v}\right)$ $t_m = t_s + \dfrac{1}{p+q} \ln\left(\dfrac{q}{p}\right)$ Iterative numerical methods needed to be performed for system solution.	M — market capacity t_s — time when product/service is introduced, $B(t_s) = 0$. Δt — time period needed for penetration grows to the level v v — chosen level of penetration (e.g., 90%, 95% or 99%); $0 < v < 1$ t_m — time of sales maximum	$M, t_s, \Delta t,$ $t_m \in \{\beta_i\}; u \in \{\gamma_i\}$ To enable higher diversity it is allowed to assume that for $p > q$, t_m exists even before t_s. Limitations: Same limitations as for the Bass model.

Table 2.   (*Continued*)

Model	Parameters	Comments
Richards Model $R(t; M, a, b, c)$ $= \dfrac{M}{[1 + e^{-a(t-b)}]^c}$	M — market capacity a — growth rate parameter b — time shift parameter c — shape parameter which controls vertical position of sales maximum $R(t_m)$. Relative position $R(t_m)/M$ is in range: $e^{-1} < \dfrac{R(t_m)}{M}$ $= \left(\dfrac{c}{1+c}\right)^c < 1$ For $c = 1$ the model is identical to the Logistic model.	$M \in \{\beta_i\}; a, b, c \in \{\alpha_i\}$ Time of sales maximum t_m depends on a, b and c: $t_m = b + \dfrac{\ln c}{a}$ Limitations: Similar to the Logistic model, unsuitable for modelling the beginning phase of P/SLC. Minimal value of $R(t_I)/M$ arises for $c \to \infty$ and cannot be smaller than $e^{-1} \approx 0.368$. Maximal value is without restriction, i.e., $R(t_I)/M \to 1$ for $c \to 0$.

Measurement errors of input time series data and explanatory parameters can be associated with their uncertainties and accordingly represented by particular confidence intervals. Consequently, forecasting result can be represented by a prediction interval between pessimistic and optimistic values. Range depends on a determined confidence level, which is typically 95%. Furthermore, sensitivity analysis of model parameters (especially explanatory parameters) should be deployed to examine what effect their variations have on the forecasting result.

Frequently used measures of the differences between values obtained by a model $f(t_i)$ and the values actually observed (time series data) $N(t_i)$, $i = 1, \ldots, n$ are given in Table 4.

These measures can be used as criteria for comparing and selecting growth models. If *MAE, MAPE, RMSE* are lower or r is higher, the growth model better fits input data. Note that high *MAPE* does not mean poor fit on entire interval, but indicates that there are

Table 3.   Models for the later phases of product/service life cycle.

Model	Parameters	Comments
Shifted Logistic Model $$LS(t; M, a, t_m, s)$$ $$= s + \frac{M-s}{1+e^{-a(t-t_m)}}$$	M — market capacity a — growth rate parameter t_m — time of sales maximum s — vertical shift	$M, t_m \in \{\beta_i\}; a, s \in \{\alpha_i\}$ Suitable for modelling of successive segments with monotone growth (or monotone decline). For $a > 0$, $M > c$ models growth and $M < c$ models decline. For $a > 0$, $M > 0$ and $c < 0$ Shifted logistic model is identical to the Bass model.
Bi-logistic $$BL(t) = M_0$$ $$+ \frac{M_1 - M_0}{1 + e^{-a(t-b)}}$$ $$+ \frac{M_2 - M_1}{1 + \left(\frac{1}{u} - 1\right)^{1 - 2(t - t_S)/\Delta t}}$$	M_0, M_1, a, b — model parameters for the current P/SLC segment (see Shifted logistic model) $M_2, t_s, \Delta t, u$ — model parameters for the first successive P/SLC segment (see Logistic model through two fixed points)	$M_0, M_1, M_2, t_s, \Delta t \in \{\beta_i\};$ $a, b \in \{\alpha_i\}; u \in \{\gamma_i\}$ Suitable for modelling of the current P/SLC segment and forecasting of the first successive segment P/SLC in the future.
Multi-Logistic Model $$ML(t) = M_0$$ $$+ \frac{M_1 - M_0}{1 + e^{-a_1(t - b_1)}}$$ $$+ \frac{M_2 - M_1}{1 + e^{-a_2(t - b_2)}}$$ $$+ \cdots + \frac{M_n - M_{n-1}}{1 + e^{-a_n(t - b_n)}}$$	The sum of discrete logistic growth models requires three parameters M_i, a_i, and b_i per item (see Logistic model).	Multi-logistic model is suitable for modelling of the entire P/SLC. A large set of known data points is needed, which limits

(Continued)

Table 3.	(*Continued*)

Model	Parameters	Comments
	Increments $M_i - M_{i-1}$ represent market capacity changes related to individual P/SLC segment.	application of the Multi-logistic model for the forecasting purposes.

Table 4.	Measures of accuracy.

Mean Absolute Error	$MAE = \frac{1}{n} \sum\limits_{i=1}^{n} |f(t_i) - N(t_i)|$
Mean Absolute Percentage Error	$MAPE = \frac{1}{n} \sum\limits_{i=1}^{n} \frac{|f(t_i)-N(t_i)|}{N(t_i)} [\%]$
Root Mean Squared Error	$RMSE = \sqrt{\frac{1}{n} \sum\limits_{i=1}^{n} [f(t_i) - N(t_i)]^2}$
Correlation coefficient, $0 < r < 1$	$r = \sqrt{1 - \dfrac{\sum\limits_{i=1}^{n} [f(t_i)-N(t_i)]^2}{\sum\limits_{i=1}^{n} [\overline{N}-N(t_i)]^2}} ; \quad \overline{N} = \frac{1}{n} \sum\limits_{i=1}^{n} N(t_i)$

larger differences between data obtained by a model and input data in cases when input data have small values.

In addition, the appropriateness of growth models for the forecasting purposes may be chosen as follows. Determine the model parameters based on the reduced dataset $\{t_i, N(t_i)\}, i = 1, \ldots, m$; $k < m < n$, and then calculate measures of accuracy only for the remaining points $\{t_i, N(t_i)\}, i = m + 1, \ldots, n$. According to the values obtained for measures of accuracy, the most appropriate forecasting model can be selected. Similar procedure can be used for determination of suitable weight scheme for the chosen model in cases when the weighted least squared method is used.

References

Makridakis, S, S Wheelwright and R Hyndman (1998). *Forecasting: Methods and Applications*, 3rd edn. New York: Wiley.

Meade, N and T Islam (2006). Modelling and forecasting the diffusion of innovation-A 25-year review. *International Journal of Forecasting*, 22(3), 519–545.

Meyer, SP and JH Ausubel (1999). Carrying capacity: A model with logistically varying limits. *Technological Forecasting and Social Change*, 61(3), 209–214.

Myung, IJ (2003). Tutorial on maximum likelihood estimation. *Journal of Mathematical Psychology*, 47(1), 90–100.

Sokele, M (2008). Growth models for the forecasting of new product market adoption. *Telektronikk*, 104(3/4), 144–154.

Chapter 19

PROMETHEE: TECHNICAL DETAILS AND DEVELOPMENTS, AND ITS ROLE IN PERFORMANCE MANAGEMENT

Malcolm J. Beynon
Cardiff Business School, Cardiff University,
Colum Drive, Cardiff, CF10 3EU
beynonmj@cardiff.ac.uk

Harry Barton
Nottingham Business School,
Nottingham Trent University, Burton Street,
Nottingham, NG1 4BU
harry.barton@ntu.ac.uk

The Preference Ranking Organisation Method for Enrichment Evaluations (PROMETHEE) method offers a way to undertake the ranking of a finite set of decision alternatives based on values from a number of criteria. As an outranking method it is a multi-criteria decision aid in the ranking process. This chapter outlines the rudiments of the PROMETHEE method, and applies it in a tutorial problem, including the presentation of example numerical calculations. The inclusion of an uncertainty based analysis with PROMETHEE in the presented text demonstrates the developmental potential of PROMETHEE. The problem considered throughout the chapter concerns the relative performance ranking of individual police forces in a region of the UK, based on their levels of sanction detections (clean-up rates).

Keywords: Criteria; decision alternatives; multi-criteria; outranking; PROMETHEE; ranking.

1. Introduction

The Preference Ranking Organisation Method for Enrichment Evaluations (PROMETHEE) method, was introduced by Brans (1982) and initially further developed by Vincke and Brans (1985) and Brans *et al.* (1984, 1986). It is an outranking method, used as a multi-criteria decision aid to rank a finite set of decision alternatives, based on evidence from a selection of criteria. In simple terms, outranking methods are a class of ordinal ranking algorithms for multi-criterion decision making, which rather than building complex utility functions, determine the preferences of alternatives by progressively comparing them on each criterion.

The PROMETHEE method is considered quite simple in approach, employed since it is characterised by simplicity and clarity to a decision-maker (Brans *et al.*, 1986), and with a transparent computational procedure (Georgopoulou *et al.*, 1998). Put simply, the ranking achieved using PROMETHEE produces a series of final 'net' values which are used to rank alternatives, found from the aggregation of constituent 'criterion' values, which express the levels of preference of the alternatives over the different criteria. It is noted, there exist other ranking methods, such as ELECTRE (Beccali *et al.*, 1998; Figueira, 2009) and TOPSIS (Lai *et al.*, 1994; Abo-Sinna and Amer, 2005), which similarly perform an ordinal ranking of alternatives.

The popularity of the PROMETHEE method can be evidenced by the range of applications employing it. This is fully appreciated by reading the survey article Behzadian *et al.* (2010), where, for example, they identify a number of PROMETHEE based papers in the management areas of; Environment Management (Queiruga *et al.*, 2008; Kapepula *et al.*, 2007), Hydrology and Water Management (Hajkowicz and Collins, 2007; Simon *et al.*, 2006), Business and Financial Management (Albadvi *et al.*, 2007; Mavrotas *et al.*, 2006) and Energy Management (Doukas *et al.*, 2006; Zhou *et al.*, 2006).

Beyond the original PROMETHEE analysis, to illustrate its technical progression, details of a development on the PROMETHEE method is also included in this chapter, namely the role of PROMETHEE in perceived improvement analyses (Hyde *et al.*, 2003; Hyde and Maier, 2006). Other developments of PROMETHEE have been undertaken, not included in this chapter, they include; fuzzy PROMETHEE where there is perceived imprecision in the criterion values describing alternatives (Goumas and Lygerou, 2000). The PROMETHEE method has also been used in conjunction with other methods, such as the Analytic Hierarchy Process, both in crisp and fuzzy environments (see Macharis *et al.*, 2004; Kundakci, 2011) and in relation to neural networks (Yi-Chung, 2010). It has also been compared to more general methodologies, such as multi-attribute utility theory (Wang, 2010).

This chapter offers an understanding of the application of PROMETHEE within a pertinent management problem, namely performance management. The specific example problem considered is the relative performance ranking of individual police forces, here the police forces making up the east England region in the UK. The performance in this case is measured by each police force's levels of sanction detections (percentage levels of clear-up rates). There have been periodic governmental and pedagogical studies of the constituent police forces in the UK. The government sponsored Spottiswoode (2000) report identified the need for more efficiency based measurements. Conversely, Her Majesty's Inspectorate of Constabulary has adhered to the more output only driven performance measurement approaches (HMIC, 2003).

To clearly demonstrate the pertinence of the need to be able to rank alternatives, a further example of the impacting nature of ranking in management is briefly described here. In the case of forced ranking within an organisation (Scullen *et al.*, 2005), the bottom 10% (for example) of a workforce could be systematically removed, and replaced with perceived better employees. One view on forced ranking systems is that they help to bring truth into the performance management process (Grote, 2005). Clearly, if the PROMETHEE method formed part of the performance ranking system, the improvement analysis, could be used to offer direction to those less performing (possibly in bottom 10%) employees. While the described issue is impacting in terms of employee retention, it clearly demonstrates the role of ranking in management.

Where appropriate, explicit calculations are given to offer clear insights into the mathematical rudiments of the PROMETHEE method. Hence, it is hoped, this chapter offers details in a tutorial form for the reader, enabling their employment of PROMETHEE in future studies.

2. Description of PROMETHEE and Developments

The background presented in this chapter is a description of the PROMETHEE method along with an example of its technical development, namely to enable rank improvement analysis.

2.1. *PROMETHEE*

PROMETHEE was introduced by Brans *et al.* (1984, 1986) to preference rank a set of decision alternatives, based on their values over a number of different criteria. Put simply, a ranking of alternatives is established based on the accumulative preference comparisons of pairs of alternatives' values over the different criteria (using generalised preference functions).

More formally, to express the preference structure of N alternatives $(a_1, \ldots, a_N)$ and to withdraw the scaling effects of the different K criteria considered $(c_1, \ldots, c_K)$, with PROMETHEE, generalised criterion preference functions are defined, $P_k(\cdot, \cdot)(k = 1, \ldots, K)$. Each is a function of the difference between criterion values of pairs of alternatives (from $a_1, \ldots, a_N$), where $P_k(a_i, a_j) \in [0, 1]$ confers the directed intensity of the preference of alternative a_i over a_j, with respect to a single criterion c_k. The often exposed limiting qualitative interpretations to the $P_k(a_i, a_j)$ values are (from Brans *et al.*, 1986);

$P_k(a_i, a_j) = 0 \Leftrightarrow a_i$ is not better than a_j with respect to criterion c_k,

$P_k(a_i, a_j) = 1 \Leftrightarrow a_i$ is 'strictly' better than a_j with respect to criterion c_k.

This qualitative interpretation highlights that at least one of the values, $P_k(a_i, a_j)$ and $P_k(a_j, a_i)$ will be zero, depending on whether

a_i or a_j is the more preferred between them. Expressing the $P_k(a_i, a_j)$ by:

$$P_k(a_i, a_j) = \begin{cases} H(d) & a_i - a_j > 0, \\ 0 & a_i - a_j \leq 0, \end{cases}$$

where $a_i - a_j > 0$ and $a_i - a_j \leq 0$ refer to whether a_i or a_j is the more preferred on that criterion (taking into account the direction of preferment of the criterion values), and $d = v(a_i) - v(a_j)$ is the specific difference between the criterion values of the alternatives a_i and a_j. The extant research studies have worked on the utilisation of six types of generalised preference functions for $H(d)$. Their names, labels (also required parameters) and graphical representations are given as (Brans *et al.*, 1986):

I — Usual (-)

II — Quasi (q)

III — Linear preference (p)

IV — Level (p, q)

V — Linear preference and indifference (p, q)

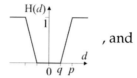 , and

VI — Gaussian (σ)

The graphical representations shown for the generalised preference functions highlight an important point, namely that some of them are continuous (III, V and VI) and the others not continuous (I, II and IV), with respect to the $P_k(a_i, a_j)$ value over the $v(a_i) - v(a_j)$ domain. The non-continuous feature means that small changes to criteria values may mean a dramatic change in the associated preference function values (see later).

The augmentation of the numerical preference values throughout the operation of PROMETHEE is described through the notion of flows. A *criterion flow* $\phi_k(a_i)$ value for an alternative a_i from a criterion c_k can be defined by:

$$\phi_k(a_i) = \sum_{a_j \in A} \{ P_k(a_i, a_j) - P_k(a_j, a_i) \},$$

where A is the set of N alternatives, $a_1, \ldots, a_N$, considered, it follows $-(N - 1) \leq \phi_k(a_i) \leq N - 1$ and $\sum_{a_i \in A} \phi_k(a_i) = 0$ (the bounds are due to not normalising by $(N - 1)$ in each case). In words, a criterion flow represents the preference of an alternative over the other $(N - 1)$ alternatives, with respect to a single criterion. A subsequent *net flow* $\phi(a_i)$ value is defined by:

$$\phi(a_i) = \sum_{k=1}^{K} w_k \phi_k(a_i),$$

where $w_k, k = 1, \ldots, K$ denotes the relative importance of the criterion c_k (the criteria importance weights). The conditions, $-(N-1) \leq \phi(a_i) \leq N-1$ and $\sum_{a_i \in A} \phi(a_i) = 0$, similarly hold for the net flow values (when w_k are normalised so they sum to one). The magnitudes of the net flow values subsequently exposit the relevant rank order of the N alternatives considered. The larger an alternative's net flow value, the higher its rank position.

It is worth noting, this form of PROMETHEE, is PROMETHEE II, where the difference values $P_k(a_i, a_j) - P_k(a_j, a_i)$ are used, whereas in PROMETHEE I partial ranking of the alternatives are found based on the sums of $P_k(a_i, a_j)$ and $P_k(a_j, a_i)$ considered separately (see Martín *et al.*, 2003). Following Fernández-Castro and Jiménez (2005) these two forms were developed into PROMETHEE III and PROMETHEE IV, using fuzzy integer linear programming.

Given the technical details presented on the PROMETHEE methods, the assumptions associated with its employment are succinctly described in De Keyser and Peeters (1996), and summarised into the following five propositions:

(a) PROMETHEE methods may only be applied if the decision maker can express their preference between two actions on a given criterion on a ratio scale.
(b) PROMETHEE methods may only be applied if the decision maker can express the importance they attach to the criteria on a ratio scale.
(c) The weights of the criteria express trade-offs between the criteria.
(d) PROMETHEE methods may only be used with criteria where the differences between evaluations are meaningful.
(e) It is not possible to take discordance into account when constructing the outrank relations of PROMETHEE methods.

2.1.1. *Rank Improvement Analysis (here using Trigonometric Differential Evolution)*

An associated issue with PROMETHEE, recently considered, is the uncertainty in the ranking results found using PROMETHEE (Hyde *et al.*, 2003), re-defined here as the consideration of the rank improve-ment of those alternatives ranked below the top ranked alternative. Hyde and Maier (2006) investigated the possibility of changes to the criteria values of an alternative and the concomitant criteria importance weights, which reversed the ranks of two alternatives. Considering only changes to criteria values and concentrating on the rank improvement of an alternative a_{r_1}, what changes of the r_1th ranked alternative's criteria values are necessary so its net flow value is larger than or equal to that of the r_2th ranked, in technical terms $\phi(a_{r_1}) \geq \phi(a_{r_2})$.

The minimum changes necessary to achieve this change in rank order are evaluated by minimising some distance function (d_{r_1,r_2}) between the original and proposed criteria values of the considered alternative. Here the Euclidean distance measure function d_{r_1,r_2} is employed, given by (from Hyde and Maier, 2006):

$$d_{r_1,r_2} = \sqrt{\sum_{k=1}^{K} (v^i_{r_1,k} - v^o_{r_1,k})^2},$$

where $v^i_{r_1,k}$ and $v^o_{r_1,k}$ are the initial (original) and optimised (proposed) criteria values. Without further external knowledge on the ranges of the criterion values, the changes to the criteria values of the r_1th ranked alternative are kept within known domains, given by $LL_{v,k} \leq v^o_{r_1,k} \leq UL_{v,k}$, where $[LL_{v,k}, UL_{v,k}]$ is the allowed interval domain of the kth criterion value, for example given by the minimum and maximum values known over each criterion. It follows that the improvement analysis problem can be described as a constraint optimisation problem. Further, with limited knowledge on the con-sidered criteria, the alternatives' criteria values can be standardised, so the impact of different sizes of difference between the criteria values are consistent (further knowledge may negate the need for standardisation).

When there is the presence of non-continuous preference func-tions, the requirement for $\phi(a_{r_1}) \geq \phi(a_{r_2})$ may not be strong enough. That is, small changes in the proposed criteria values may cause disproportionate changes in the resultant net flow value (as in Hyde and Maier, 2006), so other alternatives may take the desired rank position (since $\sum_{a_i \in A} \phi(a_i) = 0$). A stronger condition is simply that the new $\phi(a_{r_1})$ value affords the desired rank position for the considered alternative.

The constrained optimisation problem formulated within the rank improvement analysis using PROMETHEE is solved here using Trigonometric Differential Evolution (TDE) (Storn and Price, 1997; Fan and Lampinen, 2003). The domain of TDE is the continuous space made up of the K criteria domains. For an alternative, its series of criteria values are represented as a point in this continuous space (target vector). In TDE, a population of NP parameter vectors, $\overrightarrow{y_i^G}$, $i = 1, \ldots, NP$, is considered at each generation G of the progression to an optimum solution, measured through a defined objective function (OB — d_{r_1, r_2} in this chapter).

Starting with an initial population, TDE generates new target vectors by adding to a third member the difference between two other members (this change subject to a crossover operator). If the resulting vector yields a lower OB value, then a predetermined population member takes its place. A further operation takes into account the OB values associated with the three vectors $\overrightarrow{y_{r_1}^G}$, $\overrightarrow{y_{r_2}^G}$ and $\overrightarrow{y_{r_3}^G}$ chosen, used to perturb the trial vector. This trigonometric operation, which is the development in TDE (Fan and Lampinen, 2003) from the original differential evolution (Storn and Price, 1997), on occasions, takes the place of the original mutation (described previously) using a 'trigonometric mutation probability' parameter M_t, where a random value less than M_t implies the use of the trigonometric mutation.

The progression of the construction of new generations continues until a satisfactory OB value is achieved. This may mean a required level has been attained or a zero decrease in the OB value is identified (over a number of generations). Here, the concomitant parameters employed were; amplification control $F = 0.99$, crossover constant $CR = 0.85$, trigonometric mutation probability $M_t = 0.05$ and number of parameter vectors $NP = 10\times$ number of control variables $= 50$ (see Fan and Lampinen, 2003).

3. PROMETHEE Analysis of Police Performance Problem

The issue of performance measurement and target setting has been one of the central planks of the government's reform agenda of the UK public services. In the UK, the Government's emphasis is on improving the performance of public services, and on the police service in particular (Barton, 2003). Such measurement has relied to a large extent upon data provided by the police on reported crime rates and crime clear-up rates (known as sanction detections — percentage of crimes for which someone is charged, summonsed, receives a caution or other formal sanction). These levels have been maintained as critical indicators of performance and have historically constituted the main form of information for evaluating police services (Dadds and Scheide, 2000).

Performance measurement is seen to be more robust if it is based on the outcomes we are seeking to achieve (Home Office, 2005). Five sanction detections (criteria) are utilised here to describe the performance of each police force (published in the Home Office Statistical Bulletin, Home Office, 2005), namely; Violence against the person (Vap), Sexual offences (Sxo), Burglary (Bgy), and Offences against vehicles (OaV). These sanction detections have been used in similar studies, with evidence approving and not approving of their usage also published (see Thanassoulis, 1995; Drake and Simper, 2005).

The police forces considered in this police performance problem make up the East of England region of the UK, namely the six police forces: Bedfordshire (Bfds), Cambridgeshire (Cmbs), Essex (Essx), Hertfordshire (Hfds), Norfolk (Nflk), and Suffolk (Sflk). The details of these six police forces are reported in Table 1.

In Table 1, brief inspection of the sanction detection levels across the different police forces highlights variations in their performance (discussed more specifically later).

3.1. *PROMETHEE analyses of police performance dataset*

The intention of the PROMETHEE method, as described previously, is to identify a rank ordering of alternatives (the police forces Bfds,

Table 1. Criteria details (sanction detections levels — %) of considered police forces.

Police Force	VaP	SxO	Rby	Bgy	OaV
Bedfordshire	45	29	23	11	8
Cambridgeshire	46	30	21	11	13
Essex	56	24	18	15	16
Hertfordshire	59	30	27	18	13
Norfolk	54	31	29	20	18
Suffolk	52	27	31	15	12
Mean	52.000	28.500	24.833	15.000	13.333
Standard deviation	5.066	2.363	4.561	3.317	3.145

Cmbs, Essx, Hfds, Nflk, and Sflk), based on their values over a number of associated criteria (the sanction detections VaP, SxO, Rby, Bgy, and OaV). This subsection of the chapter reports a standard PROMETHEE analysis on the police performance dataset.

In this exposition of the application of PROMETHEE in the police performance problem, the five criteria, sanction detections VaP, SxO, Rby, Bgy and OaV, are considered of equal importance ($w_k = 1/5, k = 1, \ldots, 5$). This is without loss of generality of different levels of importance being assigned to the different criteria considered.

The PROMETHEE method was then employed, with the criterion flow values ($\phi_k(\cdot)$) found for the six police forces on each criterion, and then the subsequent net flow values ($\phi(\cdot)$) evaluated (see the description of the PROMETHEE), see Table 2.

Table 2. Criterion and net flow values for preference of the six police forces.

Vehicle	$\phi_{VaP}(\cdot)$	$\phi_{SxO}(\cdot)$	$\phi_{Rby}(\cdot)$	$\phi_{Bgy}(\cdot)$	$\phi_{OaV}(\cdot)$	$\phi(\cdot)$	Rank
Bedfordshire	−3.311	0.722	−1.140	−2.901	−3.944	−2.115	6
Cambridgeshire	−3.018	1.514	−2.171	−2.901	−0.316	−1.378	5
Essex	1.945	−4.355	−3.432	0.019	2.063	−0.752	4
Hertfordshire	3.102	1.514	1.345	2.290	−0.316	1.587	2
Norfolk	1.121	2.221	2.310	3.474	3.450	2.515	1
Suffolk	0.161	−1.616	3.088	0.019	−0.937	0.143	3

Table 3. $P_{Rby}(a_i, a_j)$ values evaluated during the comparison of the Bfds alternative with the others, over the criterion Rby (d values presented are $v(Bfds) - v(a_j), v(a_j) - v(Bfds)$).

$P_{Rby}(a_i, a_j)$	Bfds	Cmbs	Essx	Hfds	Nflk	Sflk	Sum
d	—	2, −2	5, −5	−4, 4	−6, 6	−8, 8	—
$P_{Rby}(Bfds, a_j)$	—	0.092	0.452	0.000	0.000	0.000	0.544
$P_{Rby}(a_i, Bfds)$	—	0.000	0.000	0.319	0.579	0.785	1.683
$P_{Rby}(Bfds, a_j)$ $-P_{Rby}(a_i, Bfds)$	—	0.092	0.452	−0.319	−0.579	−0.785	−1.139

The details presented in Table 2, in terms of the criteria and net flow values shown, have come from the evaluation of a series of $P_k(a_i, a_j)$ preference values over the different criteria for each alternative. An example of the calculation of these $P_k(a_i, a_j)$ values is next reported in Table 3, for the calculation of $\phi_{Rby}(Bfds)$ ($= -1.140$).

The $P_{Rby}(a_i, a_j)$ values presented in Table 3 concern the comparison of the Bedfordshire police force with the others over the Rby criterion (robbery sanction detection). To demonstrate the construction of these values, the case of the individual preference value $P_{Rby}(Bfds, Cmbs)$ is considered. For $P_{Rby}(Bfds, Cmbs)$, on the criterion Rby, where $d = v(Bfds) - v(Cmbs) = 23 - 21 = 2$ and using $\sigma = 4.561$ (all from Table 1), then:

$$P_{Rby}(Bfds, Cmbs) = 1 - \exp(-d^2/2\sigma^2)$$
$$= 1 - \exp(-2^2/2 \times 4.561^2) = 1 - 0.908 = 0.092.$$

It follows, associated with this preference value, the respective complement $P_{Rby}(Cmbs, Bfds)$ is zero. The dashes given in the Bfds column in Table 3 simply register the point that there is no need to compare Bfds with itself (the resultant criteria flow value would be zero). The value in the bottom right corner of Table 3 is the respect criterion flow value for the alternative Bfds on the Rby criterion, namely $\phi_{Rby}(Bfds) = -1.140$ (the rounding accuracy inconsistency is noted).

Interpreting the criterion and net flow values reported in Table 2, they identify a preference (performance) rank ordering of the six police forces, with Norfolk (Nflk $-\phi$(Nflk) = 2.515) and Bedfordshire (Bfds $-\phi$(Bfds) = -2.115), top and bottom ranked, respectively. The criterion flow values ($\phi_k(\cdot)$) elucidate the contribution of each criterion (sanction detection %) to the net flow value of a police force and their subsequent performance ranking. In the case of the top ranked Norfolk police force, the evidence from the sanction detections in decreasing order of contribution is, Bgy (ϕ_{Bgy}(Nflk) = 3.474), OaV (3.450), Rby (2.310), SxO (2.221), and VaP (1.121).

3.2. *Performance rank improvement 'uncertainty' based analysis of six police forces*

This subsection presents an 'uncertainty' based analysis of established rank performance orderings of the six police forces of the East of England region of the UK, based on their sanction detections (criteria). Moreover, the pertinence here, with respect to the police performance problem, is the ability to identify the minimum changes necessary to the sanction detections levels of a police force that would infer an improvement to its previously established performance rank order. Within this problem it is expected that changes to the sanction detections are upwards when attempting to improve a police force performance rank order.

Throughout this subsection the police force Bedfordshire (Bfds) is considered in terms of potential changes to its sanction detections' levels and potential performance rank improvement. With its identified bottom performance rank position (sixth), there is the possibility to improve (attain) its rank position to any of the five higher rank positions. Here, the minimum changes necessary to its sanction detections' levels, to achieve the fifth, third and first rank positions are considered, subject to minimising the d_{r_1, r_2} objective function using TDE described previously (distance between standardised Bfds sanction detections' levels and its proposed levels), see Table 4 (still considering when there is equal importance between the sanction detection levels).

The results in Table 4 identify the proposed new sanction detections levels of the Bedfordshire police force, which collectively

Table 4.   Changes in sanction detections of police force Bedfordshire (Bfds) to improve its performance rank position from sixth to fifth, third and first rank positions.

Criteria	Changes to Bedfordshire (Bfds)		
	Fifth (Cmbs)	Third (Sflk)	First (Nflk)
VaP (45.0%)	46.047 (2.327%)	50.339 (11.865%)	57.406 (27.569%)
SxO (29.0%)	29.569 (1.964%)	30.485 (5.119%)	31.000 (6.895%)
Rby (23.0%)	25.028 (8.818%)	27.131 (17.959%)	30.170 (31.172%)
Bgy (11.0%)	12.035 (9.406%)	14.010 (27.362%)	18.679 (69.807%)
OaV (8.0%)	9.137 (14.213%)	10.891 (36.140%)	16.596 (107.445%)
ϕ(Bfds)	−1.48937331	−0.33081812	1.77393315
$\phi(\cdot)$	−1.48937351	−0.33081846	1.77393210
d_{r_1,r_2}	0.726 (1.714)	1.999 (2.962)	4.692 (4.804)

offer the minimum d_{r_1,r_2} from its original detection levels, subject to equating its net flow value with that of the police force it is being compared with (fifth, third and first placed police forces — shown in each column). The bracketed values are the relative changes (as a percentage) from its original sanction detection levels. The net flow values associated with the Bedfordshire police force (ϕ(Bfds)) and the comparison police forces are given to nine decimal spaces to show their almost equal values in each case, while the ϕ(Bfds) values are slightly larger, as desired to achieve the necessary improved performance rank position.

The bottom row of this table gives two distance values for each analysis (based on having standardised the sanction detections' levels), the first is the distance of the proposed new sanction detections' levels to the original set associated with the Bedfordshire police force, the second (in brackets) is the distance of the original set of sanction detections' levels of the Bedfordshire police force to those of the comparison police force (values in standardised form). In all of the analyses, the first distance value is less than the second value, and this indicates in each case that the changes described are less than what would have been necessary to exactly match the sanction detections' levels of the compared to police force. This highlights the subtlety of this analysis, where using PROMETHEE (with equal criteria importance), these are the sanction detections' levels the Bedfordshire police force should strive towards on order to improve their performance rank position.

Considering the actual results for the equating of the Bedfordshire police force with fifth placed Cambridgeshire (Cmbs), the VaP sanction detection level would need to be increased from its original 45% upto 46.047%, a 2.327% change in its level. Similar changes of 1.964%, 8.818%, 9.406% and 14.213% are necessary to the SxO, Rby, Bgy and OaV sanction detections levels, so the performance ranking of the Bedfordshire police force is equal to that of the Cambridgeshire police force. To improve to the third rank position, a further small increase in their sanction detections' levels is required. The largest of these is a 36.140% change in OaV. Considerably, more increase in the Bedfordshire's sanction detections' levels is necessary to achieve the first rank position, the largest in this case is a 107.445% change in OaV.

To further exposit the relationship between the considered Bedfordshire police force and the other police forces, a graphical presentation is next reported. It considers the changes in the net flow values associated with all the police forces, subject to the proposed changes to the sanction detections' levels of the bottom ranked Bedfordshire police force, see Fig. 1. It should be remembered that any change in value of a net flow value for one alternative (say Bfds) will mean a change in one or more net flow values of other alternatives, since the sum of them must equal zero.

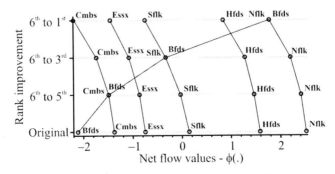

Fig. 1. Changes in net flow values of police forces when changing performance rank position of Bfds from sixth to fifth, third and first rank positions.

In Fig. 1, the graph shows the effects of improving the rank position of the bottom ranked Bedfordshire police force to the respective fifth, third and first rank positions. Describing the graph, along the y-axis is the rank position of the police force the bottom placed Bedfordshire police force was compared to (to equate net flow values), with the x-axis showing the scale of the net flow values (each circle represents a net flow value). At the base of the graph is the original net flow values associated with each police force (see Table 2). Successive horizontal lines of circles report the changes in the net flow values of the six police forces when comparing the Bedfordshire police force with other higher ranked police forces (to fifth, third and first placed rank positions).

In the graph there is a relatively more dramatic change in the net flow value associated with the Bedfordshire police force to equal that of the higher first placed Nflk police force, with lesser changes apparent to move up to the fifth (Cmbs) and third (Sflk) rank positions. There is a near uniform decrease in the net flow values associated with the other police to accommodate the improved performance rank of the Bedfordshire police force (increasing net flow value of one alternative means decrease of net flow value of one or more). This is interpreted as showing that the improvement of the Bedfordshire police force is at the expense of all the other police forces and not just one or two (including the police force it is particularly compared with) and is directly related to the constraint that the sum of the net flow values is zero.

4. Conclusions

The PROMETHEE method is known for being a multi-criteria decision making method whose approach is based on simplicity and clearness. Its description here contributes to that clearness, with ranking results evaluated and presented. As a method, which is routinely employed and developed, the development exposed here is such an example, an uncertainty based analysis termed here in terms of improvement analysis.

The considered problem to demonstrate the PROMETHEE method is police performance. The criteria used to formulate the ranking of the police forces were publicly available sanction detections' levels. Within the public sector there is prevalence for comparative analysis of organisations through their ranking, previously this was predominantly presented in the form of league tables. Successive governments (the UK) have had to balance the publics' legislative right for published rankings and the protection of those organisations being ranked against inappropriate findings.

The potential future applicability of PROMETHEE and its developments is wide ranging. The existing applications of PROMETHEE show the way in which its outranking approach can offer pertinent findings, clearly of interest in marketing and management research areas.

References

Abo-Sinna, MA and AH Amer (2005). Extensions of TOPSIS for multiobjective large-scale nonlinear programming problems. *Applied Mathematics and Computation*, 162, 243–256.

Albadvi, A, SK Chaharsooghi and A Esfahanipour (2007). Decision making in stock trading: An application of PROMETHEE. *European Journal of Operational Research*, 177, 673–683.

Barton, H (2003). Understanding occupational (sub) culture — a precursor for reform: The case of the police service in England and Wales. *The International Journal of Public Sector Management*, 16(5), 346–358.

Beccali, M, M Cellura and D Ardente (1998). Decision making in energy planning: The ELECTRE multicriteria analysis approach compare to a fuzzy-Sets methodology. *Energy Conversion and Management*, 39(16–18), 1869–1881.

Behzadian, M, RB Kazemzadeh, A Albadvi and M Aghdasi (2010). PROMETHEE: A comprehensive literature review on methodologies and applications. *European Journal of Operational Research*, 200, 198–215.

Brans, JP (1982). Lingenierie de la decision. Elaboration dinstruments daide a la decision. Methode PROMETHEE. In *Laide a la Decision: Nature, Instrument set Perspectives Davenir*, R Nadeau and M Landry (eds.), pp. 183–214. Canada: Presses de Universite Laval, Qu ebec.

Brans, JP, B Mareschal and PH Vincke (1984). PROMETHEE: A new family of outranking methods in MCDM. In *International Federation of Operational Research Studies (IFORS 84)*, JP Brans (ed.), pp. 470–490. Amsterdam: North Holland.

Brans, JP, PH Vincke and B Mareschal (1986). How to select and how to rank projects: The PROMETHEE method. *European Journal of Operational Research*, 24, 228–238.

Dadds, V and T Scheide (2000). Police performance and activity measurement. *Trends and Issues in Crime and Criminal Justice Series*, 180, 1–6.

De Keyser, W and P Peeters (1996). A note on the use of PROMETHEE multicriteria methods. *European Journal of Operational Research*, 89, 457–461.

Doukas, H, KD Patlitzianas and J Psarras (2006). Supporting sustainable electricity technologies in Greece using MCDM. *Resources Policy*, 31, 129–136.

Drake, LM and R Simper (2005). The measurement of police force efficiency: An assessment of U.K. home office policy. *Contemporary Economic Policy*, 23(4), 465–482.

Fan, H-Y and J Lampinen (2003). A trigonometric mutation operation to differential evolution. *Journal of Global Optimization*, 27, 105–129.

Fernández-Castro, AS and M Jiménez (2005). PROMETHEE: an extension through fuzzy mathematical programming. *Journal of the Operational Research Society*, 56, 119–122.

Figueira, JR, S Greco and B Roy (2009). ELECTRE methods with interaction between criteria: An extension of the concordance index. *European Journal of Operational Research*, 199(2), 478–495.

Georgopoulou, E, Y Sarafidis and D Diakoulaki (1998). Design and implementation of a group DSS for sustaining renewable energies exploitation. *European Journal of Operational Research*, 109, 483–500.

Goumas, M and V Lygerou (2000). An extension of the PROMETHEE method for decision making in fuzzy environment: Ranking of alternative energy exploitation projects. *European Journal of Operational Research*, 123, 606–613.

Grote, D (2005). *Forced Ranking: Making Performance Management Work*. Boston, Massachusetts: Harvard Business School Press.

Hajkowicz, S and K Collins (2007). A review of multiple criteria analysis for water resource planning and management. *Water Resource Management*, 21, 1553–1566.

HMIC (2003). *Annual Report 2002–2003*. London: HMSO.

Home Office (2005). Official Web Site. Available at http://www.homeoffice.gov.uk/ [accessed on 16 May 2011].

Hyde, KM, HR Maier and CB Colby (2003). Incorporating uncertainty in the PROMETHEE MCDA Method. *Journal of Multi-Criteria Decisions Analysis*, 12, 245–259.

Hyde, KM and HR Maier (2006). Distance-based and stochastic uncertainty analysis for multi-criteria decision analysis in Excel using Visual Basic for Applications. *Environmental Modelling & Software*, 21(12), 1695–1710.

Kapepula, KM, G Colson, K Sabri and T Thonart (2007). A multiple criteria analysis for household solid waste management in the urban community of Dakar. *Waste Management*, 27 (11), 1690–1705.

Kundakci, N (2011). Notebook selection with the combination of FAHP and PROMETHEE methods. *Journal of Multiple-Valued Logic and Soft Computing*, 17(1), 25–45.

Lai, YJ, TY Liu and CL Hwang (1994). TOPSIS for MODM. *European Journal of Operational Research*, 76, 486–500.

Macharis, C, J Springael, K De Brucker and A Verbeke (2004). PROMETHEE and AHP: The design of operational synergies in multicriteria analysis. Strengthening PROMETHEE with ideas of AHP. *European Journal of Operational Research*, 153, 307–317.

Martín, JM, W Fajardo, A Blanco and I Requena (2003). Constructing linguistic versions for the multicriteria decision support systems preference ranking organization method for enrichment evaluation I and II. *International Journal of Intelligent Systems*, 18(7), 711–731.

Mavrotas, G, D Diakoulaki and Y Caloghirou (2006). Project prioritization under policy restrictions. A combination of MCDA with 0–1 programming. *European Journal of Operational Research*, 171, 296–308.

Queiruga, D, G Walther, J Gonza'lez-Benito and T Spengler (2008). Evaluation of sites for the location of WEEE recycling plants in Spain. *Waste Management*, 28(1), 181–190.

Scullen, SE, PK Bergey and L Aiman-Smith (2005). Forced distribution rating systems and the improvement of workforce potential: A baseline simulation. *Personnel Psychology*, 58, 1–32.

Simon, U, R Bruggemann, H Behrendt, E Shulenberger and S Pudenz (2006). METEOR: A step-by-step procedure to explore effects of indicator aggregation in multi criteria decision aiding–application to water management in Berlin, Germany. *Acta Hydrochimica et Hydrobiologica*, 34, 126–136.

Spottiswoode, C (2000). *Improving Police Performance*. London: Public Services Productivity Panel, H. M. Treasury.

Storn, R and K Price (1997). Differential evolution-A simple and efficient heuristic for global optimisation over continuous spaces. *Journal of Global Optimisation*, 11, 341–359.

Thanassoulis, E (1995). Assessing police forces in England and Wales using data envelopment analysis. *European Journal of Operational Research*, 87, 641–657.

Vincke, JP and PH Brans (1985). A preference ranking organization method. The ROMETHEE method for MCDM. *Management Science*, 31, 641–656.

Wang, M (2010). The comparison between MAUT and PROMETHEE. In *IEEM2010-IEEE Int. Conf. Industrial Engineering and Engineering Management*, pp. 735–757. Macao

Yi-Chung, H (2010). A single-layer perceptron with PROMETHEE methods using novel preference indices. *Neurocomputing*, 73(16–18), 2920–2927.

Zhou, P, BW Ang and KL Poh (2006). Decision analysis in energy and environmental modeling: An update. *Energy*, 31, 2604–2622.

Chapter 20

CLIQUE COMMUNITIES IN SOCIAL NETWORKS

Luís Cavique
Universidade Aberta, Portugal
lcavique@univ-ab.pt

Armando B. Mendes
Universidade Açores, Portugal
amendes@uac.pt

Jorge M.A. Santos
Universidade Évora, Portugal
jmas@uevora.pt

There is a pressing need for new pattern recognition tools and statistical methods to quantify large graphs and predict the behaviour of network systems, due to the large amount of data which can be extracted from the web. In this work a graph mining metric, based on k-clique communities, is used, allowing a better understanding of the network structure. The proposed metric shows that for different graph families correspond different k-clique sequences.

Keywords: Data mining; graph mining; social networks.

1. Introduction

After Berners-Lee's (2006) communication on the three ages of the Web in the International World Wide Web Conference WWW2006, there has been an explosion of interest in the social networks associated with Web 2.0 in an attempt to improve socialising and come up with a new model for knowledge management. Even though Tim Berners-Lee had imagined a read-and-write Web, the Web was originally a read-only medium for the majority of the users. As Mika (2007) describes it, the Web of the 90s was much like the combination of a phone book and the yellow pages, a mix of individual postings and corporate catalogues, and instilled a little sense of community among its users.

Social Network Analysis is a very relevant technique that has emerged in modern sociology, and which studies the interaction between individuals and organisations. See Scott and Carrington (2011) and Wasserman and Faust (1995) for the theoretical basis and key techniques in social networks.

The idea of 'social network' was loosely used for over a century to connote complex sets of relationships between members of social systems at all scales, from interpersonal to international (Freeman, 2004). In 1954, J. A. Barnes used the term systematically to denote patterns of ties, and is normally considered the father of that expression. However, the visual approach to measuring social relationships using graphs, known as sociograms, was presented by Moreno (1934). In Moreno's network, the nodes represent individuals, while the edges stand for personal relationships. This scientific area of sociology tries to explain how diffusion of innovation works, why alliances and conflicts are generated in groups, how the leadership emerges and how the group structure affects the group efficacy (Mika, 2007).

A major development on the structure of social networks came from a remarkable experiment by the American psychologist Stanley Milgram (Milgram, 1967). Milgram's experiment consisted in sending letters from people in Nebraska, in the Midwest, to people in Boston, on the East Coast, where the latter were instructed to pass on the letters, by hand, to someone else they knew. The letters that reached the destination were passed by around six people. Milgram concluded that the experiment showed that, on average, Americans are no more than six steps away from each other. This experiment led to the concepts of the six degrees of separation and the notion of small-world.

An interesting example of a small-world is the 'Erdös Number' (Grossman *et al.*, 2007). Erdös is the most prolific mathematician, being author of more than 1,500 papers with more than 500 co-authors. Erdös is the number zero and the researchers who worked with him are called Erdös number 'one'. The co-authors of Erdös number 'one' are the Erdös number 'two', and so on, building one of the oldest small-world known. The work of Erdös and Renyi (1959) describes interesting properties of random graphs. A brand new interest has been revived with the Watts and Strogatz (1998) model, published in the *Nature* journal, which studies graphs with small-world properties and power-law degree distribution.

The social network analysts need to survey each person about their friends, ask for their approval to publish the data and keep a trace of that population for years. Also, the applications, implemented on internet, that uses the concept of establishing links between friends and friends of friends, like Facebook or LinkedIn (LinkedIn Corporation), provide the required data. According to Linton Freeman's comprehensive Development of Social Network Analysis, the key factors defining the modern field of social network analysis are: The insight that the structure of networks affects the outcome of aggregate actions, and the methodological approach that uses systematic empirical data, graphic representation, and mathematical and computational models to analyse networks. These attributes of social network analysis were established through the work of scientists from the fields of psychology, anthropology, and mathematics over the last decades (Freeman, 2004).

The visualisation of a small number of vertices can be completely mapped. However, when the number of vertices and edges increases, the visualisation becomes incomprehensible. The large amount of data extracted from the Internet is not compatible with the complete drawing. There is a pressing need for new pattern recognition tools and statistical methods to quantify large graphs and predict the behaviour of network systems.

Graph mining can be defined as the science and the art of extracting useful knowledge, like patterns and outliers provided, respectively, by repeated and sporadic data, from large graphs or complex networks (Faloutsos *et al.*, 1999; Cook and Holder, 2007). As these authors put it, there are many differences between graphs; however, some patterns show up regularly, the main ones appearing to be: The small worlds, the degree distribution and the community mining.

In this chapter, the clique communities are studied using the graph partition approach, based on the k-clique structure. A k-clique is a relaxed clique, i.e., a k-clique is a quasi-complete sub-graph. A k-clique in a graph is a sub-graph where the distance between any two vertices is no greater than k. It is a relevant structure to consider when analysing large graphs like the ones arising in social network analysis.

The proposed Socratic questioning is the following: How many k-clique communities are needed to cover the whole graph? This work is part of a larger project on common knowledge of proverbs whose previous results were published in Mendes *et al.* (2010).

2. Graph Theory Concepts

The representation of social networks has been quite influenced by graph theory. In the social networks, the set of vertices (or nodes) correspond to the 'actors' (i.e., people, companies, social actors) and the set of edges to the 'ties' (i.e., relationships, associations, links).

The sociologic applications of cohesive subgroups can include groups such as work groups, sport teams, political party, religious cults, or hidden structures like criminal gangs and terrorist cells. In this section, some concepts about cohesive subgroups like cliques and relaxed cliques, such as k-clique, k-club/k-clan and k-plex, are explained.

2.1. *Graph notation*

Graph theory has many applications and has been used for centuries. The book by Berge (1958), called 'Théorie des Graphes e ses Aplications', published many of the knowledge known at the time. A latter edition, in 1973, established a very common notation in graph theory literature that is also used in this chapter.

In this notation, an undirected graph is represented by $G = (V,A)$, where $A \subseteq [V]^2$ is a pair in which $V(G)$ represents the set of vertices or nodes, and $A(G)$, the set of links or edges. An edge can be also represented by $\{i,j\} \in A(G)$, where i and j are the two connected vertices. The number of vertices $V(G)$ can be represented by $|V(G)|$ and the graph called of order n if $V(G) = \{1,2,\ldots,n\}$ and so, $|V(G)| = n$. The number of arcs m is given by the cardinality of $A(G)$, i.e., $|A(G)|$. If two vertices are joined by an edge, they are adjacent.

A graph $G' = (V', A')$ is a sub-graph of the graph $G = (V,A)$ if $V' \subseteq V$ and $A' \subseteq A$. We can also say that if C is a proper subset of V, than $G' = G-C$ denotes the sub-graph induced from G by deleting all vertices in C and their incident edges. In Fig. 1, the graph G' is a sub-graph induced by G, while G'' is not, as only edges are missing.

In Social Network Analysis, the order of the end-vertices of an edge is usually irrelevant and so, we have to work only with undirected graphs. In directed graphs, each directed edge (usually, called arc), has an origin and a destination, and is represented by an ordered pair. In social network contexts, the direction of an edge is not relevant; what is important is to acknowledge the existence, or not, of a link between the edges.

2.2. *Clique*

Given an undirected graph $G = (V, E)$, where V denotes the set of vertices and E, the set of edges, the graph $G_1 = (V_1, E_1)$ is called a sub-graph of G, if $V_1 \subseteq V$, $E_1 \subseteq E$ and for every edge $(v_i, v_j) \in E_1$, the vertices $v_i, v_j \in V_1$. A sub-graph G_1 is said to be complete, if there is an edge for each pair of vertices. In fact, a clique is a complete

Fig. 1.   Graph G and two sub-graphs G' and G".

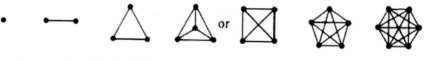

Fig. 2.   Cliques with 1, 2, 3, 4, 5 and 6 verticles.

sub-graph, which means that in a clique, each member has direct ties with each other member or node. Some simple examples of these very cohesive structures are shown in Fig. 2. A clique is maximal, if it is not contained in any other clique. The clique number of a graph is equal to the cardinality of the largest clique of G and it is obtained by solving the maximum clique NP-hard problem.

The clique structure, where there must be an edge for each pair of vertices, shows many restrictions in real life modelling and is uncommon in social networks. So, alternative approaches for little more relaxed cohesive groups were suggested, such as k-clique, k-clan/k-club and k-plex.

2.3.   *k-clique*

Luce (1950) introduced the distance base cohesion groups called k-clique, where k is the maximum path length between each pair of vertices. A k-clique is a subset of vertices C such that, for every i, $j \in C$, the distance $d(i, j) \leq k$. The one-clique is identical to a clique, because the distance between the vertices is one edge. The two-clique is the maximal complete sub-graph with a path length of one or two edges. The path distance of two can be exemplified by the 'friend of a friend' connection in social relationships. In social websites, like the LinkedIn, each member can reach his own connections as well as the ones two and three degrees away. The increase of the value k corresponds to a gradual relaxation of the criterion of clique membership. See Fig. 3.

2.4.   *k-clan and k-club*

A limitation of the k-clique concept is that some vertices may be distant from the group, i.e., the distance between two nodes, may

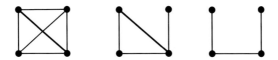

Fig. 3.   Examples with four nodes one-clique, two-clique and three-clique.

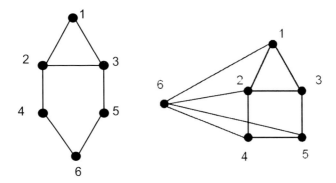

Fig. 4.   Two-clans, two-clubs (left) and three-plex (right).

correspond to a path involving nodes that do not belong to the k-clique. To overcome this handicap Alba (1973) and Mokken (1979) introduced the diameter-based cohesion group concepts called k-club and k-clan. The length of the shortest path between vertices u and v in G is denoted by the distance d(u,v). The diameter of G is given by diam(G) = max d(u, v) for all u,v$\in$ V. To find all k-clan, all the k-cliques S^i must be found first, and then the restriction diam(G[S])$\leq k$ applied to remove the undesired k-cliques. In Fig. 4, on the left, the two-clique $\{1,2,3,4,5\}$ was removed because d(4,5) = 3, i.e., the path 4–6–5 is not possible as node 6 does not belong to the sub-graph with the two-cliques. Another approach to these diameter models is the k-club, which is defined as a subset of vertices S such that diam(G[S])$\leq k$. In the left graph of Fig. 4, can be found two two-cliques: $\{1,2,3,4,5\}$ and $\{2,3,4,5,6\}$, one two-clan: $\{2,3,4,5,6\}$ and three two-clubs: $\{1,2,3,4\}$, $\{1,2,3,5\}$, and $\{2,3,4,5,6\}$.

2.5. *k-plex*

An alternative way of relaxing a clique is the *k*-plex concept which takes into account the vertices degree. The degree of a vertex of a graph is the number of edges incident on the vertex, and is denoted by deg(v). The maximum degree of a graph G is the maximum degree of its vertices and is denoted by $\Delta(G)$. On the other hand, the minimum degree is the minimum degree of its vertices and is denoted by $\delta(G)$. A subset of vertices S is said to be a *k*-plex, if the minimum degree in the induced sub-graph $\delta(G[S]) \geq |S| - k$. In Fig. 4, on the right, the graph has six vertices and so, $|S| = 6$ and the degree of vertices one, three, four and five does not exceed the value three. Thus, the minimum degree in the induced sub-graph $\delta(G[S])$ is three. For $|S| = 6, k = 3$ is obtained.

3. The Two Phase Algorithm

Complex network and graph mining metrics are essentially based on low complexity computational procedures, like the diameter of the graph, the degree distribution of the nodes and connectivity checking, underestimating the knowledge of the graph structure components.

On the other hand, in the literature, many algorithms have been developed for network communities. One of the first studies is given by the Kernighan and Lin (1970) algorithm, which finds a partition of the nodes into two disjoint subsets A and B of equal size, such that the sum of the weights of the edges between nodes in A and B is minimised. Recent studies, based on physics method, introduced the concept of clique percolation (Derenyi *et al.*, 2005), where the network is viewed as a union of cliques.

In order to find the *k*-clique communities, a two-phase algorithm is proposed. First, all the maximal *k*-cliques in the graph are found. Second, the best subset of the *k*-cliques is chosen to cover the vertices of the graph.

To find all the maximal *k*-cliques in the graph, we use the *k*-th power of the graph G in such a way that we can use an already well-known algorithm, the maximum clique algorithm. The procedures described in the next flowchart starts by transforming the graph and applying next a maximum clique algorithm and finally, in phase two, applying a set covering algorithm.

Algorithm 1.   The Two-Phase Algorithm.

Input: distance k and graph G
Output: k-clique cover
1. Find all maximal k-cliques in graph G
1.1. The kth power of graph G
1.2. Apply maximum clique algorithm
2. Find the cover of G with k-cliques
2.1. Apply set covering algorithm

3.1.   *Maximal k-cliques in graph G*

The transformation of a graph G(V,E) into a graph such that for every $i,j \in V$, the distance $d(i, j) \leq k$, is denoted by graph $G(V,E)^k$.

The $G(V,E)^k$ is obtained using the k-th power of the graph G with the same set of vertices as G and a new edge between two vertices if there is a path of length at most k between them (Skiena, 1990).

The Maximum Clique is a NP-hard problem that aims to find the largest complete sub-graph in a given graph. In this approach, we intend to find a lower bound for the maximisation problem, based on the heuristics proposed by Johnson (1974) and in the meta-heuristic that uses Tabu Search developed by Soriano and Gendreau (1996). Part of the work described in this section can also be found in Cavique *et al.* (2002) and Cavique and Luz (2009).

We define A(S) as the set of vertices that are adjacent to vertices of a current solution S. Let $n = |S|$ be the cardinality of a clique S and $A^k(S)$ the subset of vertices with k arcs incident in S. A(S) can be divided into subgroups $A(S) = \cup A^k(S)$, $k = 1, \ldots, n$.

The cardinality of the vertex set $|V|$ is equal to the sum of the adjacent vertices A(S) and the non-adjacent ones $A^0(S)$, plus $|S|$, resulting in $|V| = \Sigma|A^k(S)| + n, k = 0, \ldots, n$. For a given solution S, we define a neighbourhood N(S) if it generates a feasible solution S'.

In this work we are going to use three neighbourhood structures. For the next flowchart consider the following notation:

$$N^+(S) = \{S' : S' = S \cup \{v^i\}, v^i \in A^n(S)\},$$
$$N^-(S) = \{S' : S' = S \setminus \{v^i\}, v^i \in S\},$$
$$N^0(S) = \{S' : S' = S \cup \{v^i\} \setminus \{v^k\}, v^i \in A^{n-1}(S), v^k \in S\},$$

where S is the current solution, S*, the highest cardinality maximal clique found so far, T, the Tabu list and N(S), the neighbourhood structures.

Algorithm 2. The Tabu Heuristic for the Maximum Clique Problem.

Input: graph G^k, complete sub-graph S
Output: clique S*
1. T= Ø; S* = S;
2. while not end condition
2.1.   if $(N^+(S) \setminus T \neq$ null) choose the maximum S'
2.2.   else if $(N^0(S) \setminus T \neq$ null) choose the maximum S'; update T
2.2.1.   else choose the maximum S' in $N^-(S)$; update T
2.3.   update S = S'
2.4.   if $(|S| > |S*|)$ S* = S;
3. end while;
4. return S*;

Finding a maximal clique in a graph G^k is the same as finding a maximal k-clique in a graph G. To generate a large set of maximal k-cliques, a multi-start algorithm is used, which calls the Tabu Heuristic for Maximum Clique Problem.

3.2.   The k-cliques cover

To understand the structure of a clique community of a network in the previous work (Cavique *et al.*, 2009), the minimum set covering formulation was used.

The detailed analysis of the resulting solution, the set of k-cliques, an excess of over-coverings can be found, which makes it hard to

	1	2	3	4	5	6	7	8	9	10	11	12	13	14	15
1		128	132	122	122	139	147	123	125	130	138	140	150	144	155
2			151	138	145	158	153	147	142	151	154	160	161	152	161
3				173	171	182	181	174	174	180	186	191	194	184	193
4					181	176	172	188	185	184	194	196	197	197	196
5						181	170	197	191	186	196	199	193	197	195
6							183	181	183	189	196	199	200	191	200
7								174	180	181	192	192	201	195	206
8									191	192	201	204	197	201	200
9										187	206	201	203	204	205
10											203	209	202	197	203
11												216	217	215	219
12													220	212	223
13														222	231
14															226
15															

Fig. 5. Bridges between the 15-set of k-cliques in the $k3$-Erdos-97–1 dataset.

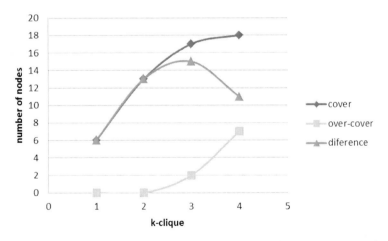

Fig. 6. Best trade-off solution happens when the difference is maximal.

interpret the clique communities. For each pair of k-cliques, the nodes that belong to both k-cliques, are called 'bridges' between the two communities. In the next figure, the matrix shows the bridges between the 15 k-cliques, with k equal three, for the Erdos-97-1 dataset, where the large density of connections does not allow for a clear interpretation of the network.

The minimum set covering algorithm generates 15 k-cliques, which covers all the 283 nodes, but over-covering 252 nodes.

In this chapter, we propose a trade-off between the covered and over-covered nodes. The new metric finds the best solution when the number of covered nodes does not exceed the number of over-covered ones. In other words, the best solution is found when the difference between covered and over-covered nodes is maximal.

The k-clique cover algorithm implementation is composed of a constructive step and a reduction step.

The input for the k-clique cover is a matrix where each line corresponds to a node of the graph and each column, a k-clique covering a certain number of nodes.

In the constructive step, the Clique Cover heuristic, proposed by Kellerman (1973) and improved by Chvatal (1979), is used.

We consider the following notation: M[line, column] or M[vertex, k-clique] for the input matrix, C for the cost vector of each column, V for the vertex set of G(V,E) and S for the set covering solution.

Algorithm 3.   The Heruistic for the k-Clique Covering.

Input: M [line, column], C, V
Output: the cover S
1. Initialise $R = M$, $S = \emptyset$,
// Constructive Step
2. While $R \neq \emptyset$ do
2.1.   Choose the best line i*$\in$R such as $|M(i^*,j)| = \min |M(i,j)| \forall j$
2.2.   Choose the best column j* that covers line i*
2.3.   Update R and S, $R = R \backslash M(i,j^*) \forall i$, $S = S \cup \{j^*\}$
3. End while
4. Sort the cover S by descending order of costs
5. For each Si do if (S\Si is still a cover) then $S = S \backslash Si$
// Reduction Step
6. While (over-cover > cover) do
6.1.   Choose the column j* such as (over-cover > cover)
6.2.   Remove column j*
7. End While
8. Return S

In the constructive step, for each iteration, it is chosen a line to be covered and the best column that covers that line. Then, the solution S and the remaining vertex R, are updated. The chosen line is usually the line that is more difficult to cover, i.e., the line that corresponds to fewer columns. After reaching the cover set, the second step is for removing redundancy, by sorting the cover in descending order of cost and checking if each k-clique is really essential.

In the reduction step, the best trade-off solution is found by removing the most over-covered k-cliques, i.e., the k-cliques with a high degree of nodes over-covering.

This heuristic can be improved using a Tabu Search heuristic, by alternating the constructive step with the removal of the most expensive columns, finding a trajectory of solutions, as presented in Gomes *et al.* (2006).

The solution obtained with the reduction step, decreases the number of k-cliques that covered all the nodes, allowing for a better interpretation of the network. The sub-covered (or not-covered) nodes are treated as outlier nodes and thus not considered in the clique community analysis.

In order to get a better interpretability of the network data, this analysis considers the k-cliques covered nodes as communities, the over-covered nodes, as bridges between the communities and the not-cover nodes, as outlier (or marginal) nodes.

3.3. *Two numeric examples*

In this section, two numeric examples will be presented to show the constructive and the reduction steps.

To exemplify the constructive step, given a graph with five vertices and four edges with E = $\{(1,2),(2,3),(3,4),(4,5)\}$, the second power of the graph, $k=2$, a new graph with five vertices and seven edges is obtained with k-E = $\{(1,2),(1,3),(2,3),(2,4),(3,4), (3,5),(4,5)\}$.

Running a multi-start algorithm with the maximum clique problem, three maximal cliques of size 3 can be easily identified: $(1,2,3), (2,3,4)$ and $(3,4,5)$. See Fig. 8.

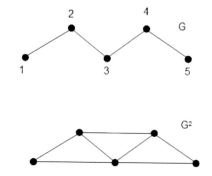

Fig. 7.   Example of a graph G and its transformation into a G2.

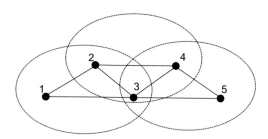

Fig. 8.   *k*-clique generation example.

nodes				over
	C1	C2	C3	covered
active	1	0	1	
1	1			
2	1	1		
3	1	1	1	1
4		1	1	
5			1	

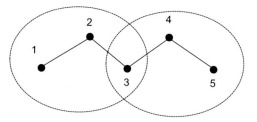

Fig. 9.   Two-sets of two-cliques cover the whole graph.

Finally, running the *k*-cliques cover, in the constructive step of phase 2, two subgroups are found that cover all the vertices. The two-cliques cover is equal to two. Notice that the vertex number 3 appears in the two sets. In social network analysis, this is called a 'bridge'. Indeed, node 3, with distance 2 can reach any other vertex. See Fig. 9.

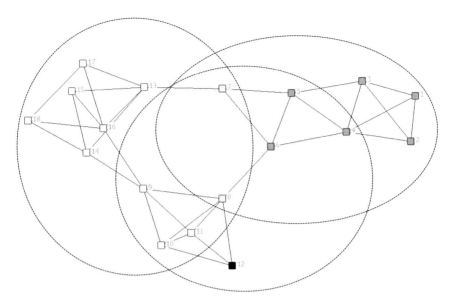

Fig. 10.   Three-sets of three-cliques are needed to cover the graph.

The previous figure presents the two subsets solution, using a matrix representation and a graph. For large graphs and a large number of subsets, the graph visualisation gets worse. In these cases, a better general view is attained, using the matrix representation, which is the output of the set covering heuristic.

To show the reduction step of phase 2, let us use a graph with 18 nodes that has a diameter equal to six. To cover the whole graph with three-cliques, three-sets are needed. See Fig. 10.

The result of the constructive step is three-sets/columns of three-clique. In the reduction step, the columns with a larger difference between the covered-nodes and the non-covered nodes, will be removed. In Fig. 11, one column will be removed, and the final result is a two-sets of three-cliques, with two nodes as bridges (7 and 8) and one marginal node, the node 12.

4.   Applying the Algorithm to Actual Datasets

To validate the two-phase algorithm, two groups of datasets were used, the Erdös graphs and some clique DIMACS (1995) benchmark

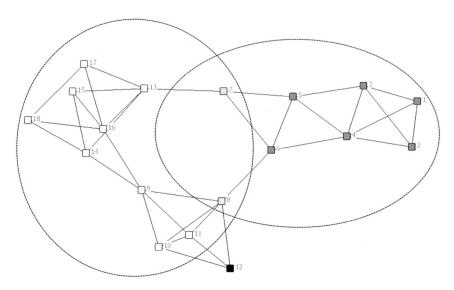

Fig. 11.   Two-sets of three-clique are needed to cover the graph.

instances. In the Erdös graphs, each node corresponds to a researcher, and two nodes are adjacent if the researchers published together. The graphs are named 'ERDOS-x-y', where 'x' represents the last two digits of the year that the graphs were created, and 'y', the maximum distance from Erdös to each vertex in the graph. The second group of graphs contains some clique instances from the second DIMACS challenge. These include the 'brock' graphs, which contain cliques 'hidden' within much smaller cliques, making it hard to discover cliques in these graphs. The 'c-fat' graphs are a result of fault diagnosis data.

For the analysis of each graph, we consider the number of nodes, the diameter and the cardinality of the set of k-cliques in the constructive and reduction steps, varying k from 'one' to the diameter, as showed in Table 1.

In the table, the cardinality of the k-clique cover shows a significant reduction between the two steps: constructive and reduction steps.

For the Erdos-98-1 and Erdos-99-1, with the diameter of seven, the graphs are covered with only one-set of five-cliques. These values exemplify the difference between k-cliques and k-clans; these graphs

Table 1. Sequence of k-clique covers in the constructive step and reduction step.

Graph	Nr nodes	Diameter	Cardinality x of the k-clique cover (constructive step; reduction step)									
			$k=1$	$k=2$	$k=3$	$k=4$	$k=5$	$k=6$	$k=7$	$k=9$	$k=18$	$k=40$
test	18	6	8;7	4;3	3;2	2;1	2;1	1;1	—	—	—	—
erdos-97-1	472	6	9;4	8;1	15;1	10;3	4;3	1;1	—	—	—	—
erdos-98-1	485	7	8;4	10;1	12;1	9;3	1;1	1;1	1;1	—	—	—
erdos-99-1	492	7	8;4	11;1	12;1	9;3	1;1	1;1	1;1	—	—	—
brock200_1	200	2	24;4	1;1	—	—	—	—	—	—	—	—
brock200_2	200	2	26;9	1;1	—	—	—	—	—	—	—	—
brock400_1	400	2	26;5	1;1	—	—	—	—	—	—	—	—
brock400_2	400	2	23;4	1;1	—	—	—	—	—	—	—	—
c-fat200-1	200	18	28;16	26;10	23;7	20;7	15;5	13;5	12;4	10;4	1;1	—
c-fat200-2	200	9	15;10	11;7	7;5	4;4	4;3	6;2	6;2	1;1	—	—
c-fat500-1	500	40	28;16	26;10	23;8	20;7	18;6	17;5	16;5	14;4	8;2	1;1

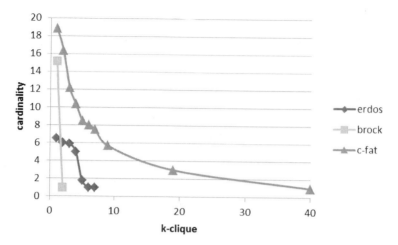

Fig. 12.   Average *k*-clique cardinally for the graph families.

are five-cliques but not five-clans because the diameter is equal to seven.

The 'brock' graphs, known as hiding cliques, have a diameter equal to two, and to cover the graph, one-set of two-cliques is enough. Most of the DIMACS instances present this profile. On the other hand, the 'c-fat' graphs have the diameter larger than seven, generating long sequences of *k*-clique cover.

In the proposed metric, the sequence of *k*-clique covers identifies families of graphs and seems to be very promising in social network analysis. The *k*-clique sequence returns a different pattern for each family of networks. In Fig. 12, the average *k*-clique cardinality is shown for the different family graphs.

To answer the initial question about how many *k*-cliques communities are needed to cover the whole graph, it is done. The social network analyst should choose the best *k* for his study.

Additional information can be retrieved, like the covered nodes, over-covered nodes and the non-covered nodes, as shown in Table 2, the number of nodes in the bridges, exemplified in Fig. 13, and the *k*-clique composition.

Table 2.   Detailed information.

File	k1-brock400_2
Columns	4
Total number of lines	400
Covered lines	50
Over-covered lines	13
Non-covered lines	66
Empty lines	271

	1	2	3	4
1		4	4	5
2			5	2
3				3
4				

Fig. 13.   Bridges between the four-sets of k-cliques in the k1-brock400_2 dataset.

5.   Conclusions

Given the large amount of data provided by the Web 2.0, there is a pressing need to obtain new metrics to better understand the network structure; how their communities are organised and the way they evolve over time.

Complex network and graph mining metrics are essentially based on low complexity computational procedures like the diameter of the graph, clustering coefficient and the degree distribution of the nodes. The connected communities in the social networks have, essentially, been studied in two contexts: global metrics like the clustering coefficient and the node groups, such as the graph partitions and clique communities.

In this work, the concept of relaxed clique is extended to the whole graph, to achieve a general view, by covering the network with k-cliques. A graph mining metric based on k-clique communities, allows for a better understanding of the network structure.

In order to get a good interpretability of the network data, this analysis considers the k-clique covered nodes as communities, the over-covered nodes as bridges between the communities and the not-covered nodes as outlier nodes. The k-clique cover algorithm implementation is composed of a constructive step and a reduction step.

The sequence of k-clique communities is presented, where the diameter and the community structure components are combined. The sequence analysis shows that different graph families have different structures.

Social networks do not usually exceed a hundred nodes. In this work, the proposed two-phase algorithm deals with graphs with hundreds of nodes, with a running time performance of a few seconds. Even though this performance may be adequate for practical applications, it is important to study the scalability of the algorithms for much bigger networks like the ones we can find in complex system areas.

With these tools, the social network analyst can measure the basic performance of the networks, study thoroughly the communities of the network by choosing the best k for his/her study.

References

Alba, RD (1973). A graph-theoretic definition of a sociometric clique. *Journal of Mathematical Sociology*, 3(3), 113–126.

Berge, C (1958). *Théorie des Graphes et ses Applications*. Paris: Dunod.

Berners-Lee, T (2006). The next wave of the web plenary panel. In *15th International World Wide Web Conference*, WWW2006. Scotland: Edinburgh.

Cavique, L, AB Mendes and JMA Santos (2009). An algorithm to discover the k-Clique cover in networks. In *Progress in Artificial Intelligence*, L Seabra Lopes *et al.* (eds.), pp. 363–373. *EPIA 2009*, LNAI 5816. Berlin, Heidelberg: Springer-Verlag.

Cavique, L and CJ Luz (2009). A heuristic for the stability number of a graph based on convex quadratic programming and tabu search. *Journal of Mathematical Sciences*, 161(6), 944–955.

Cavique, L, C Rego and I Themido (2002). A scatter search algorithm for the maximum clique problem. In *Essays and Surveys in Meta-heuristics*, C Ribeiro and P Hansen (eds.), pp. 227–244. Dordrecht, The Netherlands: Kluwer Academic Pubs.

Chvatal, V (1979). A greedy heuristic for the set-covering problem. *Mathematics of Operations Research*, 4(4), 233–235.

Cook, DJ and LB Holder (eds.) (2007). *Mining Graph Data*. London: John Wiley & Sons.

DIMACS (1995). Maximum clique, graph coloring, and satisfiability. *Second DIMACS implementation challenge*. Available at http://dimacs.rutgers.edu/Challenges/ [accessed on March 2011].

Derenyi, I, G Palla and T Vicsek (2005). Clique percolation in random networks. *Physical Review Letters*, 94(16), 160202.

Erdös, P and A Renyi (1959). On random graphs. *Publicationes Mathematicae*, 6, 290–297.

Faloutsos, M, P Faloutsos and C Faloutsos (1999). On power-law relationships of the Internet topology. In *Proc. SIGCOMM*, pp. 251–262.

Floyd, RW (1962). Algorithm 97: Shortest Path. *Communications of the ACM*, 5(5), 345.

Freeman, LC (2004). *The Development of Social Network Analysis: A Study in the Sociology of Science*. Vancouver: Empirical Press.

Gomes, MC, L Cavique and IH Themido (2006). The crew timetabling problem: An extension of the crew scheduling problem. *Annals of Operations Research*, 144(144), 111–132.

Grossman, J, P Ion and RD Castro (2007). The Erdös number Project. Available at http://www.oakland.edu/enp/ [accessed on March 2011].

Johnson, DS (1974). Approximation algorithms for combinatorial problems. *Journal of Computer and Systems Sciences*, 9(9), 256–278.

Kellerman, E (1973). Determination of keyword conflict. *IBM Technical Disclosure Bulletin*, 16(2), 544–546.

Kernighan, BW and S Lin (1970). An efficient heuristic procedure for partitioning graphs. *Bell Systems Technical Journal*, 49, 291–307.

Luce, RD (1950). Connectivity and generalized cliques in sociometric group structure. *Psychometrika*, 15(15), 159–190.

Mendes, A, M Funk and L Cavique (2010). Knowledge discovery in the virtual social network due to common knowledge of proverbs. In *Proc. DMIN'10*, MG Weiss and R Stahlbock (eds.), pp. 213–219, 6th edn. USA: CSREA Press.

Mika, P (2007). *Social Networks and the Semantic Web*. New York: Springer-Verlag.

Milgram, S (1967). The small world problem. *Psychology Today*, 1(1), 60–67.

Mokken, RJ (1979). Cliques, clubs and clans. *Quality & Quantity*, 13(13), 161–173.

Moreno, JL (1934). *Who Shall Survive?* Washington D.C: Nervous and Mental Disease Publishing Company.

Scott, JP and P Carrington (eds.) (2011). *The SAGE Handbook of Social Network Analysis*. London: Sage Pubs.

Skiena, S (1990). *Implementing Discrete Mathematics: Combinatorics and Graph Theory with Mathematica*. Reading, MA: Addison-Wesley.

Soriano, P and M Gendreau (1996). Tabu search algorithms for the maximum clique. In *Clique, Coloring and Satisfiability, Second Implementation Challenge DIMACS*, DS Johnson and MA Trick (eds.), pp. 221–242. American Mathematical Society.

Wang, N, S Parthasarathy, K-L Tan and AKH Tung (2008). CSV: Visualizing and mining cohesive subgraphs, In *ACM SIGMOD '08 Proceedings*. Vancover, Canada.

Watts, DJ and SH Strogatz (1998). Collective dynamics of small-world networks. *Nature*, 393(393), 409–410.

Wasserman, S and K Faust (1995). *Social Network Analysis: Methods and Applications*. Cambridge: Cambridge University Press.

Chapter 21

CONCLUSION

In the social sciences, quantitative research refers to the systematic empirical investigation of social phenomena via statistical, mathematical, or computational techniques. The objective of quantitative research is to develop and employ mathematical models, theories and/or hypotheses pertaining to phenomena. The process of measurement is central to quantitative research because it provides the fundamental connection between empirical observation and mathematical expression of quantitative relationships. Quantitative data is any data that is in numerical form such as statistics, percentages, etc. In layman's terms, this means that the quantitative researcher asks a specific, narrow question and collects numerical data from participants to answer the question. The researcher analyses the data with the help of statistics. The researcher is hoping the numbers will yield an unbiased result that can be generalised to some larger population.

Quantitative research is used widely in social sciences such as in marketing and management. In the social sciences, the 'quantitative' term relates to empirical methods, originating in both philosophical positivism and the history of statistics. Quantitative methods can be used to verify which research hypotheses are true.

Modelling involves developing physical, conceptual or computer based representation of systems. Scientists build models to replicate systems in the real world through simplification, to perform an experiment that cannot be done in the real world or to assemble several known ideas into a coherent whole to build and test hypotheses. Computer modelling is a relatively new scientific research method, but it is based on the same principles as physical and conceptual modelling.

Quantitative research synthesis methods can be used to examine theoretical models for substantive research questions. Model-drive syntheses can address more complex questions than have typically been addressed in quantitative reviews in a more systematic and organised manner than in a traditional narrative review.

Quantitative analysis requires the representation of the problem using a mathematical model. Mathematical modelling is a critical part of the quantitative approach to decision making. Many times decision makers use their practical knowledge to transform an optimum solution into an implementable solution.

Most people are not experts in predicting the outcome of the system governed by stochastic processes and quantitative modelling. Although many software tools exist to model such processes, hardly any attention is paid to the analysis of quantitative aspects to support or optimise the outcomes. A substantial number of users do not have confidence in the assumptions of the models. High quality solutions are often missed any may create other problems (e.g., making the organisation more resistant to the introduction of future changes).

In the current era, when new modelling and mathematical techniques appear, one question inevitably is: Why one more and which one quantitative model in particular? Indeed, one of the major challenges any researcher has to cope with is the practical implementation of statistical, computer, or mathematical models.

Business modelling is a vast arena of research and practice, which is gaining increasing important in the rapid development of e-commerce, globalisation, and in particular, the movement toward global e-business. The ability to utilise advanced computing technology to model, analyse and simulate various aspects of ever-changing businesses has made a significant impact on the way businesses are designed and run these days. With the current global e-business and e-commerce initiatives, it has become important that all businesses carefully validate their business objectives, requirements, and strategies through a careful process of formal business modelling. It is important for effective enterprise decision making to have clear, concise business models that allow the extraction of critical value from business processes and specify the rules to be globally enforced. Particularly in e-business specifications, the need to be unambiguous, accurate, and complete becomes even greater, because there may be no human mediator or agent to reply on in complex or unforeseen situations.

Quantitative modelling seems admirably suited to help managers in their strategic decision making on operations management issues. Market competition and recent progress in date collection and data storage techniques have increased the importance of quantitative modelling. Modelling has become an important part of research and development across many fields of study, having evolved from a tool to a discipline in less than two decades. There is the need to give an overview of quantitative analysis methods and models, as quantitative modelling enables to devise specific management problems. Recently, quantitative modelling has received a lot of attention. Modelling framework and software tools enhance the performance of business. Quantitative models provide diagramming techniques to document business process for growth.

The field of marketing and management has undergone immense changes over the past decade, and those changes are driving an increasing need for data analysis. Marketing management combines both art and science: Managers must combine creative thinking with rigorous analysis when making decision. Increasing financial pressures demand that managers deliver ROI from their investments; therefore, quantifying the effects is imperative. At the same time, customer relationship management (CRM) software and emerging Web 2.0 applications are providing managers with reams of data about their customers.

The marketing and management analysis toolkits are a suit of analytical tools that managers can use to inform decision-making. Each toolkit includes a technical note that outlines the analysis technique and provides examples of how it is used in marketing and management and shows mathematical formulas used in the technique.

The marketing and management toolkits were designed to provide a quantitative foundation for analysing decisions and an analytical structure and process for completing a project.

How can a potential user distinguish between a quantitative model that may be of some real value and one that is not? The model builder rarely provides much help, since most are advocates of their own work and tend to lose their objective toward the model. Therefore, an independent evaluation is necessary to judge the true usefulness of the model.

The usefulness of a quantitative model depends on both 'acceptability' and 'quality'. Acceptability refers to approval by those in the organisation who would actually use the model, while quality refers to the ability to provide better predictions or decisions. A model must score well on both characteristics if it is to be judged useful. A high-quality model that is not accepted is of no value. Usually, some trade-offs must be made between quality and acceptability.

For all practical purposes, quality and acceptability must be viewed in relative terms. That is, these concepts can only be examined by a comparison of alternative models. A model is said to be 'good' if it is better than alternative models. Among the alternative models would certainly be included the way in which these predictions or decisions are currently being made. In most cases, the current method is based entirely upon the judgement of a manger. Woolsey, for example, examined four applications of complex computer models and claimed that they were inferior to the decisions currently being made subjectively. In one case, for example, two 'little old ladies' did far better than a complex and expensive computer model.

Finally, it is important that the evaluation of both quality and acceptability be carried out but an unbiased evaluator. Quality and acceptability are characteristics that may depend not only upon the model but also upon the situation. This is yet another reason why the potential user should carry out his own examination of the model.

When evaluating acceptability, one must consider both whether the model will be used and, if used, how it will be used. High quality solutions are often misused and may create other problems (e.g., make the organisations more resistant to the introduction of further changes). On the other hand, low-quality solutions are often high in acceptability.

1. Evaluating Quality

The evaluation of quality calls for an examination for four key stages as illustrated in Fig. 1. The first stage relates the 'real world' to the assumptions of the models: Are the assumptions reasonable and comprehensive? The second stage relates the model's assumptions to the final form of the model. Does the model follow logically from the assumptions? Is it possible for a mathematician to derive the same model given the initial date, can the outputs be replicated? And the fourth stage relates the outputs to the real world: Do the benefits of the model (e.g., better predictions, better assessments of risk, or better decision making) justify the costs of the model?

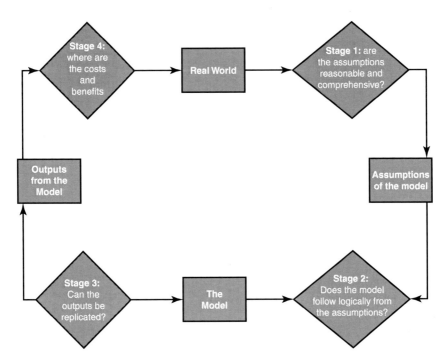

Fig. 1.   Examination of four key stages.

1.1. Stage 1: Relationship of the Real World to the Assumptions

The first step in the assessment of the assumptions is to review written documents in order to develop an explicit listing of the key assumptions. This list may be checked by conducting interviews with the advocates of the model. The assumptions are then tested for reasonableness against: (1) empirical evidence, (2) judgements of managers, and (3) assessments by the evaluator. Admittedly, this procedure is rather crude; however, the objective at this stage is merely to identify 'highly unreasonable' assumptions.

1.2. Stage 2: Relationships of the Assumptions to the Model

Stage 2 involves an examination of the logical structure of the model. This calls for a systematic check of the mathematics used to go from the basic assumptions to the final form of the model. This stage sometimes requires a good mathematician, especially where the model is complex.

Stage 2 should expose any implicit assumptions underlying the model. Sophisticated techniques such as mathematical programming and simulation often tend to obscure the assumptions which underlie their use. Indeed, the mystique which surrounds the complex solution may serve to give it credibility beyond that which it rightly deserves.

1.3. Stage 3: Relationships of the Model to the Outputs

Stage 3 is merely a routine auditing step. Given the model and the data, is it possible to replicate the output? One takes a sample of the data used and enters it into the model that the advocates claim to have used. The procedure is analogous to the financial audit.

1.4. Stage 4: Relationship between the Real World and the Outputs

Stage 4 is concerned with the value of the models outputs as compared with the outputs of other models. This stage of analysis is generally the most important one for assessing the quality of a model.

It is recommended that Stage 4 not be dealt with directly; rather, it should be broken into parts using a cost-benefit framework. An outline of one possible approach is provided below.

1.5. *Costs*

Initial development (money and time)
    Maintenance (money and time)
    User (ease in understanding, time to get results, need for expert assistance)

1.6. *Benefits*

Predictive accuracy
    Ability to assess uncertainty
    Identification of improved policies
    Learning (the model improves as experience is gained)
    Ability to asses effects of alternative policies
    Adaptability (can adapt as the environment changes)

These areas should help to provide for a more complete assessment of costs and benefits.

The assessment of costs is usually straightforward, other than the fact that costs are typically underestimated. The assessment of benefits is much more complex. Evaluators for the model should attempt to gain information on each area of benefits. In the final analysis, however, much will depend on the evaluators' to place some relative weights upon the various types of benefits.

There are many ways in which to obtain information on each of the costs and benefits. Tests of outputs in extreme situations are useful in determining whether a model is able to predict over a wide range of situations.

Once the four stages of the analysis are completed, it is necessary to consider their net effect. At this point it is suggested than an explicit summary be prepared. This summary would compare the proposed model with its various competitors.

It is rare for any one model to completely dominate another model on all the criteria. In the more typical case, where different models are judges to be superior on different criteria, the manager must decide on the relative importance of the various stages of analysis. The authors would suggest that the most important of the criteria is the cost-benefit analysis of the outputs. Beyond this, however, they have no simple solutions.

The potential user of a model should not depend entirely upon the models advocates for an assessment of the model. Rather, he/she should carry out his/her own analysis. The framework, which is summarised in Fig. 1, helps to provide a systematic, comprehensive, and explicit evaluation of a model. The framework may be used for the analysis of any quantitative model.

Process modelling and design require predicting the accuracy of analytical model output values. For any analytical model which requires many input parameters, only a few parameters values are known and the rest, in the most cases, are assumed as best case values. A quantitative value for each parameter in the analytical model, ranking in importance, is required to validate the model output. The accuracy of an analytical model can be estimated quantitatively using the uncertainty and sensitivity analysis.

Analytical models are used in numerous applications in science and engineering to predict and analyse the behaviour of a system or equipment. The individual input parameters can be exact, measured, predicted, or assumed. Model accuracy is also a critical parameter for robust process modelling and design calculations. The model accuracy is highly correlated to the accuracy of different parameters involved in the formulation of the model and their effect on the output of the model. While modelling real physical systems, a set of assumptions and validations are often made without knowing the exact quantified impact of the individual parameter.

The parametric importance and its quantitative contribution towards the model can be estimated using an uncertainty and sensitivity model. The model accuracy is highly correlated to the accuracy of measurement of different parameters involved in the formulation and their effect on the output of the model. To estimate the effect of input parameters, uncertainty and sensitivity analysis provides a good platform.

The parameters with the highest importance of the ones that affect the output of the model, the most, contribute more to model accuracy. The inputs to the model, most generally, are the input parameters at design condition values, and at maximum and minimum range values. The model accuracy prediction based on defined parameters can serve as a preliminary measure to process design and parameter control.

Parameter sensitivity is the amount of variation in the model output in response to changes in the parameter inputs. Minor changes in some input parameters may make considerable changes to the model results, while larger changes to other parameters may have significant effect on results. Parameter sensitivity can identify the parameters that have the largest effect on output for model calibration by linearising the analytical model and also which deserve the most attention, accuracy, or research during data collection.

INDEX